The Economist
BUSINESS
TRAVELLER'S
GUIDES

GERMANY

The Economist
BUSINESS
TRAVELLER'S
GUIDES

GERMANY

The
Economist
PUBLICATIONS

PRENTICE HALL PRESS
NEW YORK

This edition published in the United States and Canada in 1988 by Prentice Hall Press
A division of Simon & Schuster, Inc.
Gulf + Western Building
One Gulf + Western Plaza
New York, New York 10023

The publishers welcome corrections and suggestions from business travellers; please write to The Editor, *The Economist Business Traveller's Guides,* 40 Duke Street, London W1A 1DW, United Kingdom.

Series Editor Stephen Brough
Assistant Series Editor Brigid Avison
Editors John Farndon (*overview*); Moira Johnston, Rachel Stewart (*travel*)
Designer Alistair Plumb
Sub-editors Maggie Daykin, Georgina Evans
Editorial assistants Mary Pickles, Bettina Whilems
Researchers Stephen Irving, Barbara Tombs
Design assistants Clare Bryan, Lynn Hector
Indexer Fiona Barr

Maps and diagrams by Oxford Illustrators
Typeset by SB Datagraphics, Colchester, England
Printed in Italy by Arnoldo Mondadori, Verona

Contributors *overview* John Ardagh, Jonathan Carr, Patricia Clough, Nick Colchester, Malcolm Crawford, Darrell Delamaide, Jonathan Fenby, Andrew Fisher, Mario Kakabadse, Don Kirk, Roon Lewald, Tom Lucie, Terry McCarthy, Willie Morgan, James O'Toole, Robert Silver, Haig Simonian, Peggy Trautmann; *travel* Norman Bartlett, Peter Graham, Angus McGeogh, Gillian Thomas

Consultants Barbara Anders, Michael Stocks, Max Worcester

Library of Congress Cataloging-in-Publication Data
The Economist business traveller's guides. Germany.
  Includes index.
  1. Germany (West) – Description and travel – Guide-books. 2. Business travel – Germany (West) – Guide-books.
  I. Economist (London, England)
DD258.25.E25   1988
914.3'04878   87-32890
ISBN 0-13-234956-6

Contents

Glossary

BDA West German employers' federation.

BDI Federation of West German industry.

Bund West Germany at the national (federal) level, hence *Bundesbank* (the central bank of the federal government); *Bundespost* (the federal postal and communications monopoly), *Bundesrat* (the upper house of the federal government), the *Bundestag* (the lower house of the federal government).

Bundesrepublik Deutschland Federal Republic of Germany – that is, West Germany.

CAP Common agricultural policy of the EC.

Codetermination The legally established principle of worker participation in management (*Mitbestimmung*).

DDR or *Deutsche Demokratische Republik.* German Democratic Republic – that is, East Germany.

DGB West German federation of unions, embracing the 17 industry unions.

DIN Deutsche Industrie Normen Product standards set by various German industry organizations and incorporated in the DIN catalogue.

EC European Community, also known as the Common Market. Founded in 1957; by 1987 had 12 members: Belgium, Denmark, Eire, France, Greece, Italy, Luxembourg, the Netherlands, Portugal, Spain, the UK and West Germany.

EFTA European Free Trade Association: Norway, Sweden, Austria, Iceland, Switzerland and, with associate membership, Finland.

EMS European monetary system, created in 1979 to aid management of the exchange rates between European currencies.

Gastarbeiter Guestworker. Immigrants mainly from southeast Europe invited into West Germany to help in times of labour shortage.

GATT General Agreement on Tariffs and Trade. Instituted in 1947 to liberalize trade and prevent discrimination. Over 100 countries are signatories.

GDP Gross Domestic Product. The best measure of a country's economic performance, GDP is the total value of a country's annual output of goods and services. It is normally valued at market prices; GDP can, however, be calculated at factor cost, by subtracting indirect taxes and adding subsidies. To eliminate the effects of inflation, GDP growth is usually expressed in constant prices.

GNP Gross National Product. A country's GDP plus residents' income from investments abroad minus income accruing to nonresidents from investments in the country.

Green Plan Federal schemes for rural regeneration.

Land (plural *Länder*). One of the states within the Federal Republic. Not including West Berlin, there are ten altogether: Baden-Württemberg, Bavaria (Bayern), Bremen, Hamburg, Hesse (Hessen), Lower Saxony (Niedersachsen), North Rhine-Westphalia (Nordrhein-Westfalen), Rhineland-Palatinate (Rheinland-Pfalz), Saarland and Schleswig-Holstein.

Mehrwertsteuer Value-added tax.

NATO North Atlantic Treaty Organization. The alliance for the defence of the West against the Soviet Union. Formed in 1949, it includes the USA and Canada and most West European nations with the notable exception of France which withdrew in 1966.

OPEC Organization of Petroleum-Exporting Countries.

Ostpolitik The West German policy for improving relations with Communist countries to the east of the Iron Curtain, notably East Germany.

Social market economy The West German version of capitalism with a social conscience.

UBGGs Unternehmensbeteiligungs-gesellschaften Venture capital units set up by the banks which may take share options in unlisted companies.

Using the guide

The Economist Business Traveller's Guide to Germany is an encyclopedia of business and travel information. If in doubt about where to look for specific information, consult either the Contents list or the Index.

City guides

Each city guide follows a standard format: information and advice on arriving, getting around, city areas, hotels, restaurants, bars, entertainment, shopping, sightseeing, sports and fitness, and a directory of local business and other facilities such as secretarial and translation agencies, couriers, hospitals with emergency departments, and florists. There is also a map of the city centre locating recommended hotels, restaurants and other important addresses.

For easy reference, all main entries for hotels, restaurants and sights are listed alphabetically.

Abbreviations

Credit and charge cards AE American Express; DC Diners Club; MC MasterCard (Access, Eurocard); V Visa.

Figures Millions are abbreviated to m; billions (meaning one thousand million) to bn.

Publisher's note

Although *The Economist Business Traveller's Guide to Germany* is intended first and foremost to provide practical information for business people travelling *in* Germany, the general information will also be helpful to anyone doing business with Germany, wherever and however that business may be conducted.

Price bands

Price bands are denoted by symbols (see below). These correspond approximately to the following actual prices at the time of going to press. (Although the actual prices will inevitably go up, the relative price category is likely to remain the same.)

Hotels

(one person occupying a standard room, including service and tax at 15%)

$\boxed{DM}$	up to DM75
$\boxed{DM}$/	DM75–150
$\boxed{DM}$//	DM150–200
$\boxed{DM}$///	DM200–275
$\boxed{DM}$////	over DM275

Restaurants

(typical meal, including half a bottle of house wine, coffee and service)

$\boxed{DM}$	up to DM45
$\boxed{DM}$/	DM45–70
$\boxed{DM}$//	DM70–90
$\boxed{DM}$///	DM90–120
$\boxed{DM}$////	over DM120

INTRODUCTION

Many people in West Germany today are talking of a second "economic miracle" (*Wirtschaftswunder*), a sustained spell of prosperity and economic vigour akin to that of the 1950s and 60s that transformed the country from a war-torn wasteland to the world's third largest economy. It is easy to see why they are so confident. The country's trade and current accounts are heavily in surplus; the inflation rate (below 1% in 1987) is tiny even by strict German standards; and the D-mark is as sturdy as ever.

Irritatingly for foreigners, this remarkable performance seems to be sustained with little of the once-notorious teutonic strain and stress. The Germans pay themselves some of the highest wages in the world, take very long holidays abroad, and their cities are full of evidence of an increasingly relaxed attitude to life.

But there remain underlying problems which make talk of a second "miracle" seem overdone. It would be more accurate to say that the German economy is in a third postwar phase of development, a phase in which new opportunities and new stresses are emerging.

A phoenix from the ashes

The first phase was Germany's remarkable recovery following the founding of the Federal Republic in 1949: two decades which saw the country rapidly rebuilt from the rubble of defeat, the striking success of brilliant German entrepreneurs like Grundig, and the formation of strong and disciplined trade unions.

Throughout this period the country was governed by Christian Democrat-led coalitions. The second phase began in 1969 when the Christian Democrats were driven from office by the centre-left alliance of Social and Free Democrats, pledged, among other things, to (costly) programmes for social reform. At the same time there was a reaction among the young against the profit and success motive underlying the *Wirtschaftswunder*, a reaction symbolized by the popularity of careers in teaching and sociology rather than engineering or science.

Faltering progress

West Germany coasted through the first oil crisis in the mid-1970s better than its neighbours. But the second oil shock at the end of the decade exposed economic weaknesses, such as the low profit-sales ratios and weak capital base of many German firms, which had been masked by more or less steady growth. Many companies went bankrupt, and even famous firms like AEG-Telefunken came close to collapse. Between 1979 and 1981, the country's trade surplus plummeted, the current account plunged into deficit and some foreign critics began to claim that the miracle was going down the drain.

That was a big exaggeration. But the recession prompted a serious reappraisal which helped to bring a new Christian Democrat-led government to power in 1982; the economy moved into its third phase. The new chancellor, Helmut Kohl, pledged that there would be a *Wende*, an economic and (as he put it) spiritual turnaround in which the state's role would be pruned and private initiative allowed to flourish.

The great *Wende*?

The Kohl government's record since 1982 has been mixed. On the credit side, it has braked its borrowing, streamlined its schemes to promote research and technology, cut corporate and personal tax a little, and planned a more comprehensive tax reform for 1990. In parallel, the Bundesbank, the independent central bank, has liberalized the German capital market, encouraged financial innovation and promoted reform of the country's antiquated stock market. Young people are turning back to careers in industry and commerce; setting up one's own business is fashionable again, and venture capital outfits are emerging to help entrepreneurs.

The record on privatization is less impressive. Some major state holdings (like the VEBA energy concern and the VIAG industrial group) were sold to the public, but coalition squabbling blocked faster progress. Only in 1987 did the government start to take modest steps to shake up the Bundespost, the huge and inflexible federal post and telecommunications enterprise. State subsidies have risen despite government promises of cuts and social security benefits have been trimmed, not slashed. The state quota (public sector spending as a share of GNP) was a mere 3% (from 50%) between 1982 and 1986.

Slowly but surely

Complaints and problems abound. Many in business grumble because there has not been a more pronounced *Wende* under Herr Kohl. The trade unions stress bitterly that, despite the government's repeated pledges to cut unemployment, the jobless total has for years averaged well over 2m (9% of the dependent labour force). Moreover, trading partners criticize the big German trade surpluses and constantly urge Bonn to do more to boost the economy. Since Herr Kohl came to power, GNP growth has averaged only around 2% annually, and prospects for anything much faster look poor. One handicap is that West Germany has the lowest birth rate in the world and faces the challenge of an ageing population. That may ease unemployment in the 1990s, but presents problems for pension payments, health insurance and so on.

Despite all this, Germany continues to grow economically, is still increasingly prosperous, and the traditional virtues are still intact. The country has a diligent and well-trained labour force, responsible trade unions, a good infrastructure and not least a federal system which helps promote regional development and pride. Some yearn for a little more daring, and a swifter pace of change. But the broad, slow swings in political and economic emphasis since the war show that is not the modern German way.

The Economic Scene

Natural resources

Germany has always shown a remarkable capacity to make the most of what it has, and lack of natural resources has never been seen as a major obstacle to economic progress. Cut off from 60% of German prewar farming land in the 1945 settlement, for example, the Federal Republic rose to the challenge by boosting agricultural productivity more than sevenfold. The oil crisis of the early 1970s, meanwhile, spurred the country to reduce its dependence on imported oil by more than a fifth.

Agriculture

Farm production now accounts for barely 1.5% of GDP, and employs little over 1% of the workforce. But the huge gains in productivity since the war, especially in meat, dairy products, wheat, sugar beet and wine, mean that Germany produces enough of most basic commodities to satisfy 85% of home need. Indeed, Germany is the world's fourth largest exporter of food and drink – although it is also one of the biggest importers.

The 1980s, however, have seen German farming in a state of crisis, as farm incomes shrink and the government wrangles with its EC partners over cuts in Common Agricultural Policy (CAP) subsidies to the nation's thousands of small farms. An emotional charge is added to the issues, moreover, by the Germans' concern over a vanishing way of life.

Leaving the land As in other EC countries, the farming population in Germany has shrunk dramatically over the last four decades. Since 1950, three out of four farmers have left the land, and the number involved full-time in agriculture has dropped below 900,000.

Part-time farmers One of the most striking, and controversial, features of the German farming scene is the high number of part-time farmers; some 40% of all farms, and most of those under 1.6 ha/4 acres, are worked by people who have jobs elsewhere. Farms like these, which persist especially in the south, generate cash incomes of less than DM4,000, and a factory or office job provides the bulk of family income.

Small farms As farmers leave the land, so the number of farms is dropping dramatically, from 1.6m in 1950 to 740,000 in the mid-1980s. Yet Germany's unusual inheritance laws, bequeathed by Napoleon, have left the country a legacy of tiny farms. Well over a third of all farms are less than 1.5 ha/4 acres, and the average farm size is only 15 ha/40 acres.

The preponderance of small farms is seen as the central paradox of German farming, throwbacks to another era persisting in one of the world's most modern industrial economies. Consequently, land consolidation has remained a keystone of government rural regeneration projects or green plans since the early 1950s.

Poor relations? Low farm incomes are a major source of worry. After rising some 7% a year in real terms until 1975, average annual farm incomes have dropped steadily ever since; in 1986, they stood at just DM25,250.

Major battles now rage around the issue of farm subsidies, and the farming lobby, especially in the south, has been so effective at putting the farmers' case that the Ministry for Agriculture and Nourishment is often known in Bonn as the Ministry for the Nourishment of Agriculture. German farmers were major recipients of CAP subsidies and felt badly let down by the economy drive of the mid-1980s and the introduction of the milk production quotas. But their outrage at the dismantling of the "monetary compensatory amounts" (MCAS), designed to protect farmers from exchange-rate movements, was so fierce that the German government was, uniquely, able to persuade the EC to let them compensate farmers from the proceeds of a rise in tax on farm produce from 8% to 13%.

Forestry
With almost a third of the country covered by woodlands, forestry is a major industry, employing some 800,000 and providing Germany with almost half its total timber needs. The woodlands are also a leisure and tourist resource. About 55% of woodlands are in state hands; the remainder is owned privately but subject to very strict regulations. Private owners are not allowed to clear woods without a licence and must replant thinning areas. Private woods are also, by law, freely open to all. Since a 1983 report showed that more than a third of all trees were sick, woodland conservation has been a key political issue.

Fishing
The fishing fleets of the north coast supply little more than a third of the country's fish consumption. They are now facing competition even on their own fishing grounds, as fishing fleets from other EC countries are free to fish as equals in 266km/200-mile zones. Between 1983 and 1985, the number of vessels registered dropped by almost a tenth, while in 1985 the catch was more than a third down on the previous year.

Minerals
West Germany has a useful rather than rich mineral resource base. Iron ore to supply the steel industry is largely imported; the native iron ore extraction industry is in long-term decline. But Germany has useful deposits of potash, quartz, lava sand, refractory clay, gypsum and limestone, and is a major producer of lead, zinc, aluminium and copper.

Coal mining accounts for 80% of employment in mining but, with almost all easily workable deposits of hard coal in the Ruhr exhausted, the industry is shrinking. Output of hard coal slumped from more than 110m tonnes/122m US tons in 1970 to 81m/89m in 1986, and it now supplies just 20% of the country's energy needs (compared to 35% in 1970). At the same time, early retirement schemes have cut employment in the industry from 225,000 to barely 160,000. Production of lignite (brown coal) from fields near Cologne and the Harz foothills continues to rise and, in 1985, reached 121m tonnes/133m US tons. But its low energy value means that it still supplies only 10% of all energy needs.

Over the last 20 years, the government has been closely involved in the industry, and it was on its initiative that 40 mines were merged in 1969 to form the vast Ruhrkohle conglomerate which produces more than 75% of German hard coal. The idea was to guarantee a secure supply of coal, and to keep miners working by enabling them to move easily to another mine when one closed down. Subsidies to the steel industry favour domestic coal, while the electric utilities must contribute to a fund designed to reduce the cost difference between domestic and imported coal. The volume of coal imported is also restricted. The mood which produced the 90/90 Concept in 1980, however – a guarantee to produce 90m tonnes of coal a year by 1990 – has evaporated. There are increasing demands at home and abroad for cuts in subsidies and a relaxation on import controls.

Oil and gas Germany has only small oil reserves: offshore near Schleswig-Holstein and the Ems estuary, and on shore in the North German plain and Alpine foothills. Imports account for 94% of German oil consumption. Output of natural gas, however, is considerable, supplying 35–40% of domestic consumption.

Human resources

There are some 61m people living in West Germany, making it the most populous country in Europe. It is also one of the most densely populated and urbanized, with more than 60% of Germans living in towns of over 20,000. But the 1980s have seen growth slow almost to a standstill, and before long the population may actually begin to shrink.

A diminishing population

For more than a decade, West Germany's birth rate has been the lowest in the world and it is getting lower all the time. Each year, for every seven Germans who die, only six are born, and the average German family now has just 1.3 children. If the population has not actually begun to dwindle already – as many believe it has – then it is only a matter of time before it does. Only an influx of foreign immigrants has kept the overall population rising at all during the 1980s, and immigration has now slowed to a trickle. Some believe there will be fewer than 40m West Germans altogether by the year 2030.

Surprisingly, no-one knows precisely what the population of West Germany is; nor have they for many years. There has not been a proper census since 1973; public outcry over possible invasion of privacy delayed the 1983 census until 1987, and the results have still to be published.

Baby talk Whatever the reason for the dropping birth rate – and many have been mooted, including anxiety about the future, the rise in the number of women working and even *Kinderfeindlichkeit* (dislike of children) – the trend is causing Germans deep concern. Just how anxious they are was revealed when the Kohl government launched a programme to encourage parents towards a target of 200,000 extra babies a year. But improved maternity benefits and a range of other baby-boosting measures have as yet had little impact.

Holding back growth? The gradual decline in the population has been cited as one reason why the economy is not officially expected to expand by more than around 2.5% annually until well into the 1990s. With fewer young people entering the job market, companies are having to spend more money on retraining employees to cope with new technology. The number of people looking to start new apprenticeships is already sliding. In 1986, there were fewer than 730,000 candidates for 716,000 training places; by the mid 1990s, the number of candidates will drop to 500,000. Some industries, especially in the engineering sector, could run into major hiring difficulties.

Long-term doubts In the long term, the declining birth rate and diminishing population will reduce the strain on Germany's pressured environment, but many observers are worried by the prospect of an increasingly old and smaller workforce. By the turn of the century, the share of the labour market accounted for by people under the age of 30 is likely to be just 20%, compared with more than 33% now. German industry, which has already automated heavily to reduce labour costs, will have to move even farther down the labour-saving road.

Moreover, as people live longer, the number of old people is likely to increase considerably. In the year 2,000, it is estimated, there will be 47 people of pensionable age for every 100 in work, and the average age of the population will be almost 42. Many wonder how the country will support so many economically inactive people and, at the same time, provide the extra healthcare and welfare all these elderly people will inevitably need.

Population movement

Ever since World War II, Germany's rural population has dwindled steadily, as poor farm incomes drive people to seek work in the towns. Paradoxically, however, the past 20 years or so have seen increasing suburbanization of the countryside around the major cities. One in two Germans now live in the semi-rural suburbs (the *Verdichtungsräume*) around the major cities, and every day millions of Germans drive in from small villages and isolated houses to work in town. Significantly, it is the small and medium-sized towns, not the big cities, which have grown most in recent decades. With no dominant capital to act as a focus for growth, development in Germany has been markedly provincial.

Moving south The most heavily populated area remains the old industrial heartland around the Ruhr and the lower Rhein, where town after town sprawl together to form an almost continuous conurbation. But as the traditional industries have declined here, and in other northern industrial centres, so more Germans have moved south, drawn by the booming high-tech and motor industries and pleasant environment of Bavaria and Baden-Württemberg. So far the numbers involved have been small, for Germans have shown a marked reluctance to leave home in search of work, but the drift to the south is expected to gain momentum in the future.

Unemployment

In the 1980s, for the first time, unemployment in Germany has become a major cause for concern. Indeed, in the mid-1980s, more than 70% of voters considered it the crucial election issue. Throughout the decade, the number of jobless has risen intermittently, but with little sign of a major reversal until recently. By 1986, unemployment was running at 9%, and there were more than 2.2m out of work. The bulk of the job losses have been attributed to the contraction of employment in heavy industry, which has been barely offset by gains in the service sector. But another factor has been the flood of new entrants to the job market as those born in the 1960s baby boom came of age. It will not be until well into the 1990s that the decline in birth rate has an impact on unemployment.

Population Pyramid 1985

Age Groups	Male (in millions)	Female
0–4	1.4	1.3
5–9	1.3	1.2
10–14	1.6	1.5
15–19	2.4	2.3
20–24	2.5	2.4
25–29	2.1	2.0
30–34	1.9	1.9
35–39	1.7	1.6
40–44	2.0	2.0
45–49	2.2	2.2
50–54	1.7	1.7
55–59	1.6	1.9
60–64	1.3	2.0
65+	3.0	5.8

Source: Statistisches Bundesamt

Young and old

The devastating effects of two world wars are still working their way through the population. A dearth of people in their mid-40s and early 50s reflects the few births during the war years, while a surplus of women over the age of 60 is largely due to war casualties. A third "missing generation," of people in their late 60s, dates from the drop in births during the economic crisis of 1932.

Two baby booms, one in the years after the war and one in the 1960s, have also created two distinct bulges in the age pyramid. A high proportion of Germans are now around the age of 40, and an especially large number are in their mid-20s. Many political analysts firmly attribute the Green party's mid-1980s electoral successes to the coming of age of those born in the 1960s.

International trade

West Germany is one of the world's giants when it comes to international trade. Its visible exports (DM526bn in 1986) are second to none, and its imports are surpassed only by those of the USA. But the continuing strength of the D-mark has damaged exports, and in 1986 annual exports failed to rise for only the second time since the mid-1950s. There are now signs that West Germany's traditionally highly visible trade surplus may be starting to narrow.

The surplus

West Germany's export performance during the 1980s has been consistently impressive. But many believe the country's dependence on exports is excessive. While exports are equivalent to just over 11% of Japan's GNP and under 10% of the USA's, they account for almost a third of West Germany's (32.8% in 1986). This is why the level of the visible trade surplus excites such keen interest both at home and abroad.

Abroad, economics ministers want the German economy to act as a motor for growth elsewhere, but they want the trade surplus to narrow and imports to grow faster in real terms than exports. There are signs that this is now happening. Although in 1986 the surplus reached a record DM113bn, the figures disguise a perceptible narrowing of the gap in real terms. Exports actually dropped that year in both volume and value, for the first time in many years. And while there was a drop in the value of imports, this was largely due to the sharp dip in prices, assisted by the fall in oil prices and the weak dollar. Imports were significantly up in volume, and, at 1985 prices, the surplus would have been cut by DM20bn. Now, Germany's trade surplus may be shrinking in value as well as volume, as exports stagnate and imports boom.

Key exports

As might be expected, manufactures dominate Germany's export trade, and finished goods account for 70% of Germany's export earnings.

Despite faltering on the home market in the face of foreign competition, the German motor industry remains the country's largest earner overseas by far. In 1986, export sales of road vehicles brought in not far short of DM100bn, almost a fifth of Germany's total export earnings.

Machinery of all kinds – office equipment, machine tools, textile machines, pumps and so on – brings in DM80bn or so a year while electrical equipment, another healthily growing sector, is also a big earner, worth a further 8% or so of Germany's export earnings. Other important export areas include chemicals, food and drink and, some way behind, iron and steel.

On the whole, Germany's finished goods exports – particularly in capital goods – have held up well in recent years, despite the strength of the D-mark. Exports of consumer goods continue to grow, albeit slowly, as German industry has reaped the benefit of its reputation for quality and sophistication. But profit margins have been trimmed. And exports of raw and semi-processed goods have been badly hit by the strength of the currency and have slumped in both value and volume in recent years.

Key imports

Germany's imports, currently expanding at 6% a year, are much more evenly distributed throughout the various sectors, and primary goods play a far more prominent role.

Food and drink remain the biggest single import sector, accounting for about 14% by value. Chemicals and other raw materials for industry are also important. But recent years have seen finished goods claiming an increasingly large slice of the cake, helped along by the strong D-mark and the booming German consumer market. A decade ago, finished goods made up only a third of German imports; now they account for half.

Despite German efforts to reduce dependency on foreign energy, the low worldwide price of oil and gas has undercut domestic energy, and imports of oil and gas have risen sharply in the past few years.

Invisible trade

The seeming inevitability of Germany's surplus in visible trade is matched by an equally inevitable deficit in invisible trade. It is not that Germany has a poor export record in services. The German-based armed forces of the USA and other NATO countries, for instance, put DM20bn a year into the country, while the state-owned Lufthansa and other German airlines bring in a healthy sum. But Germans love to take their holidays abroad, and, when they go, they take their money with them. Currently, tourism drains some DM30bn net from the country each year, and this total is rising steadily. In the long term, too, Germany has a deficit in fees, licences, royalties, personal services and insurance, too, although one recent year, 1986, saw insurance strongly in credit.

Trading partners

Trade in the EC Almost half German exports are sold within the EC, and EC members remain among Germany's most important and most reliable trading partners. Germany's trading relationship with its neighbour, France, is crucial. France is not only Germany's leading export market, taking almost 12% of all foreign sales; it is also the source of more than 11% of Germany's imports.

The lack of tariffs between EC countries, their proximity and Community policy fosters strong trading links with other EC members as well. The Netherlands, the UK, Italy, and Belgium (with Luxembourg) each take around 7–8% of German exports. Significantly, the balance of trade within the EC is tipping increasingly in favour of West Germany, growing from DM31.6bn in 1985 to DM51.4bn in 1986. This is particularly marked in the case of the UK. But German trade with EC partners is showing signs of slackening, and only in Italy, and in new members Spain and Portugal are exports buoyant, but on the whole it is holding up well.

Transatlantic trade The USA, too, occupies a prominent position in German trade, and, until recently, offered a booming market for German cars. The USA is Germany's second largest single export destination, taking over 10% of all foreign sales. The weakness of the dollar undermined German exports to the USA a little, but US exports to Germany tumbled much faster, opening a wide trade surplus in Germany's favour.

Trade with the poorer nations It is Germany's trade with the less heavily industrialized countries that has really slumped in recent years, as these countries have simply run out of money to buy German goods. They now take less than a quarter of all German exports.

In 1982, German exports to the OPEC countries were worth some DM38bn; by 1986 they were worth barely DM18bn. Exports to OPEC dropped by 30% in one year alone (1985–86). That same year, exports to non-OPEC developing countries tumbled 8% too.

Equally marked has been the slump in trade with Comecon, mainly because falling oil and gas prices have undermined the Soviet Union's purchasing power. Exports to Comecon have dwindled to account for less than 4% of all German exports (about the same as Sweden).

The nation's finances

The long-running debate in German financial circles on how much to stimulate the economy has given the nation's finances a rather erratic twist in the 1980s. Much of the fluctuation can be put down to changing ideas and personalities, and varying pressure from the outside world. But there is no doubt that the nation's unique financial organization, with its elaborate dovetailing of federal, state and local budgets, has also played its part.

Massaging the economy

Throughout the 1980s the Bonn government has been under pressure from abroad to take steps to boost the Germany economic growth. A little judicious pump-priming and reflation, foreign finance ministers feel, would do wonders for the German economy, and so the world as a whole. Finance minister Gerhard Stoltenberg has tried to resist the overtures. But an increasingly sluggish economy and rising unemployment have forced the government to take at least limited action.

Tax-cuts The Kohl government's answer has been a series of tax-cuts. The first plan, dating from the mid 1980s, was to lop off DM9bn from the 1986 tax bill and a further DM10bn in 1988. Both figures have since been overtaken, however, as parts of the schemes have been brought forward and combined with newer proposals. As a result, the nation's finances have become extremely fluid. In 1987, the government proposed tax reforms in 1990 designed to slice DM44bn off the income tax bill. DM25bn is to be raised by public spending cuts; the remaining DM19bn may come from increases in indirect taxes or, perhaps, from cuts in subsidies. But while the Free Democrat arm of the government coalition, led by the economics minister Martin Bangemann, has supported the cuts, many Christian Democrats do not, and the picture may change yet again. Many people doubt that the government will actually be able to put their plan into practice. The input of the various *Land* and local

governments is bound to confuse the issue further. Many *Land* governments are worried by "irresponsible" tax-cuts which will leave them with a smaller slice of the financial cake, and will fight against them tooth and nail.

The deficit Opponents of the tax-cuts argue that they will help pile up potentially destabilizing budgetary deficits. Deficits have been rising sharply in recent years and have become a key issue in federal finances. In 1987, the actual budget deficit was expected to reach DM29bn against the previous year's forecast of DM23bn, as a result of sluggish growth and low inflation. The worry is that tax-cuts may increase the deficits in future.

Meanwhile, Germany's overall public sector deficit is also on the rise, with projections of DM55.5bn for 1988 and well over DM65bn by 1990. As a result, public debt has been soaring. At the end of the 1970s, the public sector government was DM206bn in the red; by 1983, it owed DM341bn; and by the end of 1986, DM415bn.

A three-tier system

Spending more than DM900bn every year, West Germany's public finance structure is a vast and unwieldy system stretching across the three tiers of government: the federal government in Bonn, the 11 *Land* governments and the numerous local authorities. All three levels set their own budgets independently and have their own sources of revenue, but there are large – and contentious – areas of overlap. Naturally, spending priorities vary considerably from tier to tier and with the political colour of the party in power, and so different arms of the government can often pursue directly competing financial policies. To achieve at least a semblance of concerted action, the federal finance minister gathers together the 11 finance ministers from the *Länder* and representatives from the local authorities in regular meetings of the financial planning council (*Finanzplanungsrat*); often the head of the Bundesbank will attend too. But how effective these meetings are is a matter of debate.

How the cake is cut Each tier of government has its own particular sources of revenue. The federal government, for instance, imposes tax on tobacco, while the *Länder* collect motor vehicle tax, and local authorities levy real estate tax. But they also receive a slice of the national revenue as well.

As a rule, the federal government and the *Länder* each take a little over 40% of revenue from income tax, while local authorities take the rest. Sales tax goes roughly two-thirds to the federal government and one-third to the *Länder* (not local authorities). Under the Equalization Law (*Finanzausgleich*) tax revenues are automatically redistributed among the *Länder* so that no *Land* ends up with 5% more or less than all the others.

Usually, the federal government ends up with about 27% of all public revenues (DM236bn in 1985), while the *Länder* get about 26% (DM226bn), and the local authorities just under 19% (DM164bn). The remaining 28% (DM242bn) is in the social security system.

Where the money goes The division of financial responsibility between the various tiers of government is often obscured by political rivalries. But essentially: the federal government pays for things best handled at a national level, such as defence, transport, communication and elements of social security such as social insurance; the states pay for education, the police and so on; local authorities pay for hospitals and leisure facilities, the utilities and some social welfare payments. Within these areas, each authority is free to set its own budget.

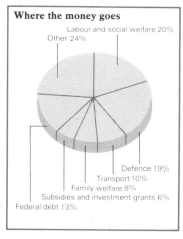

Where the money goes

Labour and social welfare 20%
Other 24%
Defence 19%
Transport 10%
Family welfare 8%
Subsidies and investment grants 6%
Federal debt 13%

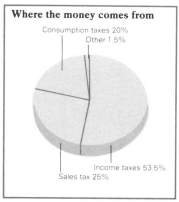

Where the money comes from

Consumption taxes 20%
Other 1.5%
Income taxes 53.5%
Sales tax 25%

The Industrial Scene

Industry and investment

Slowly and tentatively, the giant West German industrial machine is regaining some of the momentum it lost in the early 1980s. Although certain sectors, notably iron and steel, are still in deep trouble, and the continuing strength of the D-mark is a real handicap in the vital export markets, German industry has on the whole proved more flexible than some feared, and is learning to adjust well to the changing world economic climate.

Shifting gear

After almost three highly successful decades, the West German industrial machine entered the 1980s showing distinct signs of stress. Escalating oil prices exposed the weak capital base and low profit-sales ratios of many firms. Energetic competition from Japan and the Far East sliced deeply into markets both at home and abroad, especially in consumer goods, steel and ships. And, to their profound concern, the Germans found themselves losing the technological race in electronics to the Japanese and Americans.

Although some companies went bankrupt, unemployment climbed to 2m and the country's trade surplus dipped, it was not the full-scale crisis some suggested, but it provoked a major re-appraisal. The changes begun in the early 1980s will dictate the pattern of German industry at least until the end of the decade.

Small but special One of the keys to the re-alignment of German industry in the 1980s has been the flexibility of the thousands of small and medium-sized firms who between them account for half Germany's exports in capital goods. They are winning through by tailoring their products precisely to suit customers and continually refining and updating to offer the best and most sophisticated products that money can buy. Especially visible in the precision instruments industry, these small firms have been quick to make the most of new

technology in their own operations, and to employ the latest microelectronics in their products.

Restructuring at the top In every industry, the message is the same. To combat mounting production costs, businesses must shift their emphasis from big sales and small profit margins to smaller sales and big profits – in other words, move from bulk goods to high value-added specializations. The strenuous efforts of industrial giants to rise to the challenge has spawned a wave of job cuts, rationalizations, mergers and acquisitions, as the big firms try to buy their way into new areas and abandon old. High-tech firms have been popular targets, and Daimler-Benz's purchase of first the electronics company AEG-Telefunken, then the aero-engine makers MTU and finally the aerospace firm Dornier is a sign of things to come. But although these changes have been dramatic, there is little sense of haste about them; West German firms have always moved cautiously, and the steadiness of the economy has bought them plenty of breathing space.

Investing abroad With high production costs at home and the strong D-mark undermining exports, many firms have decided that the way to sustain foreign sales is to set up operations abroad. Accordingly, German firms from Siemens to BASF have been buying overseas bases in the USA, and to a much lesser extent in Japan.

Problems

There can be no doubt that many businesses are readjusting confidently to the changing world situation. But some sectors, such as steel and shipbuilding, are finding the necessary changes painful, and it is not certain they can be made at all. Moreover, there remain a number of problems that are undermining faith in the strength of German industry.

Costs and productivity German industry faces some of the highest production costs in the world. Workers are among the highest paid in the world, have some of the longest holidays, and each year seem to achieve further reductions in the working week. It is no wonder then that German industry spends more on labour-saving than job-creating, and that factory automation is one of the main thrusts of industrial progress.

Poor investment German industry's investment record in the 1980s has been poor. While it has been adept at building up huge cash piles, it has been rather laggardly at ploughing it all back in investment. Gross new investment, which was 26% of GNP in the 1970s, is now down to 20%, and to make matters worse, over 35% of this money is spent simply replacing worn out equipment rather than buying new – that compares badly with the 1970s, when all but a fraction of investment was on new items.

Service deficiency With exports falling, many people believe that Germany will have to generate growth internally in future, and in this respect service industries may be crucial. Yet West Germany has been uniquely slow among the developed nations at building up its service industries, and still relies to an unusual extent on manufacturing for its economic vitality. Financial and leisure-related services such as travel agencies are doing well, but Germany seems to have missed out altogether on the expansion of services such as insurance, hotels, catering and so on that have become such an integral part of economic growth in the USA and the UK. Most observers believe that, if service industries are to flourish, the government must act quickly to lift the suffocating rules and regulations that control services in Germany.

The Green movement Over the past decade, German consciousness of the environmental hazards of industry has been raised to such a pitch that many observers believe it poses a serious threat to certain sectors. Costs of guarding against ecological damage are escalating in the chemical and power industries in particular, and it is said some firms may even leave the country if anti-pollution pressure gets any more intense.

Growth industries

Cars and chemicals, along with machine tools, are highlighted as the areas most likely to do well over the next few years. But it may be high-tech and the German consumer that prove to be the keys to the country's industrial future.

Spending power The late 1980s have seen German affluence at last reflected in raised consumer spending, and the boom in consumer spending is expected to be a prime engine for economic growth over the next few years. The retail sector is already beginning to pick up, and related industries are bound to follow suit. Yet German industry as a whole is only poorly oriented to the consumer market and, at the moment, it is importers who are benefiting more than domestic producers.

High-tech Sophisticated and expensive, the high-tech industries are seen as one of the great hopes of West German industry, and the country is pouring billions of D-marks into R&D. Siemens, Mannesman, Daimler-Benz and Bosch are just a few of the companies which have invested heavily in high technology to secure their futures.

The motor industry

Motor manufacturing is the flagship of West German industry, a symbol both of its strength and its vulnerability. The motor industry is strong because it has made the most of Germany's reputation for sophisticated, high quality products. It is vulnerable because the strong yen is pushing Japanese car makers into the same high quality market. Already some 30% of German home car sales have been won by importers; half of these, and easily the fastest growing portion, are Japanese.

Industry prospects

In the early 1980s, the strong dollar and a booming US economy helped foster an export drive that kept motor manufacture clearly in front as German's leading industrial sector. Spearheaded by Daimler-Benz and BMW, the German industry scored notable successes in the US market at a time when other European car makers were being forced on to the defensive by the Japanese. By 1986 Daimler-Benz was selling over 100,000 luxury cars a year in the USA, and even the small Porsche company was selling half its select output of 50,000 cars there.

The mid-1980s saw the benefits of lower oil prices flow through to the German consumer who, encouraged by temporary tax incentives to boost the sale of cars running on unleaded petrol, provided a strong home market, and sales reached a record 2.83m in 1986.

Successes like these pushed employment in the industry to a peak of 838,000 in 1986, despite the increasing automation of German factories. Industry sales reached DM194.2bn that year, and brought in over DM90bn in export earnings.
Future doubts In the late 1980s, however, clouds have begun to appear on the horizon. After decades of inexorable growth, the German economy is beginning to stagnate, hitting home sales. Yet at the same time, the D-mark has regained the uncomfortable strength that has driven the car makers' strategy since the breakdown of the fixed exchange rate system in the early 1970s.

The result is that vehicle output by the German industry is now drifting back down to around 4m per year from a peak of 4.3m in 1986. An impressive 60% of these (some 2.4m) will still go for export. But home sales may be down to 1.6m, though this is still two out of every three cars sold in West Germany. And employment in the industry is expected to stagnate, if not shrink.

High tech and high quality

German car makers have long been aware that they are poorly placed to challenge the Japanese and Koreans in the mass market. German labour costs are too high – a problem accentuated by the strong D-mark. So BMW, Porsche and Daimler-Benz in particular have aimed instead at the growing minority of buyers who want exclusivity, sophistication and superb engineering from their car and are prepared to pay the price.

High-tech has become a key selling point in export markets, and West Germany has held on to its position as world leader in automotive design – in contrast to, say, cameras, where it surrendered its lead to Japan in the 1960s. Effective fuel injection, engine electronics, anti-skid braking, small car diesel, four-wheel drive: all of these became car-market phenomena under West German badges. Robert Bosch, the Stuttgart based electronics group, was the brains behind many of these advances, spreading its favours evenly between the different German manufacturers.

The German car industry spends billions of D-marks a year on research and development in a bid to keep the innovations flowing. Daimler-Benz spends almost DM4bn a year on research, while Volkswagen alone employs some 500 computer systems analysts to help keep its place in the technology race. At Volkswagen, the technology is central to the production as well as the end product. Indeed, VW were pioneers in the use of industrial robots, and 25% of the final assembly for the bestselling Golf (called the Rabbit in the USA) is fully automatic.

Foreign moves
German car makers are now confronted by two serious concerns: the continuing high cost of labour in Germany, and the challenge of increasingly sophisticated and well-built cars from Japan and Japanese plants abroad.

Going abroad Car makers' concerns about the sheer cost of producing cars in Germany are reflected in the strategy of the US multinationals, Ford and General Motors (Opel), GM having shifted overall management of its European operations away from Frankfurt to Zurich. The Opel Kadett is soon to be built under license by Korea's Daewoo Motor Company. Some Opel models are now flowing from Britain to West Germany for the first time, and some Opels for European sale may soon be built in the USA. Ford, too, may be shifting supply, and even design, of some of its cars for Europe to the USA. Meanwhile, VW is investing heavily in its SEAT plants in Spain, where its smallest model, the Polo, can be built at increasing cost savings as the D-mark strengthens; average labour costs for VW in Spain are about half those in Germany.

The Japanese challenge West Germany has always let Japanese cars into the country freely, but the strain of competition is at last beginning to tell. German car makers are now beginning to move towards joint ventures with the Japanese. Ford Europe is already looking to Mazda

for help in developing its smaller models, while Toyota may well be taking up spare capacity at VW's Hanover plant to build 2,500 light commercial vehicles a month. A battle royal for technological sophistication between the Germans and the Japanese is in store, featuring such novelties as active suspension, ceramic engine parts, four wheel steering, and car navigation and guidance systems.

The major companies
The giants of the German industry are Daimler-Benz and Volkswagen, both of which are among West Germany's biggest companies (see *The top ten companies.*)

Having long been one of the leaders in the technological race, BMW is managing to offer a wide range of models of its sophisticated cars, despite a relatively small output. But its market niche, sporting saloons, is coming under siege. The rallying success of the four-wheel drive Quattro gave Audi, an independent subsidiary of VW, a tremendous boost. Audi is now the third largest exporter of luxury cars to the USA, behind Volvo and Daimler-Benz, but ahead of BMW.

Daimler, too, is squeezing BMW with its outstandingly successful 190, and there are doubts about how long BMW can continue to thrive independently. Like the much smaller Porsche company, BMW remains totally German, but rumours, denied by the company, have been circulating that BMW may be persuaded to join forces with a heavyweight producer abroad.

The GM subsidiary Opel, meanwhile, has begun to revive its flagging fortunes by moving into the same luxury car market which has proved so lucrative for other German car makers. The Omega, developed at a cost of a billion or so D-marks, is now one of the best selling cars in Germany, holding over 20% of the market in its class, second only to the Mercedes.

Mechanical engineering

One of West Germany's two biggest industries (with the motor industry), mechanical engineering has in the past been a barometer for the state of the country's economy. Export-dependent and comprising thousands of small firms, the industry is acutely sensitive to shifts in economic mood, falling into recession in the early 1980s and booming again mid-decade. Today, with exports sagging and domestic demand stagnating, the outlook for the industry can only be described as "changeable."

Changing fortunes

The early 1980s were an unnerving time for the West German engineering industry. Output slumped as the world recession bit into foreign sales and buyers at home cut back on investment. But late in 1984, the industry's flagging fortunes began to revive. Spurred by a strong dollar and a thriving US manufacturing industry, the German engineering firms began to work at full capacity once again. With exports to the USA soaring by 24% in 1985 alone, a mood of confidence spread through the industry, and investment in new microelectronic production technology gathered pace.

Late in 1986, the bubble burst, and the industry began to lose momentum. First, sales in the vital export markets dropped sharply, as the high D-mark and falling dollar sapped German competitiveness and overseas demand shrunk. Now the domestic market is showing signs of stagnation too. Output was expected to drop more than 2% in 1987, and the prospects are for further contraction. Increasingly, the industry is pinning its hopes on factory automation and product innovation.

Automation Like all German industries, mechanical engineering is handicapped by high labour costs. With the biggest workforce of any sector (1.1m), engineering is labour intensive, and expensive labour is an acute disadvantage. More than any other industry, engineering suffers from a shortage of skilled labour, and a dwindling number of new entrants

to the workforce (see *Human resources*) – problems aggravated by the cuts in the working week recently achieved by the major engineering unions. Part of the solution lies in automation, and firms have invested heavily in this area, but automation requires increasingly skilled workers, and it remains to be seen whether the industry can train enough to meet its needs in the future.

Innovation Often unable to compete with overseas makers such as the Japanese in cheap, mass-produced machines, West German engineers rely for their success on exploiting (and creating) small, specialized niches. As a result, German engineering firms are shifting steadily to a high-technology approach, often abandoning their traditional products altogether. Mannesmann, for example, has shifted from steel pipes to hydraulics and now telecoms. This trend has been accompanied by a small but perceptible drift of the industry away from the old manufacturing belts in the lower Rhein and the Ruhr towards the south.

Varying success

In such a diverse industry, it is inevitable that some areas do better than others. One of the success stories of recent years has been the dramatic turnround of the textile machinery industry. After a slump lasting almost a decade, the industry entered a boom in 1983 which shows few signs of abating. Output climbed 70% to DM6.7bn in the three years to 1986 and is still rising, especially for spinning and weaving machines, with order books full until 1989. As so often in German industry, the keys to success have been quality, sophistication and automation.

Other areas performing well are plastic moulding and printing equipment, again with an emphasis on microelectronics, while orders for refrigeration and heating equipment and materials handling (including conveyor belts) are consistently healthy. Areas of the industry with less scope for sophistication, such as agricultural machinery and basic machine tools, are doing much less well, while the demand for turbines, where the MAN company has strong interests, has slumped with the world's shipbuilding industry.

Small family firms

The over-riding characteristic of the West German mechanical engineering industry is diversity. Although it is often the big firms that make the headlines, a large share of the industry is in the hands of small family firms scattered across the country, making everything from fork-lift trucks to knitting needles. The industry association, the VDMA, has 2,600 members, each typically with a staff of 300–400. Indeed 90% of German engineering firms employ fewer than 500.

Niche marketing The proliferation of small firms is a reflection of the unusual nature of the engineering market, with its demand for thousands of specialized "niche" products which the West German industry, with its small, specialist firms, is well-equipped to supply. While the Japanese can often swamp the market for cheap, mass-produced machine tools, they tend to lose out to the West Germans on equipment with exact, individual demands.

The big companies

Although the vast majority of German engineering firms are small, a handful of big companies tend to dominate the sales figures.

MAN power With annual sales of almost DM15bn, MAN is West Germany's biggest mechanical engineering firm, making a wide variety of products, but with a booming heavy vehicles sector. Formed when GHH took over its subsidiary MAN, the company is currently scoring considerable successes abroad, in contrast to many other big German heavy industry groups. Export sales rose by 22% in the year to mid-1987 alone and are now worth almost DM8bn. However, profits remain slim at barely DM130m.

Other big firms include the power-engineering group Deutsche Babcock and Metallgesellschaft which, through its subsidiaries such as Lurgi, supplies anti-pollution devices and caters for the oil industry.

Gildemeister, West Germany's biggest machine tool group, now seems back on its feet again after years in the doldrums, and its strategy for recovery may hold pointers for the future of German engineering. In the early 1980s, the collapse of the market in multi-spindle lathes and competition from the Japanese had Gildemeister up against the ropes. With a slimmed-down workforce and an array of sophisticated new products, however, Gildemeister has managed to turn round its fortunes. The keys to its success have been computer numerical control cutting machines, and its "turnkey" management systems for integrated factories.

Steel fugitives Among the biggest engineering concerns are a range of steel companies who entered the field to broaden the base of their operations. The steel giants Thyssen and Krupp, for instance, now earn about DM30bn and DM15bn a year respectively from engineering sales, more than a quarter of all their sales. A smaller arrival from the steel world is Klöckner, which is battling with the arms manufacturer Krauss Maffei for market leadership in injection moulding machines.

Chemicals

The West German chemicals industry is one of the biggest in the world, and it has played a crucial role in the development of the economy; it still contributes more than 10% of exports. But after hitting a peak in 1983, growth faltered, and in the mid-1980s sales began to droop. A host of factors have been blamed for the slowdown – including the weak dollar and fluctuating oil prices. But the German chemicals firms are responding well, restructuring on an unprecedented scale to shift their operations away from the weak bulk chemicals sector into the more profitable specialty chemicals market. They are also investing vigorously in research.

Changing direction

Throughout the 1970s, the German chemicals companies geared up to meet an expected big rise in demand and sales. When the early 1980s brought a sharp downturn instead, they found themselves with far more capacity on their hands than they needed. In 1982, more than a third of the industry's capacity stood idle. But the Germans were much quicker to respond to the crisis than their counterparts in the USA who were confronting a similar problem, and soon embarked on a wholesale restructuring of their operations, pruning excess capacity and moving into new and more profitable areas.

Cutting back Since the early 1980s, the German chemicals industry has cut back swiftly and effectively on excess capacity and by 1985 it was working at over 85% capacity. Cuts in basic plastics manufacture have been severe. Between 1982 and 1985, BASF lopped 50% off its polyethylene capacity, while Hoechst pruned its by 40%. Similarly, BASF, responding to the popular taste for natural fibres, reduced its dependence for sales on fibres (its star sector in the 1950s) from 8% to 3%, and moved out of dyestuffs. So timely and effective have these moves been that the German chemicals industry has not had to shed jobs. Indeed, in 1987 it was able to increase employment by 10,000 to 565,000.

New directions Falling oil prices in the mid-1980s have given the German chemicals companies a temporary respite, but they recognize that they are at a long-term disadvantage compared to the oil-rich states of the Gulf and the Third World. Moreover, their competitiveness in overseas markets is being undermined by the strength of the D-mark and the weakness of the dollar. As a result, the German chemicals industry is increasingly shifting its focus towards specialty chemicals.

Among the potential growth areas are top-quality plastics and polymers, special synthetic fibres, pesticides and pharmaceuticals. Each of the major companies is spending heavily in research in a bid to develop new products; BASF is pouring cash into its research to find plastics that will conduct electricity, while all the big three groups are developing engineering plastics for aerospace.

Global moves

Relying on exports for almost two-thirds of their sales, the big companies have become increasingly internationalized, and they now have to be seen as global rather than purely German firms. Between 1976 and 1985, the foreign assets of the big three firms mushroomed by a huge DM16bn, while their domestic assets grew by less than DM4bn. Bayer and Hoechst in particular have been steadily reducing their reliance on the home market throughout the 1980s, and less than 30% of their sales are now in Germany. Sales to the Third World and Japan have constituted a static proportion of global turnover. But all the big three have been making deep inroads in the US market, and it is clear they intend to penetrate further here.

With the D-mark continuing to put the dollar in the shade, the German companies have sought to boost their capacity within the USA. In 1985, BASF bought the big American paints manufacturer Inmont in a deal costing $1bn. The reduced interest of BASF in the home market was revealed when it then disposed of Inmont's West German operation to ICI, its main rival in vehicle finishes in the UK.

The following year, Hoechst swooped in to snatch the US cable and fibres giant Celanese for $2.8bn, the biggest takeover in German history. The purchase made Hoechst the biggest chemicals conglomerate in the world. The move seemed to reverse Hoechst's move away from basic chemicals, but the company's chairman Wolfgang Hilger argued that it gave the company a strong base in the USA and a foothold in advanced fibres and engineering plastics.

Bayer, formerly the biggest, most aggressive of the three in the USA (23% of its sales are there), has stayed comparatively quiet – although its recent repurchase for $25m of the right to use its own name on the US market may be a sign of things to come. Bayer has targeted the vast Japanese market for its expansion plans. Its annual sales in the country are already almost DM2bn a year, and the company intends to invest more than DM200m in the next few years.

The big firms
The German chemical industry is dominated by three giant concerns: Hoechst, Bayer and BASF. All three were split off by the Allies after the war from the giant chemical conglomerate IG Farben, but each is now individually bigger than Farben ever was (see *The top ten companies*).

Beyond the big three there are a number of other substantial companies, including Henkel, makers of Persil detergent. Along with Colgate-Palmolive, Henkel dominates the West German toiletries market, and in 1987 it signalled its intention to move into France in a big way with its purchase of the cleaning products firm Lesieur-Cotelle, immediately selling half its share in the company to Colgate-Palmolive to begin a joint venture. Reflecting the trend among the big three, Henkel's profits rose 28% in 1986, while its sales dropped 5%. Another large German toiletries firm, Blendax, was recently swallowed up by Procter and Gamble, leaving most of the remaining substantial chemicals companies in pharmaceuticals, including Merck, Schering (known for its oral contraceptives), Böhringer-Ingelheim and Böhringer-Mannheim.

Environment
As the Green movement has gained in strength and influence in the 1980s, so the chemicals companies have found themselves under increasingly vehement attack for polluting the environment. In 1986, a spillage of toxic chemicals into the Rhein after a fire at the Swiss Sandoz firm's warehouse in Basle seemed to confirm the ecologists' worst fears about chemicals companies.

The pressure on chemical companies to clean up their act is already intense, and likely to increase. They now spend some DM4.5bn a year on environmental protection, and each of the big three has a full-time environment officer. Insurance against environmental accidents is becoming very expensive. Meanwhile, the government plans to impose tough controls on new chemicals plants and force firms to report even minor accidents. Many observers are worried that as anti-pollution pressure at home grows, so chemicals firms will take more and more of their investment abroad.

Electronics and electrical engineering

In the early 1980s, the West German electronics and electrical engineering industries found themselves falling behind in the technological race, to the Japanese in electronics and the USA in data processing, and the country's share of the international electrical goods market plummeted. German pride, as well as business, was hurt, and since then the industry has made strenuous efforts to catch up, pouring millions of D-marks into R&D. Just how fruitful these efforts have been remains to be seen, for while German firms have scored notable triumphs in particular niches, the strength of the D-mark continues to squeeze business abroad and undermine competitiveness at home.

Industry structure

The West German electrical industry is dominated by two vast groups, Siemens and Robert Bosch, who between them account for more than half the sales by the industry (see also *The top ten companies*). The next largest firm, Nixdorf, achieves sales barely a tenth of the size of Siemens, and the influence of the two giants on the German industry is huge.

A number of key areas have been identified as crucial to the future of the West German electrical industry. *Factory automation* has been a consistent winner for the West German electrical industry, and Siemens in particular is investing heavily in both CAD (computer-aided design) and CAM (computer-aided manufacture) systems. But factory automation only really comes into its own when CAD and CAM and computerized stock control systems can be linked together to form a fully integrated factory. And both the Japanese and the Americans (General Motors' MAP system, for example) have a clear lead in integrated systems. Many believe the only way West German firms can compete with the giant multinationals such as IBM and Honeywell is by collaborative projects with European neighbours. A sign of things to come may be the CNMA project, which includes Siemens and Nixdorf as well as fellow Europeans like Olivetti and GEC.

Semiconductors For many years,

West German electronics firms allowed Japan and the USA to surge far ahead in the semiconductors industry, the Japanese consumer electronics industry and the American data processing industry consuming chips at a prodigious rate. But semiconductors are now emerging as the key element in all sectors of the electronics industry and the Germans are realizing that their reliance on US and Japanese suppliers may be a serious handicap – especially as the increasing complexity of chips means that for optimum performance chips should be tailor-made for each application. The Germans have a long way to go to catch up, however, and they are pinning their hopes on a collaborative project between Siemens and the Dutch Philips company – one of the few big European chipmakers – to develop an advanced "megabit" memory chip. Siemens plans to use the chips in factory automation, medical technology and car electronics. The company has already poured well over DM2.5bn into the project, but production at its new factory at Regensburg in Bavaria is way behind schedule, and the project is proving a real drain on company resources.

Medical technology Another important area for the future is medical diagnostic equipment. The market in Nuclear Magnetic Resonance (NMR) scanners alone is already worth DM1bn a year worldwide and is expected to grow rapidly. Siemens in particular is making great strides in this field, and a few years ago took over a US medical technology firm to provide a firm base for its operations there. The continuing adverse D-mark/dollar ratio, however, has hit Siemens' US sales of medical equipment badly and the sector is now consistently making substantial losses.

Consumer electronics After some years in the doldrums, the German consumer electronics industry is beginning to look healthy again, lifted by the consumer spending boom in Germany. The market was apparently saturated, but Germans now seem willing to buy new products provided they show signs of innovation. After trimming its workforce and automating in the lean years, Grundig, for example, is now turning heavy losses into small but significant profits on its audiovisual equipment.

Defence electronics Although many European governments are cutting their spending on defence electronics, it remains a highly lucrative market, as Daimler-Benz recognized when they took over the leading German firm AEG in 1986. In the past, German firms have been in the forefront of defence electronics technology, but the advantageous position of US firms in relation to huge US defence contracts may eventually tell on them. Increasingly, the Germans are coming to rely on European collaborative projects, such as the four-nation Eurofighter (EFA) and the Franco-German PAH-2 anti-tank helicopter, all of which are fraught with problems.

The computer industry

Computer hardware For the past decade, the West Germans have been steadily slipping behind US and Japanese firms in their share of the computer hardware market, and as the worldwide growth of the industry begins to slacken, German firms are being forced increasingly onto the defensive. For some firms, collaboration seems to be the only way to avoid being pushed into narrow niches. Siemens, the biggest European computer firm with over 5% of all sales in Europe (compared with IBM's 22%), has had an arrangement with the Japanese Fuji company for marketing Fuji's machines in Germany, while BASF, Germany's fourth biggest company, has a similar deal with Hitachi. In 1987, both BASF and Siemens amalgamated their IBM-compatible computer businesses. The bright spark of the West German computer industry, however, is Nixdorf, whose sales are booming. The key to its success has been to focus its efforts on a number of well-defined sectors of the market, notably banking and retail computer networks. With a huge order from Montgomery Ward, the USA's fifth largest retailer, and orders from Austrian banks and the German, British and Norwegian postal services, Nixdorf's future looks bright.

Computer software Long among the world leaders, West German software companies have come under increasing pressure from the US giants such as Lotus and Microsoft. On the spot in the world's largest market, the US firms capitalized by selling standard software packages in vast quantities. The Germans have little chance in competing at this game, and are beginning to concentrate on the market for specialized, custom-made software; the leading German firm, Software AG, prides itself on its good customer relations and the "user-friendliness" of its software. Nevertheless, Software AG's famous Adabas database management systems established such a long technological lead when it was launched in the 1970s that the US houses are only just beginning to catch up. And Software AG is currently working on a way of including sophisticated expert systems in standard business software applications.

Iron and steel

Once the powerhouse of the economy, the West German iron and steel industry is in trouble. A boom in the mid 1980s evaporated as quickly as a summer shower, and the industry is back into the spiral of decline that began more than 20 years ago. Yet the German iron and steel industry is still the world's third largest, beaten only by Japan and the USA.

Changing fortunes

The bad years In the late 1970s and early 1980s, declining demand for steel products combined with unprecedented competition from cheap non-European steel to tear great holes in the German steel industry. Output plummeted by a third in just six years as the steelmakers made great efforts to cut excess capacity, and 100,000 steelworkers – more than a quarter of the workforce – lost their jobs. Yet despite their efforts, Germany's steelworks were running at just 54% capacity in 1982, and the industry was making a loss of DM80 on every ton of steel it made.

1983 saw the industry at its nadir. The steel-producing regions were plunged into a round of mass lay-offs, desperate pleas for state aid and abortive merger talks. Korf Stahl went bust and steel centres like Hattingen in the Ruhr, where Thyssen closed its mill, threatened to turn into ghost towns.

The good years In 1984 and 1985, the industry staged a remarkable comeback, aided by a buoyant domestic economy and thriving construction and car industries, both major steel-buyers. As export sales to the USA boomed, Germany's steel trade surplus reached new heights. For the first time since 1977, Hoesch shares paid dividends, and Thyssen's mass-steel operations turned round a profit of DM691m in 1985. Earlier streamlining, it seemed, was paying off, and the top companies poured money into new technology, such as electric furnaces and continuous casting.

Downcast steel The recovery proved short-lived and, as the D-mark rose against the dollar, exports failed, cheap imports took 40% of the home market and output slumped almost to 1983 levels. By 1987, the profits of the mid-1980s had evaporated, huge job losses were threatened, and the Bavarian steel firm Maximilianshuette ("Maxhuette") collapsed.

The steelmakers complain about the strong D-mark, about being squeezed out of the protected US market, and about EC subsidies to European rivals – subsidies which are, according to Thyssen boss Heinz Kriwet, creating "unprecedented" price competition in the European market. But these are only minor components of a more fundamental problem: the fact that the world is producing too much crude steel. Whatever the reasons for the industry's problems, few doubt that it must contract and reorganize on a drastic scale – and do it quickly – if it is to remain competitive.

In October 1987, the federal government reached a key agreement with the steel unions led by IG Metall under which 30,000 industry jobs would go by 1989, bringing the workforce down to just 157,000 (compared with 330,000 at the end of the 1970s). In return, the government is providing DM600m in social aid for redundant steelworkers; the steelmakers must find about DM1.2bn.

Strategies for the future

New products Like many German industries, the steel industry is making the most of its technological know-how in shifting its emphasis from bulk steel to higher value-added specialized products. In Europe and the USA, enhancements are very much in vogue: steel is made light or thinner, or galvanized and coated with additives such as plastics, nickel or zinc, which make it more malleable, less liable to rust or more heat resistant. Technology is playing a part in production, too, and West Germany has led the world in cutting energy costs by accelerating the traditional energy-intensive smelting process.

Mergers For years, the top steelmakers have talked of joining forces to improve their competitiveness, but most of the merger talk has been idle. A few years ago a Deutsche Bank scheme to forge Klöckner, Hoesch and Salzgitter into a Ruhr group and Thyssen and Krupp into a Rhein group foundered on petty rivalries and government-unwillingness to bear the costs. The threat of a foreign presence in southern Germany, however, may force the big firms to act together to save Maxhuette. And in 1987, Krupp, Klöckner and Thyssen announced a plan to merge their forged product activities into a joint company, in which each will have a one-third stake. This, they hope, will help the companies weather the effects of over-capacity in the forge sector stemming from a drop in orders from makers of power stations and from shipyards.

Diversification The largest steel firm, Thyssen, has bought itself into new businesses, such as machine tools and even trading and services. Barely a third of Thyssen's sales now come from steel. Both Krupp and Hoesch are spreading their operations into industrial automation, while Krupp is developing new plastics processing capacity. Hoesch is even trying its hand at computer software.

The EC and subsidies

The relationship between the EC and German steelmakers is highly volatile. On the one hand, the EC, according to the Germans, is continuing to pump subsidies into the steel businesses of

their EC rivals despite a 1985 agreement to end subsidies. The EC plan to cut 20m tonnes/22m US tons of surplus EC steel capacity will also, they say, hit the "efficient" German producers especially hard. On the other hand, the EC agreed in 1987 to retain the steel production quota system which the Germans believe is helping to stop them being undercut by their subsidized rivals.

Other Europeans complain that West Germany does subsidize its steel industry, not only directly, but through help to the coal industry. Over the years, the federal and state governments, under pressure from the unions, the SPD and the steelmakers, have also handed out hundreds of millions of D-marks in rescue packages. Late in 1987, for example, the Bonn government began to seek EC approval for a DM180m regional development grant to help areas worst affected by the steel crisis. In view of the Kohl government's plans to cut aid, however, subsidies will remain a controversial subject.

Industry structure

The steel industry remains in predominantly private hands, and the biggest firm, Thyssen, and third biggest, Krupp Stahl, are both family concerns. The only state enterprise is Peine-Salzgitter, which accounts for barely 10% of the sector's output, and may soon be privatized. The giant Thyssen group, centred in Duisburg (see *The top ten companies*) makes twice as much steel as its nearest rival and over 30% of all German steel. Hoesch, Klöckner and Krupp each produce 10–12%.

The industry remains concentrated in North Rhine-Westphalia, especially the Ruhr, with Thyssen in Duisburg and Krupp in Rheinhausen in the west, and Hoesch in Dortmund in the east. But steel is still made in significant quantities in the Saarland, Bavaria, Lower Saxony and Bremen, where Klöckner is based.

Precision instruments

The West German precision instrument industry exhibits all the qualities that have sustained the country's economic success through the 1980s. Small firms make high-quality, highly sophisticated products at high prices that sell to professional and industrial users simply because they are the best that money can buy.

An export-led industry

Precision instruments makers in West Germany employ 130,000 people, almost 20% of them in firms of fewer than 50. Exports make up 70% of the turnover of these small companies and, in the optics and laboratory equipment sector, 90%, which makes them unusually sensitive to exchange rate fluctuations. Of these exports, 66% go to Europe, and 20% to the USA.

Small is beautiful With the exception of ophthalmic products, such as spectacles and contact lenses, most precision products are small, specialized capital goods on which the efficiency of whole projects, factories or hospitals depend. The buyer of such products is far more interested in quality than price, and in the dedication and track-record of the supplier more than its size. This, then, is a business where West Germany's small companies have their best chance to compete, where the skills of the workforce come in most useful, and where exports are still marketable despite the strength of the D-mark and high pay of German workers.

Photographic equipment
Germany once led the world with its photographic equipment, and the product was one of the Federal Republic's earliest consumer export successes. It then became the first consumer business to be conquered and dominated by the Japanese. Now the West German photographic equipment makers have dug themselves in strongly again, finding a niche in exporting sophisticated products geared to the professional market. Still cameras and movie cameras are made by Rollei, Linhof, Minox, Ernst Leitz and Robot;

darkroom and film processing equipment by Agfa-Gevaert.

Optical and laboratory equipment In the optical and laboratory equipment sector, the march of technology has played into the hands of Germany's old-established optical skills. The progressive miniaturization of electronic circuitry needs optics of very high precision to reduce the blueprints of electronic chips to minuscule size, a business in which Carl Zeiss excels. The increasing use of the laser as a tool, a measuring device and a transmitter of information down optic fibres provides opportunities for firms such as Messer-Griesheim and is sure to be developed further.

Precision guidance Rather left behind in the development of electronic technology, West Germany has made a strong comeback by adapting electronics to precision guidance. Thus drawing-office equipment from Albert Nestler and Franz Kuhlmann is computer-guided, and Zeiss's high-precision, multi-dimensional measuring equipment calculates and displays dimensions electronically as well.

Process control With instruments for controlling processes, the customer is particularly anxious that the equipment and after-sales service is reliable. Here the West German reputation for reliability scores heavily, and companies such as Eckardt and Bopp & Reuther do very well.

Medical equipment In the medical equipment business, one of the best-known firms is Draegerwerk. Again, this small company ploughs an enormous proportion of its turnover back into research and development.

Communications

With the size of the world telecoms market set to triple over the next decade, West German communications firms are spending heavily on R&D in a bid to stay ahead of the pack. But while firms such as Siemens are undoubtedly world leaders, the industry fears that with West Germany's telecoms still firmly in the grasp of the Bundespost the country is falling behind its fast deregulating international rivals.

Bundespost

With annual sales of DM50bn and 547,000 employees, the state-owned Bundespost is Europe's largest services enterprise. It has a complete monopoly over West Germany's national communications networks, including everything from telephones to television cables. But the Bonn government has come under increasing pressure to break up the Bundespost's monopoly. Critics say the Bundespost's centralized, bureaucratic structure is slow and conservative when dynamism and innovation are imperative if Germany is not to be left behind in the telecoms race. Moreover, the Bundespost's service is among the most expensive in the world and, according to a report by McKinsey, high-speed data transmission costs 15 times as much in Germany as the USA. With costs this high, it is no wonder that some international services firms are moving out of the country.

A government report published in September 1987 recommended ending the Bundespost's monopoly on telecoms services and the supply of equipment (*Endgeräte*) such as telephones and telex machines, but retaining its control of the network and telephone services. However, the government faces fierce opposition even to these changes, none of which will begin until the end of the decade. In the meantime, the Bundespost is upping its spending on new technology, creating DM30bn of business. Its procurement policy remains strict, and its tendency to favour German firms has been vehemently criticized by foreign competitors.

Siemens and ISDN

For Siemens, now the world's third largest telecoms manufacturing company, the Bundespost's support has been crucial. Recently, Siemens and the Bundespost have collaborated on the development of a digital commmunications network called ISDN (integrated services network), a universal integrated telephone and telex network which makes it possible to transfer speech, video images, texts and data. The ISDN network is to form the basis of West Germany's future telecommunications infrastructure and, according to some, the parallel development of intra-office networks capable of ISDN has given the West German communications industry a world lead in the telecoms war.

Office networks

Spearheading West Germany's bid for world communications markets are intra-office systems. Leading German manufacturers Telenorma, Nixdorf, Detewe and SEL had installed 6,300 systems by 1987, and the pace is likely to accelerate. Some buyers are hesitating, though, knowing that future business may depend upon installing the right system.

Mergers and takeovers

Many West German firms are talking of collaboration and takeovers to achieve economies of scale. In 1987, Siemens was involved in a bitter struggle with the US giant AT&T for control of the second French switching gear manufacturer CGCT, a prize which was eventually won by the Swedish firm Ericsson.

The top ten companies

Daimler-Benz

Today, Daimler's empire embraces everything from vehicles and aircraft to gas turbines, medical equipment and toasters. The 1985–86 takeover spree which netted the Dornier aerospace group, engine and turbine manufacturer MTU and the AEG electrical and electronics combine was widely interpreted as signalling Daimler-Benz's intention to become a generalized high-technology company. The group's continued solid performance, except in the troubled trucks sector, has belied signs of mild indigestion in the wake of these takeovers, symptoms which provoked major shareholder Deutsche Bank to nudge out chairman Werner Breitschwerdt in favour of deputy Edzard Reuter.

Volkswagen

Europe's biggest car maker is doing well despite a sensational foreign currency deal scandal in 1987 which forced the government to postpone a plan to sell off its 16% stake in the firm. Healthy cash reserves enabled VW to absorb losses due to the scandal of DM473m and chairman Cahl H. Hahn seems firmly back in control. With a 14.7% slice of the European market and the leading 28.6% of the home market, VW and its upmarket subsidiary Audi boosted worldwide sales to a record 2.5m cars in 1986. There are still problems with its Brazilian wing, but VW hopes that the soaring foreign sales of its new Spanish acquisition SEAT and a Latin American joint venture with Ford will improve the situation.

Siemens

West Germany's biggest electricals firm, Siemens is investing heavily in future-oriented technology. A 50% increase in capital spending in 1987 (to DM600m a year) focused on microelectronics. The company also expanded its production facilities for personal computers, peripheral equipment, production automation gear and automotive engineering products. An increased US market share should follow Siemens's takeovers in both telecommunications and medical technology, where it is already a world leader. However, it remains tied to a number of sluggish markets; a 14% drop in sales in 1985–86 was due largely to its sagging power station business.

BASF

The largest of the big three chemical companies, BASF has been pushing deeper into high value-added products. It has also embraced consumer goods like magnetic audio tapes, as well as paints, plastics, pharmaceuticals and agricultural products. Via its Wintershall AG oil and gas subsidiary, BASF is the only German chemicals company to supply most of its own raw materials. But low oil prices are taking a toll on this strategic asset, and in 1986 company sales were 8.8% down as oil, gas, fertilizer and bulk chemicals sales faltered. Nevertheless, BASF is boosting investments to expand its worldwide activities. A major target for growth is the USA, where sales grew 42% in 1986.

Bayer

Earning nearly 80% of its sales outside West Germany, Bayer is spending more than DM2bn on R&D to speed its progress into higher value-added products and now boasts that 40% of sales are generated by new products. Key research projects include new pharmaceuticals and photo-electronics for information systems. Chief sales sectors are polymers (16%), inorganic (21%) and organic (14%) chemicals, drugs (15%), agricultural products (14%) and photographic products (17%). Besides its Agfa-Gevaert photographic subsidiary, key investments include US subsidiaries Mobay Corp and Miles Laboratories. Unhampered by oil activities, Bayer is weathering oil price and weak dollar problems better than BASF.

VEBA

VEBA is the largest home-owned energy supplier in Germany and the final sale in 1987 of the government's stake in VEBA was the biggest ever flotation on the German stock market. Its PreussenElektra subsidiary's 42 electric power plants generate 25% of the company's sales, while its oil and petrol arm, including the VEBA Oel exploration and refining subsidiary and a majority holding in Aral, Germany's biggest gas station chain, account for a further 25%. But expansion of activities such as chemicals (11.8%), trading (30%) and transport (5%) have broadened VEBA into a holding group for over 500 companies.

Hoechst

Like its two bigger chemical rivals, Hoechst is homing in on the fast-growing US market in its expansion efforts, taking over Celanese in 1986. Hoechst is now an internationally oriented chemicals company with major foreign holdings in many other places besides the USA including Roussel Uclaf SA in Paris. Its biggest sales are in pharmaceuticals, with other products ranging from plastics, colouring agents, fibres and agricultural technology to foils, plant engineering and information technology. Sales have been hit by the weak dollar and low oil prices, but high investment and R&D spending are expected to boost future sales in areas like technical ceramics and biogenetic technology.

Thyssen

Europe's largest privately-owned steel producer, Thyssen has diversified via mergers and takeovers. Now a strong services and trading group under Thyssen Handelsunion accounts for 40% of company sales, and products from railway engines to machine tools generate a further 25%. Nevertheless, steel and stainless steel still provide a third of the company's revenues, and have been rocked by the European steel industry crisis.

Although steel capacity has been halved and DM1bn invested in plant modernization every year since 1974, steel profits are still way down.

RWE

Europe's biggest private electricity producer, RWE generates 40% of West German public sector power needs. Electricity provides 56% of sales, but the company also owns 96% of German lignite production through its Rheinische Braunkohlenwerke subsidiary. Other interests include major stakes in a big construction company (Hochtief) and a highly profitable printing machine manufacturer (Heidelberger Druckmaschinen). But the growth in demand for electricity seems to have ended, while low oil prices are encouraging industrial clients to switch to in-house oil-fired generation. The reaction of RWE is to tighten its belt by delaying planned investments, or cutting them altogether.

Robert Bosch

Electrical equipment maker Robert Bosch has built an innovative, high-growth image supplying sophisticated components to Germany's car industry. Car parts account for 53% of Bosch's sales, and the proportion is growing by the year, spurred by rising sales of its pioneering electronic anti-skid braking system (ABS) and fuel injection equipment. Traditionally strong in car radios via its Blaupunkt subsidiary, Bosch has restructured its communications sector into three groups (private, public and mobile communications) to reach new markets, including satellite receiving gear, broadband nets, user terminals for digital integrated services networks and new electronic functions for cars. With US subsidiary Robert Bosch Corp accounting for 10% of Bosch sales, the company is investing heavily in the USA to control the weak dollar, focusing on fuel injection and anti-lock braking systems.

The Political Scene

The government of the nation

Founded only in 1949, the Federal Republic has already given the people of West Germany the longest experience of democracy in German history, and the political system that emerged after World War II is proving more resilient than many had believed possible. West Germany's political structure today may be complex, but it has shown itself capable of providing strong leadership, moderation and steadiness.

The Basic Law

West Germany's constitution, known as the Basic Law (*Grundgesetz*), was never intended as anything but a temporary measure, a transitional structure to tide the country over until the day when East and West were reunited. But as the prospect of reunification has faded, the Basic Law has become the foundation for political life in an increasingly mature and permanent state.

A fundamental feature of the West German system is the country's federal structure, which splits political power between the federal government in Bonn and 10 state (*Länder*) governments, each with its own constitution – West Berlin is a special case. Equally significant is the division, inspired in part by the US Constitution, of the government into three separate arms: the legislature (the Bundestag and Bundesrat), the executive (the chancellor, cabinet and bureaucracy) and the judiciary. Articles 1–17 of the Basic Law also enshrine guarantees of a range of inalienable human rights, such as equality before the law and freedom of speech.

Envisioned only as a provisional document, the original version of the Basic Law was by no means perfect; it has already proved necessary to amend it more than 30 times since 1949. Nevertheless, it has been successful in providing a framework for a newly-formed state which is widely accepted by its citizens, and which has kept Germany free of constitutional crisis.

The Bundestag

As in the UK and USA, the German parliament is split into two houses, the Bundestag and Bundesrat. But the lower of the two, the Bundestag, has ten times as many members and is much more important. It is also the only part of the German government that is directly elected (see *The parties*). Sitting temporarily in what was once a waterworks, the atmosphere of the Bundestag is much more down-to-earth and business-like than its equivalents in Britain and the USA. And the functional setting is reflected in the restrained and serious – some might say dull – way in which it conducts its business.

The Bundestag has a minimum of 496 deputies – plus 22 non-voting observers from West Berlin – each returned in a general election for a term of four years, although the government may call an early election if it loses its majority in the house, after referring its case to the Federal Constitutional Court.

Changing role The Basic Law assigned to the Bundestag a dominant role in the lawmaking process, besides the task of electing chancellor, and all bills are introduced here. Yet in the past it has often been put thoroughly in the shade by a strong chancellor; during the Adenauer era in particular, the house was little more than a rubber stamp for executive initiatives.

Since the late 1960s, however, the Bundestag has begun to adopt a higher profile. The house now expects to be consulted thoroughly during the preplanning stage of every bill, and has expanded its staff to provide expert back-up. It is also involving the public more in its day-to-day business. Public hearings for committees are now common, and televized debates attract substantial audiences.

Parties and factions Party discipline in the Bundestag is tight, particularly among the two major parties, and 90% of all votes split along party lines. Yet the federal nature of West German politics means that regional loyalties are never far from the surface, and no-one can forget that the block of 50 or so CSU deputies on the conservative benches are from Bavaria.

The whole chamber is divided into strongly organized factions (*Fraktionen*), each affiliated to a particular interest – Catholic labour groups, Protestant groups, the agriculture lobby, women's organizations and so on. These factions are a recognized part of the chamber hierarchy, and each *Fraktion* is given its due place on various Bundestag bodies. The size of a *Fraktion* governs, for example, how many places it is allocated on each committee and how strongly it is represented on key bodies like the Council of Elders and the Presidium.

The committees The Bundestag's 19 standing committees examine in detail and report on every bill submitted to the house, and their findings can carry considerable weight. The Bundestag committees still play a less prominent role than US congressional committees. They have fewer resources and, in the past at least, have tended to see their role as one of collaboration with the executive – a tendency underlined by the partisan basis of committee membership. Investigative committees, especially, are often toothless. But some committee members are now beginning to take a more aggressive line. A few years ago, one Bundestag committee, led by a Green party lawyer, delved into the

funding of political parties by big business concerns, notably the giant Flick company, in a way that would have been unthinkable in the Adenauer era.

The Bundesrat

The upper house of the German parliament, the Bundesrat, is where *Länder* interests are represented. Each of the various *Länder* governments sends three to five of the 41 delegates, depending on population. Naturally, the *Länder* tend to choose delegates of their own political persuasion, so the party composition of the chamber reflects the balance of power in the states.

Under the Basic Law, the Bundesrat has to approve all laws which affect the interests of the states, and can actually initiate laws, although it has rarely done so. Traditionally, it has played a minor role in the legislative process and remains more an administrative than an overtly political body – although this may be changing (see *The reins of power*). Indeed, delegates usually get state civil servants to deputize for them in the chamber, except at the monthly plenary sessions; and on the Bundesrat's committees, where much of the house's work is done, deputizing bureaucrats typically outnumber elected politicians 15 to 1.

The chancellor and the government

As head of the federal government and chief executive, the West German chancellor (*Bundeskanzler*) plays a dominating role in the day-to-day politics of the country. He (there have been no female chancellors) is not directly elected, but gains his high office essentially as leader of the majority party in the Bundestag. He is actually nominated by the federal president and then elected by the Bundestag, but this is a formality; the president will only nominate a chancellor candidate who has the backing of the majority in the Bundestag.

There is actually nothing in the constitution to say when the chancellorship should change hands; the chancellor can be removed only when the Bundestag manage to muster a majority for an alternative candidate. Usually this happens in the wake of a general election, but the incumbent chancellor, Helmut Kohl, acceded to the office in 1982 when the tiny Free Democrat party defected from their coalition partners, the SPD, to support Herr Kohl's CDU/CSU party. Kohl called an immediate election, however, to legitimize his position.

The cabinet contains the heads of all the various ministries, typically 16, sometimes with the addition of a few ministers-without-portfolios. Chancellors like to appoint ministers of their own political colour, but the prevalence of coalition governments in recent years has meant that cabinet posts must be awarded as much on the basis of party strengths as on the chancellor's own preferences. It has become established practice, first under Herr Schmidt and now under Herr Kohl, that the Free Democrats should hold two senior ministries – foreign affairs and economics. The Bavarian allies of the Christian Democrats expect at least one senior position (the interior ministry in Herr Kohl's government), as well as a ministry of special interest to them, such as agriculture. As a result, the government can often present a far from united front, as different ministers follow different party lines. Even the chancellor may leak criticisms of his ministers to the press via his top aides.

The chancellor's office has grown in size and importance in recent years, and the staff is now 400-strong. The chancellor relies on it to provide the accurate, up-to-date information and analysis he needs to lay down policy guidelines, and among its key officials the chancellor may find his closest friends and advisers. These officials have considerable influence on government policy.

The minister's house Within his or her own "house" or ministry, a cabinet minister is, in theory, in complete command, and the power structure is rigidly hierarchical. At the top of the tree are the various political appointees arriving with each change in government – the minister and his two state secretaries, plus half a dozen or so department heads. Beneath them are the various ranks of permanent civil servants (*Beamte*).

The key policy-making units in each ministry are the 100 or so sections, each staffed by three to seven *Beamte* and responsible for a particular policy area. The unusual practice of making section heads (*Referenten*) both personally and legally responsible for their own decisions has bred a preference within the sections for low-risk, short-term projects – a preference which political leaders committed to major political innovations, yet relying on the advice of these experts, sometimes find immensely frustrating.

The federal president

The West German presidency is largely a ceremonial job. Elected for five years by a special federal convention made up from the Bundestag and state parliaments, the president does little but sign the bills before they become law and act as head of state. A fleeting attempt by one president, Walter Scheel, to increase the authority of his office in the mid-1970s came to nothing. However, a determined and respected president, such as the current incumbent Richard von Weizsäcker, can make his influence as a spokesman for the nation deeply felt. On the difficult occasion of the 40th anniversary of the Nazi defeat, for example, Herr von Weizsäcker's speech far outshone the pedestrian efforts of Helmut Kohl, and the text immediately became a best-selling pamphlet.

The courts

At the peak of German's labyrinthine legal structure sits the Federal Constitutional Court (*Bundesverfassungsgericht*). Defined as the guardian of the constitution, it has a status and role in many ways similar to the US Supreme Court. But, unlike the Supreme Court, the Federal Constitutional Court has two senates, one dealing with individual liberties and one with political wrangles, each containing eight judges elected by the Bundestag and Bundesrat. The pivotal role of the Court in determining the legality of political decisions has made appointments as judges highly sought after. Whenever a vacancy arises, there is the inevitable jockeying for influence among the parties and the elite Bundestag judicial selection committee is heavily lobbied.

Like its US counterpart, the Court has made some controversial decisions in its time, and has never shrunk from confrontations with the government. But a number of its decisions have bolstered democracy in a restrictive rather than liberal sense – approving, for instance, the banning of "radicals" from civil service jobs in the 1970s.

The federal system

The division of responsibilities between state and federal governments is complex and constantly fluctuating. According to the Basic Law, the *Land* governments take charge of everything not specifically assigned to the Bund (defence, foreign affairs, currency, etc) and have broad legislative powers in fields such as education, police, culture, the environment and local government. But while national laws in areas such as labour and criminal law are voted by the Bundestag in Bonn, they are actually applied by individual states within their own borders, and there is often considerable leeway for the *Länder* to interpret these laws in their own way. The *Länder* can also exert a considerable influence on the turn of events in Bonn through their delegates in the Bundesrat.

State finances The division of finances between Bund and *Land* is, if anything, more intricate than the division of power, and a cause of almost as much contention. Generally speaking, the *Länder* receive half the proceeds of income and corporation tax collected within the state, and a third of the sales tax. But since some states are rich (such as Baden-Württemberg) and others are poor (such as Schleswig-Holstein), money is redistributed among them under the Equalization Law (*Finanzausgleichsgesetz*) – though just who gives and who receives is a source of considerable conflict.

Some poorer states have managed to prise subsidies out of the federal government in recent years, despite its declared aim to cut back such payments. Some states have even gone a step farther afield and opened "embassies" of their own in Brussels to lobby for EC cash.

Regional or national power? For most state prime ministers, the attractions of moving to a national political job in Bonn are few. Only a handful of very senior posts in the federal cabinet offer the power they already enjoy at a regional level. When Franz Josef Strauss failed in his bid for the chancellorship in 1980, he returned to Bavaria rather than remain in Bonn in anything but the top job. His southern neighbour Lothar Späth, prime minister of Baden-Württemberg, has been spoken of as a potential chancellor, but nobody expects him to move to Bonn for a preliminary training period in federal government.

West Berlin West Berliners now elect a city parliament and administration, but ultimate authority in the city rests with the occupying Allies. The city sends 22 deputies to the Bundestag in Bonn, but they cannot take part in the plenary votes on legislation or in the vote for the federal chancellor.

The reins of power

Such a prominent role did the chancellor and the executive play in the government of the Federal Republic in its formative years that the political system has been described as a "chancellor democracy." But as the German political system has matured, so the complexity of its power network has grown, and the chancellor's control over events is now tempered by rival factions both within and without the political hierarchy, and by the competing claims of the *Länder*.

Chancellor democracy

The pattern of chancellor power was set by the first chancellor of the Federal Republic, Konrad Adenauer, in his long tenure, from 1949 to 1963. Through personal charisma, and a compliant Bundestag, rather than by any power granted under the constitution, Adenauer was able to exert a high degree of control over the cabinet, the bureaucracy and his party, and effectively bypass parliament in many key policy decisions. If subsequent chancellors have fallen short of this level of control, Adenauer's period in office nonetheless left them with a substantial legacy of accrued power.

The guiding hand There is no doubt that a strong chancellor sets the political agenda, and is the guiding hand behind many of the legislative initiatives which emanate from the executive. As leader of the majority party in the Bundestag, he is in a commanding position to see legislation through, especially as party discipline tends to be tight, and the extensive network of party connections running through parliament, regional and local governments and the bureaucracy underlines his authority. Moreover, the increasingly technical and complex nature of legislation has helped tilt the balance of power further in favour of the "experts," while the need for speed and secrecy in foreign affairs enables the executive to make the running.

Limits to power The main threat to a chancellor stems from worries about his ability to win elections. But recent chancellors, including Helmut Kohl, have not always been able to push their legislative programme through exactly as they want. Pressure from within the bureaucracy, and even his own party, can severely limit the chancellor's freedom to manoeuvre, as can the demands of his coalition partners. And if he has only a slim majority in the Bundestag, he may face real problems getting bills through the house. With a majority of less than 12, Willy Brandt's first government from 1969 to 1972 managed to push through only 75% of its proposals; under his second government, returned in 1972 with a healthy majority, the proportion shot up to 93%. A hostile Bundesrat may pose even more problems.

Cabinet rivals

Article 65 of the Basic Law leaves the power relationship of the chancellor and his ministers open to interpretation. The chancellor is supposed to lay down general policy guidelines, but "within this policy, each minister conducts the affairs of his department independently and under his own responsibility." Adenauer gave his ministers almost no leeway, but subsequent chancellors have not always found it so easy.

Chancellors naturally try to appoint ministers sympathetic to their own policy direction, but this is not always possible. Coalition government in particular has helped many ministers to exercise an appreciable degree of functional independence. The leading Free Democrat of the 1970s and 1980s,

Hans-Dietrich Genscher, who served as foreign minister under both Helmut Schmidt and Helmut Kohl, established considerable latitude in shaping foreign policy.

In cabinet meetings, the balance of power often lies with the chancellor. Agreement is generally reached by consensus, but the chancellor's vehement support for a measure virtually guarantees its adoption and he can effectively torpedo any proposal he strongly disagrees with by his power of veto. However, this power is only rarely invoked.

Parliamentary power

The influence of the Bundestag on policy-making is complex and subtle, and the constant lobbying and discussion, both formal and informal, between the government, the Bundestag committees, various *Fraktionen* and individual deputies means that it is almost impossible to be entirely sure where the decisive voice lies. Government bills are rarely thrown out, but they are often much modified before they are presented in the house.

The chancellor's party majority in the Bundestag, underpinned by corresponding majorities on the committees, means that he tends to have the support of the house as a whole. Even when he loses his majority – usually when the FDP switch their allegiance – a vote of no-confidence succeeds in driving him out of office only if an alternative candidate can raise enough support. However, the house has become increasingly assertive in recent years and is now demanding more accountability from the government. *Question time* in the Bundestag is by no means as boisterous as the British equivalent, but deputies now appreciate its value for putting the government on the spot. Besides question time, a group of deputies can demand an *Aktuelle Stunde* (topical hour) to grill the government on a key policy area, and petitions from 25 or more deputies require a "small inquiry."

Investigative committees The Bundestag has the right to set up a committee to investigate any area of government activity, and this committee can demand the appearance of any government official. But the partisan composition of the committees inclines them to avoid uncovering anything that might embarrass the government.

A hostile Bundesrat

The powers of the Bundesrat under the constitution are limited. But a hostile majority in the upper house can be a thorn in the side of the chancellor, as Helmut Schmidt found to his cost in the 1970s, when the CDU/CSU held the balance of power in the Bundesrat. The Bundesrat has power of veto only over legislation directly affecting the states' areas of responsibility, such as education and the police. But since the states can claim they are responsible for any law that they have to put into practice, the Bundesrat now has to approve nearly two-thirds of all legislation – despite an important constitutional court ruling in 1974 that it had no power over amendments to existing legislation. A veto in the Bundesrat can usually be overridden by the lower house, but it can delay the progress of legislation or force major changes.

Interest groups

The consensual basis of German politics has given lobbyists – or, rather, official organizations – an unusual influence in the policy-making process. Many Bundestag deputies directly represent interest and occupation groups, while organizations such as the employers' and industrial federations, the BDA and the BDI, as well as the trade union federation (the DGB), can count on parliamentary support from a sympathetic block in the house. Advocates of sectional interests are highly visible on the Bundestag's committees.

Party politics

West German politics are dominated by two big party groupings: the Christian Democrats (CDU) with its Bavarian Christian Socialist partner (CSU), and the Social Democrats (SPD). But the country's unique electoral system, with its second, party-list vote, has enabled two other parties, the Free Democrats (FDP) and the Greens, to gain a foothold.

The party state

The German parties are such a fundamental, institutionalized part of the political scene that they are written into the constitution. Indeed, the state will sponsor any party that can muster more than 0.5% of the vote at a general election. Even in the mid-1970s, the state was shelling out some DM120m a year in subsidies to the parties, and state funding amounts to a third of the total income of the major parties (even more for the minority parties). The other side to the coin is that only those parties who conform to the constitution are admitted to the system – which is why the Communists and neo-Nazis were banned in the 1950s. And independents are all but non-existent.

Coalition government

Despite the rivalry of two clearly defined major parties, the Federal Republic has for many years now been ruled by coalitions at the national level. Both the CDU/CSU and the SPD have, in recent elections, always fallen short of an absolute majority in the Bundestag and so have had to turn to coalition with the Free Democrats. From 1969 to 1982, the Free Democrats lent their support to a coalition government with the SPD. When they withdrew their support in 1982, the SPD fell from power, and since then they have been part of a coalition government led by the CDU/CSU.

The electorate has used the party list vote so often to ensure coalition governments that it is clear West Germans feel most comfortable with a cabinet in which a small party can act as a brake on whichever of the two major parties tops the poll. But

coalitions can paralyze decision-making, inhibit clear leadership and give the strong – or wily – leaders of small parties undue influence.

Christian Democratic Union

Operating in conjunction with the CSU in Bavaria, the CDU has held power for more than two thirds of the Federal Republic's life. It was originally based on alliance of Catholics and Protestants formed in the wake of Hitler's defeat at a time when people wished to build bridges across the faiths. But it has never really adopted any binding ideology – except strong commitments both to the market economy and to NATO. Indeed, it has always been seen as a "pragmatic" party, willing to change its policies to stay in tune with voters.

The CDU's traditional support comes from among the conservative professional classes, and older Catholics as well. But it also contains a more liberal element, based in the industrial Ruhr, and a few right-wingers whose influence is less than their ability to grab headlines.

The CDU's Bavarian ally, the Christian Social Union (CSU), is a more natural home for right-wingers. Under the leadership of Franz Josef Strauss, the CSU has staked out a distinct position for itself as a vehement defender of law and order, an ardent promoter of private business and a supporter of US foreign policies.

The Social Democratic Party

After abandoning Marxism at a historic party conference in Bad Godesberg in 1959, the SPD enjoyed 13 years of uninterrupted power between 1969 and 1982. But since then the Social Democrats have fallen victim to problem familiar to other European socialist parties. Economic prosperity and social change have eroded their traditional working class base, while at the same time, the rise of the Greens has cut the party's support among young voters.

The SPD retains regional strongholds in the north of the country, particularly in areas of heavy industry and high unemployment. But it is weak in much of the south, where new technology booms. With the retirement of the inspirational Willy Brandt as party chairman, and the failure of the party's moderate 1987 chancellor candidate, the SPD is hoping that Hans-Jochen Vogel can provide the new leadership which can offer a sound alternative to the CDU without frightening middle-of-the-road voters.

The Free Democratic Party
Although rarely polling more than 10% of the national vote, the liberal Free Democrats have sat in every federal cabinet since 1949. Holding the balance of power between the two major parties, the FDP have maintained their grip on a number of important cabinet posts. A small party with a low membership and a few rich supporters, the FDP owes its survival at the top to its ability to respond to the national mood with a flexibility the big parties can't match.

The Greens
Ecologically-minded and anti-nuclear, the Greens are the most lively of the parties. But their anti-establishment tactics can distract attention from serious ideas about protecting the environment and limiting the pursuit of economic

---

Elections to the Bundestag
West Germany's electoral system is a complex blend of constituency voting and proportional representation and, when Germans go to the polls, they have two votes to cast: one for a constituency candidate (*Erststimme*) and the other for a party (*Zweitstimme*), or rather a list of candidates put up by each party in every state. The constituency vote gives every voter a local representative; the party vote determines the final composition of the Bundestag. Victors of the 248 local contests automatically take up seats in the house. The remaining seats are divided among the parties according to the proportion of votes cast for them in the party vote. Sometimes, a party wins more local seats than it is entitled to on the party vote. When this happens, the party retains its local seats and the number of deputies in the chamber is increased to restore the correct balance between the parties.
The 5% barrier A ruling that

parties polling less than 5% of the party list vote cannot enter the Bundestag effectively excludes independents and extremists. On the other hand, any party which does scale the 5% barrier is represented in the house even if it has won no local contests whatsoever. Thus a handful of Free Democrats have been returned in every election since 1949 – yet the party has never triumphed in a single constituency. The Greens maintain their foothold in the Bundestag on the same basis.
Using the system Turnout in German elections is higher than anywhere else in Europe, and many Germans now make the most of their double vote to do some sophisticated "ticket splitting," opting for one of the big parties in local contests and a smaller party on the party list. Candidates, too, make the most of the system. Those high in the party hierarchy push for a place near the top of the party list. That way they can be sure of a seat even if they fail in the first ballot.

growth. After a some success at the state level, the Greens first entered the Bundestag in 1983, riding in on the 5% rule, and in 1987 upped their share of the vote by 40%. But they are now racked by internal divisions between the "Realos" (realists), who believe they must join forces with the SPD if they are to have any real influence, and the "Fundis" (fundamentalists) who think any such a link would be a betrayal.

International alignments and national security

West Germany has been described as an economic giant but a political dwarf. The legacy of the Kaisers and Hitler has made governments in Bonn acutely sensitive to suggestions that they might be throwing their weight around, while political differences within the coalition governments have often made it hard to maintain a clear foreign policy. West Germany is a committed member of the Western Alliance and the European Community, but its potential international influence has yet to be fully realized.

The Western Alliance

Since its creation, the Federal Republic has been firmly wedded to the ideal of international cooperation and, despite occasional murmurings of discontent from the Greens and left-wing Social Democrats, it is one of the most loyal members of the Western Alliance. The deployment of American medium-range nuclear missiles in the country in the early 1980s provoked widespread protest in Germany, and the Allies feared that West Germany might swing towards neutralism. But Germany's exposed position on Europe's political fault-line binds it securely to NATO, and as yet the idea of a non-aligned zone in mid-Europe has little force.

Good Europeans

Post-war West German governments have been equally keen on developing West European political co-operation. Inhibited about pursuing a specifically German line abroad, chancellors and foreign ministers in Bonn have often seen the European Community as a vehicle for them to play a much greater role in international affairs. On the whole, however, these aspirations have come to nothing, and talk in Bonn of greater European unity is often just well-meaning vagueness.

Francophilia Much more concrete than the European ideal is the real and strengthening bond with the French, confirmed in a treaty signed in 1963. This pairing is now the key link in Western Europe. Yet it is not without problems for Bonn. France's individualistic defence and foreign policies pose the Germans from time to time with an agonizing choice between Paris or Washington. In view of the US nuclear umbrella, it is hardly surprising that Germany's favours usually fall on Washington.

Ostpolitik

Loyalty to the Western Alliance and the large US military presence in the country have not prevented West Germany from pursuing detente with Eastern Europe. A series of treaties signed in the early 1970s regularized relations with the USSR, Poland, Czechoslovakia and East Germany. Progress since then has been slow, but the policy of re-establishing ties with the East – *Ostpolitik* – is now an accepted part of German thinking, although the Bonn government is all too well aware that their relationship with their Communist neighbours is at the mercy of the changeable USA-USSR relationship.

Fellow Germans Many West Germans still harbour the idea of eventual reunification with East Germany. Bonn makes large cash payments to the East Germans to buy relaxations in travel restrictions between the two countries, and any sign of a thaw in inter-German relations provides a boost for the government at home. Yet despite a treaty between the two countries signed in 1972 and frequent signs of accord, the heavily-armed frontier and the Berlin Wall make it all too clear that the East is prepared to maintain the split by force.

National security
Situated on the frontline between East and West, West Germany is seen by the NATO powers as the lynchpin of Europe's defence against the Soviet threat, and it is the most heavily militarized country in the Alliance. There are not far short of 900,000 troops constantly on active service within the Federal Republic, and more than 40,000 separate military installations. A measure of the country's state of readiness is the fact that all public transport is designed with military use in mind. Despite this, it is enshrined in Germany's constitution that its armed forces are for defensive purposes only. Any measure putting them on a footing construed as offensive is fiercely criticized.
The German armed forces Until the 1950s, Germany was not allowed its own army under the terms of the post-war settlement. Since the ban was lifted, however, it has built up the biggest army in Western Europe, 495,000-strong. There is also a further 150,000 in reserve, plus 400,000 ex-conscripts brought back each year for refresher training. About half the army are conscripts; the rest are mostly volunteers. Only 13% are professionals. In theory, every young German receives army training, but many are able to avoid the draft. Recently, the country's falling birth rate forced the government to take the controversial step of extending military service from 15 to 18 months as from 1989 to maintain the army's strength.

NATO forces Stationed permanently in West Germany are almost 400,000 foreign servicemen from six NATO countries: the USA, the UK, Belgium, the Netherlands, Canada and Denmark. Each country (including Germany itself) is responsible for the defence of a particular sector of the country's eastern border, with the Germans and Americans guarding the south, and Germans and the rest the north. Every September, the NATO forces hold a massive exercise covering millions of acres.
By far the largest foreign contingent (more than 230,000 men) is from the USA, and the enormous American presence is a source of controversy. Simple anti-Americanism is now much diminished but many defense experts are worried that the huge US budget deficit may persuade the USA it can no longer afford to pay so heavily for the defense of Europe. Some politicians argue that departing US troops need not be replaced. Others urge further cooperation with European neighbours – a view echoed by many in France and the UK. In 1987, Chancellor Kohl proposed a joint French and German brigade; a few months later a highly-publicized joint exercise saw a French force on manoeuvres in Germany.
The nuclear arms issue has been a political hot potato ever since the 72 medium-range Pershing II missiles arrived from the USA in the early 1980s. And Chancellor Kohl's surprise announcement that Germany would be willing to lose these missiles was one of the major factors behind the success of the 1987 INF treaty between the USA and USSR. The removal of the American missiles will give a boost to those who have been arguing for a joint European nuclear deterrent, independent from the USA. But talks are bound to raise the awkward question of whether, for the first time, Germany should have its finger on the nuclear trigger.

The Business Scene

Government and business

For a country often held up as a prime example of the free-market economy, Germany has an array of links between government and business that are quite remarkable in their depth and extent. State ownership and state holdings in business are extensive. Subsidies are among the highest in Europe. Rules controlling business are far-reaching and strictly enforced. Taxes on business are very high. And there is a tangled web of interlocking interests and personal connections reaching into every corner of German business. The Kohl government came to power in 1983, pledging to roll back the state and allow business to flourish in private. But the range of conflicting interests within the state has made it impossible to put all their plans into practice, and the government's record has been distinctly patchy.

State ownership

The sheer size and scope of state ownership in West Germany often surprises foreigners. Besides the truly nationalized public services – post and telecommunications, the railways, and the alcohol trade, for example – the federal government has stakes of over 25% in almost 500 German companies, plus smaller stakes in many more. Its largest single holding (100%) is in the once-troubled steel company Salzgitter, but it has majority holdings in dozens of others, including the mining company Saarbergwerke and the airline Lufthansa. Indeed, until it sold off its stake in the giant energy and chemicals group VEBA, the federal government had substantial holdings in companies that between them employed more than 0.5m people.

The individual *Land* governments too have substantial stakes in many firms. The government of Lower Saxony, for example, has a 20% share in Volkswagen (the federal government has 16% too) and in most *Länder* ownership of the *Landesbanken* is divided equally between the state government and the savings banks.

Privatization Headway on privatization under the Kohl government has been faltering. Late in 1987, the finance minister, Herr Stoltenberg, could claim to have disposed of major government stakes in over 50 companies since 1983, but many of his privatization plans have run aground, as opposing interests surface within the coalition government and without.

Among the government's successes have been the two-stage sell-off of its stake in VEBA, which netted DM3.3bn, and its disposal of 45% of IVG and 40% of VIAG. But in 1987 the proposed sale of the government's 16% stake in Volkswagen had to be put on ice when the company was implicated in a huge foreign exchange fraud.

Meanwhile, the subject of Lufthansa, West Germany's flag airline in which the government has a 75% holding, has become a political hot potato. The Free Democrat wing of the coalition has put pressure on Herr Stoltenberg to go ahead with his plans to sell a 20% holding. But the plan has been consistently blocked by Franz Josef Strauss, the minister-president of Bavaria, ostensibly because the airline is a "symbol of German efficiency and European technology," but possibly because he wants to ensure Lufthansa buys Airbus which are partly made in

Bavaria. Just how state governments can exert their power in business was shown when the Bayerische Landesbank, half-owned by the Bavarian government, announced that it would take up the Federal Government's rights in a proposed share issue by Lufthansa if the Federal Government chose not to buy them.

Nevertheless, further privatizations are planned, including the DSL bank and Deutsche Pfandbriefanstalt (see *Banks and other financial institutions*). The disposal of the Bundespost remains a very distant prospect.

Regulation and deregulation

From the powerful anti-cartel laws to the rules which forbid shops to open late or on Sundays, the business scene in the Federal Republic is among the most thoroughly regulated in the world. The Kohl government has promised to ease up some of these rules, and in 1986 received from the Kiel Economics Institute a vast report suggesting possible deregulations. Perhaps the most significant plan that has been mooted is the break up of the Bundespost's monopoly on telecommunications (see *Communications*), but this is likely to face considerable opposition. The Free Democrat wing of the government has been championing the cause of relaxing rules on shopping hours, but the CSU in Bavaria, along with the associations of small retailers and the unions, is sure to fight against it tooth and nail. An interesting development in 1987 was the Federal Cartel Office's ruling that the federal agency that awards concessions on the *Autobahnen* could not refuse bids from McDonald's.

Progress on deregulation has been most dramatic in the financial markets, where the Bundesbank has been able to push through a number of changes to open up the market (see *Financial markets*).

Subsidies

Subsidies in Germany are not as substantial as in some countries, but they are certainly high, and are continuing to rise, despite the Kohl government's promises. In 1986, subsidies in West Germany, either through tax concessions or direct grants, were worth some DM120bn, more than 6% of the GNP.

The bulk of subsidies go to the service industries, notably the railways, plus agriculture and housing. Subsidies per head are largest in agriculture: the average German farmer receives hand-outs of DM13,500 a year. Manufacturing as a whole gets little, but certain sectors, such as coal, steel and shipbuilding, do especially well. And West Berlin is given DM8.9bn a year to help attract industry.

The government has said that it plans to find DM19bn for its 1990 tax reforms by cutting subsidies. But the range of opposition in the country means that it will be almost impossible to make large cuts in any sector. Indeed, in 1987 Herr Stoltenberg was forced to yield to pressure to up subsidies to farmers and the steel industry.

One of the obstacles to cuts is the degree to which subsidies have become entrenched in *Länder*, notably North Rhein-Westphalia, and the state governments strongly resist any moves to cut their support for business, cuts which might mean they lose business to neighbours, or, worse still, lose votes.

Taxes

West Germany has some of the highest taxes on business in the world, with corporate income tax running at 56%. The Kohl government's planned tax reforms will cut the rate by just 3%, and late in 1987 it announced its intention to re-introduce a 10% withholding tax on interest income in 1989. It also shelved the long-promised abolition of the stock-exchange turnover tax, a tax which many financiers feel costs billions of D-marks worth of potential trade in securities.

Power in business

Business power in West Germany is concentrated firmly in the hands of the big banks and the official institutions – industry associations, trade unions and the political hierarchy – that earn the epithet "Germany Incorporated." But there are signs that banking power, long regarded as excessive, may finally be on the wane.

Banking power

It is hard to overestimate the hold of the banks, and especially the big banks, on the German business scene. A web of financial links, holdings and personal contacts extends their control deep into the heart of almost every company in the country, and the hegemony over German business of the Deutsche Bank in particular is inescapable.

The levers of power Banks can exercise their influence through a variety of channels, and it is this that gives them such power. As universal banks (see *Banks and other financial institutions*), for instance, they are the sole financial intermediaries of any significance and, with so little equity-funding in Germany, they are usually the prime source of business finance as well. Moreover, if a company should go public and raise money on the stock market, the banks often buy the majority shareholding. Deutsche Bank, West Germany's biggest bank, is the largest shareholder in Daimler-Benz, the country's biggest business.

As if this were not enough, the banks also have their top executives sitting on the supervisory boards, often as chairman; they exert considerable power at annual shareholders' meetings by controlling the automatic proxy vote of shares held in custody by them (*Depotstimmrecht*), which is nearly all those owned by private investors; and they act as financial advisers to shareholders who bank with them. While Deutsche Bank holds only 28% of Daimler-Benz shares, it holds *Depotstimmrecht* over some 30% more, and issues advice to many of the remaining shareholders – and Deutsche executives sit on Daimler's supervisory board, with Bank boss

Alfred Herrhausen at the head.

Out of house The intertwining of banks and business is formalized in the "house bank" relationship, in which most German companies are assigned to one or another of the big banks. Even though a new generation of financial managers is willing to shop around for bank services, the house bank tradition is strong, and there is considerable pressure from the banks to maintain the links; banks can be quite severe in "punishing" those who try to break away. Nevertheless, many German companies are currently sitting on huge cash piles, and have no need for bank loans. Moreover, many firms are now turning to securities rather than bank loans to raise finance. All these changes are gradually weakening the hold of the banks.

The Bundesbank

The Bundesbank commands great respect in West Germany, and as its head Otto Pöhl is one of the most influential men in the country. Although its direct powers are not as wide as those of the US Federal Reserve, the high esteem in which the Bundesbank is held means that those in business listen carefully to its line. Its reputation is enhanced by its highly visible independence.

Germany Incorporated

Traditional German deference to authority has helped invest immense influence in established institutions, and the triangular grouping of organizations representing government, business and labour interests has led some critics to label the country "Germany Incorporated." Consensus is very much the ideal, and all the organizations see Germany as a country based on social enterprise. In other words, strong-arm tactics are misplaced, and the three organizations frequently meet to establish a common policy on, for example, the coal industry's problems – a practice which can leave those outside the official hierarchy feeling distinctly powerless.

The industry associations In theory, the most influential of the industry associations is the umbrella Federation of German Industry (BDI), but its power to alter the course of events depends very much on who is in charge – partly because its ability to put a coherent case is often hampered by the fact that it represents both large and small companies. Conversely, the Association of German Chambers of Commerce has much less actual authority than the BDI, but the personal charisma of chairman Otto Wolf means no-one can ignore it.

The unions The relationship between management and the unions has been good. But this is not to say the unions are quiescent, nor weak, in any way. They have considerable authority, both by negotiating industry contracts at a state level, and by their control over worker representation on company supervisory boards (see *Employment*) – although this is a power the Kohl government is hoping to curtail. Central to the power of the unions is their sheer size – IG Metall, with 2.5m members, is the non-Communist world's largest union – and the fact that they each represent an entire industry. If a union takes action, the whole industry is affected. On the other hand, if agreement is reached in one key state, such as Bavaria, it tends to set the pattern for the rest of the country.

Politicians

Underlying the official links between government and business is an intricate and powerful network of personal ties and overlapping interests. The revolving door which allows easy switching between public office and business is not as well developed as in many countries, but is evident at all levels of the political hierarchy, and many leading political figures, especially at the state level, have direct interests in business.

The web of interlocking interests in the Bavarian government of Franz Josef Strauss and the banking institutions of Munich are particularly intricate. Bavaria's finance minister Herr Streibl, for example, is also head of the supervisory board of Munich's largest bank, the Bayerische Landesbank, in which the Bavarian government owns a 50% stake, while his predecessor as minister is the bank's chief executive. Another ex-Bavarian minister and friend of the Minister-President is head of the Landeszentralbank. Herr Strauss himself sits on the board of many prominent companies. And so it goes on. But it is often only foreigners who see such connections as liable to create conflicts of interest. Many Germans tend to regard them as mutually beneficial, and essential to the smooth relationship of government and business.

The media

On the whole, the press sees itself as part of the business establishment, and rarely toes anything but the established line. Business news often emanates from cosy press evenings around a blazing fire in a Harz mountain retreat. But two weekly magazines, *Der Spiegel* and *Stern*, base their circulation on delving below the surface. They are often the first with any major business news, and so can often make or break a deal. And in uncovering scandals, they can bring down the heads of the biggest companies. The biggest business scandal of the 1980s, involving bribes to politicians by the giant Flick company, was revealed and pursued relentlessly by *Der Spiegel* and *Stern*.

The business framework

Outwardly, Germany is a land of progressive free enterprise, but scratching the surface reveals a business scene as formal, conservative and highly regulated as any in the world. Not only is there a welter of legislative and administrative rules to contend with; there are complex – and even more "binding" – relationships which limit a company's freedom of manoeuvre. Stringent anti-cartel laws (imposed by the Allies after 1945) and recent moves towards deregulation cannot disguise the basic aversion in German business to the notion of unrestricted competition long upheld in the USA and now establishing itself in the UK.

Business structures

Business organization in Germany is, in many ways, very old-fashioned. Some of the world's largest and most successful international corporations are German, but the German business scene remains largely in the grip of the old family-owned firms. And it is the families, along with the big banks, who still direct companies' fortunes – not the shareholders. Only 0.13% of German enterprises are publicly quoted on the stock market.

Businesses in Germany can be run under any one of an array of legal guises. But the overwhelming majority choose to operate as private limited companies (*Gesellschaft mit beschraenkter Haftung* – GmbH), although various forms of partnership are also popular. Only the few big firms seeking a listing on the stock market, or needing a large capital base, bother to go through the rigmarole of setting up as a stock company or public corporation (*Aktiengesellschaft* – AG). At the beginning of 1987, there were some 350,000 GmbHs in Germany, compared with just 2,190 AGs.

The GmbH

Some of the largest firms in Germany are GmbHs, such BASF, but it is small and medium-sized companies which have found this form of organization especially attractive. The appeal of the GmbH lies in the legal framework; regulations covering both the way a GmbH is set up, and the way it is run, tend to be far less strict than those for AGs.

A GmbH can, in theory, be started by just one person, who is allowed to be both the sole shareholder and the sole director. A minimum of DM50,000 capital is legally required for incorporation, but only half of this actually has to be paid up before registration. And a GmbH needs to specify its major activities in its charter in only the most cursory terms. Setting up as a GmbH can cost as little as DM300. For a company with a share capital of DM1m, it would cost roughly DM7,000; to form an AG might cost three times as much.

Running a GmbH is generally far simpler, too. Maintenance formalities are less complex than for an AG, and a supervisory board is required only if the company employs more than 500 people. Moreover, until recently, most GmbHs did not have to appoint an independent auditor or report annual accounts. But with the implementation of the EC 4th Directive from 1987, the regulations affecting GmbHs are becoming tighter. Most significantly, any firm with more than DM8m in sales, a balance sheet totalling at least DM3.9m, and more than 51 employees is now obliged to submit to an annual audit and publish its accounts.

The AG

The legal obligations upon AGs are complex, demanding and expensive, and discourage all but the largest companies from operating in this form.

To set up as an AG, businesses need more than DM100,000 capital, of which at least 25% must be fully paid up before registration. And for a company with DM1m capital, the cost of formation is rarely less than DM20,000. Moreover, a company operating as an AG must not only have at least five shareholders; it must also have two boards, one being the usual board of managers (*Vorstand*), and the other being a supervisory board (*Aufsichtsrat*) (see *Corporate hierarchies* and *Employment*).

The creation of an *Aufsichtsrat* is compulsory for all AGs – GmbHs need one only if they have more than 500 employees. It must have a minimum of three members and a maximum of 10, 16 or 20 for companies with capital up to DM3m, up to DM20m and above DM20m, respectively.

Forming an AG Before incorporation as an AG, the founders must appoint the first supervisory board, which, in turn, appoints the board of managers. Articles of association stating the company's name and objectives, amount of share capital, denominations of shares and types, and composition of the boards must then be certified by a court or a notary public.

To incorporate, the company must register with the commercial, provincial or district court where it is based, filing at the same time all the certified documents, the founders' report on the formation of the company, and proof of payment of the shares. Only when 25% of the share capital has been paid up, and the company's articles of association are registered in the Commercial Register at the local courts, does the stock company or AG come into being.

Partnerships

Partnerships in Germany operate under a number of different guises,

varying in popularity.

Kommanditgesellschaft – KG (limited commercial partnerships) are relatively common in Germany, although by no means as popular as they are in the USA and UK. The basic KG consists of one or more limited partners.

GmbH & Co KG Another common form of limited partnership, the GmbH & Co KG has a limited liability company as its general partner instead of an individual with unlimited liability. In fact, shareholders of the GmbH may also be, and usually are, the other limited partners, so that the entire partnership effectively has limited liability. The advantage over a simple GmbH – which also has limited liability – is that whereas the GmbH is taxed at corporate rates and the shareholders are taxed on distributions, the GmbH & Co KG is fiscally transparent, so that its members are taxed separately on their share of the profits made by the partnership. Moreover, GmbHs and Co KGs escape the EC's 4th Directive, which requires medium-sized and large GmbHs to have their accounts and audits published.

Kommanditgesellschaft auf Aktien – KGaA The third common form of limited partnership, KGaAs have shareholders and have elements of both a stock corporation and a partnership. A KGaA is a separate legal entity in which the liability of the shareholders is limited to the amount of their investment in the company. Only a small number of German companies have chosen to work as KGaAs, but the giant chemical concern Henkel is among them.

Going public

Public corporations are something of a rarity in West Germany. Traditionally, German industry has looked to the banks for long-term financial support rather than to the stock market – a habit reinforced by old emotional ties with families, and a natural reluctance of privately owned firms to open up their books (and hidden reserves) to public scrutiny. Moreover, the few firms prepared to break the traditional mould and go public have often been put off by the high costs, excessive bureaucracy and stringent disclosure rules of an official listing on the stock exchange.

There are some signs, however, that attitudes are changing, and recent attempts to attract companies to the market have met with some success. In 1983, some 12 firms joined the stock market. The following year the computer giant Nixdorf issued 20% of its capital stock, and since then a number of other well-known private companies have taken the plunge, among them the cosmetics firm Wella, the sports equipment makers Puma and the car makers Porsche. In 1986, significantly, the huge industrial group Feldmühle-Nobel (formerly Flick) was joined on the market by a number of much smaller concerns, such as Edding, and the fashion firm Escada.

Yet there is still tremendous caution over the notion of going public in Germany. Very often, the free float of shares in public issues is limited; the same universal banks that supported the companies while they were privately owned usually take a firm, long-term stake when they go public. Issues of non-voting preference shares are also common; shareholder power is strictly the preserve of the banks.

There were 24 new listings in 1986, compared with only 29 in the period 1977-83, but this still only brings the total number of companies listed on the country's stock exchanges to 465, barely one quarter of Germany's AGs. This compares with an increase over the past 15 years in the number of GmbHs, which have leapt from fewer than 70,000 to almost 350,000. Nevertheless, many more German companies are now considering tapping the stock market for funds.

Even international firms based in Germany have, in the past, maintained a somewhat ambivalent attitude towards the stock market, using a listing as a public relations device rather than as a means of raising capital. But there are signs that this attitude, too, is changing. New listings of foreign firms on German exchanges average about ten a year but are expected to grow in number.

Listing procedures The first step for any company, German or foreign, seeking a listing on an exchange is to establish a relationship with a German bank. The bank will form a consortium to underwrite the share issue and will offer it to private and institutional investors alike. The bank not only handles the listing and initial purchase or sale of shares but also engages in *Kurspflege* (maintaining an orderly market) of the securities. Multiple listing of large companies in Germany is common.

Issuing shares is costly. Fees are higher than in other countries and may amount to as much as 10% of the value of the issue. Costs, which include banks' and auditors' services, listing fees, public relations and advertising can range from 4 to 7% of the capital that is received. Porsche, for example, is known to have paid its banks DM6m for its 1984 listing. The costs of listing securities are the same for all German exchanges.

Application for admission of a security to a stock exchange must be made by the sponsoring bank, which must be a member of the exchange. Foreign securities are usually introduced by one of the big three banks (see *Banks and financial institutions*).

Listing requirements Every application for a stock market listing must be accompanied by a prospectus signed by the sponsoring bank and the issuing company, and must contain all the factual and legal information needed for an intelligent evaluation of the security: details of the company's organizational structure, its history, names of its management and supervisory board, and balance sheets and profit and loss statements for the past five years. The same rules generally apply equally to both foreign and local securities, but the German authorities do permit some exceptions.

Any company planning to list its shares on a German exhange should be prepared to submit a detailed prospectus, proof of the right to issue securities, a copy of its bylaws and articles of association, annual reports for the past three years and a specimen of the stock certificate.

The *Börsenzulassungsgebühr*, or exchange admission fee, is charged on a sliding scale from DM30m (on the nominal capital up to DM20m) to DM100m per million (on more than DM50m). But foreign companies can often negotiate a reduction of 30–60%, since only a small percentage of their issued shares wil be traded in Germany. General Motors, for example, which was liable to pay DM200,000 at each of Germany's eight exchanges, reportedly settled for half that amount.

Foreign investment

No other major industrialized nation is, in theory, as open to foreign business as Germany. Germany imposes virtually no restrictions or controls on foreign investment, and is one of the few countries in the world that has no permanent currency or administrative authority to oversee foreign business ventures.

There is no limit on either the percentage of equity or the amount a foreigner may invest. Nor is there any restriction on real-estate purchases by foreigners or foreign-owned companies. Foreign investors do need special licences for certain businesses, such as passenger transport, insurance and savings banks – but so too do German firms.

There are no exchange control requirements on normal commercial transactions or the transfer of dividends and profits. The same is true for the transfer of interest on foreign private loans, the remittance of royalties and fees, the repatriation of capital and the repayment of principal on foreign private loans.

Branches and subsidiaries For a variety of reasons, most foreign firms operating in Germany tend to work through local subsidiaries rather than establishing branches – mainly to reduce tax liabilities and to avoid the complicated accounting procedures that apply to branches. But foreign firms using a German subsidiary must be sure it is registered in the Commercial Register at the local court before it starts to do any business; under German law, any deal entered into by the subsidiary before registration remains the liability of the parent company alone, something one US firm found to its cost when it was sued over a real-estate contract entered into before its German subsidiary was listed.

If a foreign firm does wish to set up a branch, the procedure is basically similar to that for German investors. However, the firm must obtain prior permission from the local provincial government (*Landesregierung*). There are rarely any objections.

Monopolies, mergers and acquisitions

Compared with the UK and USA the German mergers and acquisition market is remarkably inactive and low key. This is partly because there are so few companies for sale and partly because quoted companies' shares are so well protected, making a US-type stock market raid virtually impossible. Moreover, the whole mentality of the mergers game is totally alien to the German business scene.

The concept of junk bonds embodies the kind of risk completely foreign to the traditional German business mind, while the cut and thrust of a Lord Hanson or a de

Benedetti is viewed with considerable distaste. Significantly, there is no example of a hostile takeover worth recording in the past decade, and the consensus among bankers is that no established German retail bank would be party to a hostile bid.

Making an acquisition Ironically, the problem of acquiring quoted companies on the open market in Germany lies not in the legislation – an announcement is required in Germany only after a 25% holding has been reached and surpassed, whereas in the USA disclosure is required at 5% – but rather in the scarcity of shares to purchase. Many relatively substantial companies are still not listed. German shares in any but the top 20 quoted companies are notoriously illiquid, with huge blocks of voting shares stowed away with controlling families and institutional investors. As a result, any corporation wishing to enter or expand in the German market through acquisition is forced to focus on the numerous medium-sized privately held companies on which data is exceptionally hard to come by.

If a prospective acquisition is successfully initiated and closed, the advising bank will typically charge a fee based on the purchase price (3% for the first DM10m, with additional negotiable commission above that level). Most acquisitions successfully completed in Germany have values of DM25,100m, and typically last six to seven months from approach to completion.

The regulations Germany has one of the toughest and most comprehensive anti-trust regimes outside the USA, policed by the government's competition watchdog, the Berlin-based Federal Cartel Office (FCO). Armed with the 1957 Law Against Restraints of Competition, the FCO has sweeping powers both to stop mergers and acquisitions in their tracks and, unusually, to break them asunder once they have taken place.

Monopolies and cartels are not automatically illegal, but any agreement that allows one group to abuse a dominant position in the market is banned. It is up to the FCO to decide just what constitutes an abuse of market dominance.

Typically, it regards as dominant any company with more than DM250m which corners more than one-third of the market; any three companies with DM10m turnover that take more than half the market; or any five that take more than two-thirds. Among the various abuses of market dominance, it is overpricing and underpricing that the FCO has combatted most vehemently in recent years – as five companies importing the blood preparation Factor 8 from the USA recently discovered. The five companies were alleged to have an 85% market share and to be charging five times as much for Factor 8 as it cost in the USA; after pressure from the FCO, they dropped the price by more than a third.

All big mergers (the acquisition of more than 25% of another company) have to be notified to the FCO in advance. Any agreement which seems to be horizontal, the FCO will nip sharply in the bud before it comes to fruition. It will also place limits on vertical deals that seem to interfere with free competition.

Any negative ruling can of course be appealed against first to the Berlin High Court, and then to the Supreme Court. But a prenotified merger cannot go ahead (and thus becomes impracticable in most cases), while consummated mergers may suffer from a protracted uncertainty as to whether the courts will allow them to survive or not. And an alternative appeal to the economics minister, who can overrule the FCO, will get merger candidates off the hook only in the most exceptional circumstances.

The anti-trust authority uses complex share and financial resources as criteria in evaluating a merger. The complexity of the evaluation criteria can be seen from the grounds on which the FCO may prohibit a merger: if a company with a turnover of at least DM2bn gains 5% or more of a market dominated by many small or medium-sized companies; if a company with sales of at least DM2bn acquires another firm in a dominant position in at least one significantly large market; and so on.

Tax

German taxes, particularly on retained earnings, are among the highest in the world, and will remain so even after impending tax reforms. Onto the basic federal taxes are added layers of regional and local taxes. While the same federal rates are charged all over Germany (with the exception of West Berlin), local taxes vary, and the calculations are extraordinarily complicated.

Corporate tax For resident companies, the standard rate of income tax is 56%. Under current plans it will be reduced to 50% beginning in 1990. This standard rate compares with the so-called distribution rate of 36%, which applies to profits that are distributed in the form of dividends.

In addition, a municipal trade income tax (*Gewerbesteuer*) is levied on all enterprises engaged in industrial or commercial activity in a particular municipality. This tax generally costs a company 10–20% of its annual income, and consists of two parts: a tax on adjusted business income and one on business capital. Both taxes are fully deductible for corporate tax purposes.

The basic rate of the trade tax on income (*Messzahl*) for corporations is 5%. But this base is then multiplied by a trade tax factor coefficient. Each municipality applies its own multiple, which ranges between 2 and 4.9. Although considerable differences exist, the average rate of trade tax on business income is about 17%. An exceptionally low rate of 9% applies in West Berlin.

Capital taxes Corporations pay two annual capital taxes: the national property or net worth tax

(*Vermoegenssteuer*) and the local business capital tax (*Gewerbekapitalsteuer*).

For firms resident in Germany, all domestic and foreign assets (including real estate and the value of patents), minus liabilities, are subject to an annual national net worth tax. The first DM125,000 of a resident company's net worth is exempt from this tax. The rate is currently 0.6%, and is assessed only on 75% of any excess net worth above DM125,000. Unlike the municipal trade tax on capital, the net worth tax is not deductible for corporate income tax purposes.

For the purpose of the local trade tax on business capital, the business capital is generally identical with capital as computed for national net worth tax, except for certain adjustments. The value of the real estate owned by a firm is also firmly excluded since it is taxed separately.

Taxes on dividends The normal dividend withholding tax (*Kapitalertragssteuer*) is 25% whether the shareholder is local or foreign. Foreign parent companies often pay a lower withholding tax under tax treaties.

Subsidiaries of foreign companies pay a 36% corporate tax on distributed profits, plus the 25% withholding tax (which may be reduced under tax treaties) on the remainder. Income distributed to local firms is also taxed at the corporate rate of 36% (plus the 25% dividend withholding tax when applicable), but the resident recipient is eligible for a credit on the 36% corporate tax.

Value-added tax Mehrwertsteuer is payable only by businesses with annual sales of over DM100,000. The standard rate is 14%. A reduced rate of 7% is available for certain types of goods and services, whereas exports and a number of services specified in tax law (eg banking, insurance, medical services) are zero-rated. Special rules apply to transactions involving enterprises in West Berlin.

Employment

German workers have a reputation for skill and conscientiousness, and a strong sense of company loyalty. They are also very expensive, thanks to a generous system of health insurance, pensions and other benefits, and are well protected by strong unions and strict regulations. Extensive labour laws that specify even the number of legs on office chairs (five) have helped make working conditions among the best in the world, and the German unions, ideological in words and gestures but usually pragmatic in action, have won many privileges, including a shrinking working week and up to six weeks annual holiday, with very few strikes. "Co-operative" and "working together" are words both employers and labour leaders like to use. While Chancellor Kohl's government is taking measures to curb labour union power, it will also expand employee rights in the coming years.

Changing job base

More than 600,000 jobs have been created in Germany since 1983, when the number in work sagged to 25.3m for the first time since the mid 1950s. The labour force now stands at over 26m, and is expected to grow well into the 1990s. But the extra jobs have not brought a corresponding reduction in unemployment, which continues to run at over 2m.

Jobs lost Job loss has been heaviest in the traditional heavy industries: steel, construction, coal mining, shipbuilding, and textile and clothing manufacture. Only in a few sectors, such as chemicals and plastics, is there any sign of an improvement.

Jobs gained Industry still employs vast numbers of people in Germany and there are some 4.2m working in the engineering and electrical engineering industries alone. But employment in the services, already accounting for half the workforce, continues to grow apace; by the year 2000, 60% of German jobs may be in services. Work in data processing and hospitals has grown especially rapidly, followed by leasing, market research and banking. Even in traditional manufacturing, the trend in new jobs has been away from the production line and into the office.

Skill shortage So rapid has been the adoption of new technology in both industry and the services that

many companies are crying out for skilled people, and are having to spend heavily on retraining or even recruit from far afield. Training courses have been redesigned to make them more flexible, but it will be some years before there are enough workers capable of working with the latest technology.

Part-time work Although the Bonn government has enacted strong laws to make part-time and fixed term jobs more attractive, the response has been lukewarm, and few men (though more women) have taken the scheme up. A much-heralded effort to stimulate job-sharing has been scarcely more successful.

Hidden employment One real growth area is the "shadow economy", now estimated to be worth a massive 10% of the GNP. Repairmen and painters paid in cash by home-owners and others, with no questions asked, are numerous, while many thousands of unregistered workers, some from neighbouring countries and the Eastern Bloc, are employed by the building and similar trades, despite the risk of heavy fines.

Wages, labour costs and productivity

Labour costs in Germany remain, as they have been for years, among the highest in the world and are projected to increase at 3.5% a year. Employers have been unable to exploit the current high levels of unemployment to push down pay – although absenteeism has dropped noticeably. In 1987, average industrial earnings (including benefits) climbed to a heady DM32.70 per hour, second only to Switzerland on DM33.00. This compares with DM25.10 in the USA and just DM17.60 in the UK. Moreover, non-wage benefits and bonuses boost labour costs in Germany by as much as 99% in some sectors.

Productivity continues to increase at 2.5% per year, and Germany can still out-perform its competitors in terms of work output per hour, as can Switzerland. But unit labour costs are much higher than in the USA, Japan and even the Netherlands.

Labour relations

Ever since the war, West Germany's record in labour relations has been the envy of the Western world. Sustained high wages have no doubt helped to smooth out differences between employer and employee. But so too have a powerful array of labour laws that force employers to adopt a kid-glove approach to their workforce. Until recently, all sides of the labour triangle – government, management and unions – at least paid lip service to the spirit of cooperation.

Recent discord Since Chancellor Kohl's centre-right government came to power in 1982 signs of discord have kept bubbling to the surface to disturb the traditionally cosy, consensual direction of German labour relations.

The Kohl government's approach to the unions has been ambivalent. Encouraged by the centrist labour minister Herr Blühm, it has, on the one hand, sought to build up the CDU's support amongst blue-collar workers. On the other hand, it has come down on the employer's side in a number of key disputes, and

its current plans to amend the Codetermination Law are clearly designed to curb union power.

The unions have been on the defensive in recent years, but they remain a potent force. Union membership remains relatively high, at over 7m, and the unions' control over worker representation on company boards gives them considerable influence. All workers in each sector of industry, both manual and technical, belong to a single union. Germany has just 17 unions, all coming under the umbrella of the *Deutscher Gewerkschaftsbund* (DGB), the national federation of unions in Düsseldorf. The biggest and most powerful union, IG Metall (headed by the charismatic Franz Steinkühler), claims to be the West's largest, with 2.5m members. Besides the 17 DGB unions, there are also two civil service unions, a Christian union and a police union.

Unionism retains its strongest grip in the traditional heavy industries; membership in the iron and steel and mining industries is not far short of 90%. It is weakest in the financial services sector, where membership is below 30%. Naturally, it is unions like IG Metall, IG Druck (the printers) and ÖTV (transport and public services) that tend to be the most militant. Yet in recent years even the small financial workers' union has become increasingly willing to call for industrial action.

Collective bargaining The unions' most important role is in negotiating collective wage agreements. Almost all workers' contracts in Germany are negotiated annually on an industry-wide basis at the state level between the appropriate union and the employers' association for that industry. The agreement is legally binding. Officially, such collective agreements apply only to members of the union and employers' association directly involved. In practice, they tend to have effect right across the industry.

Stoppages Full-scale strikes remain

a rarity in West Germany, and the most common form of last-resort industrial action is the work stoppage. In theory, stoppages are not supposed to take place until after the end of the "peace period" during contract negotiations, but in practice are usually held during the talks or before they even start. Stoppages may last a few minutes or many hours.

Stoppages occur on company time and property and sometimes right in the negotiation room itself. They are quicker and easier to hold than a formal strike, which must be approved by membership vote and start only after contract negotiations fail. In addition, the employer, not the union, must pay workers during a stoppage, while, during a strike, unions would have to pay – German unions have very small strike funds.

Workers in management
Many people believe the key to Germany's industrial harmony lies in the country's legal framework for worker participation in management. It has a history dating back to the 1920s, but it was under the SPD-led government of the 1970s that it really came to fruition with the 1976 Codetermination Act, which added worker representation on the *Aufsichtsrat* to the existing system of Works Councils. In some companies, worker participation is seen to inhibit management, which has to consult extensively. But in others it has led to a more open and less traditional management style, which can be highly successful in industries such as computers (notably Nixdorf) and publishing (Bertelsmann).
Works Council (*Betriebsrat*) represent employees only and may be set up in any company with more than five employees. Elected by a secret ballot, the Works Council has substantial powers to approve working hours, methods of pay, holiday schedules, job training, company rules and hiring. It must also be informed of all staffing changes although, as employers have

often insisted, "informed" does not mean "approved." Works Councils are typically involved in negotiations about hiring and firing, shift times, holidays, and especially overtime. Their priority is usually to preserve jobs in their own particular workplace. Unions often accuse them of "selling out," but they maintain their independence.
Labour courts The labour courts are one of the five branches of the judiciary (see *Law*) and their time is occupied largely with cases against dismissals and lay-offs brought to them by Works Councils. Decisions tend to go in favour of the Works Council. A local labour court must give an immediate hearing to a works council's appeal against dismissals or lay-offs, and the court may issue an order on the spot to prevent an employer acting until a formal court hearing has been held, perhaps a month or more later.

Labour courts are kept so busy that a decision which goes to final appeal, as many do, may take three or more years – which is why unions and works councils often use the courts to delay plant closures. If an employee wins an appeal to keep the job, the employer must pay compensation for loss of earnings as well as the job.
Codetermination (*Mitbestimmung*) ensures 50% worker representation on the supervisory board of all companies with over 2,000 employees, and 33% on the board of companies with over 500 employees. Many employers find this law irksome and have sought ways round it by changing the legal status of the company. The unions, for their part, claim that it does not provide for real codetermination because the casting vote lies with a chairman elected by the shareholders. The exceptions to this rule are the coal and steel industries, where a neutral chairman agreeable to both worker and shareholder representatives is co-opted. These problems have kept codetermination at the top of the political agenda for all parties.

Labour laws

Hiring and firing Under the Dismissal Protection Law and the Works Constitution Law, which apply to all firms with more than six employees, the works council must be consulted on manpower planning, dismissals, work procedure and so on. A "social plan" (severance pay) must be drawn up if ten or more employees are dismissed. If a fired employee has been with a firm for at least half a year, the dismissal may be appealed the very next day to the local labour court.

Working hours The statutory maximum working week is 40 hours, but most blue-collar workers now work less than 38.5 hours a week, and unions are campaigning for further reductions. Overtime, often difficult to arrange and officially discouraged, must always be approved by the works council, and must be paid at least 25–50% above basic.

Health insurance Contributions to the national health insurance scheme by both employer and employee are compulsory. Currently, each is expected to pay 6.25% of monthly pay. Those earning above a certain figure (DM4,275 per month in 1987) may opt for a private health scheme, to which the employer may also contribute.

Equal opportunities West Germany's constitution demands equal treatment for men and women, but there is no doubt that, in practice, they do not get it. German women still find it extraordinarily difficult to get well-paid jobs and, even though they now make up 40% of the workforce, their average hourly earnings are exceeded by men's by 40–50%. Unlike nearly every other major European nation, Germany has no special legislation to prevent discrimination against women and special units set up in *Länder* to help foster equal opportunities have as yet made little headway. In theory, employers are forbidden from taking on women to work night shifts or to do heavy lifting. In practice, many thousands of women work very late in the evening, cleaning or packing for instance.

The *Gastarbeiter* (immigrants) are, if anything, in an even worse position. Wages among the Turks in particular are very low and unemployment runs at 25%. And the law helps native Germans at the expense of the Turks.

The disabled The Bonn government is ahead of most of its European neighbours in encouraging positive discrimination in favour of the disabled, and the Labour ministry conducts a special job training programme for them. Moreover, companies are required by law to employ one seriously disabled person for every 16 able-bodied people. Yet most firms ignore this ruling, preferring to pay a small fine.

Executive pay

In 1987, managing directors and board members earned on average DM257,000 a year, including profit share, but some earned less than DM100,000 and others more than DM500,000. Heads of large departments reporting directly to the top executives averaged DM136,000, while middle management incomes range from DM60,000 to DM250,000.

Personal taxes Personal tax rates in Germany are among the highest in the world, and climb sharply for medium and upper incomes. The whole system is excessively complex, and even wage-earners have to use a tax consultant (usually provided by the union) to help them file their tax returns and locate myriad legitimate tax deductible expenses, such as job-related magazine subscriptions and contributions to charity.

The Kohl government is now seeking to reduce the tax burden. Following small tax cuts in 1986 and 1988, an extensive "tax reform" in 1990 is expected to lower the top rate from 56% to 53% and convert the progression of tax rates from the present curve to a linear system.

Banks and other financial institutions

Unlike banks in the USA or UK, West Germany's commercial banks are universal banks, offering a full range of services covering both commercial and investment banking. This, combined with their extraordinarily close ties with industry (see *Power in business*), has enabled them to maintain a strong grip on the domestic market, despite the efforts of foreign banks to gain entry.

The big three

Of the many private commercial banks in Germany, just four provide a full nationwide coverage: Deutsche Bank, Dresdner Bank, Commerzbank, and the much smaller Bank für Gemeinwirtschaft. The big three – Deutsche, Dresdner and Commerzbank – dominate the German banking scene and set the tone, although many of the larger *Landesbanken* are now beginning to rival them in size.

Deutsche Bank is the biggest and best-known of all German banks, with assets of more than $130bn. From its gleaming twin towers in Frankfurt, affectionately known as Debit and Credit, Deutsche Bank controls an enormous banking empire built up under its legendary former chairman, Dr Hermann Abs, in the years after the war. Its contacts and ties reach into every corner of German industry and it has major holdings in a range of leading companies, including Daimler-Benz, Bayer, Bosch and Siemens. The bank also claims to handle more than 20% of all Germany's foreign trade.

Outstandingly managed, Deutsche Bank has a highly decentralized structure unusual among German banks, and its regional head offices retain a considerable degree of independence. Deutsche Bank has always been renowned for its conservatism, which sometimes verges on complacency. But recent years have seen it moving into new product areas and greatly expanding its foreign operations. The bank's ground-breaking decision to set up a capital markets subsidiary in London in 1987 demonstrated that its customary caution has never stood in the way of profit.

Its decision to take a stake in Roland Berger and Partner, Germany's leading management consultancy firm, further underlined Deutsche Bank's willingness to move in new directions. The bank believes management consultancy is the vital third element it needs to develop, along with commercial and investment banking, if it is to stay among the world's leading banks.

Dresdner Bank Germany's second bank with assets of more than $100bn, the Dresdner has a long and deserved reputation as a skilled trader of treasury products. The Dresdner ran into trouble in the early 1980s with a series of mismatched loans. The assassination of one chief executive and the forced resignation of another plunged the bank further into gloom. But the cloud seems now to have passed. Dresdner's present head, the canny Dr Wolfgang Röller, is capitalizing on the bank's less stuffy image and its readiness to innovate to capture new markets.

Commerzbank is the smallest of the big three, but still has assets worth more than $70bn. It suffered even more sharply than Dresdner from loan mismatches in the early 1980s, but seems to have recovered strongly. It remains in the shadow of the Deutsche and the Dresdner, however. The current chief executive, Walter Seipp, seems determined to combat this image problem by leading from the front and the signs are that it is paying off.

Smaller commercial banks

Below the big three and the Bank für

Gemeinwirtschaft in the banking hierarchy is a whole range of smaller commercial banks operating on a regional or local level.

The biggest of the so-called regional banks – the Munich-based Bayerische Vereinsbank and Bayerische Hypotheken & Wechsel, for example – have long outgrown their regional base and have assets approaching those of the Commerzbank. These banks have branches in all the major cities, and even abroad. None yet offers a genuinely nationwide service matching the big three, however.

Small private banks have declined sharply in number over the last few decades. Yet those which remain are often out of all proportion to the size of their balance sheets.

Many of these banks are able to exploit aristocratic connections and old loyalties when marketing to private clients or fund managers, and so retain some of the most prestigious clients. Many also have a high reputation for securities trading and other specialities; a few are, unusually for Germany, strong on research. The Frankfurt-based Metzler bank is minute by national standards, but has a very high standing in German banking circles. Sal Oppenheim of Cologne and Merck, Finck of Munich are bigger and better known, and also well thought of.

The last few years have seen significant gains by private houses in business at the local level because they are equipped to offer the kind of specialized service and expertise many customers are now coming to expect.

Savings banks and Landesbanken

Part-owned by state and federal government, the savings banks and *Landesbanken* are the country's public credit institutions.

Savings banks Operating on a purely local level, Germany's 590-odd savings banks (*Sparkassen*) are almost unknown abroad but play a vital part in the smooth running of the country's finances. There is a savings bank in virtually every sizable town or village and, along with their arch-rivals the cooperative banks, savings banks handle day-to-day retail banking for millions of private and small business customers the length and breadth of the country – the kind of business once neglected by the big commercial banks. Savings banks are, by law, restricted to certain types of activity (credits, investments and money transfers) and they have, in the past, tended to focus on home loans, municipal investment and routine retail banking.

Landesbanken Owned partly by the savings banks and partly by the *Land* government, the 11 *Landesbanken* are the biggest of the public credit houses, the umbrella institutions servicing savings banks at the *Land* level and acting as clearing houses for them. Typically, the *Landesbanken* take over the kind of activities only really practical on a state level: wholesale banking, foreign exchange and trade finance.

In recent years, some *Landesbanken* have grown more ambitious and international. The giant Düsseldorf-based Westdeutsche *Landesbank* is now the third biggest bank in the country, with bigger assets even than the Commerzbank. It is now beginning to step up its investment banking operations, and has expanded abroad. The Munich-based Bayerische *Landesbank* and the slightly smaller Norddeutsche *Landesbank* are heading in the same direction. Some of the smaller *Landesbanken* share these big aims; others are content to doze.

Rationalization? The 1980s have been a worrying time for the savings banks and the smaller *Landesbanken,* as both the larger commercial banks and the elite private houses eat into their share of the market. One of the problems is that many of the public banks are just too small to offer the kind of specialized service customers now expect. So many clients, while continuing to use the savings banks for their day-to-day needs are beginning to look elsewhere for particular requirements. The fear is that eventually the savings banks will lose even their bread-and-butter business to the commercial houses, which are showing increasing interest in the local retail market.

Many of the smaller savings banks have been pooling their resources for years to make economies of scale and to ease the introduction of new technology. But for sometime now there has been a feeling that the only real way forward lies in mergers between the *Landesbanken.* The high level of political involvement in the banks, however, ensures that any merger is likely to be fraught with difficulties.

The cooperative banks
Rivalling the savings banks for day-to-day retail business are the cooperative banks: the *Volksbanken* and the *Raiffeisenbanken.* There are approaching 4,000 of these industrial and agricultural credit institutions, and between them they have 20,000 branches nationwide. Like the savings banks, they are represented by umbrella institutions at the regional level, seven in total.

The top of the cooperative pyramid is the Deutsche Genossenschaftsbank (DG Bank). DG Bank is growing steadily and is now one of Germany's largest banks, with total group assets of DM112bn in 1986 (8% up on 1985). Like the big commercial banks, it has substantial holdings in industry; it recently acquired a 45% stake in the pharmaceuticals wholesale group Andraea-Noris Zahn, for example. And its international securities operations are expanding rapidly.

Federal credit
The two leading federally-owned credit institutions are the Kreditanstalt für Wiederaufbau (KfW) and Deutsche Siedlungs-und Landesrentenbank (DSL Bank).

KfW was set up after the war to handle loans for reconstruction, and is now a top-notch borrower, lending low-cost funds for a range of special projects, notably those concerned with the environment. KfW's high-quality debt is becoming increasingly well known internationally.

DSL Bank used to be the main channel for government subsidies to agriculture, but it is now a universal bank in all but name. Indeed, it has made such a success of commercial banking that it is now high on the government list for privatization.

The Deutsche Bundesbank
The Frankfurt-based Deutsche Bundesbank, which coordinates the activities of 11 state central banks and over 200 branches nationwide, is Germany's central bank, and it is the federal government's prime means of implementing monetary policy. It is the Bundesbank which issues bank notes and regulates money circulation and the supply of credit.

Working with the government
The Bundesbank operates in tandem with the Treasury, and is supposed to support the government's monetary policy. But thanks to the act establishing it in 1957, it enjoys an unusual degree of independence, which it has not been afraid to exercise.

In the past, the bank's desire to keep inflation under control by keeping a tight rein on the money supply has brought it into conflict with governments keen to stoke economic growth. Relations between the current bank president, Karl-Otto Pöhl, and the Christian Democrat government of Chancellor Kohl run surprisingly smoothly, however – even though Herr Pöhl is a Social Democrat. Indeed, in 1987 the government was happy to elect Herr Pöhl for a second, eight-year term, which will make him the longest serving central bank head in the West.

The bank in action The Bundesbank's monetary policy is determined at the monthly meetings of the bank's ruling council, comprised of the bank president, seven full-time directors and the heads of the 11 state central banks. At the heart of the bank's strategy are yearly targets for the growth of the central bank money stock (CBMS), which depends on the total cash in circulation and the minimum reserves the bank decides are needed to meet domestic liabilities.

The bank has little direct control over commercial interest rates, but it can send unmistakable signals to the banks by varying its lending rate for loans to the banks secured by top-grade assets (the Lombard rate) and, more recently, by its short-term securities repurchase rate. On a day-to-day basis, the Bundesbank will intervene on the stock exchanges, where its floor traders deal in a variety of federal debt issues. By altering the balance between the supply and demand for credit in the economy, the Bundesbank thus exerts a powerful influence on commercial interest rates. It has also been known to intervene on the foreign exchange markets usually to prevent the D-mark rising too high.

Regulations Regular supervision of all banks outside the central bank system falls within the ambit of the Berlin-based Bundesaufsichtsamt für das Kreditwesen (Federal Banking Supervisory Office). In theory, this gives the government some direct influence over the way the banks work. However, it is the Bundesbank that sets the agenda when it comes to financial innovations or new lending rules.

The changing scene

Banking in Germany still tends to be conducted in an atmosphere of old-fashioned calm. Many banks are habitually cautious, suspicious of innovations such as new types of bond, and reluctant to expose themselves to risk. Bankers are often very deferential to those above them in the hierarchy, and there is often a gentlemen's agreement among banks not to poach each other's clients. Naturally, competition between the banks has been somewhat muted in the past; the leading banks all tended to offer similar products at similar prices. Outsiders often feel that the German banking scene is a club to which they are not admitted.

There are signs, however, that the German banks may at last be starting

---

Credit cards and Eurocheques

The Germans lag a long way behind the Americans, the British, the French, the Dutch and many others in the gradual shift away from cash for small transactions. 96% of Germans still prefer to pay for restaurant meals in cash, as against 76% in the UK and 40% in France; and it would be a very unusual German who laid a credit card on the table at the end of the meal. The use of credit cards in Germany has been so small that none of the big German banks has bothered to adopt them. In 1986, West German wallets contained only 1.4m credit cards between them – as against more than 20m in the UK, and some 200m in the USA – and virtually all of these were issued by foreign companies: American Express, Eurocard, Diners Club and Visa.

For 20 years, the big German banks have nailed their colours to the Eurocheque but it has never caught on outside Germany, partly because of disputes over charges. Now even German customers are becoming impatient with the credit limit of just DM400 per cheque. The credit card companies are finally beginning to make headway, and in 1987, much to the big banks' chagrin, a group of retailers and hoteliers issued their own credit card, the *Deutsche Kreditkarte.*

to slough off their traditional complacency. One contributory factor is the depressed demand for funds to industry as the D-mark remains strong abroad and the pace of growth slackens at home. Firms such as Daimler-Benz are sitting on so much cash that all they need from the banks is advice on how best to invest it. Some firms are even beginning to by-pass the banks and go to the stock market for funds.

Moreover, the general conservatism of the big banks has sometimes given more adventurous newcomers the edge in areas such as foreign exchange and investment banking where innovation counts as much as contacts. Munich in particular has a number of smaller houses which have made a mark in fund management and venture capital. Even foreign banks are making some progress in these specialized areas.

A third factor is the liberalization of the country's money markets (see *Financial markets*) which has accelerated the tempo of banking in Frankfurt in particular. The influx of banks from abroad may prove especially significant.

Foreign invasion The presence of foreign banks in Germany is nothing new. US banks like Citibank, Chase Manhattan and Morgan Guaranty have been established in Frankfurt almost since the war, when the city was the centre of the US occupation zone, while Japanese banks followed Japanese manufacturers to Düsseldorf more than 20 years ago. But the liberalization of Germany's money markets which began in the mid 1980s has triggered an unprecedented influx of international investment banks into Germany. Among the more prominent new arrivals have been the elite Wall Street banks such as Salomon Brothers and Morgan Stanley, and a number of leading Swiss banks. With the final lifting of the ban on foreign banks lead-managing D-mark Eurobond issues, Japanese banks may also make their mark.

As yet, however, only Crédit Suisse-First Boston, who had the foresight to buy a small German subsidiary (Effectenbank), have made any serious headway against the firmly entrenched big German banks. But the German banks have been shocked to find themselves suddenly facing competition from foreign banks for bond issues by formerly loyal clients. Another effect has been to expose them to a hitherto unfamiliar problem: a shortage of suitable staff. Employees traditionally stayed loyal to a bank for life. Now foreign banks are tempting talent away with fat salaries. The response from the German banks has been very low key, but most analysts predict that soon they will have to move more positively.

Venture capital

Venture capital has always been hard to obtain in Germany. The first German venture capital group, WFG Deutsche Gesellschaft für Wagniskapital, was set up by the federal government and a number of leading banks as long ago as 1976, but its fortunes have been mixed and its impact limited. In 1987 Germany had just 25 venture capital firms, compared with 550 in the US and 110 in the UK. Under a new law designed to stimulate the growth of venture capital, the banks are allowed to establish UBGGs. Since then, most of the big banks, starting with the Deutsche Bank, have formed their own UBGGs which can take share options in unlisted companies. So far, however, the policy of most of the UBGGs has been rather conservative, and it has been up to the smaller groups, notably foreign-inspired ventures, to provide capital for high-risk projects.

Financial markets

Until just a few years ago, German money markets were bound by such cramping restrictions that few foreign banks could or would trade in them, while the German equity markets, equally hedged by restrictions, were described by critics as small and boring. In the mid-1980s, however, the Germans became aware that they were in danger of being left behind, as new financial developments came thick and fast in London and, more disturbingly for the Germans, in Paris and Zurich too. Since then the Bundesbank has begun to push through a series of measures liberalizing the financial markets to inject them with new life.

The stock exchanges

West Germany has eight separate stock exchanges trading in equities and bonds, and they are all highly independent and sometimes mutually suspicious. At the top of the tree is Frankfurt, which accounts for 50% of German stock and bond turnover. Düsseldorf follows with 20%, while Hamburg and Munich, with 7–10% each, squabble over who comes next. Stuttgart, Berlin and Hanover deal with about 4%, while the tiny Bremen bourse handles just 2%.

A market for all Before 1987, there were three different levels of market on each exchange: a top tier for companies with an official listing (*Amtlicher Handel*); and two others for unlisted companies, one a semi-official regulated free market (*geregelter Freiverkehr*), the other unregulated (*ungeregelter Freiverkehr*). Many medium-sized companies find the rigmarole and cost of an official listing too demanding yet the legal framework of the two unlisted markets too uncertain, so are put off going public altogether. To combat this problem, a new market level, the *geregelter Markt* was introduced in May 1987. This offers similar legal standing to the official market at much less cost and without so many awkward rules. Ultimately, it is expected to replace the *geregelter Freiverkehr*.

The traders

German interest in the stock exchanges has always been fairly muted. Individual German investors buy more shares than they used to but still very few. Similarly, the big institutional investors, such as the insurers, are moving into the market only slowly; barely 12% of the insurance companies funds go on equities. It was foreign buyers who were behind the surge in German shares in the mid 1980s, and foreigners are now believed to hold a quarter of all German shares. This makes the market rather vulnerable to currency swings.

Opening up the markets

Some years ago, the Bundesbank, worried by the flow of trade to London, embarked on a string of financial reforms. In April 1984 it abolished the "withholding" tax foreigners had to pay on interest when investing in government bonds. A year later, it decided new financial instruments like floating-rate notes (FRNS), zero-coupon bonds, swaps and Euronote facilities were acceptable after all. By 1987, foreign banks with a German base could lead-manage D-mark Eurobonds, and join the consortium underwriting federal bonds.

All these reforms boosted the presence of foreign banks in Frankfurt. Many German bankers still feel, however, that trade in DM bonds will go on draining away to London unless the *Börsenumsatzsteuer*, the stock exchange turnover tax, is abolished. Moreover, with no futures market, there is no chance of hedging, which keeps trading risky.

Insurance

The West German insurance market is the third largest in the world, writing almost 10% of world insurance business, and it is growing larger by the year. Germany is also a world leader in reinsurance.

Insurance companies

There are more than 480 insurance companies active in Germany at present, including foreign subsidiaries and public groups, plus around 20 reinsurance firms. But more than half of all premiums are handled by just 12 groups.

Allianz, sometimes seen as the insurance equivalent of Deutsche Bank, is by far the largest, with gross premiums in 1986 of DM25bn. Europe's biggest insurer, it has been rapidly expanding its foreign operations with the purchase of companies such as Britain's Cornhill and Italy's RAS.

Germany's second insurance company, Munich Re, is much smaller than Allianz, but still huge by European standards. It is the world's leading reinsurer, and also owns stakes in a number of German direct insurers.

Interdependence German insurance is something of a maze, for there is a web of defensive cross-holdings between leading companies. There is a little unravelling of the web as some insurers divest their minority stakes in competitors. But the important cross-holdings, notably the reciprocal 25% between Allianz and Munich Re, remain intact.

The top five

	Gross premiums 1986
	DMbn
Allianz	25.0
Munich Re	11.8
Gerling Konzern	5.0
Victoria Life	3.8
Aachener & Münchener	3.3

The insurance market

The German insurance market is as buoyant as ever, with growth in nearly all sectors. Life, which is the largest sector with 40% of all premiums, is expanding particularly rapidly, and all the leading insurance companies have life subsidiaries. Reinsurance is growing steadily too, while accident and casualty is thriving, thanks largely to the continuing rise in car ownership. Steady premiums have also ensured that private health insurance stays competitive against state schemes.

Investment strategies The insurance companies' investment moves are notoriously unadventurous. Most assets are ploughed into federal or communal fixed-interest bonds, and they invest little more than 6% of their money in equities. However, their investment portfolios are growing rapidly, and in 1985 earned a profit of DM45bn on an investment of DM500bn, roughly half what they received from premiums. The "special funds" that are run by the banks for the insurance companies have grown especially fast.

Prospects A worrying prospect for the life companies is the big wave of policies about to mature with the sharp peak in the population's age profile (see *Human resources*). The test will be to keep the maturing funds within the insurance net rather than allowing them to slip away to the banks and private fund managers. The companies will need to strengthen their investment departments if they are to be in a position to offer competitive investment funds of their own. Indicative of things to come may be Aachener & Münchener's purchase of a controlling stake in the Bank für Gemeinwirtschaft as a prelude to developing a financial services group – although it caused much consternation among German insurers at the time.

Law

Germans are among the most litigious people in the world. In 1985 more than 21m cases were heard in German courts. One reason for the German readiness to go to court is the fact that they have so many courts to go to. Another is that they have so many laws that there is plenty to go to court about. Legal scholars aptly describe Germany as a *Rechtsstaat*, a "law state," for the structure and jurisdiction of the German judiciary offers extensive legal protection, with advanced forms of redress for private grievances against the state and against private business, especially in data, consumer and environmental protection.

The German legal system

The German legal system is highly codified, which means that it depends entirely on written law. There is, in theory at least, little scope for a judge to interpret the law, and case precedents are much less important than in many countries. The judge's task is simply to administer the code and apply the written law to each case as it is presented.

One affect of this is to virtually eliminate the adversarial approach on which the US and UK courts are based, with defence and prosecution advocating their case to a neutral judge or jury. Instead, all participants – judge, defense and prosecution – are there to uncover the truth, and many foreigners are surprised by the active, inquisitorial approach often taken by judges.

The basic civil, commercial and criminal codes that the judges adhere to date in essence from the Empire days of the last century, but they have since been fleshed out by statute and thoroughly revised since 1949. These codes form the basis of a unified system that applies right across the country. While Germany's politics are fragmented and decentralized, its laws are the same everywhere in the country.

The courts

Like the laws, the German court system is a unified structure, and separate state and federal courts like those in the USA do not exist; state and federal courts are all part of the same hierarchy. But the hierarchy has two arms: the regular courts dealing with ordinary civil and criminal cases; and the specialized courts.

The regular courts are organized on four levels: local (*Amtsgerichte*), district (*Landesgerichte*), appeal (*Oberlandesgerichte*) and, at the top of the pyramid, the federal court (*Bundesgerichtshof*). Located in most decent-sized towns, the 500 or so local courts have just one judge – unlike the district and appeal courts which work in panels of three, four or even five – and handle minor civil matters and petty criminal offences, plus functions such as bankruptcy supervision. The 90-odd district courts are the main criminal and civil courts, while the 20 Oberlandesgerichte are the main courts of appeal. Final appeal is to the federal appeals court in Karlsruhe, where more than 100 judges work in 20 or so panels.

Detailed rules govern which court will hear a case. Monetary claims of less than DM5,000, for instance, go to the local courts, but can be appealed to the district court, while only where there is more than DM40,000 in the balance or where the law is in question can the case be appealed all the way to the federal courts.

Specialized courts In addition to the regular courts, a hierarchy of specialized courts handles administrative, labour, social matters, plus, at the national level only, fiscal, tax and patent cases. Dispensing quick and relatively inexpensive justice, these courts are widely used by Germans to redress grievances against the authorities or against private business. The administrative courts have played a major part in blocking the construction of nuclear power plants, such as that at Wyhl in Baden-Württemberg in 1976, while many an employer has found redundancy plans thwarted by a decision in the labour court (see *Employment*).

Going to law

Despite the complexity of the system, the German judiciary is efficient, and civil and commercial litigation is relatively rapid. This may be one reason why so few cases are settled out of court (although another is the German tendency to play things by the book). There is no procedure for discovery of documents which in other countries stretches out the pre-trial stage; nor are there any preliminary hearings, while strict deadlines encourage the litigants to press on rapidly through the case. Severe penalties befall those who miss deadlines and suits for professional negligence often focus on lawyers who have overshot deadlines. Only if a case is appealed all the way to the federal court is litigation long and costly, taking up to two years.

The costs Fees are paid to the lawyers and the court according to the amount of the claim following a standard table. For a claim of DM100,000, the lawyer's fee is DM1,585, the court's DM812. But added to the lawyer's fee are his or her expenses plus 14% value-added tax.

The loser is required to pay all expenses for all parties in a case. This can be very costly for an individual. But many Germans belong to Rights Protection Organizations – a form of socialized legal aid financed by monthly payments – to cover legal expenses connected with home, car and family. Thus insured against the risk of incurring heavy costs, it is hardly surprising that Germans are

so ready to pursue a case in the courts. Companies and corporations, however, rarely belong to such organizations, preferring to write off legal expenses against normal running costs.

The legal profession

With almost 50,000 *Rechtsanwälte* (attorneys) and over 17,000 judges, Germany probably has more lawyers per capita of population than any country in the world, except the USA. There are also numerous public notaries entitled to handle company formation, convey land and draw up wills. But German lawyers have neither the status, nor the soaring salaries, of their counterparts in the USA.

Training Both attorneys and judges are considered part of the overall system of justice, and go through the same initial training. After 3–5 years study at university, all law students who pass the state exams spend $2\frac{1}{2}$ years as a *Referendar* in the civil service, gaining in practical experience as an attorney, in the state prosecution service and in the judiciary. Passing a further state exam qualifies the student to practise law.

Once qualified, the lawyer must decide on a career path: private practice, a business career, the civil service or the judiciary. Once committed, there is no going back, although attorneys can and do move into business and vice versa. Despite the gruelling training period and the rigour of the exams, West Germany actually has a glut of lawyers and many are unable to practise.

Law firms The average law firm in Germany is very small, with just 4–6 partners; only a handful of firms have more than 20. Firms and individual attorneys are only registered to practise in one Land and cannot merge across state boundaries. As a result, even the largest partnerships have to "correspond" with other firms in different regions to give their clients a full, national service.

Accountancy

Staid and somewhat elitist, German accountancy has traditionally held itself aloof from the hurly-burly of the commercial world. But the impact on the home market of the Big Eight US-UK accounting firms, not afraid to publicize themselves nor the wide range of services they can offer, has shaken the profession badly. At the same time, a spate of far-reaching new regulations threatens to transform old working practices. The larger firms are now realizing that they must adopt a more dynamic approach.

The profession

At the top of the professional tree are the *Wirtschaftsprüfer* (WPs), the publicly certified accountants who, until recently, were the only people allowed to perform statutory audits. Typically, it takes as long as eight to ten years to qualify as a WP. But, once qualified, WPs join an exclusive and highly-paid elite.

There are 5,000 WPs in Germany – compared with 100,000 FCAs in the UK and more than 350,000 CPAs in the USA. This is essentially because, in the past, German commercial law has not demanded extensive financial disclosures from companies. Even today, annual accounts for the big banks are notable more for what they hide than what they reveal. Until 1987, only the largest German companies were legally obliged to carry out a full annual audit.

Nevertheless, WPs are closely bound by a variety of strict rules governing financial statements, and there is little room for the exercise of professional discretion. An auditor's report is no more than a certification that the accounting records, the annual accounts and the directors' report comply with the law and the company statutes.

Besides the tiny clique of WPs, West Germany has many thousands of *Steuerberater* (StB), working either singly or in small firms. StBs have few formal qualifications and, until recently, acted largely as tax advisers and book-keepers for small companies not needing a full audit. However, the EC 4th Company Law directive of 1987 vastly increased the number of companies required to have an annual audit. To cope with the extra workload, the government has thrown company audits wide open. No longer are statutory audits the sole prerogative of the WP. Now an audit can be performed by any StB who has passed a simple exam.

The firms

German accountancy is still largely in the hands of myriad small limited companies. There are big companies in Germany, but they have not achieved quite the same dominance that the Big Eight have achieved in the US-UK. There are signs that the picture is changing, however, as competitive pressures force traditionally staid German accountancy firms to branch out in new directions. Many medium-sized firms are now pooling their resources to enable them to offer a much wider range of services, including management consultancy and financial advice. The recent merger of the largest German accountancy firm Deutsche Treuhand (DTG) and the giant US-UK firm, Peat Marwick, was also seen as a sign of things to come.

Foreign intruders

In recent years, the old German accountancy firms have fought a running battle with the US-UK Big Eight. The internationals are marketing their services aggressively and often highly effectively, but the German firms still maintain an unshakeable grip on the domestic audit market. To combat prejudice against foreign firms, Price Waterhouse set up a subsidiary with a German name, while receptionists at Arthur Andersen answer the phone "Artur Andersen" to give the firm's name a Germanic ring. But no major German company is yet audited by a foreign firm. However, German accountancy firms are poorly equipped for dealing with clients on an international basis. So to hold on to the audit market for the multinationals, all the large domestic German accounting firms have had to forge links with the internationals. Moreover, the Big Eight, particularly Arthur Andersen and KMG Peat Marwick, have made huge advances in the field of management consultancy and financial advice, marketing their services in an up-front style the Germans are only just beginning to learn.

New images and roles
Spurred by the success of the Big Eight's high profile strategy, German firms are gradually losing their traditional distaste for marketing. Most German firms now publish their own brochures, and some hold conferences to publicize their name. And the *Bundeskartellamt*, the anti-trust commission, is studying whether the profession's ban on advertising is anti-competitive.

Management consultancy is seen as ripe for explosive growth among German accountancy firms. It is still in its infancy at the moment, as German companies have always preferred to solve all their problems inhouse. But this is changing, and the large accountancy firms are following the US-UK lead and trying to build up their consultancy base.

So far, German accountants have confined their consultancy operations largely within narrow limits: general financial and audit-related advice, as well as information systems consultancy. The profession has been reluctant to move into areas not directly related to accounting

expertise, such as market analysis, head-hunting or strategic business advice. But this is likely to change – largely because accountants will not be able to hold on to their brightest consultant if the types of work they can do are so restricted.

Top German firms
Deutsche Treuhand (DTG) is the largest accounting firm in Germany, with a fee income in 1986 of well over DM200m. DTG's long list of blue chip German clients is envied by all the US-UK Big Eight.

Treuarbeit is owned by the federal government and all the individual states, and relies on public sector accounts for more than half its work. The firm is trying hard to shed government involvement, but the government has shown little willingness to sell its stake.

Treuhand Vereinigung is affiliated to Coopers & Lybrand. The firm is strongly developed in the provinces and has one of the largest regional networks of offices.

Arthur Andersen is the biggest of the foreign firms, and is universally regarded as the most aggressive accountancy firm of all in winning new business. Particularly strong in information systems consultancy.

Schitag is well placed in Stuttgart to benefit from Germany's high-tech industries, but has been slow to build up its management consultancy. Affiliated to Arthur Young.

Treuverkehr is not as highly rated by competitors as in the past. But it still audits the Deutsche Bank, probably Germany's most prestigious client.

Deloitte Haskins & Sells is an amalgamation of three German firms led by Wollert Elmendorff in Düsseldorf. It is strong in financial services, and has a reputation for quality work.

Wilbera is owned partly by the German local authorities and partly by Treuarbeit. It is one of the few firms with a consulting arm that has a large number of non-accounting industry specialists.

Advertising and PR

The continued affluence of German society and a gradual erosion of traditional reserve about consumer spending have helped stimulate growth in the German advertising and PR industries in the 1980s. But marketing practices remain markedly conservative, and industry progress may yet founder as the growth of the German economy begins to flag and stifling government codes on advertising stay in place.

Growth areas

Throughout the 1980s, spending on advertising has risen at 5% every year. Driving this boom have been four principal stimuli: the continued growth in consumer spending; the spread of communications and computer technology in German offices; the increasingly high profile of financial institutions; and intense competition in sectors such as the automobile industry.

Corporate advertising may well begin to take off, too, as more and more companies go public and want to establish a strong corporate identity. Instinctively low key, German corporate publicity may yet acquire the slick, image-conscious look of its American and British counterparts.

Media trends

Most German advertising appears in print, and the broadcast media still play a relatively small part. Daily newspapers not only grab the lion's share of the advertising cake (35% of all spending on advertising) but are actually extending their grip. Consumer magazines, too, take a substantial share (about 5%), while direct marketing and the trade press take about 10% each.

Television advertising is hampered by strict codes, and has as yet been able to take little more than 10% of the market. The two state-owned television networks, for example, are allowed only four strictly timed blocks of commercials per day, set at hours when only children and grandmothers are watching: that is, before 8pm in the evening, and never on Sundays or public holidays.

New private TV stations have as yet made little impact but, as cable TV grows apace, the legislators may be persuaded to relax the rules. Already some semi-comparative messages are appearing in TV commercials. The industry watchdog (the *Werberat*), however, keeps a sharp eye on the protection of public morality and will probably ensure that any relaxation is very gradual.

If television advertising does begin to surge, the most likely victims will be among the consumer magazines. Competition here is already intense, and there are often vicious circulation battles among the big four publishing houses (Heinrich Bauer, Gruner & Jahr, Springer and Burda) which between them capture 70% of the advertising revenue in this market.

The agencies

The traditional reticence of the German industry has allowed foreign-controlled advertising companies a dominant position. The top nine agencies are: Team/BBDO, SSC & B Lintas, Ogilvy & Mather, McCann Erickson, J. Walter Thompson, Young & Rubicam, Grey, Saatchi & Saatchi Compton and Doyle Dane Bernbach. Together these agencies take a third of all billings. There is an undercurrent of up-and-coming and adventurous homegrown agencies, such as Baums, Mang & Zimmerman and Scholz & Friends, but they will have their work cut out to dent the international agencies' control. In the long run, though, it will be the medium-sized, non-specialist agencies that may be squeezed out.

Importing, market entry and distribution

Importing well over DM400bn of goods and services a year, West Germany is one of the world's largest and most lucrative markets, and, for the right products, there is a wealth of opportunities. In theory, the German market is wide open. The government is firmly wedded to free trade. But in practice there is a range of less obvious problems confronting foreigners trying to break into the German market, not least of which are the exacting official product specifications and standards.

Import tariffs and duties

West Germany has one of the most liberal trading regimes in the world, and there are few restrictions, quotas or licences applying to imported goods, except for a few sensitive products from East Germany, South-East Asian countries and Japan.

Tariffs Almost half German imports are from other EC members, and on most of these there are no tariffs whatsoever. The few exceptions are certain foodstuffs and agricultural products, which may be subject to levies and "compensatory amounts" granted under the EC Common Agricultural Policy; these tend to vary with world prices.

Tariffs from non-EC members may also be low or non-existent if the country has associated or preferential status. Goods from EFTA countries are effectively tariff-free, barring a few sensitive products, and tariffs are low or non-existent on goods from a range of less developed countries.

All goods are classified under the Customs Co-operation Council Nomenclature (formerly the Brussels nomenclature), and customs duties are based on the customs valuation. This usually depends on the cif port of entry invoice price, although if the sole agent, German-based subsidiary or branch has been granted exceptionally low prices or price reductions the customs valuation may be increased.

Import taxes All imports to West Germany are subject to Import Turnover Tax (*Einfuhrumsatzsteuer*). But this does not penalize overseas producers any more than domestic

German producers, for it is set at exactly the same rate as the value-added tax (*Merhwertsteuer*) payable on all goods made within the Federal Republic by both German and foreign producers. Import Turnover Tax, like VAT, is set at 14% for most goods, payable on the cif port of entry value plus customs and excise duty and cost of transportation to the first destination in Germany; food and books are charged only at 7%. Foreign businesses can avoid this tax by ensuring that delivery is completed before the goods pass through the customs barrier. Conversely, if goods are brought in and assembled inside Germany, the company is legally obliged to notify the tax authorities and pay domestic VAT.

Excise duties are in force at various rates on many products including spirits, sparkling wine, beer, tobacco, tea, coffee, sugar, salt, perfume and lighting.

Samples Small commercial samples and specimens of little value (except for alcohol and tobacco) can be brought in duty-free provided they are easy to recognize as such – officials may require that samples be made unsaleable (eg by tearing or marking). Samples may also be taken into Germany if the import duty is deposited with customs officials until the samples are taken out of the country again. Another ploy is to use an ATA carnet, leaving a refundable deposit or guarantee with the issuing authority abroad; this is the only route with printed matter and advertising materials.

Controls and standards

Like most countries, Germany places prohibitions and restrictions on imports of certain sensitive goods, including food and alcohol, matches containing yellow phosphorus, DDT, and live animals. And there are licences in force on a variety of products from particular origins. About 25% of imports from East Germany require a licence. Bilateral voluntary limits are also set on steel imports into the EC from 15 major European, Asian and South American producers. Other quotas are in force against textiles, especially from the Far East, under the Multifibre Arrangement. Under the Lomé Convention, quotas apply to various products, including bananas and rum, from 66 less developed countries.

DIN standards For many importers, however, the real barrier to getting goods on to the German market is neither duties nor quotas but rather Germany's exacting standards system, enshrined in the Deutsche Industrie Normen (DIN). There are more than 25,000 of these DIN norms, covering everything from cycle clips to circuit breakers, and they are among the toughest in the world. A few years ago, the French officially complained that DIN standards were so rigorous, and so tailored to German producers, that they were unfairly obstructing French sales in Germany. But when asked to come up with a list of specific grievances, Paris failed to do so. Nevertheless, the German government has started to relax the DIN system in recent years, and has cut down the number of different standards.

DIN standards are actually established by hundreds of industrial associations, from the German Association of Electrical Engineers (VDE), which checks electrical appliances, to the FKN, which checks juice cartons. But complementing the DIN system, and adding immeasurably to the complexity of

the German certification system, are some 45,000 additional industrial standards.

Although there is actually no legal obligation for producers to meet DIN or any other standards, it is a genuine market necessity to do so because German law holds distributors legally responsible for the safety of every product they sell. Moreover, employers and employees must by law comply with Accident Prevention Regulations which specify that only "safe" equipment can be used in the workplace. Of course, the legal proof of "safety" is the appropriate DIN test certificate.

GS-tested Mail order purchasing is very popular in Germany, and many of the larger mail order companies have their own product testing facilities, controlled by 40 government-authorized bodies, which issue GS (*Geprüfte Sicherheit* – "Tested for safety") marks. Such certification by mail order companies and other retailers is performed primarily to ensure the products they sell are safe as required by law, but there is no doubt that the German consumer is also deeply distrustful of any product, particularly a foreign-made product, which has not been officially approved.

Identifying opportunities

Germany's potential as a market for foreign business is underlined by the expectation that imports will be the fastest growing component of the GNP at least until the end of the decade. Already, foreign producers hold a large, and even dominating, share of the German market in certain goods, especially consumer goods. In 1986, foreign producers took a huge 81% of all domestic sales of toys, sports gear and jewellery, 66% of computer sales, 65% of textiles and 56% of precision and optical instruments. Even in industrial products foreigners can make a considerable impact, taking 40% of the German iron and steel market, 37% of chemicals, 29% of electrical engineering and 27% of machinery.

The key markets The booming market for consumer goods offers the greatest opportunities, and this is expected to grow by more than 3% a year until well into the 1990s. But services should not be overlooked, for sales in this sector are expected to expand faster than those in any other at least until the early 1990s.

Finding a niche For many companies, the secret of success, particularly on the highly competitive consumer market, is to identify and exploit a narrow market segment. To identify this niche, on-the-spot market research is virtually essential. Regional variations in consumer spending patterns are much more marked in Germany than many similar-sized countries, and importers should always seek local advice to establish whether their product goes down well in a particular area. Even domestic producers usually pick a "Nielsen" area to test their product prior to launch.

Foreign producers should always be prepared to see the market from the German point of view and adapt their product accordingly. Companies in high technology should consider collaboration, even a joint venture, with a German partner – through the EC's EUREKA programme, for example. Another window of opportunity is the franchise system which has been expanding rapidly in Germany for a wide range of goods and services including DIY, car repair and computer hardware, software and training centres.

Trade fairs Even for domestic firms, trade fairs are a crucial part of selling in Germany; for foreigners, they provide perhaps the best possible gateway to the market. But it is essential to avoid exhibiting until the product is completely ready for the German market.

Sources of information There are many official and quasi-official sources of information. Your own embassy in Bonn, and trade departments at home, are good starting points. The German embassy in your country and, where available, a local German chamber of commerce, are also valuable sources. A central source of literature in English is the German Foreign Trade Information Office (Postfach 10 80 07, Köln 1), which produces a helpful publication called *How to approach the German market*, and another on *Import Duties, Taxes and Import Regulations.*

Adapting to the market

Any firm trying to break into the sophisticated and fiercely competitive German market must maintain consistently high product standards. Germans are prepared to pay high prices for their purchases, but demand high quality in return.

In recent years, moreover, German consumers have become increasingly design-conscious, and conspicuously good design, stylish but highly functional, is becoming a hallmark of products succeeding on the German market.

Avoiding stereotypes Importers often have to surmount national prejudices if they are to succeed in Germany. US producers, especially, have to overcome a reputation for shoddiness; British producers have to prove they are not prone to deliver late. German manufacture now seems to be such a positive guarantee of quality for domestic consumers that many foreign companies decide to set up their own manufacturing plant or at least final assembly plant in Germany, not only giving them proximity to German customers, but also the marketing bonus of labelling their products "Made in Germany."

Packaging and labelling For most commodities, there are few special regulations for packaging and labelling unless German words are used, in which case the country of origin must be indicated. But for consumer goods, meeting all the regulations can be quite a problem. For a start, all prepackaged consumer goods must conform to particular categories of size, pricing and packaging under the Prepackaging Order (*Fertigpackungsverordnung*). Food and drugs, which are covered by special foodstuff (*Lebensmittelgesetz*) and drugs (*Arzneimittelgesetz*) laws, are particularly sensitive areas. Food must be labelled strictly in accordance with the Foodstuffs Marking Order (*Lebensmittel-Kennzeichnungsverordnung*), while drugs must be registered with the Federal Health Office (*Bundesgesundheitsamt*). Under the Textiles Marketing Law (*Textilkennzeichnungsgesetz*), the raw material content must be indicated on all textile products.

Using an agent

It is possible to sell direct to the major buying organizations in West Germany. But by far the majority of trade in West Germany is handled by agents, and buyers are used to placing orders with agents who pay regular visits.

German agents are, on the whole, extremely efficient at marketing, especially to large outlets, and their knowledge of buyers and purchasing habits can be invaluable to foreign producers wishing to enter the market in Germany. Most can safely be left to handle sales and distribution from beginning to end. Nevertheless, it pays suppliers to put in an appearance with the buyers at least once a year.

More than 60% of German agents work on commission, although there are also agents who work on consignment, agents who carry stock on their own account, and importers. But agents covering the whole country are few and far between, and most importers are obliged to appoint half a dozen or so to act for them in various regions. This is not quite the drawback it sounds, for there are considerable differences in regional

purchasing habits, and a local agent should have a thorough knowledge of local tastes.

Problems and pitfalls Agents usually handle several suppliers in the same product area, so it is important to establish just what the agent will do. Agents should also be given a detailed brief of a supplier's products, a rundown of advertising and marketing plans, a written agreement of terms of delivery, payment and so on.

Strict regulations, soon to be established on an EC-wide basis, govern the relationship between agent and supplier. But the German Agency Law tends to protect the agent more than the supplier, so it is vital to consult a German lawyer before signing a contract. Sample contracts and German law on such agreements are available in various languages from the agents' and brokers' national association: Centralvereinigung Deutscher Handelsvertreter-und Handelsmakler-Verbände, Geleniusstr 1, Köln 41. National embassies in Bonn often provide valuable advice on choosing an agent.

Franchises and licences In fields such as high fashion and cosmetics, franchise agreements are the most effective ways of overcoming the problems of dealing with specialized independent retailers. But it is important to consult a lawyer before entering into any franchise or licence agreement; deals may for instance run into problems with either EC or West German anti-cartel law.

There are two principal types of licence in Germany: the simple and the exclusive. With an exclusive licence, the licensee can only grant one licence in any area; with a simple licence, any number can be granted. The cost of licences varies from sector to sector. In electrical goods, for example, a licence fee of between 0.5% and 5% is considered "fair;" in machinery, 0.33% to 10% would be fair; for drug licences, fees would be between 2% and 10%.

Distribution

West Germany's transport network is very sophisticated, and goods can be taken in numerous different ways, such as: via Frankfurt Airport, the world's largest cargo airport outside the USA; through the seaports of Hamburg, Bremen and Bremerhaven, which all offer freeport facilities; by river, especially the Rhein (via Rotterdam) and the Danube; across Germany's extensive land borders on the famous *Autobahnen* and the Federal Railway.

The railways Carrying 36% by weight of all German freight, the state-owned rail network retains the edge over road-haulage for long-distance freight. A vast quantity of track was destroyed in the war, encouraging extensive modernization, and 41% of the network is now electrified. Recent investment has focused on high speed and frequent freight service throughout the country, while other freight innovations include extensive container facilities and "piggyback" traffic.

The roads Road haulage, which accounts for 37% of German freight traffic, is in the hands of numerous private companies, but is subject to very strict regulations and tariffs, calibrated by weight and distance (the RKT). The basic modernization of the *Autobahn* network is largely complete. But Germany's roads are exceptionally crowded, and the accident rate high.

The waterways of West Germany are heavily used for bulk goods, and carry almost a quarter of all German freight. The Rhein carries over 60% of all German waterborne traffic, and it may be soon be linked to Germany's other main water conduit, the Danube. The Europa project, scheduled for completion in 1989 or 1990, will bridge the gap between these two great rivers, linking the North Sea to the Black Sea.

Frankfurt Airport Germany's high-cost, high-tech industries have brought airfreight increasingly to the fore in recent years, although the proportion of freight moved by air is still tiny. Frankfurt Airport in particular has become a magnet for companies, attracting offices, warehouses and even factories to the Rhein/Main area.

Warehousing goods in Germany for an agent to draw on at will is a strong selling point. Warehoused goods can remain the property of the foreign exporter until the agent withdraws them. In government-run bonded warehouses, no import duty or tax needs to be paid until the goods are actually withdrawn; on goods stored in private open warehouses, taxes and duties must already have been paid.

Freight forwarders cannot provide the same breadth of service as agents or importers, but many will handle all the documentation for you as well as physical transportation. One of the largest freight forwarders, Kuehne and Nagel, for example, can do everything from door-to-door haulage and combined sea, air and river transport to quality control and making sure delivery is on time. Other large companies include Hapag-Lloyd and Schenker and Co.

Wholesalers and retailers There is no single all-embracing distribution system in Germany, and the main offices for even the large chains of wholesalers and retailers are scattered across the country. This is why an agent is so important. Nevertheless, the high proportion of foreign goods sold means that even the smallest retailers are often familiar with import procedures and can offer advice.

Well over three-quarters of all trade buying in Germany is attributable to the ten biggest "umbrella" organizations, often combining retailing and wholesaling functions. But despite this concentration of buying power, foreign importers may find themselves having to deal with numerous local representatives.

Business Awareness

Foreigners arriving in Germany from the hectic cut-and-thrust of business in cities like London and New York often find the style of business here sluggish and suffocating. Germans like doing things by the book – their own book – and take their time coming to decisions. But behind their apparently slow and conservative approach lies a thoroughness and efficiency which foreigners would do well to respect.

Business attitudes

There has been a fitful debate in recent years over whether West Germans have "gone lazy," and grumbles about the decline of the work ethic are often voiced in the conservative press. It is certainly true that Germans are working fewer hours than they used to. In 1960, for example, Germans worked a total of 56bn hours; in 1986, they worked just 43bn. Moreover, they now work shorter hours than any other major industrial nation: 1,708 hours a year on average, compared with 1,771 in France, 1,778 in the UK, 1,912 in the USA and an exhausting 2,156 in Japan. And they also have an average of 39 days' paid holiday a year (including public holidays), compared with 34 in France, 33 in the UK and just 23 in the USA. But the discipline and thoroughness of the German office ensures that working time is used efficiently; there is certainly much less time spent socializing and "time-filling" than in some other countries.

German attitudes to work have relaxed a great deal in recent years with increasing prosperity and changing social patterns. But there is no doubt that the work ethic does still retain a powerful hold on German business life, especially in the Protestant north, and among older, more traditionally-minded Germans being out of work can still carry an enormous social stigma; even today, apocryphal tales are told of executives who have lost their jobs hiding their shame by leaving their homes each morning dressed in their office clothes and not returning until the end of the day. It is significant that the German word for "lazy" (*faul*) means "foul" and "putrid," as well as simply "idle."

Working hours

Official business hours are 9 to 5, but executives are usually at their desks by 8, except in the big cities (Munich, Frankfurt, Düsseldorf and Hamburg). Here, some executives may delay their arrival a little to avoid the daily rush-hour, which hits a peak just before 7, when many factories start work, and is largely over by 8. Executives in the huge chemical and auto companies located in factory towns may well keep factory hours and start even before 8.

Once in the office, executives get down to work straight away, and 8.30 appointments are by no means uncommon. Bankers, however, tend not to be "in" until after 9, although they may well be at their desks much earlier.

The business day is typically over by 5, with office workers up to department management leaving as they arrived: on time. Many higher level managers, however, leave their offices a little later, especially in the north, although they are usually gone by 7. For many a German manager, this period between 5 and 7 is precious. It is the only time when he or she can work uninterrupted. Moreover, it is the time to place transatlantic calls to catch the New Yorker before lunch. In the south in particular, there is a growing trend to leaving early on Friday afternoon.

Business lunches The early start effectively precludes New York/London-style power breakfasts, while business dinners are a rarity in Germany. So lunch has a special place in German business, although even lunch invitations are rarer than in France and the UK. Lunch tends to be taken early, often at noon, and is hardly ever longer than 90 minutes – an hour is standard. Company canteens tend to be very good, and foreign clients will often be entertained here rather than in an outside restaurant. Such occasions are primarily social rather than business-oriented, and few deals, if any, are clinched over the midday meal. Nevertheless, business lunches are popular with German executives, and the inclusion of a tax on business expenses in government tax reform plans has provoked a good deal of grumbling.

Outside work

German executives make a point of keeping their business and private lives separate. Although willing to work hard when necessary, they are disinclined to work long overtime hours, and the marathon "work-ins" often encountered in US corporations have never been in vogue in Germany. The Germans' methodical working habits mean such efforts are rarely needed anyway.

Once they have left work, executives usually head for home straight away. In some of the big cities, they may stay for a brief drink while the rush-hour traffic dies down, but they will be off as soon as the roads clear.

Contact at home A high proportion of German executives live well away from their workplace, often miles out in the country. This no doubt encourages the tendency to make straight for home after work. It also reinforces the separation between work and home.

German managers very rarely take work home, and they do not expect to take business calls at home. If such a call is genuinely essential, begin by briefly apologizing, and explaining the urgency. Should the spouse answer, be sure to apologize for the intrusion before asking for your business partner.

Holidays are very important. It is not abnormal for even top executives to take a full four weeks' vacation in the summer, plus a week or two skiing in the winter. These, and weekends, are jealously guarded, and business rarely if ever intrudes.

Work habits

The comfortable, long-term tenure of most jobs and the well-established solidity of most companies mean the atmosphere in German offices is rarely dynamic. Go-getting visitors from London or New York may find receptionists efficient but aggravatingly slow. And this apparent sluggishness extends to higher ranks.

Visitors often assume that the formality of office relationships, and the endless rules and regulations, must make German offices tense, cold places to work in. Yet Germans are used to these formalities and rules, and the generally slower operation breeds a working environment that is as relaxed and easy-going as that of any of the more freewheeling companies abroad. It is a mistake to assume that relaxation means casualness; Germans are simply taking their time to do things thoroughly and methodically.

The pace of business

Because no single West German city functions as the business and financial centre for the whole country, the atmosphere tends to be much more relaxed than in metropolises like New York, London or Paris. Traffic is rarely a problem; a top manager in Frankfurt can drive from the underground garage at his office to his home in the outlying Taunus woods in less than half an hour even in rush-hour. In the smaller cities and towns, where many important German companies are headquartered, the pace of business is positively rural.

Stay-at-home German executives are very attached to their homes. Many companies find it almost impossible to persuade top personnel to go abroad, and almost as hard to get them to agree to moves within Germany. When many foreign banks tried to expand their operations in Frankfurt in the wake of recent financial deregulation, they found it remarkably difficult to lure enough qualified staff to the city, even with hefty financial inducements. One US company located its new German headquarters in Munich because they were told (rightly) that it is the one city German executives would be willing to move to.

Nonetheless, managers are often willing to consider a long distance "commute," from Frankfurt to Bonn, for instance, or even further. The relatively small size of the country, the well-developed *Autobahn* system with no speed limit, and chauffeured Mercedes limousines lend German executives a very fluid notion of distance.

The social scene The upper echelons of German business form a very close-knit community, and this extends to social life in the major business centres. Dinner parties are very important, but as a rule not open to outsiders. Skiing vacations with associates are another way of nurturing business relationships, while Sylt, a chic North Sea island resort off the northwest coast, is so popular in summer for the business and cultural elite that some companies maintain a house there for executives.

Corporate hierarchies
The AG's twin boards
The most distinctive feature of the management hierarchy in AGs, large public corporations (see *The business framework*), is the complete division of supervision and management between two boards, the *Aufsichtsrat* (supervisory board) and the *Vorstand* (management board).

The Aufsichtsrat corresponds to the board of directors, but is composed exclusively of outside directors. Often these are top executives from the big banks, whether or not the bank has a substantial shareholding, and it often has. Others may be lawyers or representatives of big corporations. Such directors, elected by the shareholders, constitute half the board membership. Because of Germany's *Mitbestimmung* (worker-participation in management) system, the other half are worker representatives elected by the workforce. In the event of a deadlock, the casting vote rests with the chairman, elected by the shareholders.

The *Aufsichtsrat* is not involved in the day-to-day running of the company, but has the power to appoint (and remove) managers on the *Vorstand* and must approve all important investments or strategic moves. It also exercises a restraining influence on the managers, ensuring their actions do not conflict with the interests of either employees or shareholders. In practice, the *Vorstand* often has the last word on policy matters, but the influence of the *Aufsichtsrat* is considerable.

The Vorstand is responsible for managing the company as a whole. Typically, it has six *Vorstandsmitglieder* (management board members), headed by a *Vorsitzender* (chairman) or a *Sprecher* (spokesman). Management board members are sometimes described in English as "directors" or "senior vice presidents," but this is not quite accurate.

Each board member is responsible for a division or functional department. Occasionally, *Vorstand* members will have dual responsibility, acting as head of, say, both the heavy equipment division and corporate personnel, although

this is becoming very rare. The point
to remember about the *Vorstand*,
however, is that, although individual
members may supervise particular
areas, it is the management board as
a whole which has authority and
responsibility for company
management. In other words,
important decisions are not made by
individual managers but by the board
together. *Vorstandsvorsitzende* are
often called "chairmen" or "chief
executives" in English, and may have
acquired similar authority to their
US or UK counterparts. But they
have no official authority over the
board; legally they are first among
equals.

The practical effect of this is that
many companies want to make
decisions with a consensus or the
backing of an overwhelming majority
of the board. A half, or even a whole,
day each week might be given over to
the *Vorstandssitzung*, the meeting
where important issues are decided
upon.

This joint decision-making process
is often difficult to appreciate for
those accustomed to doing business
in countries with a strictly individual
management hierarchy. But it is
central to an understanding of the
workings of large German
corporations. When you negotiate
with one board member, you must,
in effect, negotiate with the whole
board. This inevitably means that
German firms can take months to
reach a decision. But once a decision
is made, the company's entire
resources are deployed to make that
decision work.

Below the board
Immediately below the *Vorstand* is
the *Generalbevollmächtigte*, literally
"chief executive" but actually an
ordinary executive in line for
appointment to the board, or
fulfilling important functions such as
legal counsel. Other firms may have
instead *Hauptabteilungsleiter* who lead
major divisions or product lines.

At the next step down are the

Direktoren, who should not be
confused with "directors" in English.
The *Direktoren* are the top level of
middle management, corresponding
roughly to vice presidents in the
USA.

The hierarchy for middle
management below the *Direktoren*
varies according to the company's
internal organization. In many
companies, the next level down is
Abteilungsleiter, a department head
who would typically be in charge of
three or four groups managed by
Gruppenleiter. The lowest ranking
officers of the company are the
Prokuristen, the literal meaning of
which implies they have the power to
sign for the company, although this
is not necessarily the case.

Other hierarchies
Although the lower parts of the
hierarchy tend to be much the same
in all kinds of companies, only public
companies have to have the twin
board arrangement.

In private companies the
Aufsichtsrat is either totally absent, or
takes the form of a *Beirat*, a board
which acts only in advisory capacity.
The company is really run by a group
of general managers called the
Geschäftsführung, chaired by the
Vorsitzende der Geschäftsführung;
individual members are called
Geschäftsführer.

Partnerships have yet another
higher management structure.
KGaAs (see *The business framework*)
are headed by *Geschäftsinhaber*
(managing partners) alone, while
small KGs are generally under the
control of a *Kommanditist*. Only the
very largest partnerships will have
a *Hauptabteilungsleiter* or
Generalbevollmächtigte immediately
below.

Women in business
Germany is very backward in
encouraging women to follow
business careers – even more so than
other European countries, which
generally trail well behind the USA

in this respect. Male chauvinism is still prevalent throughout Germany, but it is particularly marked in the business world.

Women are not only rare in the higher echelons of management, but hardly ever achieve any real responsibility in business at all. It is estimated that in banking, business and industry, barely 2% of all top positions are occupied by women.

Most women acknowledge that their chances of surmounting the highly conservative attitudes of their male colleagues and climbing the management hierarchy are slim. The few women who do reach the top usually inherit their position from a husband or father – or start the business themselves. It is significant that three out of four new businesses started in Germany in the last few years are headed by women. The success of Jil Sanders's fashion business was seen as a real sign of hope for women.

Women have made successful careers in publishing, public relations and even politics, but their progress in big business is limited. Several German cities and *Länder* have established special departments to deal with women's rights, but they have only just begun to deal with basic issues like discrimination in hiring and pay. It will be many years before they can even start to tackle the problem of women's lack of progress up the business management hierarchy.

Clearly, the lack of women in senior positions in German firms means that any foreign businesswoman is immediately in an isolated position. The male executives she meets will invariably behave in a deferential and gentlemanly manner. But she may have to fight hard to be taken seriously. Her German clients will often quietly expect her to consult her (male) boss before making a decision, and only take her word for an answer out of politeness. Fortunately, such attitudes are becoming rarer.

The business method

German companies tend to operate in a very methodical and logical manner, pursuing each policy through well-established routes and routines. They do things by the book, and they generally expect their clients to do the same.

Underlying this methodical approach is a deeply serious, even moral, attitude to business. Personal gain, in the sense of "making a million" or "getting rich quick" is much less a motivation in German business than it is in many countries. Steady growth, solidity, and minimization of risks are the hallmarks of the German business approach, for both companies and individuals, and financial probity and conservatism are very much in evidence in all German business dealings.

Many German business people find the freewheeling, cut-and-thrust business method increasingly coming to the fore in the USA not only unsound but positively shocking. West Germany has reluctantly opened up its market to floating-rate borrowing, but continues to discourage ingenuity in creating complex new financing structures like those appearing frequently in New York or London.

Outsiders may regard these attitudes as old-fashioned but it pays to defer to them when doing business in Germany. The Germans rarely respect anyone with a rough and ready attitude to business, and have a natural distrust of innovation. Any sign of unsteadiness will undermine confidence in a business partner.

Self-sufficiency

Confident that they have all the resources they need at their own disposal, German companies are notoriously reluctant to seek advice from outsiders – perhaps because the technical background of many top managers fosters the impression that no-one can tell them anything about their own business that they do not know already.

Management consultants have made some headway in company reorganizations, but German business is far less inclined to use outside consultants or ancillary services than its counterparts in the USA and other major industrial nations. If a thorough study is needed, most large companies try to do their research in house. There are rumblings of change, however, and Deutsche Bank's purchase of a large stake in a management consultant company, Roland Berger and Partner, may be a sign of things to come.

Playing the game

Personal connections and loyalties have always tended to set the tone for German business and, historically, it has shown a pronounced tendency to cartellization. Competition is genuinely fierce in most sectors, and is guaranteed by not only EC rules but also national anti-cartel laws which are the toughest in the world (see *The business framework*). Yet dealing takes place within an intricate framework of unwritten rules that are usually strictly observed. Although cartels and agreements are expressly forbidden, foreigners often find it hard to break into the network of connections; most soon learn to play it the German way.

In banking in particular, executives pay due deference to the hierarchy and tend to look to the top for a lead. It is a daring and unusual small bank which tries to upstage the Deutsche Bank in public view. Foreigners who try pointedly to subvert these traditional relationships may find the ranks closing against them.

Headhunting and company loyalty German companies value loyalty highly, and the top people in most firms generally have many years faithful company service behind them. Poaching of talent from rival firms is rare, and headhunting can still cause surprise and outrage, as

foreign banks moving into Frankfurt found when they tried to buy staff with handsome salaries.

Business meetings

The progress of telecommunications has done nothing to diminish the importance of face-to-face contact in German business. German executives expect to meet business partners in person, even if the initial contact is by letter, and meetings are a crucial element in the advance of any business deal.

The first meeting Meetings generally take place in the company's offices, typically in a small private conference room. One-to-one meetings are a rarity; a senior executive will invite subordinates from the relevant departments to attend. It is vital to be punctual; arrival even a few minutes late creates a bad impression.

Meetings are formal and somewhat distant, but it is nonetheless a personal contact, and polite questions and pleasantries precede getting down to business.

Handling meetings In most meetings, there is a clear host/guest relationship, and the host is expected to take the lead. As guest, you are expected to answer questions patiently; any attempt to force the pace may be regarded as impolite. You may find your German host confident almost to the point of arrogance, but a correspondingly aggressive response rarely earns respect, or business.

Whatever personal rivalries exist within the company will generally be well-hidden from visitors, and it is inadvisable to attempt to exploit any differences of opinion which do become evident.

Germans have a habit of playing things close to the chest, and it is often very difficult to tell how things are going behind the customary politeness. But the German need for thoroughness may provide a clue. If they are interested, your German business partners will continue the meeting for hours examining the proposals in detail. If they bring the meeting to a close in much less than an hour, you can be fairly sure you have done badly.

Trade fairs

Trade fairs play an important part in the business scene, and large numbers of fairs take place each year, from the huge industrial fair in Hanover each spring to the Frankfurt book fair, the world's largest, in autumn. Preparing and attending these fairs take up a considerable amount of management time, for many deals are arranged at them.

For foreign businesses, Germany's trade fairs provide a wonderful opportunity to make business contacts, especially for those trading in capital goods and high technology equipment. It is vital to prepare the ground beforehand by obtaining the catalogue and writing to arrange a meeting with all those firms that you want to see.

Hospitality

The clear separation between business and pleasure prevalent in German life extends to business entertaining as well. Business meals are by no means as common as they are in the USA and UK, and they tend to be strictly social occasions. Social contacts are important in German business, but they tend to be very exclusive, clubby affairs, and foreigners are only rarely invited to join in.

If you are invited for a meal, it is most likely to be for lunch. Business dinners may occasionally be arranged to fit in with a tight schedule, but as a rule, an invitation to an evening meal implies a very high level of contact or a very advanced association. Similarly, foreign business partners are rarely expected to wine and dine their German clients, if only because the dearth of top-quality restaurants, even in the major cities, makes it difficult to find a venue. Before you invite a client to dinner, make sure you know where you can eat.

Business etiquette

Although in recent years there has been a move towards a more relaxed style of behaviour, Germans remain very mannerly and very formal.

Forms of address As a rule, people use full surnames on both business and social occasions, even when they know each other fairly well. Germans almost invariably address even familiar colleagues in the office as "Herr Schmidt" or "Frau Schwartz" (*Fräulein* is now normally used only for young girls, rarely for unmarried women). If the person has a title – and in Germany professional rank often rates as a title – that is used instead of the surname, as in "Herr Professor" or "Frau Direktorin." A German who has a title will be deeply offended if you do not use it – although it is a worse mistake to address someone as "Herr Doktor" when he has no such title.

Similarly the distinction between the formal *Sie* and informal *Du* for "you" is still important and *Sie* is used in all business dealings. The difference may not be evident when dealing in English, but it is still very much in the mind of the German interlocutor. It is wise never to use *Du* with acquaintances unless they specifically suggest it.

Greetings Germans always shake hands when greeting or taking leave of each other. On formal occasions, women should be prepared for a proffered hand to be raised to the lips and kissed. But kissing hands is not expected of foreigners who would not do it at home.

Dressing for business In a country not known for its adventurous dress-sense, German business attire is very sedate and restrained. Almost all men in business wear dark suits, sober ties and white shirts; the few women tend to wear an equally conservative suit and white blouse. Blazers, sportscoats and light-coloured suits are very rarely worn by senior

German executives, except perhaps in very hot summers – but even then they will swelter away in tie and jacket rather than stripping to shirtsleeves.

Gifts Substantial gifts between business partners are looked upon with considerable distaste by most German executives. If you feel you want to make a gesture of appreciation towards a host who has treated you exceptionally well, your gift should be small and simple. A pen of reasonable quality, but not expensive, might do.

The business media
The national dailies
Leading the field among the dailies for its business coverage is the *Frankfurter Allgemeine Zeitung* (FAZ). A serious general newspaper based in Frankfurt but distributed across the country, it is one of only three German dailies that sells nationwide (the others are the Axel Springer stablemates *Bild*, aimed squarely at the popular market, and *Die Welt*, a more restrained affair). The FAZ devotes an entire section every day to business, and its editorial stance is keenly attuned to the views of the business community. *Die Welt* also carries a substantial business section, and is widely read by those in business in Germany, as is the highly-respected Munich daily *Süddeutsche Zeitung*.

Specialist papers
Handelsblatt is the leading specialist business daily and its coverage is comprehensive and thoughtful. Readership of *Handelsblatt* among executives is high, and it has something approaching the status the *Financial Times* and the *Wall Street Journal* have in their home markets.

The daily devoted to the stock market, *Börsenzeitung*, is reckoned to be extremely reliable in its financial reporting, while the *Nachrichten für Aussenhandel* is unrivalled for the range and completeness of its foreign trade reporting.

Business in the magazines
Although there are many magazines specializing in business, the only magazine German executives feel they really must read is *Der Spiegel*, the country's leading general news magazine. It often takes a highly critical stance in its business coverage, and is usually the first to break the news of crises or scandals affecting business.

Newsletters and specialist magazines There is a raft of newsletters more or less oriented towards the stock market, and these vary considerably in their usefulness. By far the most influential is *Der Platow Brief*, which appears two or three times a week. The main business magazines, the weekly *Wirtschaftswoche* and the monthlies *Capital* and *Industriemagazin*, are popular with middle management, while *Manager Magazin*, a monthly controlled by *Der Spiegel*, has a reputation matching its famous parent's for its hard-hitting and often controversial editorial line.

News agencies
Of the many economic and business news agencies in West Germany, *Vereinigte Wirtschaftdienste* (VWD) is the most important. Along with a ticker and screen service, VWD publishes a score of specialized industry reports on a daily basis. Two UK agencies, AP Dow Jones/Telerate and Reuters, are also widely used.

Business on the air
German televison and radio programming on business is solid and competent rather than inspiring. But its mass audience target tends to dilute the coverage, and it often has little real depth. The daily news broadcasts give scant attention to business, rarely referring to anything more than movements in exchange rates or major changes in government economic policy. Unlike in the USA and many other European countries, the stock market receives barely a mention on television news.

Cultural Awareness

A historical perspective

Through the long centuries before the 1860s, Germany was not a unified nation but a loose collection of sovereign entities, numbering at one period over 300. During this time the Germans failed to develop any strong tradition of democracy. Yet they were for the most part peaceful and law-abiding, less often invaders than invaded, and ruled over by scores of princes, counts and other potentates. Then after Bismarck finally unified the country, a new militarism came to the fore, as aggressive rulers sought to expand Germany out of its rather cramped position at the heart of Europe, with disastrous results, culminating in Hitler's propulsion of the country into World War II.

One major price that the Germans have paid for this is that their country is now divided, with one-quarter of it under Communist rule. But, in the West democracy has at last taken root. For years after 1945, the Germans understandably did not want to look at their history, preferring to try to blot out the past and make a clean new start. But today they feel sufficiently secure to take a fresh interest in the heritage that has shaped them.

10BC–AD10 The Romans, who have already established colonies at Augsburg, Trier and Cologne, extend their rule to the Elbe. They are then forced back to the Rhein by a revolt of their subject tribes, the *Germani*.

800–814 Charlemagne (Karl der Grosse) becomes emperor of much of Western Europe; he sets up his court at Aachen, and is the first ruler to assemble the German tribes into some unity, albeit short-lived.

1241 Led by Lübeck, several North German towns unite in a trading federation, the Hanseatic League, while the rest of the country remains feudal and divided.

1517 Start of the Protestant Reformation, leading to the peasants' revolt of 1524.

1618–48 Germany is ravaged by the Thirty Years' War between Catholics and Protestants, ending in the Peace of Westphalia.

1740–86 Frederick the Great, king of Prussia, an enlightened despot, sets the path for Prussian ascendancy over the other German states.

1862 Bismarck becomes prime minister of Prussia, then defeats Austria (1866) and France (1870–1) and unifies all Germany under the Prussian crown.

1914–18 Under Kaiser Wilhelm II, Germany in alliance with Austria declares war on Russia and France, but is ultimately defeated; the Treaty of Versailles imposes heavy reparations.

1933 After the failures of the Weimar Republic and the steady rise of the Nazi Party, Adolf Hitler becomes chancellor and exploits his position to seize full power and suspend civil rights.

1938–9 Hitler annexes Austria. At Munich, France and Britain agree to his taking the Sudetenland; soon afterwards German troops occupy the rest of Czechoslovakia.

1939 Hitler invades Poland, whereupon Britain and France declare war against Germany; France is defeated in June 1940.

1945 A beaten Germany is occupied by the Allies; the Russians then begin to turn their zone into a separate Communist state.

1948–9 The Russians blockade West Berlin, hoping to subjugate it: they are foiled by the Allied airlift and the spirit of the Berliners.

1949 The Federal Republic of West Germany is created, and later joins NATO (1955) and becomes a founder member of the EC (1957). Konrad Adenauer becomes the

Republic's first chancellor and continues to dominate West German politics until his retirement in 1963.

1961 East Germany builds the Berlin Wall.

1969–1970 Willy Brandt, social democrat, becomes chancellor and concludes agreements with the Soviet bloc that lead to much easier relations with East Germany.

1972 Decisive election victory for the social democrats enables them to embark on major social reforms.

1974 A senior official in the chancellor's office, Günter Guillaume, is found to be an East German spy. Willy Brandt resigns and Helmut Schmidt becomes chancellor.

1979 The German economy begins to falter seriously for the first time since the war.

1982 Continued economic problems undermine the SPD-FDP coalition and the conservative CDU return to power under Helmut Kohl.

1983 A general election confirms the CDU in office and sees the Greens emerge as a force in West German politics.

1985 The country is divided over US President Reagan's judgement in deciding to visit Bitburg cemetery, which contains the remains of 49 SS troops.

1987 First visit to the Federal Republic by the East German president Erich Honecker.

The Reformation Martin Luther's revolt against the corrupt practices of the papacy may have been well justified, initially. But his reform movement soon created its own harshly authoritative conservatism, which was to mark Germany deeply. It also served to divide the country into two warring camps, Catholic and Protestant, leading to the devastating Thirty Years' War that killed more than one German in three.

The rise of Prussia Under the Hohenzollern dynasty, and Frederick the Great (1740–86) in particular, Prussia emerged as the dominant force in Germany. Prussia's disciplined, efficient army and bureaucracy not only brought the country territorial conquests but also reflected the principles of the *Aufklärung* (Enlightenment) which were to lead, through the philosophies of Kant and then Herder, to the cult of State power championed by Hegel in the early 19th century. There was little room in Prussian politics for the liberal values then sweeping Europe, and the country demanded great sacrifices of its people. But with the rise of the Hohenzollerns, the Austrian Habsburg Empire at last faced a serious rival for power within Germany.

Unification under Bismarck
Since Germany has a certain cultural, linguistic and ethnic unity, and thus has always had the makings of a real nation, its political unification was a logical step, however belated. But it happened in a less than happy manner: through the remarkable diplomatic manoeuverings of the Prussian chancellor Otto von Bismarck, and a series of Prussian military successes – over Denmark (1864), Austria (1866) and France (1871) – a Prussian elitist caste, militaristic, legalistic and intolerant of democracy, imposed its will on the rest of Germany. Unification paved the way for industrial revolution and Bismarck, it is true, did help to modernize Germany even in the social field, by creating welfare services for the new industrial masses. But the ambition of the Hohenzollern dynasty plunged Europe into war.

Weimar and the Nazis The miseries of Germany in the 1920s and early 1930s, first rocketing inflation and then unemployment reaching 6m, were certainly due in part to the harshness of the Versailles Treaty. But the so-called Weimar Republic (created in 1919 by an assembly convened at Weimar) proved weak and incapable; its leaders lacked experience and its Constitution was feeble. So the burgeoning Nazi party was free to exploit popular discontent, including the panic fears of Bolshevism and of Jewish money-making. The resulting holocaust needs no retelling.

Post-war renewal Emerging from the *Stunde Null* (zero hour) of post-war devastation, the republic born in Bonn in 1949 was able to avoid repeating the mistakes of Weimar: it had a far more effective Constitution, it benefited from the authoritative and moderate leadership of Chancellor Adenauer, and this time the Western victors' policy was far more constructive. By dedicated hard work the Germans rebuilt their shattered economy, while the old political feuding gave way to a new spirit of consensus that permitted democracy at last to flourish.

Nationality and beliefs

West Germany is a well-ordered and wealthy society in which life, on the whole, is comfortable and pleasant. Its people are well-educated, often well-travelled and receptive to ideas and influences from abroad. Many understand and willingly speak foreign languages, principally English. Uncompromising protest and civil disobedience movements are often a reaction against the disastrous submissiveness of the previous generation to the Nazi regime, while a deep preoccupation with peace and arms control reflects the country's exposed position on the frontier between East and West.

What is Germany?

With the Second World War and its consequences, the Germans suffered a trauma unparalleled in modern history. After such a brief period as a unified state, patriotism had become repugnant, national identity was shattered. With large territories lost to Poland and the Soviet Union and the rest divided between the East and West blocs, the question "what is Germany?" is debated frequently and always inconclusively. Officially,

every West German government is committed by the Constitution to work for reunification – which East Germany flatly rejects. But despite the official stance, most West Germans do not believe reunification will come in their lifetime. Once again Germany is not a state but an abstract concept, based on language, a common culture and history.

Digesting the Nazi legacy The early postwar decades were marked by a virtual taboo on talking about the Nazi period. But this has changed greatly in the past 10 or 15 years, as the guilty generation dies away or retires from active life. Today the subject is discussed freely and copiously in public, especially in the media, and is taught fairly objectively in schools, while many towns have staged big exhibitions of life under the Nazis. The result of this new openness is that people are now more candid. Some elderly ones go in for self-justification while many young ones vocally resent being made to feel guilty for events of another age. Most Germans today, however, do accept that the past must never be forgotten and that the nation must still bear some historic responsibility. Millions go on visits of humility to Dachau, Belsen and other camps. "Neo-Nazism" is a fringe phenomenon with little impact, restricted to handfuls of nostalgic ss veterans and young extremist thugs, plus a few loony idealists.

Patriotism and national identity A recent Gallup international survey that put the question, "Do you feel proud to be (American, Italian, etc)?," found only 21% of Germans answering "yes," far fewer than Americans (80%), Britons (55%) or French (33%). If the main explanation is shame about the past, another could be that a German's strongest loyalties often tend to be local or regional, rather than national; many a Bavarian will declare that he feels Bavarian first and German only second. Some observers have recently detected a new rise in national sentiment but this appears to be focused on cultural identity rather than politics, or else takes the form of pride in sporting or economic successes.

Regionalism From the time Germanic tribes pushed out the Celts and settled in this part of Europe around the 2nd century BC, until its unification a little more than 100 years ago, Germany was a varied collection of tribes, then of individual states. This diversity and decentralization was deliberately perpetuated in West Germany after the war with a federation of 10 *Länder*. This arrangement suits local temperaments and loyalties well, for the cool, reserved farmers of Schleswig-Holstein are very different from the baroque, beer-swilling Bavarians, while the disciplined people of Lower Saxony look down a bit on the happy-go-lucky Rheinlanders. Northern regions, particularly the city-states of Hamburg and Bremen, tend to be more progressive, while the south, especially Bavaria, is basically conservative. Another division is religion: the area south of Bavaria, Westphalia and the whole area on either side of the Rhein are predominantly Catholic, while Swabia and most of north Germany are mainly Protestant.

The lack of a real capital city to act as a magnet for talent, a cultural melting-pot and a show-case for the world has bred a better quality of regional life. Munich and Hamburg, for instance, have a much richer and more self-contained cultural and social life, stronger traditions and identity than most other medium-sized European cities. Leading industries, too, are often found in little towns or the deepest countryside, where local farmers work shifts and executives have comfortable but unostentatious homes way off the beaten track.

Local characteristics and habits were watered down by the upheaval of World War II and, in particular,

the influx of millions of refugees from Germany's eastern territories at the end of the war. Nevertheless, a regional accent and local patriotism are a source of pride rather than a sign of homespun provincialism.

Religion and race

Although religion has a diminishing influence on life, most West Germans belong, at least nominally, to a church and almost exactly half are Catholic, half Protestant (about 26.5m each). They pay contributions to their church, which the state automatically collects along with their taxes, and can opt out only if they apply formally in writing. Over 90% of Germans still pay these taxes, and the churches receive an income of some DM10bn a year, which they spend on running a vast array of schools, hospitals and welfare bodies. This helps to give the churches considerable influence in public affairs, although church attendance has long been in steady decline. The old Catholic/Protestant conflicts that long bedevilled German history have largely disappeared, and a friendly ecumenicism is in vogue. Instead, there are sharp dissensions *within* each of the Churches. Among Catholics, these are between old and new guards on subjects such as abortion. And in Protestant ranks there is a schism between the politically-minded leftists, who want the Church to commit itself on nuclear and other issues, and the conservative neo-pietists who believe that Christianity should steer clear of politics and secular matters.

Racial issues There are about 4.5m foreigners living in West Germany, some 1.4m of them Turks. The vast majority of them came in the post-war boom years in response to the demand for labour as *Gastarbeiter* (guest workers), although more recently large numbers came in from Third World countries, making use of West Germany's liberal asylum laws. While the Italians, Portuguese, Greeks and Yugoslavs were absorbed fairly easily, the Turks have tended to live in ghettos and often find it difficult to get anything but the lowest paid, menial jobs. A right-wing tabloid press still occasionally whips up the feelings against Turks, and young German thugs have occasionally used violence. But there are signs that the Germans are at last beginning to tolerate, if not welcome, the presence of these people in their midst, and many organizations and individuals, notably Christians and Greens, go out of their way to help and befriend them.

There are about 30,000 Jews living in West Germany, only a fraction of the number living in the German Reich before the rise of Nazism. They form about 65 religious communities, of which West Berlin, with 6,500, is the biggest. Anti-semitism still rears its head from time to time, but on the whole the Jewish population now is accepted and assimilated. Any public official making an anti-semitic remark is likely to be drummed out of office.

Attitudes

National attitudes and characteristics regarded as typically "German" have been changing with the years. The image of Germans as authoritarian, overdisciplined, conformist and even aggressive is no longer accurate. Permissive upbringing has already produced a generation quite different from its elders, while the atmosphere in schools, the workplace and the home is more relaxed and friendly. Work, top of most peoples' list of priorities for many years, slipped to fourth place in the early 1980s, after such considerations as family, leisure and friendship. Public authorities now have a human face, most bureaucrats regard themselves as public servants, and the armed forces and police have consciously cultivated a democratic, civilian image.

Nevertheless, by comparison with other Western countries West Germany can still seem over-orderly,

legalistic, prone to red tape and an official pernicketiness which can drive foreigners to distraction. People living in blocks of flats or housing estates are confronted at all turns by signs forbidding children's games, dog-walking, playing music or hanging out washing, while regulations limit the frequency of baths or parties, and impose the clearing of snow or fallen leaves from paths and steps. Passers-by spontaneously interfere if a motorist parks untidily or a pedestrian dares to cross at red even if there is no traffic in sight.

Class and community

The war not only devastated the country but also broke down class distinctions. Many people lost everything; most had to start again from scratch. Of course the new wealth acquired since then has been unevenly shared; wage differentials, though less than in most West European countries, still average 4.5 between the head of a firm and an unskilled worker. Even so, Germany today appears as a land of freedom of opportunity rather than of vested privilege, a somewhat *nouveau riche* society closer in some ways to the USA than to the old European order, and the prevailing ethos in public life is lower-middle class. Workers have been losing their class solidarity and sense of grievance and exclusion; they have adopted bourgeois life-styles, in their clothes, and their cars, even if their cultural tastes often remain distinct. Speech accent in Germany varies much more by region than by social class.

In this new semi-classless world, oddly enough, the one group that retains its identity most sharply is the old aristocracy. Today it has no formal status, but the 50,000 or so members of the old noble families still frequently use their titles. They cling together socially: yet they are much respected in public and often they win influential jobs. Many a firm is eager to have the prestige of a *Graf* or *Prinz* on its board.

Families, sex and morality

Over the years, family ties have been weakening and most children now prefer to live away from home once they become wage-earners. As the very low birth rate indicates (see *Human resources*), most young couples today have only one or at most two children, and many prefer to remain childless. If one factor here is the German's "cultural pessimism" and lack of faith in the future, other reasons are more practical: the difficulties of combining a job with motherhood, and the troubles that couples with small children often have in finding a place to live.

The institution of marriage is in decline in Germany. The annual total of weddings has fallen by 40% since 1962, and many couples do not bother to get married. In the 18–35 age group, two in five are living together unwed, and this is socially accepted. The rise in public tolerance extends also to unmarried mothers and homosexuals, while divorce has been made easier and now terminates about one marriage in three. But the sharp rise in teenage promiscuity notable in the 1960s and 1970s has now ended, and there is a swing back to seriousness and the steady couple – a trend recently accentuated by the spread of AIDS. Abortion was legalized in 1974 and is now free on the health service. But a woman must first convince a panel of doctors that she has a good reason for her abortion, and this can still be not at all easy in Catholic areas.

The generation gap

Postwar German youth was generally submissive to the established order prior to the 1968 student revolts. Ever since then, and especially since the rise of the Greens in the early 1980s, a large section of youth has vigorously contested what it sees as the greedy materialism and bourgeois conformism of its parents and elders. Yet if the generation gap has seemed sharper in Germany than in most other Western countries, it is less a conflict of generations than of two dramatically opposed ideologies and lifestyles, and there are plenty of deserters both ways across the age divide. Many of the most vehement radicals and Greens are now middle-aged, while the very young generation emerging from its teens contains a surprisingly large careerist element.

Women's equality

Under the Federal Republic's Basic Law, men and women are regarded as equals. But women did not win full legal equality until 1977, with the repeal of an old law that permitted a wife to take a job only if her husband agreed. And today, though in theory they have full rights, many women still feel discriminated against. Like others who try to change the entrenched social order in Germany, the first feminists, nicknamed "*Emanzen*," were greeted with hostility and ridicule, particularly in the male-dominated press. But this did not stop the movement spreading. Women are moving in large numbers into most professions, every second woman is in employment and women make up 37.4% of the workforce, but the odds are still against their reaching the top.

In politics, since the war, virtually no woman has reached a position of prominence; and if since 1980 their representation in the Bundestag has climbed from 7 to 15.4%, this has been largely due to the progress of the female-dominated Green party. An important turning-point in political attitudes came in the early 1980s, when the ruling conservative Christian Democrat Party realized that women, traditionally its most faithful voters, were abandoning it in droves for the more feminist-minded Social Democrats. Since then it has cautiously embraced modern women's concerns and given the Minister for Health, Family and Youth a brief to champion women's interests. Whatever the reasons, most people agree that German women have now thrown off their old frumpish *Kinder, Kirche, Küche* (children, church and cooking) image and are demanding far more from life. Nowhere is this better illustrated than in women's fashion. Once noted primarily for their "sensible" shoes, raincoats and trilby hats, German women are now among the best-dressed in Europe, although preferring a sporty, classical style rather than Latin chic.

Lifestyles

The standard of living in West Germany is one of the highest in the world, and it is very important to its people. Even the slightest warning of economic trouble ahead prompts a disciplined belt-tightening among a population who have known, or been told by its parents, of the horrors of economic ruin. Soundings into the ambiguous attitude of West Germans towards reunification in recent years have found that while a majority would be prepared to accept neutrality in exchange for reunification, far fewer would sacrifice their standard of living for the same end.

Home life

The Germans today are very comfortably housed, and the shortages of the postwar years have been solved. But home prices in cities have risen so high that a young couple with little capital must expect to spend a large share of their income on a mortgage or rent. Although only 40% of homes are owner-occupied, most Germans prefer when they can to live in their own little house with a garden, rather than in a rented flat. They also tend to prefer new buildings to old ones. After the war, the desire to make a break with the past was such that much older housing spared by the bombing was hurriedly torn down; villagers destroyed their pretty cottages and built stereotyped new villas, easier to heat, or they covered half-timbered façades with fancy new plastic walls, considered more chic. However, in

the past few years a new ecological era has brought a new concern for traditional values. Such half-timbered houses as have survived are now being carefully restored rather than pulled down, and some people are again looking for old homes of character – but there are not many left.

Possessions Germans are among the affluent people in the world, and this is reflected in the consistently high level of consumer spending. Ownership of the latest home electronics, such as videos and compact disc players, is widespread, while homes are well stocked with modern consumer durables: 96% of German homes have a refrigerator, 81% a washing machine, 56% a deep freeze; 61% of families own a car and 18% two cars or more.

Food The Germans used to be renowned for their hefty appetites, and their waistlines proved the point. But today they are far more health-conscious, and rising prosperity has brought a big shift from heavy carbohydrates to a more balanced diet. The middle classes are also showing a new interest in gastronomy, prompted by foreign holidays and the presence of so many "exotic" restaurants run by immigrants from Greece, Italy, etc. In smart restaurants, French *nouvelle cuisine* has made its inevitable inroads. Cooking has become a modish hobby, although often it is the husband who dons his apron to try out new recipes. One cookbook has been the biggest seller of any title except the Bible.

Drink The Germans remain the world's heaviest beer drinkers after the Belgians (145 litres per head per year). Wine consumption has trebled since the war, to 21 litres annually per head – helped by the fact that it is not taxed and a simple table wine costs less than orange juice. But sales of soft drinks and mineral waters have also risen sharply, especially among young people. Although spirit drinking has declined, gin and whisky are still the smart drinks to offer guests in bourgeois homes. Among workers and farmers especially, the most popular remains Schnaps, still the main route to alcoholism. But a tightening of the drink-and-drive rules means that this and other fire-waters are consumed less recklessly. These laws are strictly applied, and tend to make drivers very abstemious at social functions.

Evening leisure As lunch, with a hot main dish, is the principal meal of the day in most families, in the evening they are more likely to eat *Abendbrot*, a modest supper of sliced meats, cheese, salad, etc. Television is watched a good deal. On fine evenings, many people will make for a wine-tavern or beer-garden, maybe taking a picnic meal with them to eat outdoors on the trestle tables; in colder weather, *Kneipen* (pubs) are popular. In this very musical nation, the charming old tradition of family *Hausmusik* is being revived after a period of decline; at a middle-class social evening, the host and hostess and their teenage children will sometimes perform quartets for their guests. Germany also has 14,500 choral societies – another popular leisure activity.

Most home entertaining is quite simple: a few friends are invited for a snack, or a glass or two of wine with cakes, and everyone sits round in a circle. The complete dinner party is rare, as is the stand-up cocktail party. More lavish entertainment is usually reserved for the celebration of birthdays or other anniversaries; the Germans set great store by these ceremonies. The warmly emotional family Christmas remains an important ritual, when homes are decorated with holly and candles, an Advent Wreath, and maybe a crib.

Leisure

Culture Very generous *Land* and city subsidies for the performing arts mean that even small cities support their own opera company, orchestra and sometimes even a ballet, and most small towns have a repertory theatre. The middle classes tend to take their culture-going seriously, as a matter not just of entertainment but of self-improvement. Social snobbery and convention can be involved too; people want to be seen at the right cultural events, and they like to dress smartly for the occasion. This applies especially to opera-going among the older generation; younger people and students often prefer the fringe and "alternative" cultural scenes that are liveliest in Berlin and Frankfurt. Music remains the Germans' first love, followed by theatre. Cinema is rather a poor relation of the arts, hampered by the fact that foreign films are nearly always dubbed, not sub-titled. Museum-going has hugely increased in popularity recently, and many new museums of modern art have been built with public money.

Sport Energetic outdoor sports with a keep-fit rationale have become something of a cult, and one German in three now belongs to a sports club, of which there are 50,000. Football is especially popular, followed by gymnastics, swimming and skiing; tennis, once a preserve of the upper classes, has now spread widely, given a boost by the fame of two young tennis stars, Boris Becker and Steffi Graf. Horse riding, too, has come back into vogue.

Clubs Traditional *Vereine* (clubs and associations) play a big role in local social life. There are clubs for every kind of hobby, such as pigeon-racing; many small towns and villages also have their ancient *Schützenvereine* (rifle clubs), each with its own banners, uniforms and special ceremonials. Members tend to spend more time lifting beer-glasses than rifles. The local *Trachtenvereine* in Bavaria are devoted to the wearing of traditional costumes.

The big public festivals tend to centre round wine-making and the brewing of beer. Best known of them is Munich's *Oktoberfest*, which dates from 1810.

Holidays Once a home, a car and a

degree of comfort have been acquired, most Germans next look to travel, traditionally the hallmark of a cultured person and now also a sign of economic success. For the majority this means flocking to the beaches of the Mediterranean or the Atlantic, or hiking in the mountains, but for the more educated and adventurous it could well mean a cultural tour of China or the wilder regions of South America, with diligent reading-up beforehand. Two thirds of German holidays are spent abroad, and more Germans travel abroad than any other nationality, including the Americans. Indeed, Germans' spending on holidays abroad is a major source of the country's invisible trade deficit.

Spa cures The Germans are also the world's leading spa-goers, by far: but here they stay within their own borders, for Germany has more than 200 designated spa resorts, mostly in the pleasant hills of the south. Over 6m people go on a cure each year, nearly all of them reimbursed by an indulgent health insurance system. Veteran *curistes* often find time for some late-flowering romance: one key rule of cures is that you must not bring your spouse with you, since a complete break from home is part of the treatment. Of course this can lead to trouble; the *Kurschatten* (spa romance) is a common German phenomenon, and the divorce lawyers are familiar with it.

Education

Without its education system, West Germany's rise to its position as the world's third strongest economic power would have been impossible. The German universities of the 19th century were an inspiration and model for many countries, but much of the present-day economic success is based on a thorough system of vocational training which is carefully dovetailed into high school education. Qualifications, whether educational, technical or academic, are an essential requisite for a career, to the

extent that talent can go unrecognized unless it is accompanied by an appropriate certificate. The pressure to succeed is intense and a sad side-effect is a steady rate of suicides among teenagers who feel they cannot cope.

School

Schooling, vocational education and, to a great extent, higher education are in the hands of the *Länder* and its pattern therefore varies from one to another. On major matters the *Länder* are supposed to coordinate their policies. This tends to make overall reform more difficult, for they often fail to agree. Yet reform is badly needed, as it has not proved easy to adapt the German scholastic tradition to modern needs.

Triple streaming 95% of pupils are in state (ie *Land*) rather than private schools. Four out of five children go first to a *Kindergarten*, then from age 6 to 11 to a *Grundschule* (primary school) and are then divided into three streams on the basis of ability. The brighter or more academic ones go to a *Gymnasium* (grammar school) that prepares for university; the middle range go to a *Realschule* that offers a general education till 16, usually leading to a vocational college or apprenticeship; the least gifted attend a *Hauptschule* that gives practical preparation for the job market or the extensive apprenticeship system that serves German industry so well. This triple streaming has been criticized for its alleged social divisiveness: but attempts to introduce "comprehensives" (*Gesamtschule*) in Social Democrat-controlled states have not always worked well.

At about 19, most *Gymnasium* pupils take the rigorous *Abitur* examination that is essential for university entrance. Despite endless professorial complaints of falling standards, the *Abitur* has recently been made easier: but it still demands much hard study, and German schools are still noted for the seriousness and quality of the teaching, the high level of pupil motivation, and the avoidance of early specialization. But if young minds are superbly taught *inside* the classroom, schools by tradition put very little stress on character-building or training for civic responsibility; these are felt to be the tasks of parents, and maybe also of the churches. The classroom day generally ends at 1pm, and nearly all sport and club and cultural activity takes place outside a school framework. Hence state schools tend to be austere, utilitarian places, lacking any warm sense of community. Some middle-class parents have reacted by sending their children to private schools – notably the *Waldorfschule* founded by the late Rudolf Steiner. The 80 *Waldorfschulen* put less stress on academic work and more on cultural and group activities that develop the full creative personality.

After school, about 74% of the pupils go on to vocational training under a "dual system" involving both firms and the state. They spend part of their time in practical training in a firm, the other half at a vocational training school learning both vocational and general subjects. The course usually ends after three years with a state-recognized exam. If they wish, those who complete the course can go on to more advanced technical and vocational training colleges.

Universities The 54 universities, tightly controlled by the *Land* governments, have little autonomy, and they are all run in much the same way, so that today there is little difference between a distinguished ancient university such as Heidelberg or Tübingen and a modern campus such as Bochum or Dortmund. German universities suffered a notorious malaise during the 1960s, culminating in the 1968 student revolt against professorial autocracy and fusty hierarchy. Then came years of chaos and sporadic leftist unrest,

but today order has returned. The senior professors are back in control, but they have learned to be more open-minded and easygoing.

Today's overriding problem is that of student numbers which have risen since 1959 from 200,000 to an excessive 1.3m. The flow is hard to control, for politically it is not easy to modify the rooted German tradition whereby anyone with the *Abitur* has the right to a university place, in any faculty of his or her choice. True, a limit has recently been imposed on entry to some subjects such as medicine, pharmacy and law. And with the sharp rise in graduate unemployment, some *Abitur*-gainers are now opting for vocational colleges which offer better job prospects. But faculty numbers are still kept high by the way students in Germany can usually stretch out their studies for as long as they like.

All this leads to overcrowding, underfunding, a bad student/teacher ratio, harrassed staff and lonely, ill-supervised students, and a general apathy and lowering of standards. And universities have become increasingly parochial, for almost all students today meekly enrol in the one nearest to home; the old migratory tradition of spending, say, a year at Göttingen and then another at Freiburg has almost disappeared. In face of this gloomy situation, the Kohl government began to sanction the creation of small, private fee-paying universities, elitest in nature, and often geared towards business studies. Several have now been set up. This marks a sharp break with German tradition, but is possibly the best way out of the crisis.

City by City

The map below shows the cities featured in the city by city guide. Each city follows a standard format and there is a map locating recommended hotels and restaurants, and important buildings and sights. The official name for West Germany is Bundesrepublik Deutschland (BR Deutschland). The official name for East Germany is Deutsche Demokratische Republik (DDR).

BERLIN

City codes zip 1000 ☎ 030

Geographically and politically, West Berlin is unique. Marooned in East German territory, it is separated by the Wall from East Berlin, the other half of the former Prussian and German capital. It became a political pawn during the Cold War tension of the 1950s, which eventually led to the building of the Wall in 1961, but since the Four Power Agreement of 1971 West Berlin has ceased to live in the eye of East-West confrontation.

Although West Berlin is strictly speaking a *Land* of the Federal Republic, its deputies in Bonn have only limited voting rights. It has its own parliament, which elects a governing mayor (currently the young and ambitious Eberhard Diepgen). Bonn, in theory at least, has no direct say in the affairs of West Berlin, since the supreme authority over the city is still enjoyed by the "protecting powers," France, Great Britain and the United States.

West Berlin's geographical position and curious status have had a direct bearing on its economic and social life. After World War II, almost all the major German companies that had had their headquarters in Berlin moved to the safety of other West German cities, and even after the easing of tension in 1971 they were reluctant to return. From 1970 to 1983, jobs in its manufacturing industry fell by 40%.

Yet West Berlin's output has risen steadily because of the heavy subsidies from Bonn to compensate for the disadvantages of its location and keep it as a showcase for Western values. Just over half its budget is now provided by West Germany, much of the money providing generous incentives to lure companies to the city. Recently, long-standing Berlin-based employers such as Siemens, AEG, Schering and Daimler-Benz were joined by West Germany's most successful computer company, Nixdorf. A start-up company drive to attract high-tech industries to Wedding has met with some success.

People are also encouraged to move to West Berlin. Not only does the city offer 30% lower personal taxes and other advantages, but its residents are not liable to military service. This has prompted many Greens and nonconformists to migrate to the city. They have set up a counter-culture in Kreuzberg and Neukölln, where they live in relative harmony with the large colony of Turkish workers. Berlin has a long tradition of immigration: at the end of the 17th century there was a massive influx of French Huguenots; they were later followed by Polish and Bohemian refugees.

West Berlin's diverse attractions have reversed population trends over the last five years, increasing the numbers by 50,000 to 1.9m. Over that same period, only about 30,000 new jobs were created and unemployment is higher here than in the country as a whole. Meanwhile, the rest of West Germany, put out by what it regards as the "feather-bedding" of West Berlin, waits expectantly for the next trick to be pulled out of the hat by the Berliners, famous in politics as in business for always having an eye to the main chance.

Arriving

Although most visitors from West Germany drive to Berlin, many business travellers prefer to fly there. There are scheduled flights to and from all major West German cities and about 20 world business capitals. Air passengers are not subject to East German controls. Regular but not very comfortable trains run between Berlin and Hamburg, Hanover, Frankfurt and Nuremberg. Passport control and the issue of transit visas are carried out on the train. Four *Autobahn* transit routes connect West Germany with Berlin: vehicles arriving from Hamburg (E15) enter Berlin at the Heiligensee checkpoint; those arriving from Hanover (E8), central West Germany (E63 and E6), and Nuremberg (E6) cross at the Drewitz/Dreilinden checkpoint. Drivers are advised to obey East German regulations (for example, no speeding, no hitchhikers). The speed limit, rigidly enforced, is 100km. Commercial traffic also goes by inland waterway.

Berlin-Tegel airport

Berlin-Tegel airport was originally intended to complement Berlin-Tempelhof airport, but in 1975 became the city's only civilian airport when Tempelhof was reserved almost exclusively for military use. Only five major airlines operate out of Berlin-Tegel (PanAm, TWA, British Airways, Air France and Dan Air; Lufthansa is not permitted to fly to West Berlin). There are daily services to 16 West German cities, including very frequent flights to and from Hamburg, Frankfurt and Munich. Cities served by direct international scheduled flights include Amsterdam, Basle, Brussels, Copenhagen, Geneva, Glasgow, London, Manchester, Nice, Oslo, Paris and Zürich.

The single terminal is compact and convenient. Its drive-in system means there is a very short distance between aircraft, passport control

and the taxi rank and airport bus stop. Its facilities include currency exchange bureaux (which close just before the arrival of last flights), seven cafés and restaurants, a post office, conference rooms ☎ 41013232 and a branch of the tourist office, which runs a hotel reservation service. Airport information ☎ 41012307; freight inquiries ☎ 41011.

Nearby hotel *Novotel Berlin-Airport*, Kurt-Schumacher-Damm 202, B51 ☎ 41060 ⓉⓍ 181605 • AE DC MC V. Attractive modern hotel with good conference facilities, outdoor pool, sauna and solarium. Free airport shuttle service.

City link The airport is 7km/4 miles north of the city centre, which can be reached by bus or, better, by taxi.
Taxi There are normally plenty of taxis immediately outside the main hall of the terminal. The journey into town takes about 15min. Telephone reservations ☎ 6902, 261026, 216060 and 240202.
Limousine Limousine Service ☎ 3015040; Minex ☎ 8533091.
Car rental It is more convenient to rent a car at the airport, where Avis, Europcar, Hertz and interRent have desks, although they also have city offices.
Bus There is no airport bus. City bus no. 9 runs between the airport and the centre (Kurfürstendamm, Zoo and Budapester Strasse) but the journey is rather slow (25–35min). Tickets (cheap) may be bought from the driver.

Railway station

Bahnhof Zoologischer Garten (almost always abbreviated to Bahnhof Zoo) is West Berlin's main rail terminus, but still looks the suburban station it once was. Many trains continue into East Berlin and beyond, so do not be fooled by the station's appearance into thinking you have not yet arrived at your destination. Although the East German rail authorities who, paradoxically, run Bahnhof Zoo, have at last begun to renovate the terminus, it has few facilities apart from a currency exchange bureau (outside the station building) and a post office. There is a taxi rank in front of the station, and very good *U-Bahn* and *S-Bahn* train connections to all parts of the city. For those with not too much baggage, the station is within walking distance of several major hotels. Timetable inquiries ☎ 19419.

Getting around
The centre of Berlin, around the Europa Center and the eastern end of Kurfürstendamm, is where most of the major hotels are located. It is fairly compact and can be easily negotiated on foot. Outside this area you will need to take a taxi or use public transport.

Taxis Berlin has 350 taxi ranks, several big radio cab firms, little traffic congestion and fares are about 15% lower than in the rest of West Germany. Radio taxis ☎ 6902, 261026, 216060, and 240202.
Limousines *Limousine Service* ☎ 3015040; *Minex* ☎ 8533091.
Driving Driving and parking do not present major problems although there are one-way streets. Car rental *Avis* ☎ 2611881, *Budget* ☎ 41012886, *interRent* ☎ 41013368, *Europcar* ☎ 2137097.
Walking Almost all streets are lined with trees, so walking is enjoyable except when smog periodically descends on the city. But take care to avoid the maroon cycle tracks.
Subway, bus The extensive and integrated network of fast and clean *U-Bahn* and *S-Bahn* trains and frequent buses is easy to use. You must buy tickets, which are interchangeable, from one of the many vending machines before boarding a vehicle or from the bus driver. The simplest solution is to

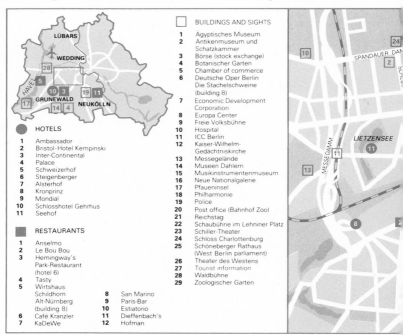

LÜBARS
WEDDING
GRUNEWALD
NEUKÖLLN

BUILDINGS AND SIGHTS
1 Ägyptisches Museum
2 Antikenmuseum und Schatzkammer
3 Börse (stock exchange)
4 Botanischer Garten
5 Chamber of commerce
6 Deutsche Oper Berlin
  Die Stachelschweine (building 8)
7 Economic Development Corporation
8 Europa Center
9 Freie Volksbühne
10 Hospital
11 ICC Berlin
12 Kaiser-Wilhelm-Gedächtniskirche
13 Messegelände
14 Museen Dahlem
15 Musikinstrumentenmuseum
16 Neue Nationalgalerie
17 Pfaueninsel
18 Philharmonie
19 Police
20 Post office (Bahnhof Zoo)
21 Reichstag
22 Schaubühne im Lehniner Platz
23 Schiller-Theater
24 Schloss Charlottenburg
25 Schöneberger Rathaus (West Berlin parliament)
26 Theater des Westens
27 Tourist information
28 Waldbühne
29 Zoologischer Garten

SPANDAUER DAM
LIETZENSEE
MESSEDAMM

HOTELS
1 Ambassador
2 Bristol-Hotel Kempinski
3 Inter-Continental
4 Palace
5 Schweizerhof
6 Steigenberger
7 Alsterhof
8 Kronprinz
9 Mondial
10 Schlosshotel Gehrhus
11 Seehof

RESTAURANTS
1 Anselmo
2 Le Bou Bou
3 Hemingway's Park-Restaurant (hotel 6)
4 Tasty
5 Wirtshaus Schildhorn Alt-Nürnberg (building 8)
6 Café Kranzler
7 KaDeWe
8 San Marino
9 Paris-Bar
10 Estiatorio
11 Dieffenbach's
12 Hofman

buy a 24hr rover ticket, valid for all forms of transport.

Area by area

West Berlin is curiously lopsided, with its centre huddled near its eastern boundary. Most of what is now West Berlin became part of Berlin only in 1920 and was still a suburb before World War II. Although now diminished as an economic force, it remains West Germany's largest industrial city and is dotted with factories and power stations. Surprisingly perhaps, one third of its large area is made up of parks, forests and lakes.

Europa Center area The modern Europa Center, an imposing business and entertainment centre, lies at the heart of Berlin's business, shopping and hotel quarter, which includes Budapester Strasse, the eastern end of Kurfürstendamm with its many cafés, and adjoining streets.

Wedding This once rather run-down industrial area of north Berlin was recently the site of a scheme to attract new high-tech businesses.

Siemensstadt An industrial district in the west, once the headquarters of the mighty Siemens and still the base of its Berlin subsidiary.

Dahlem This museum and university quarter in southwest Berlin, along with Zehlendorf, is the newly fashionable place to live.

Grunewald This western suburb, which borders on West Berlin's largest wood (of the same name), is where, prewar, the big businessmen used to live. Full of grand villas and large gardens, it is even now a much sought-after residential area.

Kreuzberg A still war-scarred district in the southeast, Kreuzberg is the centre of Berlin's thriving alternative culture, and the home of many of the city's 130,000-strong Turkish population.

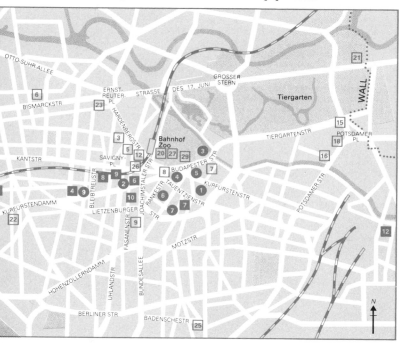

Hotels

Almost all of the major hotels are clustered in the Europa Center area. There is no problem reserving rooms. All those listed here offer IDD telephones, and can arrange for translation and secretarial help. Currency exchange and hotel parking are commonly available.

Ambassador *[DM]||*
Bayreuther Str 42–43, B30 ☎ *219020*
☎ *184259* • *AE DC MC V* • *197 rooms, 3 suites, 2 restaurants, 2 bars*
Tucked away in a quiet side street, near the KaDeWe department store, the Ambassador is a pleasant, modern hotel with good-sized, light and bright rooms. The top-floor tropical pool, complete with exotic plants and poolside bar, is very congenial. One of its restaurants, the Conti-Fischstuben (closed Sat L and Sun), deserves its reputation as the best in the city for seafood. Hairdresser • sauna, solarium, massage • 4 meeting rooms (capacity up to 200).

Bristol-Hotel Kempinski *[DM]|||*
Kurfürstendamm 27, B15 ☎ *881091*
☎ *183553* • *AE DC MC V* • *301 rooms, 33 suites, 3 restaurants, 2 bars*
Berlin's most prestigious hotel is housed in an unexciting 1950s building and has a huge, stark entrance lobby a bit like a station concourse. But otherwise it leaves nothing to be desired. Service is good; the fairly large and traditionally furnished guest rooms (two for nonsmokers) were renovated in 1987, and equipped with hairdryers. There is a roomy piano bar with leather armchairs, as well as three excellent restaurants: the Kempinski Grill (French cuisine), the Kempinski Restaurant (local dishes; closed Mon), and the Kempinski Eck, a fashionable brasserie which spreads outside onto the Kurfürstendamm (and offers special business lunches). Hairdresser, newsstand • pool, sauna, gym • 10 meeting rooms (capacity up to 600).

Inter-Continental *[DM]|||*
Budapester Str 2, B30 ☎ *26020*
☎ *184380* • *AE DC MC V* • *510 rooms,*
70 suites, 3 restaurants, 3 bars
By Berlin Zoo, the city's largest luxury hotel is in typical Inter-Continental mould: the rooms are uniform, comfortable and unremarkable, and the service (24hr) is rather impersonal but competent. While the international cuisine at its main restaurant, Zum Hugenotten, is appreciated by the top business people and politicians who eat there, its smallish tables are more suitable for informal discussions than for really important get-togethers. The large and airy Six Continents Lounge, by the entrance, is a favourite meeting place for local bankers. Shopping arcade • pool, sauna, massage, solarium • fax, computer rental, 12 meeting rooms (capacity up to 1,000).

Palace *[DM]||*
Europa Center, Budapester Str, B30
☎ *269111* ☎ *184825* • *AE DC MC V*
• *154 rooms, 6 suites, 2 restaurants, 1 bar*
Ideally situated in the Europa Center, this up-and-coming hotel has black-and-cream rooms, variations on a pink and maroon theme in its public areas, and flowers and potted plants throughout. The main restaurant, La Réserve (D only), which offers excellent French cuisine and several set menus, has both an intimate atmosphere and well-spaced tables ideal for confidential discussions. Conference facilities are good and above all comfortable. At the end of the working day, the congenial Palace Bar attracts business people from outside. Hairdryers in rooms, telephones in some bathrooms, 24hr room service • fitness centre (gym, sauna, massage, indoor and outdoor pools) • fax, 12 meeting rooms (capacity up to 550).

Schweizerhof *[DM]||||*
Budapester Str 21–31, B30 ☎ *26960*
Ⓣ *185501 • AE DC MC V • 415 rooms,
15 suites, 3 restaurants, 3 bars*
Despite being one of the biggest
major hotels in town, the
Schweizerhof has a poky entrance
lobby. Its rooms, which include
special ones for women executives
and nonsmokers, are not exactly large
either, though their furniture (partly
traditional, partly modern) and floral
decor are attractive. Unless you find
something romantic about the
occasional roar of lions in the Zoo
opposite, ask for a room at the back.
The hotel's main restaurant, the
Grill, which offers Swiss and Berlin
cuisine and specializes in game, is a
popular place for business lunches.
Newsstand, beauty salon, indoor pool
• fax, 16 meeting rooms (capacity up
to 700).

Steigenberger *[DM]||||*
Los-Angeles-Pl 1, B30 ☎ *21080*
Ⓣ *181444 • AE DC MC V • 360 rooms,
20 suites, 2 restaurants, 4 bars*
Built in 1981, this new hotel is quiet
and near the Europa Center. It
competes with the Bristol-Hotel
Kempinski for the custom of VIPs,
and boasts a presidential suite with its
own lift. The spacious rooms have a
restful decor. Business people crowd
the large Piano Bar in the evening,
and the Park-Restaurant is one of
Berlin's top eating places (see
Restaurants). 24hr room service,
shopping arcade • pool, sauna • fax,
computer rental, 12 meeting rooms
(capacity up to 500).

OTHER HOTELS
Of the other major hotels, two are
central, one is very near the
International Congress Center (ICC)
and Messegelände, and the
Kronprinz and the Schlosshotel
Gehrhus have retained something of
the atmosphere of prewar Berlin.
Alsterhof *[DM]|||* *Augsburger Str
5, B30* ☎ *219960* Ⓣ *183484 • AE DC
MC V.* A large modern hotel only
5min walk from Kurfürstendamm

and the Europa Center. It has good
conference facilities and an indoor
pool, sauna, solarium and massage.
Kronprinz *[DM]|*
Kronprinzendamm 1, B31 ☎ *896030*
Ⓣ *181459 • AE DC MC V.* The assets
of this attractive hotel (built in 1894
but well-modernized) include
excellent personalized service,
massive breakfasts and a jolly beer-
garden. It is within 15min walk of the
ICC.
Mondial *[DM]||* *Kurfürstendamm
47, B15* ☎ *884110* Ⓣ *182839 • AE DC
MC V.* A moderate-sized, modern
central hotel with an acceptable
restaurant, and an indoor pool with
jacuzzi, solarium and massage.
Schlosshotel Gehrhus *[DM]|*
Brahmsstr 4–10, B33 ☎ *8262081 • AE
DC MC V.* This secluded family hotel,
set among spacious grounds in the
Grunewald area, has kept much of
the character, if not all the
appurtenances, which it possessed
when it used to be the Palais von
Pannwitz.
Seehof *[DM]||* *Lietzensee-Ufer 11,
B19* ☎ *320020* Ⓣ *182943 • AE DC MC
V.* The most convenient hotel for the
ICC/Messegelände (5min walk), in a
bucolic location overlooking a lake
with swans. Facilities include indoor
pool, sauna and solarium.

Hotel price bands
In many hotels, particularly
older ones, room rates vary
considerably. The price bands
below represent the cost in
Deutschmarks at the time of
going to press of a typical room
for one person. Although the
actual prices will go up, the
relative price category is likely to
remain the same.

[DM]	up to *DM75*
[DM]|	*DM75–150*
[DM]||	*DM150–200*
[DM]|||	*DM200–275*
[DM]||||	over *DM275*

Restaurants

Berlin restaurants are often more interested in mood and style, and staying open late, than in gastronomic perfection, so do not expect the culinary standards of, say, Munich. The most suitable places for top-flight business entertaining are hotel restaurants (see *Hotels*), especially the Steigenberger's Park-Restaurant. Except for special events, it is not normally necessary to make reservations.

Anselmo   [DM]||||
Damaschkestr 17 ☎ 3233094 • closed Mon • AE MC V
Anselmo Bufacchi's restaurant, just off the western end of Kurfürstendamm, has long been regarded as Berlin's classiest Italian restaurant. The clean, Milanese-style decor, the modern art on display and the smartly dressed clients make this a good place for not-too-formal business occasions. The cuisine is unfussy Italian at its best, and the wine list boasts, unusually, a large contingent of excellent Italian vintages.

Le Bou Bou   [DM]|||
Kurfürstendamm 103 ☎ 8911036 • closed L exc Sat and Sun • AE MC
This high-ceilinged restaurant, round the corner from Anselmo, has a superbly austere *Jugendstil* (Art Nouveau) decor. It is a favourite lunching spot for executives from Siemens and Schering, while in the evening the candles come out and the atmosphere is more relaxed. The cuisine is a mixture of French, international and traditional German, the wine list solely French, and the service attentive.

Hemingway's   [DM]||||
Hagenstr 18 ☎ 8254571 • D only, closed Sun • AE DC MC
This exclusive restaurant is tucked away in Grunewald. Its very individual and chic decor of white wicker armchairs, white trelliswork and a huge mirror on the ceiling is just right for a not-too-formal business celebration. The chef gives his *nouvelle cuisine* one or two interesting German touches (though the small portions are decidedly unGerman). The wine list is excellent, and the bar congenial.

Park-Restaurant   [DM]||||
Steigenberger hotel ☎ 2108855 • closed Mon L, Sun D • AE DC MC V
Expect to rub shoulders with VIPs at the Park-Restaurant, the city's top restaurant for political and business entertainment. But it is as suitable for the brisk lunch as it is for protracted dining: every day a perfectly devised three-course, 60min business lunch is served. Make sure of reservations on Friday evenings for the 5-course champagne dinner (not expensive given that you can drink as much bubbly as you want). The excellent French cuisine is "modern" without being *nouvelle*, and the service impeccable.

Tasty   [DM]|
Kurfürstendamm 53 ☎ 8839444 • no credit cards
Don't be put off by the name or the café-like exterior; inside, you will find comfortable seats, beautifully designed chrome and marble tables, and a clientele to match: fashion designers and well-dressed business people. The French dishes on the short menu are refined and very skilfully executed, with the emphasis on seafood (especially lobster), and the wine list is short but well selected. Tasty has a high value-for-money ratio and is open from noon to midnight.

Wirtshaus Schildhorn   [DM]||
Strasse am Schildhorn 4a ☎ 3053111 • AE MC V
Wirtshaus Schildhorn is one of

Berlin's most countrified restaurants, on a peninsula jutting out into the lake formed by the Havel river. From the outside, it looks a little like a day-trippers' café – low, half-timbered buildings, sprawling terraces, boats for rent, a jetty for river cruisers. This is deceptive, for within it is furnished with taste and offers imaginative "New German cuisine," which may explain why it is the haunt of the well-to-do and of prominent figures in the media and arts worlds. Open daily from 10am to midnight, it is ideal for off-duty relaxation.

Good but casual

Berlin is packed with lively, casual places at which to eat, most of them open very late. Many of these establishments are clustered near the Europa Center. An invaluable standby for the quick business lunch is the very congenial *Alt-Nürnberg* ☎ 2614397, a basement restaurant in the Europa Center. The food is hearty and Bavarian, and the pine-panelled decor a most convincing replica of a tavern (private rooms available). Other good lunching places include the restaurant section of the historic *Café Kranzler*, Kurfürstendamm 18–19 ☎ 8818026, and the numerous luncheon bars in the department store *KaDeWe* (see *Shopping*).

One of the best of the many genuine Italian restaurants is *San Marino*, Savignypl 12 ☎ 3136086, which offers *pizze* and *calzoni* that are several cuts above average; in summer it is very pleasant to dine on the large and agreeable terrace which gives on to the quiet Savignyplatz. Not far from there is the fashionable and noisy *Paris-Bar* (not to be confused with Le Paris), Kantstr 152 ☎ 3138052 (closed Sun), which has good modern art on its walls and attracts off-duty business people as well as musicians and intellectuals.

Many restaurants are closed for lunch but serve dinner until very late. Fashion-conscious yuppies like the

clean white decor, temporary art exhibitions and straightforward fare at *Estiatorio*, Fasanenstr 70 ☎ 8818785. The classier western end of Kreuzberg is fast coming into fashion as a venue for relaxed dining out. Two reliable places are *Dieffenbach's*, Dieffenbachstr 11 ☎ 6945606, and *Hofmann*, Grossbeerenstr 18 ☎ 2156712, both of which offer short menus with a Mediterranean accent and are frequented by journalists, artists and professional people.

Bars

Much informal business is done in the bars of Berlin hotels. In addition to the *Bristol* in the Bristol-Hotel Kempinski, the *Six Continents Lounge* in the Inter-Continental, the *Palace Bar* in the Palace, and the *Piano Bar* in the Steigenberger (see *Hotels*), there is the *Times-Bar* (open from 6) in the Savoy Hotel, Fasanenstr 9–10, one of the best cocktail bars in town, which is frequented by stockbrokers working nearby. Late diners can also sample excellent cocktails at the smart *Le Baronet*, Kurfürstendamm 190–192 (from 8). During the day, a stylish place for a rendezvous is the *Champagne Bar* on the sixth floor of the department store KaDeWe (see *Shopping*).

Berlin has many relaxed drinking places, such as the pub-like *Kneipen*. These are packed with people who sit drinking and talking through the night. In the Europa Center area it is usually quite safe to drop into any bar, even if you are a woman on your own. Worth trying are *Die Kleine Weltlaterne* (open from 8), Nestorstr 22; *Zur Kneipe* (open from 6), Rankestr 9, and *Tiago* (open during the day as well), Knesebeckstr 15.

Entertainment

Berlin's long tradition of *Kultur*, on which it rightly prides itself, has been kept alive on both sides of the Wall by generous subsidies. In some areas, political cabaret and established theatre, for example, East Berlin has the edge. But West Berlin still has a wealth of activities and several annual festivals (theatre, classical music, jazz and film). Details of all events will be found in *Tip* and *Zitty* which come out every fortnight. The agencies in the *Wertheim* or *KaDeWe* department stores (see *Shopping*) have ticket agencies or try *Wildbad-Kiosk*, Rankestr 1 ☎ 8814507.

Theatre The three established theatres are the *Schaubühne im Lehniner Platz*, Kurfürstendamm 153 ☎ 890023, the *Schiller-Theater*, Bismarckstr 110 ☎ 3195236 and, perhaps the best, the *Freie Volksbühne*, Schaperstr 24 ☎ 8813742. Many lively events are staged by West Berlin's alternative theatre groups, such as *Grips-Theater*, Altonaer Str 23 ☎ 3933012 and *Theater am Kreuzberg*, Möckernstr 66 ☎ 7851165. In order to see some political cabaret for yourself (if your German is *very* fluent) try *Die Stachelschweine*, Europa Center ☎ 2614795.

Opera, dance Under its director Götz Friedrich, the *Deutsche Oper Berlin*, Bismarckstr 35 ☎ 3414449, has become the leading venue for opera and dance. The *Theater des Westens*, Kantstr 12 ☎ 3121022, puts on some very high-class musicals. Alternative groups to see include *Tanzfabrik*, Möckernstr 68 ☎ 7865861, *Neuköllner Oper*, Am Kottbusser Damm 79 ☎ 6933028, and *Die Etage*, Hasenheide 54 ☎ 6912095.

Cinema Berlin holds a March film festival and is one of the most rewarding West German cities for the dedicated filmgoer. It has some 80 cinemas, many of them art houses which show foreign films with German subtitles.

Music Musical life in Berlin is dominated by the towering figure of Herbert von Karajan, resident conductor of the world-famous Berlin Philharmonic Orchestra. They usually perform at the *Philharmonie*, Matthäikirchstr 1 ☎ 2614383, a modern concert hall of

unconventional design and superb acoustics. The city is also famed for its rock music and has several hundred active rock groups (for details see listings magazines). In summer, open-air performances of both classical and rock music take place at the *Waldbühne* in Ruhleben ☎ 8529056.

Nightclubs and casinos Berlin's legendary nightlife is still thriving: it boasts no less than 50 discos and a host of floor-shows (of variable quality). The more respectable discos include *Annabell's*, Fasanenstr 64 ☎ 8835220. But the really "in" place for business people who like to let their hair down after hours is *Dschungl*, Nürnberger Str 53 ☎ 246698.

There is a casino, the *Spielbank Berlin*, in the Europa Center (Budapester Strasse entrance).

Shopping

The Kurfürstendamm is commonly thought to be Berlin's top shopping street. But the really smart places to buy clothes, shoes, leather goods and so on are in adjoining streets such as Joachimstalerstrasse, Meinekestrasse, Fasanenstrasse, Uhlandstrasse and Bleibtreustrasse. The boutiques in the Europa Center are also worth exploring. Berlin has two department stores which deserve a visit, *Wertheim*, Kurfürstendamm 231, and *KaDeWe*, Tauentzienstr 21, the largest in Europe, whose staggering food department, which takes up the whole of the sixth floor, stocks some 25,000 different foods and has 22 tiny luncheon bars where you can sample the food.

Upmarket antique dealers will be found in the Eisenacher Strasse/Motzstrasse area, in the antique market housed in the converted *U-Bahn* station at Nollendorfplatz (closed Tue), and in Keithstrasse. But you are more likely to find a real bargain at the weekend flea markets, *Trödelmarkt*, Strasse des 17 Juni, and *Krempelmarkt*, Potsdamer Pl.

Sightseeing

The most familiar sights of West Berlin are not its most interesting, as Berliners would agree. The *Kaiser-Wilhelm-Gedächtniskirche* is a shored-up ruin turned into a memorial, which Berliners have nicknamed "the lipstick and powder compact," "the hollow tooth" and worse. Near it stands the 90 metre/300ft-high *Europa Center*. The broad and 3.5km/2.25 mile-long *Kurfürstendamm*, or Ku'damm, is lined with the free-standing showcases of its many shops, groups of exotic but docile punks posing for tourists, and the occasional modern monumental sculpture. The only major building of prewar central Berlin that is now in West Berlin is Germany's former parliament building, the *Reichstag*, stranded near the wall not far from the Brandenburg Gate and nicknamed the "sleeping beauty." Between the Reichstag and the Zoo lies the *Tiergarten*, a vast park with many trees, neat flowerbeds, and lakes.

West Berlin has much to offer the art-lover, with over 50 public and private galleries.

Ägyptisches Museum A superb Egyptian collection which includes the celebrated bust of Queen Nefertiti. *Schlossstr 70. Open Sat–Thu, 9–5.*

Antikenmuseum und Schatzkammer A rich collection of Greek, Cretan and Etruscan art and gold jewellery. *Schlossstr 1. Open Sat–Thu, 9–5.*

Botanischer Garten One of the largest botanical gardens in Europe, with arboretum, mountain and steppe vegetation and 16 glasshouses. *Königin-Luise-Str 6–8. Open daily 9–4.*

Museen Dahlem A complex of eight museums devoted to paintings, etchings, sculpture, ethnography, East Asian art, Islamic art, Indian art and German folklore respectively. *Arnimallee 23–27. Open Tue–Sun, 9–5.*

Musikinstrumentenmuseum European and non-European musical instruments from the 16thC to the present. *Tiergartenstr 1. Open Tue–Sat, 9–5; Sun, 10–5.*

Neue Nationalgalerie Designed by Mies van der Rohe, this museum houses a fine collection of 19thC and especially 20thC paintings (mainly German). *Potsdamer Str 50. Open Tue–Sun, 9–5.*

Schloss Charlottenburg The former summer residence of the Prussian kings (early 18thC) contains the famous rococo Golden Gallery and interesting collections of arts and crafts, porcelain and paintings. *Luisenpl. Open Tue–Sun, 9–5.*

Zoologischer Garten The Berlin Zoo, which has the largest number of animal species of any zoo in the world, has a notably successful breeding record. *Hardenbergpl. Open daily 9–7 or, in winter, until dusk.*

Suburbs

Although they live in an enclave, West Berliners are certainly not cut off from the countryside. Much of outer Berlin consists of forests, lakes and beaches, and even farmland. Places to visit include the little old village of *Alt-Lübars*, the *Havel* river, the forest of *Grunewald* and the traffic-free island of *Pfaueninsel*, which has several 18thC and early-19thC follies, peacocks, English-style landscaped gardens and rare trees. It can be reached by boat from Wannsee S-Bahn station or from Spandau.

Guided tours

Tours take anything from 30min to 4hrs. Operators include *BBS* ☎ 2134077, *BVB* ☎ 8822063, *Severin & Kühn* ☎ 8831015, and *Berolina* ☎ 8833131.

Boat excursions (sometimes with dancing on board) along the network of canals, rivers and lakes are organized by *Riedel* ☎ 6913782 (including an eye-opening summer tour starting in run-down Neukölln by the Wall and traversing the city to the Havel lake), *Winkler* ☎ 3917010 and *Stern und Kreisschiffahrt* ☎ 8038750.

East Berlin

When Berlin was divided up among the Four Powers after the last war, the heart of the city (Berlin-Mitte), where the Brandenburg Gate, Unter den Linden, and most major buildings and museums were located, became part of the eastern sector. You can go on a sightseeing trip organized by West Berlin limousine or coach operators (see *Getting around* and *Sightseeing*). These tours, lasting about 4hrs, reduce the checkpoint formalities and avoid the usual obligation to buy East German currency, but rush through the museums. If you decide to go as a pedestrian, the best crossing point is Friedrichstrasse (the terminus of *S-Bahn* 3); vehicles cross at Checkpoint Charlie. Avoid Saturday or Sunday mornings, when there can be a long wait. To cross, you need a passport, DM5 for a visa and a minimum of DM25 which is changed into East German currency and has to be spent in East Berlin. You may take Western currency with you, but you have to declare it. Your hotel will provide you with further tips and details of regulations governing your trip to East Berlin.

Sightseeing

In the 1970s, and more particularly during the years leading up to East Berlin's 750th anniversary, in 1987, the East German authorities at last began to rebuild and refurbish the many ruined public buildings and housing. After strolling up the impressively broad *Unter den Linden*, the main artery of the prewar capital, and taking a look at that hackneyed symbol of the divided city, the *Brandenburg Gate*, you should try to visit the best of East Berlin's superb museums.

Bode-Museum A rich collection ranging from Egyptian and Byzantine antiquities to coins and 14th–18thC sculpture and paintings. *Monbijou-Brücke. Open daily exc Mon, 9–6 (Thu, 9–8; Fri, 10–6).*

Pergamonmuseum One of the greatest museums of Mesopotamian, Greek and Roman antiquities in the world. It also houses impressive Islamic and Far Eastern collections. *Museumsinsel (entrance in Am Kupfergraben). Whole museum open Wed–Sun, 9–6 (Fri, 10–6); Western Asian and Architecture rooms also open Mon, 1–6 and Tue, 9–6.*

Potsdam The historic town of Potsdam, which lies in East Germany just west of West Berlin, should on no account be missed if you have a little time. It contains one of Germany's architectural gems, the rococo *Schloss Sanssouci*, built by Frederick the Great in 1747. Advance booking for tours is necessary.

Keeping fit

There are fitness centres for residents in the Bristol-Hotel Kempinski, Palace and Steigenberger (see *Hotels*); and all have pools.

Fitness centres *Engelbert Dörbandt*, Kurfürstendamm 182–3 ☎ 8826301; *Work Out Sports*, Lützowstr 105–106 ☎ 2627017.

Squash *Squash-Tennis Nord* (7 courts), Wittenauer Str 82–86 ☎ 4024031; *Squash Point Siemensstadt* (8 courts), Jugendweg 5 ☎ 3823030.

Swimming *Olympia-Schwimmstadion*, Olympischer Pl ☎ 3040676 (open air) and *Blub*, Buschkrugallee 64 ☎ 6066060 (with rapids, chutes and jacuzzis).

Tennis *Preussenpark* (11 courts), Kamenzer Damm ☎ 7751051.

Local resources

Business services

The major hotels listed can provide or organize most of the services you

are likely to need. Otherwise try
Bürotel Büroservice ☎ 8827031 or *BDS*
☎ 8029079.
Photocopying and printing
Unikopie KG ☎ 3142785.
Secretarial *A.-M. Hoffmann*
☎ 6025140.
Translation *Übersetzen Berlitz*
☎ 3239047.

Communications
Local and long-distance delivery
DHL ☎ 8315026.
Post office Bahnhof Zoo open 24hrs
(except for parcels). Tegel airport
open daily, 6.30–9.
Telex and fax *Fernmeldeamt 1*,
Winterfeldtstr 21 ☎ 2181 open 24hrs.
Fax also at all large post offices.

Conference/exhibition centres
The *ICC Berlin*, the city's
international congress centre, built in
1979 to a futuristic design, is not only
the world's biggest centre of its kind,
but its high-tech facilities are some of
the best in the world. They include
modular auditoria (maximum
capacity 5,000), 20 halls (capacity up
to 900), 80 smaller rooms, a
newsstand, post office, bank, bars,
restaurants and huge parking
facilities. Adjoining the ICC building,
and under the same management, is
the *Messegelände* (exhibition centre),
whose 15 main halls and 12 pavilions
offer about 63,000 sq metres/650,000
sq ft of display space. The congress
and exhibition centre is very
conveniently located next to the
Funkturm (radio tower) in western
Berlin, at the point where the
Autobahnen coming through the
Drewitz/Dreilinden and Heiligensee
checkpoints join up with West
Berlin's A10 ring road. Inquiries *AMK
Berlin*, Messedamm 22, B19 ☎ 30381.

Emergencies
Bureaux de change Late opening:
Post office, Tegel airport, 6.30–9;
Berliner Bank, Tegel airport, 8–10;
Wechselstube, Bahnhof Zoo (entrance
outside the station building), Mon–
Sat, 8–9; Sun, 10–6.

Hospitals 24hr emergency
department *Klinikum Westend*,
Spandauer Damm 130 ☎ 30351.
Medical emergency service ☎ 310031.
Dental emergency treatment ☎ 1141.
Pharmacies To find out which
pharmacies open late ☎ 1141.
Police Main station *Polizeipräsidium*,
Tempelhofer Damm 1 ☎ 6991.

Government offices
The *Wirtschaftsförderung Berlin*
(Berlin Economic Development
Corporation), Budapester Str 1, B30
☎ 26361, advises on incentives
available to incoming firms, and puts
out an informative booklet called
Setting up in Berlin (West).

Information sources
Business information The
*Industrie- und Handelskammer zu
Berlin* (chamber of commerce),
Hardenbergstr 16–18, B12 ☎ 31801,
is a good source of information on
local business activity, and publishes
a useful brochure called *Business
Contacts in Berlin.*
Local media *Berliner Morgenpost*
covers financial and economic news.
But the business community's
required reading, as elsewhere in
West Germany, are *Frankfurter
Allgemeine Zeitung (FAZ)* and
Handelsblatt.
Tourist information *Verkehrsamt
Berlin* (Berlin tourist office) has
three branches: Tegel airport, open
7.30–10.30 ☎ 41013145; Europa
Center (Budapester Strasse
entrance), open 7.30–10.30
☎ 2626031; Bahnhof Zoo, open 8–11
☎ 3139063. The monthly *Berlin
Programm* lists entertainments, air
and train timetables, details of
museums and so on (see also
Entertainment).

Thank-yous
Wertheim and *KaDeWe* (see
Shopping) have the biggest choice of
gifts. For that extra-special gift, try
Present Goldberg, Kurfürstendamm
12, or *Kamphüs*, Ansbacher Str 21.

BONN

City codes zip 5300 ☎ 0228

In 1949, through a quirk of history, the not very large town of Bonn became West Germany's provisional capital. Since then, as though nervous that Germany's prewar capital, Berlin, has been waiting in the wings, Bonn has retained an almost provincial atmosphere. For this reason some Germans sarcastically call it the *Bundesdorf* (federal village). Even the 1969 boundary reforms, which resulted in the tiny spa of Bad Godesberg, a little farther upriver, and Beuel, on the other side of the Rhein, being integrated into the capital, did little to increase Bonn's population. With 290,000 inhabitants, it is still only the country's 18th-largest city.

Few major industrial companies are based in Bonn, and there is little commercial activity apart from banking. Nevertheless, it is the site of the West German parliament and all the ministries, as well as being the centre of the country's foreign diplomatic and journalist representation, so business people go there to lobby, pressure, negotiate or sell themselves.

Politicians tend to spend as little time as possible in Bonn, allegedly because they find it a boring city but perhaps also because of its notoriously lethargy-producing weather. As if to compensate for this handicap, it jealously guards its reserves of chlorophyll and describes itself as Europe's greenest capital: in addition to its 490ha/1,210 acres of parks, there are numerous private gardens, with the curious result that the bird and mammal population in central Bonn differs very little from that of the surrounding countryside.

Bonn's resident human population is an odd mixture of foreign diplomatic staff, the old who come there to retire, and the young, largely fee-paying students who attend its university.

Arriving

The A555 *Autobahn* links Bonn with Cologne (26km/16 miles), which has good connections with the Ruhr to the north, and with Aachen and Belgium to the west. Bonn is connected by *Autobahn* (A565 and A61) with Koblenz and the south. The capital lies on the main Cologne–Frankfurt railway line.

Köln/Bonn airport offers a fairly extensive range of regular direct flights daily to and from major West German, European and intercontinental cities. Some visitors to Bonn may find it more convenient to fly to Frankfurt's large international airport and then take the Lufthansa Express shuttle train service to Bonn Hauptbahnhof (journey time 1hr 40min).

Köln/Bonn airport

Smallish, modern and well-equipped, the airport, which is 20km/12 miles northeast of Bonn, has two main terminals (B for scheduled flights and C for charters), as well as a private section (general aviation terminal). There are regular direct flights from London, Lyon, Madrid, Milan, Paris, Vienna, Washington and Zürich, as well as a number of German cities (Berlin, Bremen, Frankfurt, Hamburg, Hanover, Munich, Nuremberg, Saarbrücken and Stuttgart). Business travellers like the airport because embarkation/disembarkation procedures are very quick. Currency exchange facilities stay open until the last flights; the airport also has West Germany's first automatic currency exchange machine. Business facilities include 4 meeting rooms (capacity up to 120) with telephones; inquiries ☎ (02203) 402307. Airport information ☎ (02203) 404001/2.

City link The bus takes hardly any longer than a taxi and costs about one-sixth of the price. It may be worth renting a car at the airport if you have appointments in Bonn's extensive suburbs or in Cologne, or intend to tour.

Taxi There are usually plenty of taxis at the ranks in front of each terminal. Approximate cost into Bonn is DM60. Telephone reservations ☎ 555555.

Car rental Avis, Europcar, Hertz and other car rental firms have desks at the airport.

Bus Buses leave half hourly from about 7 till 11. The bus stop is by the small white tower in the middle of the airport forecourt. The journey to Bonn Hauptbahnhof takes about 25min and the fare is DM7.20.

Railway station
Bonn Hauptbahnhof is right on the edge of the old town (Altstadt). It has only two main-line platforms and is scruffy by German standards, with few facilities: a cafeteria, a newsstand and a currency exchange bureau. There are taxi ranks outside its northern (city centre) and southern (Quantiusstrasse) exits. Rail services are very frequent, with some 70 trains a day: north to Cologne (25min), the Ruhr and beyond, south to Koblenz (36min), Frankfurt (2hr), Stuttgart (nearly 4hr) and Munich (over 6hr). Trains usually stop for only two minutes. Passengers to or from Belgium and northern France have to change at Cologne. For timetable inquiries ☎ 19419.

Getting around
The very small old town area is almost entirely pedestrianized, so walking is the only way of getting around. Bonn's other major centre of activity, the so-called Regierungsviertel (government quarter), is best reached by taxi or

U-Bahn. Buses are not recommended unless you are staying long enough to become familiar with their routes. Traffic is rarely congested and finding your way around the city is straightforward.

Taxis There are ranks at all key street intersections. For reservations ☎ 555555.

Limousines *Hertz* ☎ 217041.

Driving A useful brochure, *Bonn from A to Z* (from the tourist office, Münsterstr 20), contains a map which indicates parking sites. Car rental from *Avis* ☎ 223047, *Budget* ☎ 652902, *Hertz* 217041, *interRent* ☎ 636652.

U-Bahn Convenient for getting from the city centre (Hauptbahnhof or Universität/Markt station) to the government quarter (Heussallee/Bundeshaus station).

Area by area
Bonn's vestigial business quarter is located in and around the old town, which has been largely rebuilt since World War II. On its northwest and southeast edges respectively lie the modern Stadthaus and the imposingly large main university buildings. The government quarter, which is about 2.4km/1.5 miles southeast, is scheduled to have a fine, round Bundeshaus (federal parliament building) by the end of 1989 in place of the temporary one demolished in 1987. Here, too, are the official residences of the president and chancellor and the headquarters of the political parties. Südstadt, the area between the old town and the government quarter, is a sought-after residential area.

The suburbs Many embassies and ministries are located in fashionable Bad Godesberg, 7km/4 miles southeast of Bonn's old town which, with the charming former villages surrounding it, Rüngsdorf and Muffendorf, are exclusive residential districts. Away from the river are pleasantly hilly suburbs in Venusberg, Ippendorf and east of the town of Königswinter.

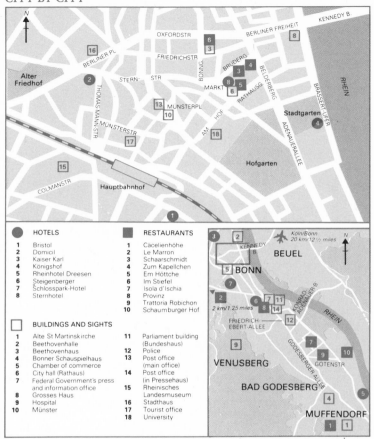

HOTELS

1 Bristol
2 Domicil
3 Kaiser Karl
4 Königshof
5 Rheinhotel Dreesen
6 Steigenberger
7 Schlosspark-Hotel
8 Sternhotel

RESTAURANTS

1 Cäcelienhöhe
2 Le Marron
3 Schaarschmidt
4 Zum Kapellchen
5 Em Höttche
6 Im Stiefel
7 Isola d'Ischia
8 Provinz
9 Trattoria Robichon
10 Schaumburger Hof

BUILDINGS AND SIGHTS

1 Alte St Martinskirche
2 Beethovenhalle
3 Beethovenhaus
4 Bonner Schauspielhaus
5 Chamber of commerce
6 City hall (Rathaus)
7 Federal Government's press and information office
8 Grosses Haus
9 Hospital
10 Münster
11 Parliament building (Bundeshaus)
12 Police
13 Post office (main office)
14 Post office (in Pressehaus)
15 Rheinisches Landesmuseum
16 Stadthaus
17 Tourist office
18 University

Hotels

Bonn has very few prestigious hotels up to high international standards, partly because visiting politicians and diplomats tend to stay in special guesthouses. Most of the major hotels are near the old town; only one, the Steigenberger, is in the government quarter. The tourist information office ☏ 773466 will help find accommodation but only within 24 hours of arrival. All of the hotels listed have IDD telephones.

Bristol [DM]|||
Prinz-Albert-Str 2, B1 ☏ *26980*
TX *8869661* • *AE DC MC V* • *105 rooms, 8 suites, 2 restaurants, 1 bar*
This modern, rather flashy hotel provides excellent service and is near the Hauptbahnhof and the old town. The rooms are fairly large and well appointed. Beauty salon, hairdresser, hat shop • pool, sauna, solarium, massage • fax, 4 meeting rooms (capacity up to 250).

Domicil *DM*|||
Thomas-Mann-Str 24–26, B1
☎ *729090* ⊤ẋ *886633 • AE DC MC V •*
closed Dec 20–Jan 4 • 39 rooms,
3 suites, 2 bars
This small, exclusive hotel on the
western edge of the old town consists
of several buildings whose interiors
have recently been strikingly
redesigned. Rooms are attractive and
functional. Within the hotel, but
under separate management, are a
good restaurant, the Krull ☎ 655300,
a coffee shop and a smart evening
bar, the Joyce. Hairdresser, 24hr
room service • sauna, solarium,
jacuzzi • 1 meeting room (capacity
up to 32).

Kaiser Karl *DM*|||
Vorgebirgsstr 56, B1 ☎ *650933*
⊤ẋ *886856 • AE DC MC V • 51 rooms,*
1 suite, 1 bar; no restaurant
This former private mansion round
an inner courtyard, next to the north
Bonn *Autobahn* interchange, is
popular with business travellers who
dislike big international hotels. Guest
rooms contain a writing table, a
second telephone in the bathroom
and a safe. The furniture is a mixture
of antiques and modern Italian.
Breakfasts are comprehensive and
there is an exclusive piano bar (open
4–1). 1 meeting room (capacity up to
100).

Königshof *DM*|||
Adenauerallee 9, B1 ☎ *26010*
⊤ẋ *886535 • Pullman • AE DC MC V •*
132 rooms, 5 suites, 1 restaurant, 1 bar
The Königshof is set in the greenery
of the Stadtgarten overlooking the
Rhein, a 5min walk from the old
town. Although fully renovated in
1982, the decor looks curiously dated,
but the rooms are reasonably sized
and airy. Its riverside restaurant,
La Belle Epoque, is a very pleasant
lunch place. Hairdryers in rooms •
4 meeting rooms (capacity up to
1,200).

Rheinhotel Dreesen *DM*|
Rheinstr 45, B2-Bad Godesberg

☎ *82020* ⊤ẋ *885417 • AE DC MC V •*
68 rooms, 1 suite, 1 restaurant, 1 bar
This charmingly old-fashioned hotel
with modern facilities enjoys a plum
location in Bad Godesberg with a
splendid view over the Rhein and the
Siebengebirge hills beyond; reserve
well ahead for a riverside room.
Famous for its Sunday *thé dansant*
and aristocratic clients, it is an ideal
place in which to combine business
and relaxation. 5 meeting rooms
(capacity up to 1,500).

Steigenberger *DM*|||
Am Bundeskanzlerpl, B1 ☎ *20191*
⊤ẋ *886363 • AE DC V • 152 rooms,*
8 suites, 2 restaurants, 2 bars
The best hotel in the government
quarter, although by no means the
best in the Steigenberger chain, this
hotel, which occupies the upper
floors of the Bonn-Center building, is
a popular choice for visiting
lobbyists. The rooms are drab, but
much business entertaining is done in
its stylish top-floor restaurant, the
Ambassador. Pool • 9 meeting rooms
(capacity up to 300).

OTHER HOTELS
Schlosspark-Hotel *DM*|
Venusbergweg 27–31, B1 ☎ *217036*
⊤ẋ *889661 • AE DC MC V.* A quiet,
roomy hotel overlooking the
Botanischer Garten and attractive
18thC Schloss Poppelsdorf.
Sternhotel *DM*| *Markt 8, B1*
☎ *654455* ⊤ẋ *886508 • AE DC MC V.*
Central Bonn hotel, with large, old-
fashioned rooms and modern
amenities. *Bonner Summer* concerts
may be held under your window
from May to September.

Out of town
If you have difficulty in finding a
room, try the riverside *Rheinhotel
Königswinter* ☎ (02223) 24051 in
Königswinter, 11km/7 miles
southeast, or the *Steigenberger
Kurhotel* ☎ (02641) 2291 in the spa
of Bad Neuenahr-Ahrweiler,
30km/19 miles south. Both are
reliable, if not distinguished.

Restaurants

A wide range of cooking styles is available, from traditional German to excellent Italian and not always well-executed French *nouvelle cuisine*. But there is a shortage of restaurants suitable for important business entertainment in the government quarter; the Ambassador in the Steigenberger hotel (see *Hotels*) is patronized by senior bankers and politicians, but more because of its convenience and classy setting than for its food. Restaurants are usually busy, and reservations are advisable.

Cäcelienhöhe [DM]//
Goldbergweg 17 ☎ *321001 • closed Sat L and Sun • AE DC MC*
This fashionable restaurant is located in the hotel of the same name in the upper part of Bad Godesberg, and affords a stunning view over the Rhein. It is particularly liked as a lunching place by Chancellor Kohl and his colleagues. The cuisine is Italian with a dash of German, and of high quality.

Le Marron [DM]//
Provinzialstr 35 ☎ *253261 • closed Sat and Sun L • AE DC MC • jacket and tie*
Certainly the most suitable restaurant in Bonn for really top-flight business entertaining. The atmosphere is rustic, with wooden beams, fireplace and bare brick walls. The inventive French cuisine and the wine list are as good as any in Bonn, and the service is amiable, if a bit leisurely.

Schaarschmidt [DM]//
Brüdergasse 14 ☎ *654407 • closed Sat L, Sun and 3 weeks in Aug • DC MC • jacket and tie*
Tables are sufficiently well-spaced for discreet conversation at this congenial restaurant, despite its tiny size. Owner-chef Michael Schaarschmidt's excellent cuisine is modern French with a few German regional touches, such as game. The wine list offers a wide range of reasonably priced Bordeaux.

Zum Kapellchen [DM]/
Brüdergasse 12 ☎ *651052 • closed Sun and Jul 10–Aug 8 • AE DC MC V*
Next to Schaarschmidt in the old town, and equally small. Newcomers and habitués (business people and politicians at lunch, actors and writers in the evening) are assured of a warm welcome by owner Fritz Rauch. The cuisine is classical French and German, with a good range of fish dishes and Franconian wines.

Good but casual
Several old German brasseries in the Altstadt serve traditional German food. The best are *Em Höttche*, Markt 4 ☎ 658596, whose spacious main dining room sports oil paintings and wood panelling (there is also a pleasant private room), and *Im Stiefel*, Bonngasse 30 ☎ 634806, also panelled but less private, since customers eat at long, scrubbed wooden tables. For an evening off in a friendly Italian restaurant try the *Isola d'Ischia*, Brandenburger Str 4a ☎ 375252. Television personalities and prominent journalists come to enjoy the excellent cuisine.

The only good casual restaurant in the government quarter is the small, rustic *Provinz*, Adenauerallee 228 ☎ 234827, which serves German home cooking (especially game) and is a haunt of SPD members and Greens. Another relaxed place, in Plittersdorf, between the government

---

Food and wine
Information and guidance on German food, including regional cooking, and on wine types and vintages are given in the *Planning and Reference* section.

---

quarter and Bad Godesberg, is
Trattoria Robichon, Gotenstr 126
☎ 373775, which serves high-quality
Italian food and has a terrace in
summer. Nearby, on the banks of the
Rhein, you will find the 18thC half-
timbered *Schaumburger Hof*, Am
Schaumburger Hof 10 ☎ 364095, a
small hotel which offers appetizing
international fare, fine wines and a
lime-shaded waterside terrace.

Out of town
There are plenty of countrified
restaurants in the immediate vicinity
of the city. They include the elegant
Herrenhaus Buchholz in Alfter,
Buchholzweg 1 ☎ (02222) 60005,
among whose customers are top
politicians and clergy. In the more
casual category is *Heimatblick* in
Bornheim-Roisdorf ☎ (02222)
60037, which is famous for asparagus
and blackberry wine; and *Gut-Sülz* in
Oberdollendorf ☎ (02223) 24178, a
delightful half-timbered building
surrounded by lawns where you can
wash down massive sandwiches with
wine from nearby vineyards, West
Germany's northernmost.

For the really special business
celebration, however, when you
require the very highest culinary
standards whatever the expense, make
for the *Goldener Pflug* near Cologne,
southeast of the Altstadt.

Bars
Generally, the best places for a
discussion over a drink are the bars of
the *Kaiser Karl* and the elegant Joyce
(evening only) in the *Domicil*. A
livelier place is *Aktuell*, in Gerhard-
von-Are-Strasse, a pub-cum-coffee
bar with a wide range of newspapers,
including a few in English.

Some restaurants are used as
drinking places outside mealtimes,
such as the *Provinz* and the
Schaumburger Hof (see *Restaurants*).
The *Nachrichten-Treff* (NT) brasserie
in the Kaiser-Passagen, off
Martinplatz, is a congenial meeting
point with its ceiling fan, leather
seats and newspapers.

Entertainment
There is a lively, varied cultural
scene and the highlight of the year is
the *Bonner Summer*, a mainly open-
air festival of free concerts (classical,
rock, jazz), dance and theatre that
runs from May to September. The
most commonly used venue for
Bonner Summer events is Markt, the
marketplace in front of the Rathaus
(old town hall). The monthly *Bonn-
Information*, put out by the tourist
information office at Münsterstr 20,
gives details. Otherwise consult the
local press. The ticket reservation
office for all municipally organized
operas and plays is at Mülheimer
Platz 1 ☎ 773666/7. Tickets for the
opera, especially when there are
famous singers, are often very hard to
come by, so you may have to rely on
your hotel concierge.
Theatre, dance, opera Bonn boasts
the greatest number of theatres, in
proportion to its population, of any
German city. Major productions are
put on by the city's two resident
companies: Oper Bonn (opera and
dance) at the splendid *Grosses Haus*,
Am Boeselagerhof 1 ☎ 728387, and
Schauspiel Bonn, at the *Bonner
Schauspielhaus*, Am Michaelshof 9, in
Bad Godesberg ☎ 82080. Tickets for
Schauspielhaus only from Karte
Kasse ☎ 773666/7, Mon–Fri, 1–3.
Music As befits the town where
Beethoven was born and Schumann
spent his last years, Bonn has a
packed schedule of concerts and
recitals. The main venue is the
modern *Beethovenhalle*, which has its
own orchestra, by the Rhein, at
Wachsbleiche 17 ☎ 631321.
Nightclubs and casinos By far the
most stylish and elegant nightspot is
the *Octagon*, Pennefeldsweg 11–15
☎ 334452. The younger crowd
prefers the brasher, louder *Biskuit-
Halle*, Siemensstr 12 ☎ 622698. The
only casino of any class within easy
reach of Bonn is the *Spielbank*,
Casinostr ☎ (02641) 2241 near the
Steigenberger Kurhotel in Bad
Neuenahr-Ahrweiler, about 30min
by car from Bonn.

Shopping
Bonn has a good selection of
upmarket shops. The two main
department stores are *Kaufhof*, on
Münsterplatz, and the slightly classier
Hertie, in Poststrasse. The best clothes
shops are in the Kaiser-Passagen
arcade, off Martinplatz, and in the
Bad Godesberg pedestrian precinct.

Sightseeing
There are no spectacular sights in
Bonn itself, but the old town's
pedestrianized streets and little
squares have considerable charm.
Most typical is the Markt, with its
market, sprawling café terraces and
rococo Rathaus. Next to the
government quarter is the huge and
well-landscaped Rheinaue park, with
its rose garden and lake.
   Three 12thC churches worth
visiting are the Münster in the old
town, the Schwarz-Rheindorf, with
its vivid frescoes, on the right bank of
the Rhein, and the tiny Alte St
Martinskirche in Muffendorf, an
unspoilt quarter of half-timbered
houses.
Beethovenhaus The house where
Beethoven was born and spent his
early years is filled with musical
instruments and other memorabilia.
*Bonngasse 20. Open Mon–Sat, 9.30–1,
3–5; Sun 10–1 (winter); Mon–Sat,
9–1, 3–6; Sun, 9–1 (summer).*
Rheinisches Landesmuseum
Collection devoted to the history of
the Rheinland, and containing the
skull of Neanderthal Man. *Colmantstr
14–16. Open Tue–Fri, 9–5 (Wed, 9–8);
Sat–Sun, 11–5.*

Guided tours
Tours of the city taking 2hr 30min
and including the Altstadt, Bad
Godesberg and Schloss Poppelsdorf,
leave from the tourist office
☎ 773466 daily Apr 5–Oct 31 and on
Saturdays for most of the rest of the
year.

Out of town
On no account miss a visit to see the
rococo splendour of the *Augustusburg*

in Brühl, about 20km/12 miles
northwest, where concerts are often
held. Cologne and its magnificent
cathedral are only 26km/16 miles to
the north.
   On the right bank of the Rhein,
behind the pleasant resort of
Königswinter, 11km/7 miles away, rise
the *Siebengebirge* (literally "seven
mountains," but hills would be a
more accurate term). One of the
peaks, the *Drachenfels* (321
metres/1,062ft high), on which
stands a ruined castle, affords a
spectacular view over Bonn. It can
be reached by rack-railway from
Königswinter. A little farther south is
the delightful half-timbered village of
Unkel. The two main river cruise
operators are *Köln-Düsseldorfer*
☎ 632134 and *Bonner
Personenschiffahrt* ☎ 363737.

Sports and keeping fit
Fitness centres Temporary
membership of fitness centres is
virtually impossible without an
introduction. However, your hotel
should be able to arrange
something.
Cycling Bonn has a very large
number of cycle tracks, notably along
the Rhein and in its parks. Bicycle
rental from *Kurscheid*, Römerstr 4
☎ 631433.
Soccer The local team is Köln FC.
Squash, tennis There are eight
squash and four tennis courts at
The Courts, Kapellenweg 61
☎ 330888.
Swimming The *Frankenbad*,
Adolfstr 45 ☎ 772469.

Local resources
Business services
The major hotels can provide or
organize most services. Otherwise
contact *Büroservice*, Bonn-Center
☎ 211177, which arranges temporary
office accommodation, typists,
secretaries, telex, fax and an
answering service.
Photocopying and printing
Bonkopie ☎ 634938 (photocopying
only), *Gather* ☎ 651566.

Translation *Translingua* ☏ 631071, *Kayser* ☏ 632461.

Communications
Local delivery *Euro-City Kurier* ☏ 613606.
Long-distance delivery *Schmidt & Kalis* ☏ 233055.
Post office Main office: Münsterpl ☏ 131. Open Mon–Fri, 8–6; Sat, 8–1; Sun, 11–12. A counter for telegrams, registered mail, long-distance phone calls and cashing of Eurocheques is open 24hr.
Telex and fax Telex available in the main post office during normal hours, and in the post office (which also has fax) in the *Pressehaus*, Heussallee 2–10 ☏ 135421, which is open Mon–Fri, 8–10, Sat, 8–2 and Sun, 2–10.

Conference/exhibition centres
Bonn has no trade fairs because of its proximity to Cologne, one of Europe's biggest exhibition venues. For congresses in Bonn in the Beethovenhalle, contact *Bonn-Kongress*, Berliner Platz 2 ☏ 773919/20.

Emergencies
Bureaux de change Late opening: *Deutsche Verkehrs-Kredit-Bank* in the Hauptbahnhof, Mon–Sat, 7.30–11.45, 12.15–6.30; Sun, 8.30–1.
Hospitals 24hr emergency treatment: *Universitätskliniken am Rhein*, Sigmund-Freud-Str 25 ☏ 2801. Emergency dental treatment: *Universitäts-Klinik für Zahn-, Mund- und Kieferkrankheiten*, Welschnonnenstr 17 ☏ 652981.
Pharmacies Open late-night on a rota; details available from any pharmacy or ☏ 11500.
Police Main station: *Polizeipräsidium*, Friedrich-Ebert-Allee 144 ☏ 151.

Government offices
The *Presse- und Informationsamt der Bundesregierung* (federal government's press and information office), Welckerstr 11 ☏ 2080, has a large number of useful brochures in English. It provides general business information and advises on political and other contacts. At the more local level of Nordrhein-Westfalen, where Bonn, the West German capital, is dependent on the state capital, Düsseldorf, approach the headquarters of the state of Nordrhein-Westfalen in that city (see *Düsseldorf*).

Information sources
Business information *Industrie-und Handelskammer* (chamber of commerce), Bonner Talweg 17 ☏ 22840, should provide information on the local business scene. For general reference, use the *Zentralbibliothek* (central library), Bottlerpl 1.
Local media The daily local papers *Bonner Rundschau* and *General-Anzeiger* have a fair amount of business coverage, both local and national.
Tourist information The tourist information office, Münsterstr 20 ☏ 773466 (open Apr–Oct, Mon–Sat, 8–9, Sun, 9.30–12.30; Nov–Mar, Mon–Sat, 8–7), whose offices are out of the way in a labyrinthine modern block, puts out the monthly *Bonn-Information* (in German only), which contains many useful addresses and telephone numbers.

Thank-yous
Many Bonn shops do not accept credit cards, so your best bet is the department stores (see *Shopping*). There are no outstanding individual gift shops and the florists tend to be very small, but there is an exceptional delicatessen: *Pfahl*, Acherstr 18 ☏ 632170.

BREMEN
City codes zip 2800 ☎ 0421

Bremen gives its name to the city and to the smallest and oldest of Germany's *Länder*. As a *Land*, Bremen includes the port of Bremerhaven, 70km/43 miles farther down the river Weser. As a city, Bremen is a major seaport and shipbuilding centre. It came into prominence in the 19th century, and now has a population of 545,000. It was the European terminus for many transatlantic liners until the 1950s. Then came the container revolution and the port suffered a decline as did its neighbour Hamburg. Unlike Hamburg, Bremen has not made the same commitment to new industry, partly because of local concern about safeguarding the environment from new industrial plants, and because this small *Land* cannot raise sufficient funds to combat the industrial decline.

The biggest employer in Bremen is Daimler-Benz with over 10,000 at its factories. Engineering is traditional in the area but deterioration in business has hit several firms associated with shipbuilding, including Bremer Vulkan, along with electrical engineers such as Lloyd Dynamowerke and Krupp Atlas. Companies with different interests fared better. Messerschmidt-Bölkow-Blohm is responsible for making major parts of the European Airbus and Europäische Raumfahrt Nord contributes to European space research.

Food processing is important. Beck's Bier, Kellogg's (German) cornflakes and Jacob's coffee are all produced in Bremen. Together with Brinkmann, in the tobacco business, they have experienced a difficult five years. Despite this varied industrial background, at 15.2% the city's unemployment level is one of the highest in Germany.

Yet Bremen hides its problems well. It has plenty of character and charm. The people have a reputation for being obstinate and unapproachable, though really they are simply cautious and courteous.

Arriving

Bremen has been an important communications centre for at least 1,000 years. Federal *Autobahn* A1 (E3) from Hamburg to the Ruhr, the so-called Hansalinie, intersects with the Hanover-Bremerhaven *Autobahn* only 10km/6 miles from the city centre. It is served by fast trains from many of Germany's major cities. There are flights to five international destinations in addition to several German ones.

Bremen airport

This provincial airport is slightly too small for the traffic it handles, but clearance formalities usually take only 15min. There is a bank which operates normal weekday hours and a restaurant, bar and bureau de change open Mon–Fri, 7.30–7.30; Sat, 7.30–3.30. Airport information ☎ 55951; freight ☎ 55927.

City link The airport is only 3.5km/2 miles south of the city centre. Streetcar route no. 5 runs about every 7min and takes 15min to the centre. There is a good 200-metre walk to the stop outside the terminal. Buy tickets (DM2.40) from the driver.

Taxi The rank in front of the terminal usually has plenty of cabs. The fare to the centre is about DM15.

Car rental Desks are in a building in front of the arrivals exit. But unless you have appointments outside Bremen a car is not necessary.

Railway station

Hauptbahnhof Direct Intercity services at hourly intervals connect with all major cities in the Ruhr, Frankfurt, Hamburg, Hanover and Cologne. There are trains every half hour to and from Bremerhaven and other nearby towns.

City streetcars and buses stop directly outside and go to all the main parts of the town. The taxi rank is to the left as you leave by the main exit. Train inquiries ☎ 19419.

Getting around

Arterial roads lead directly into the heart of the city and one, an obtrusive overhead road along the line of Hochstrasse, is an environmental disaster. However, main roads are well served by public transport and the central area is safe for walking at any time.

Taxis There are about 400 taxis in Bremen, and ranks at many points in the city; otherwise ☎ 14014.

Driving A series of *Autobahnen* almost encircle the city so driving between districts is fairly easy. However parking is difficult in the centre and one-way streets and an extensive traffic-free zone can cause confusion. Rush-hour can be fraught. Car rental agencies are at the airport apart from *Autohansa* ☎ 320051.

Walking The best way to get about in the central area is on foot. The pedestrian streets are Obernstrasse, Hutfilterstrasse, Am Markt, Böttcherstrasse, Sögestrasse, Unser Lieben Frauen Kirchhof and part of Grosse Hundestrasse.

Public transport Bremen has an efficient system of streetcars and buses. A short hop of four stops is DM1; otherwise a flat fare of DM2.40 permits a free transfer to other parts of the city, so save the ticket. Multiride and day tickets are economical. Passenger shelters at most stops display timetables and clear maps of the city showing bus and streetcar routes. Information from the Bremer Strassenbahn stand at the Hauptbahnhof ☎ 13330.

Area by area

The historic centre of the city lies between the river Weser and a series of ponds and parkland that marks the line of an old defensive dyke, Wallanlagen. There is even a

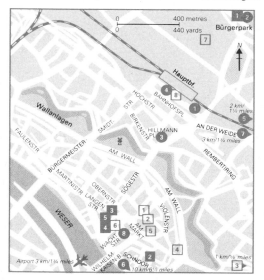

HOTELS
1 Mercure Columbus
2 Park
3 Plaza
4 Zur Post
5 Munte am Stadtwald
6 Novotel Bremer Kreuz
7 Queens Hotel
8 Ubersee

RESTAURANTS
Belvedere (hotel 3)
1 Meierei
Park (hotel 2)
2 Concordenhaus
3 Deutsches Haus
4 Flett
5 Das Kleine Lokal

BUILDINGS AND SIGHTS
1 City Hall (Rathaus)
Chamber of commerce (Handelskammer Bremen) (building 6)
2 Dom
3 Hospital
4 Police station
5 Post office
6 Schütting
7 Stadthalle
8 Tourist information

windmill here. Many of the buildings are medieval, in style if not in age. The area is extremely attractive, particularly in the Schnoor district which has quaint narrow streets. Many local government offices and shops are situated here. The main commercial office district is to the northeast, between Am Wall and the station. Here the buildings are generally modern and unappealing with one or two exceptions. Beyond the station are the delightful woods of Bürgerpark, stretching for nearly 3km/2 miles to the university and *Autobahn*. To the east and south of this are the most prestigious residential areas generally known as Parkviertel.

The suburbs
On the south side of the river there are unremarkable suburbs of low-rise apartment blocks and small villas. To the northwest is working-class Walle and the docks, and beyond Walle lie the Klöckner steel works. Farther out in Bremen-Nord, Vegesack is an old settlement with waterside inns and restaurants and riverbank walks.

Some small docks and the main manufacturing area of Osterholz, where Daimler-Benz is located, lie upstream from the city centre.

Hotels
Despite the economy's downturn, there is still investment in hotels. The opening of the Plaza in March 1985 caused several rivals to refurbish. At present rooms are plentiful so some discounting goes on. All hotels featured have IDD telephones and currency exchange.

Mercure Columbus *DM/*
Bahnhofspl 5, B1 ☎ *14161* ⊤ˣ *244688*
• *AE DC MC V* • *165 rooms, 5 suites,*
1 restaurant, 1 bar
The old and well-loved Columbus was taken over by the French Accor group in 1984. The high-windowed exterior remains the same, but the inside has been transformed with modern furnishings and fashionable decor in pink and grey. Although it is positioned on what must be one of the busiest corners in Bremen, double glazing and soft drapes keep out the noise. Sauna, solarium
• 4 meeting rooms (capacity up to 140).

Park *DM//*
Im Bürgerpark, B1 ☎ *34080*
⊤ˣ *244343* • *AE DC MC V* • *140 rooms,*
10 suites, 4 restaurants, 1 bar
The Park is a white, early 20thC building with a central section surmounted by a dome, and two side wings. Leading from a spacious lobby is a huge lounge with peaceful views across the lake and the Bürgerpark. Bedrooms are large and imaginatively furnished. Suites have antique and modern furnishings and marble bathrooms. Extras include safes and video recorders. The four restaurants interconnect, but each has an individual style: the Buten un binnen is small and businesslike, the Park, large and impressive (see *Restaurants*), the Café am Hollersee has waterside views and the Terrace is in the open air. Hairdresser, newsstand, gift shop • jogging, cycling, rowing, riding and minigolf in the park • fax, 4 meeting rooms (capacity up to 500).

Plaza *DM//*
Hillmannpl 20, B1 ☎ *17670*
⊤ˣ *246868* • *Canadian Pacific* • *AE*
DC MC V • *226 rooms, 4 suites,*
2 restaurants, 1 bar
The Plaza is an attractive, new brick-built hotel in the centre of town. It is roughly circular in shape, with a central atrium around which are the quieter but smaller rooms. The contemporary furnishings and pastel shades create an understated air of comfort. All rooms have hairdryers

and TV with access to AFN, and ten rooms are reserved for nonsmokers. One restaurant, the Belvedere, is outstanding (see *Restaurants*). Hairdresser, 30 shops including boutiques, perfumery, pharmacy • sauna, solarium • fax, 8 meeting rooms (capacity up to 750).

Zur Post   *[DM]|*
Bahnhofspl 11, B1 ☎ *30590*
⊤ˣ *244971* • *Best Western* • AE DC MC V • *199 rooms, 12 suites, 3 restaurants, 1 bar*
The Zur Post has recently been extended and refurbished, and the rooms are comfortable and well designed. The unassuming entrance leads to an inviting lobby with a 1930s flavour. The hotel is popular with business people because of its central location. One of the restaurants is in *Stube* style which fits in with the hotel's traditional image. Rooms have video and trouser

presses. Hairdresser, beauty salon, newsstand • pool, sauna, massage • 8 meeting rooms (capacity up to 120).

OTHER HOTELS

Munte am Stadtwald   *[DM]|*
Zur Munte 2, B1 ☎ *212063*
⊤ˣ *246562* • *Best Western* • AE DC MC V. Close to the university in a pretty setting overlooking the park.
Novotel Bremer Kreuz   *[DM]|*
Zum Klümoor, 2807 Achim/Uphusen
☎ *(04202) 6086* ⊤ˣ *249440* • AE DC MC V. Convenient for the industrial area and the *Autobahn*.
Queens Hotel   *[DM]||*   *August-Bebel-Allee 4, B41* ☎ *23870*
⊤ˣ *244560* • AE DC MC V. To the northeast of the city centre and a few minutes from the *Autobahn*.
Übersee   *[DM]|*   *Wachstr 27–29, B1*
☎ *36010* ⊤ˣ *246501* • AE DC MC.
Rather uninspired, but in the heart of the old town.

Restaurants

The choice of places to eat in Bremen is wide, but to be safe choose one of the large hotel restaurants. Fish is a traditional dish, although little is now of local origin. Reservations are advisable.

Belvedere   *[DM]||*
Plaza hotel ☎ *17670* • AE DC MC V • *jacket and tie*
Within two years the Belvedere rose to be ranked among the best restaurants in Germany, with its finely cooked international cuisine. The modern grey and white decor is a little stark, but the generous windows provide a view towards the old windmill. An interesting range of fixed-price meals is offered, from a seven-course dinner to an economical business lunch; the menus change daily.

Meierei   *[DM]|*
Im Bürgerpark ☎ *211922* • AE DC MC V
Run by the Park hotel, this restaurant in the century-old estate farmhouse is also in a lovely secluded tree-lined setting. The interior layout

consists of booths and alcoves, allowing privacy for confidential business discussions. The cuisine offers a choice of international dishes.

Park   *[DM]|*
Park hotel ☎ *3408556* • AE DC MC V
A beautiful lakeside setting, an excellent international menu, fine service and a wide selection of French and German wines make the Park a natural choice for either high-powered business entertaining or smart social meals. The fixed-price lunch is guaranteed to be served within 30min.

Good but casual
Concordenhaus, Hinter der Holzpforte 2 ☎ 325331, one among several small places in the quaint Schnoor area, is truly *gemütlich* (cheerful and snug). It features *nouvelle cuisine* and local

fish dishes. The *Deutsches Haus*, Am
Markt 1 ☎ 3290920 is a fine old
hostelry for eating or simply having a
drink. Also recommended for
atmosphere and the high-quality
cooking is *Flett*, Böttcherstr 3
☎ 320995. *Das Kleine Lokal*,
Besselstr 40 ☎ 71929, is small and it
serves *nouvelle cuisine*.

Bars
Only the large hotel bars are suitable
for serious discussion. The most
elegant is the *Halali Bar* in the Park
hotel and the most sophisticated the
Piano Bar in the Plaza. The small
Kleiner Ratskeller, which is in an old
building in Hinter dem Schütting, is
suitable for a more relaxed drink, as
in the *Nautilus-Bar* of Flett (see
Restaurants). And the *Bremen
Ratskeller* stores an amazing 600
German wines in its cellars in the
Rathaus, Am Markt. The *Bodega*
wine bar in Martinistr is also a
pleasant place to meet.

Entertainment
The monthly *Bremer Umschau* lists
all the shows. The tourist office
opposite the railway station ☎ 36361
has information on local events and
can make reservations. There are one
or two nightclubs near the station but
more risqué delights may be found in
Seckenhausen, a small town 20km/13
miles south of Bremen.
Theatre, dance, opera The *Bremer
Theater* and the *Schauspielhaus*, both
in Goetheplatz ☎ 3653333, feature
drama, shows, opera and ballet.
Music The Bremen Philharmonia
orchestra gives regular performances
in *Die Glocke* ☎ 326648, beside the
cathedral.
Casino Roulette and black jack are
played in the *Bremer Spielbank*,
Böttcherstr until 2am. Passports may
be asked for.

> For general information about
> German restaurants, see the
> *Planning and Reference* section.

Shopping
Bremen's very attractive traffic-free
zone has a good choice of specialized
shops and standard department
stores. Some smart shops are also
along Am Wall, opposite
Wallanlagen, and some fashionable
boutiques in the Hillmannplatz
shopping arcade beneath the Plaza
hotel. The Schnoor district is the best
area for crafts and antiques or for
window-shopping.

Sightseeing
Most of the buildings in the centre
have been carefully restored and the
whole area is a delight.
Böttcherstrasse is short but full of
interesting antique shops and small
museums in ancient buildings.
Rathaus The 15thC statue of
Roland, symbol of the city's freedom,
stands before the arcaded
Renaissance façade of the town hall
and opposite the 16thC guild
building, the Shütting. *Am Markt.
Guided tours of the Rathaus Mon–Fri,
10, 11 and 12; Sat–Sun, 11 and 12.*
Schnoor Viertel Picturesque houses
and narrow streets which are a must
for any visitor to the city.
St-Petri-Dom The cathedral's
history began with the founding of
Bremen in the 8thC, but most of the
building is 13thC. Austere and
weatherbeaten on the outside, it has a
soaring vaulted nave inside. *Open
Mon–Fri, 9–5; Sat, 9–12; Sun, 2–5
(winter months closed 1hr earlier).*

Guided tours
The local tourist office ☎ 36361
organizes harbour tours (1hr 15min),
bus tours of the town (2hr) and
walking tours (1hr 45min).

Spectator sports
A monthly guide called *Neues aus
Sport und Jazz*, can be picked up at
the tourist office opposite the
Hauptbahnhof. Some events take
place at the Stadthalle, north of the
station ☎ 3505211.
Horse-racing Mar–Nov, 1km to
4km races. *Bremer Rennverein,*

Vahrer Str 219 ☎ 463307.
Soccer Werder Bremen plays at
Weserstadion, Osterdeich ☎ 490506.

Keeping fit
No fitness centres can be
recommended and only two hotels,
Zur Post and Munte, have swimming
pools.
Golf Nonmembers can play Mon,
Thu, Fri at *Club Zu Vahn*,
Bürgermeister-Spitta-Allee
☎ 230041.
Squash *Town Squash*, Plantage 5
☎ 354084 and *Squash & Tennis
Center* Duchwitzst 47 ☎ 51626.
Swimming *Herbert-Ritze-Bad*,
Kurt Schumacher Allee ☎ 462356;
Hallenbad Universität at the
university ☎ 2182531.
Tennis *Tennis Country Club*,
Thalenhorststr 49 ☎ 487111 has
indoor and outdoor courts.

Local resources
Business services
Most hotels can arrange secretarial
help and translation to and from
English.
Photocopying *Allerding u. Co*,
Seemannstr ☎ 327676.
Printing *Appel*, Kornstr 571
☎ 873061.
Secretarial *BBS*, Neidenburger
Str 15 ☎ 4989051.
Translation *Siegfried Sander*,
Rembertistr 31 ☎ 326873, and
Lopez-Ebri, Violenstr 37 ☎ 326707.

Communications
Local delivery *XP* ☎ 534433.
Long-distance delivery *TNT*
☎ 388004, *World Couriers* ☎ 552688.
Post office Main office at
Domsheide. 24hr service at
Bahnhofsplatz 5 ☎ 3001.

Conference/exhibition centres
The major venue is the *Stadthalle* but
for information on all seminars,
conferences, conventions and
exhibitions contact the city office
Verkehrsverein Bremen at
Bahnhofspl 29, B1 ☎ 3636233
Ⓣⓧ 244854.

Emergencies
Bureau de change *Postamt 5*, An
der Weide (near station) open daily,
8–10.30.
Hospitals *Zentralkrankenhaus*,
St-Jürgen Str ☎ 4971. Emergency
doctor ☎ 19292. Emergency dentist
☎ 12233.
Pharmacies For details of
pharmacies that open late consult the
Weser-Kurier or the police.
Police Headquarters at Am Wall 201
☎ 3621.

Government offices
Senat der Freien Hansestadt Bremen
(Senate of the Free Hanseatic City of
Bremen), Rathaus, B1, external
affairs department ☎ 3612000. The
press and information department
☎ 3612396 provides details on
matters concerning the *Land*.

Information sources
Business information
Handelskammer Bremen (chamber of
commerce), Schütting, gives
information about companies here,
but for help with contacts, local
economic activity and how to do
business in Bremen a far better
source is *Verkehrsverein Bremen*
(more useful for obtaining business
information than the usual tourist
office), Bahnhofspl 29 ☎ 36361.
Local media The *Weser-Kurier* has
three or four pages of local economic
news daily. *Radio Bremen* transmits
both radio and television (as part of
the ARD regional network).
Tourist information At
Bahnhofplatz 29 outside the station.
Open Mon–Thu, 8–8; Fri, 8–10; Sat,
8–6; Sun, 9.30–3.30 ☎ 36361.

Thank-yous
Peter van den Berg operates at the
flower market near the Rathaus and
at Friedrich-Ebert-Str 152
☎ 552279. *LILAC* at Am Wall 153
☎ 325147, or *Porzellan Studio* at
Berliner Freiheit 5 ☎ 462841 are gift
shops. *W. Hasselbach & Co*,
Arsterdamm 180 ☎ 821252, provides
gift packs of fine vintages.

COLOGNE

City codes zip 5000 ☎ 0221

The people of Köln are proud that their city has been a centre of European culture and trade for 2,000 years and confident that business will continue to flourish there. Consequently, unlike their rivals in neighbouring Düsseldorf whom they regard as young and immature, they do not feel an all-consuming need to push for opportunities or to try to prove their superiority. With trade and industry taken for granted as the bedrocks of prosperity, they get on with the business of enjoying life: eating, drinking, music, theatre and making the most of their annual pre-Lent carnival.

The Romans first established Cologne's commercial and political importance, creating a network of roads to complement the river Rhein. Some 200 years ago, Germany's first chamber of trade and industry was set up here. Today the city has a population of nearly 1m, is the fourth largest in West Germany and third largest industrial centre. Its output is extremely diverse, ranging from the famous 4711 *Eau de Cologne* to Interatom nuclear reactors. Petro-chemicals has the largest sales of all sectors, though output has recently been declining. The "chemical ring" of plants around the city includes Petroleum, Esso, Shell and Rheinisch Olefin. Five major motor vehicle factories include Ford's biggest in Europe (with a workforce of 40,000), as well as KHD Tractors. Mechanical, electrical and construction engineering products are also significant, including industrial plant from Otto Wolff, cables from Felten & Guilleaume, and the Strabag construction company. There are also companies specializing in pharmaceuticals, printing and precision electronics.

Nearly a third of Cologne's companies are in the growing service sector, particularly insurance and banking. Gerling-Konzern is the biggest of 60 insurance companies with their head offices in the city. There are also 60 different banks, placing Cologne second only to Frankfurt in that sector. The media are well represented, too: four large daily local newspapers, several national magazines, the regional TV and radio station (WDR), two overseas radio services and the British Forces radio station are all based here. A major new project by the department for city development is the MediaPark, where a disused railway station is being converted into an information technology centre. Bull and Sony are its main supporters.

The city's openness to trade and industry is underlined by its thriving trade fair company KölnMesse. With 35 fairs and 800 major conferences during a typical year, hardly a week passes by without an important event, attracting 1.5m of the city's 7m business visitors. A further 13m people come as tourists, mostly during the summer.

Arriving

Cologne can be reached easily by air, rail or road. Motorways lead almost to the centre and 1,000 trains a day serve the main station. It has an international airport, though most overseas visitors fly into Düsseldorf, less than 1hr away by train.

Köln/Bonn airport
The airport has never succeeded in competing with Düsseldorf, having scheduled services to only 27 non-German cities, just 14 of them daily. Yet technically it is very advanced and is working at only half its capacity. However it has many holiday charter flights, is West Germany's second largest airport for freight and is often used when Düsseldorf is fog-bound, particularly in the autumn. The airport has a relatively small amount of traffic and so formalities do not take long. Facilities include a restaurant, a coffee bar, supermarket, hairdresser, post office, bureau de change (open Mon–Fri, 7–6.30; Sat 8.30–1, 2–6; Sun, 2–6) and a meeting room for up to 120. Passenger and freight inquiries ☎ (02203) 404001/2.
Nearby hotels *Holiday Inn*, Waldstr 200, K90 ☎ (02203) 5610 ⊤ˣ 8874665 • AE DC MC V.
City link The airport is 16km/10 miles to the southeast of the centre across the Rhein. The journey into town takes 20min, slightly longer at rush hours, 7–8.30 and 4.30–6.
Taxis There are usually plenty of taxis in the ranks in front of the terminals. Standard charges to the city centre and the trade fair grounds (the Messe) are DM30 and DM27 respectively.
Car rental Avis, Autohansa, Europcar, Hertz, interRent and Sixt have desks. It is only worthwhile renting a car if you have appointments outside the city centre.
Bus An airport bus, no. 170, runs every 20–30min, 6–11.30, to the bus station in Breslauer Platz at the south exit of the main railway station, also calling at Deutz station across the river near the trade fair grounds; fare DM3.60.

Railway station
Köln Hauptbahnhof is right in the city centre beside the cathedral and the Rhein. It is one of the busiest in West Germany with direct expresses serving principal cities all over the Continent. These include special connections for Lufthansa passengers between Düsseldorf and Frankfurt airports. The station is covered by an enormous semi-circular glass roof supported by metal girders. It has shops and a post office, open 7–10, bureau de change, open 7–9, and restaurants. Detailed arrival and departure timetables are displayed throughout the station. Car rental at Breslauer Platz entrance; taxis (always available), buses and trams in front of the main entrance; subway (*U-Bahn*) station below. Timetable inquiries ☎ 2761.

Getting around
The city centre (Innenstadt) is very compact and its main shopping area traffic free, so it is best covered on foot, though after dark the dingier streets at the side of the main station are best avoided. A car is useful for business in the suburbs or sightseeing farther afield, but traffic tends to be congested, particularly across the Rhein bridges at rush hours. Public transport serves the outer areas efficiently.
Taxis Cabs are cream coloured. You should have no trouble finding one at the main railway station or at ranks in the main squares or by making reservations ☎ 2882.
Driving Ten motorways lead onto the *Autobahn* ring which circles the city, with three running from it into the centre. Exits are clearly numbered but the traffic moves very fast except in rush hours, and a good map is essential. Outer, middle and inner ring roads run in semi-circles from the Rhein on the western left bank. There are 28 public parking areas in the city centre, where you pay as you exit; most open 7–11. During working hours, spaces are hard to find but a helpful sign system at entrances indicates the nearest with free spaces. Many of the larger hotels have garages.
All the major car rental firms have offices in the city, as well as at the airport. They also offer limousine

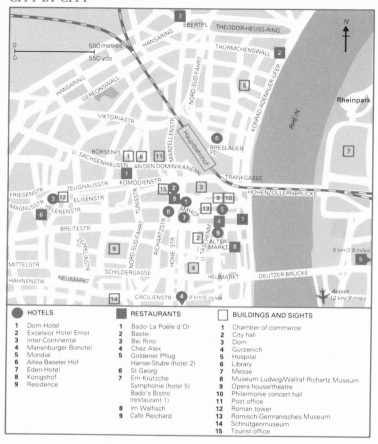

	HOTELS		RESTAURANTS		BUILDINGS AND SIGHTS
1	Dom-Hotel	1	Bado-La Poêle d'Or	1	Chamber of commerce
2	Excelsior Hotel Ernst	2	Bastei	2	City hall
3	Inter-Continental	3	Bei Rino	3	Dom
4	Marienburger Bonotel	4	Chez Alex	4	Gurzenich
5	Mondial	5	Goldener Pflug	5	Hospital
6	Altea Baseler Hof		Hanse-Stube (hotel 2)	6	Library
7	Eden-Hotel	6	St Georg	7	Messe
8	Konigshof	7	Em Krutzche	8	Museum Ludwig/Wallraf-Richartz Museum
9	Residence		Symphonie (hotel 5)	9	Opera house/theatre
			Bado's Bistro	10	Philarmonie concert hall
			(restaurant 1)	11	Post office
		8	Im Walfisch	12	Roman tower
		9	Café Reichard	13	Römisch-Germanisches Museum
				14	Schnutgenmuseum
				15	Tourist office

services; *Hertz* ☎ 01302121, *Avis* ☎ 234570.

Bus, subway and streetcar
Efficient and easy to use, public transport includes a subway (*U-Bahn*), buses and streetcars. Interchangeable tickets can be bought at subway stations or from machines at bus and streetcar stops or on board. They must be validated in the machines on board with on-the-spot fines for fare dodgers. Daily runabout tickets are a good buy and there are special visitors' tickets during trade fairs. Details of routes

and timetables can be obtained from the KVB (Kölner-Verkehrs-Betriebe) information office at the Hauptbahnhof *U-Bahn* station.
Boats Ferries cross the Rhine between the Hohenzollern Bridge and the Messe grounds on the right bank. Services every 30min May–Sep and during fairs; the journey takes 5min. Excursion motorboats operate up and down the river (Easter–Oct). Freight is sent from five dock areas and a container terminal is being built. The Messe also has a rail freight terminal.

Area by area

The city centre (Innenstadt) is enclosed by the 6.5km/4-mile semi-circular course of the old city walls on the left bank of the Rhein where the main inner ring road now runs. Within, is the city's major landmark, the cathedral whose twin towers are visible from miles around, the main offices, including insurance, bank and administration headquarters, and the largest shopping areas which are all pedestrianized. Its hub is the traffic-free cathedral square, Domkloster, with the main railway station immediately north of it, banking streets to the west and the Hohe Strasse shops to the south.

Bombing during World War II destroyed three quarters or more of the city. Most of the historic buildings that were severely damaged have been either extensively repaired or completely rebuilt. There are now modern developments, mostly plain and functional apart from the striking new arts complex with concert hall and museums overlooking the Rhein to the east of the cathedral. The old town area, the Altstadt, around the Alter Markt, a pleasant 5min walk south from the cathedral square, has succeeded in retaining much of its original character. Narrow cobbled streets are lined by small shops and restaurants in tall 14th–18thC town houses. Beside the river the Rheingarten park overlooks the steamer quays.

The suburbs

Cologne grew to 11 times its original size around 100 years ago when the old city wall boundary was dispensed with and the "new town" created. It too was laid out in a semi-circle, imaginatively incorporating the communities which already existed. Lindenthal, around the university and only just over a mile from the city centre, is a much sought after residential district, especially as it borders large areas of unspoilt woodland in the Stadtwald. Marienburg, beside the river and bounded by the southernmost section of the outer ring road, the *Militarring*, is even more desirable, with stately mansions where many leading business figures live.

The most industrial parts of the left bank are Ehrenfeld and Nippes, to the north of the city, though the Ford works and many small factories are to be found in the northern suburbs. The extensive trade fair grounds, the Messe, built in the 1920s, are opposite the city centre across the Rhein. Adjoining them is the Rheinpark which has thermal baths in its recreation centre. Behind, to the east, Deutz and Kalk are highly industrialized, many with chemical plants. The suburbs beyond are solidly working class.

Hotels

Most visitors prefer a hotel near the cathedral at the hub of the city and close to the Rhein. Although there is already a wide selection of quality hotels in the city centre, more are being built. The city's largest hotel is the Hyatt on the right bank near the trade fair grounds, while a Ramada has opened near the cathedral square in the old quarter around Friesenplatz. During the major trade fairs, when most hotels are full, the tourist office operates a shuttle service at 7pm to available rooms in the outskirts. Smart steamers on the Rhein are also used as hotels at peak times. Reservations can be made at the airport or the tourist office ☎ 2213340 and at the trade fair grounds during exhibitions ☎ 8212273. Rooms have TV and minibars, with currency exchange and 24hr room service generally available. Most hotels offer photocopying and telex.

Dom Hotel *DM*|||||
Domkloster 2a, K1 ☎ *233751*
Ⓣ *8882919* • *Trusthouse Forte* • *AE*
DC MC V • *126 rooms, 1 suite,*
1 restaurant, 1 bar
In the traffic-free square near the
cathedral. The grand and dignified
Dom has been part of the city's life
for over 125 years and attracts a
clientele of well-heeled tourists and
senior business people. Guest rooms
are attractively furnished; some have
balconies overlooking the square and
can be noisy, particularly during
open-air events. The outdoor terrace
café also looks onto the square while,
inside, the bar has comfortable
leather chairs in secluded alcoves.
The elegant restaurant has an
excellent reputation, particularly for
Rheinland dishes. Fax, 3 meeting
rooms (capacity up to 60).

Excelsior Hotel Ernst *DM*||||
Dompl, K1 ☎ *2701* Ⓣ *8882645* • *AE*
DC MC • *175 rooms, 8 suites,*
2 restaurants, 1 bar
Spacious lounges and rooms, period
furnishings and paintings, together
with the latest modern comforts, help
create an air of opulence in this late-
19thC hotel on the edge of the main
banking district. Some guest rooms
are in a new wing but the same sense
of style is maintained throughout.
Besides the Hanse-Stube (see
Restaurants), which is popular for
business meals, there is a quiet cellar
bar for informal discussions. Fax,
8 meeting rooms (capacity up to
400).

Inter-Continental *DM*||||
Helenenstr 14, K1 ☎ *2280* Ⓣ *8882212*
• *AE DC MC V* • *278 rooms, 12 suites,*
2 restaurants, 2 bars
This is an efficient hotel well used to
catering for the traveller who wants
high standards of comfort, amenities
and comprehensive business support
services. Rooms are light and airy,
and well equipped. The traditional
German Bergische Stube restaurant
has an eight-course evening menu
and hot buffet lunch. A pianist plays

in the Derby Bar, and from the
sophisticated disco and conference
rooms on the twelfth floor there are
good views of the cathedral.
Newsstand, gift shop • pool, sun
terrace, sauna, massage • fax, 13
meeting rooms (capacity up to
1,000).

Marienburger Bonotel *DM*||
Bonner Str 478–482, K51 ☎ *37020*
Ⓣ *8881515* • *AE DC MC V* • *90 rooms,*
4 suites, 1 restaurant, 1 bar
This stylish, new, privately owned
hotel is unobtrusively tucked away to
the south of the city on the main
route to the *Autobahn* ring. Popular
with those working at or visiting the
nearby TV and radio stations, it is
bright and lively, and a little flashy.
Bedrooms are welcoming and light,
with pastel furnishings and white
bathrooms. The prettily decorated
suites on a separate floor, to which
access is by special key, are suitable
for small meetings and have
whirlpool baths. Bus to and from
airport • jacuzzi, sauna, exercise
room • fax, 2 meeting rooms
(capacity up to 100).

Mondial *DM*||
Kurt-Hackenberg-Pl 1, K1 ☎ *20630*
Ⓣ *8881932* • *Pullman* • *AE DC MC V*
• *199 rooms, 5 suites, 1 restaurant,*
2 bars
This plain and functional hotel built
in the 1960s is now part of the
French Pullman group and has been
completely refurbished. Rooms are
quiet and look onto a quiet inner
courtyard; the more expensive rooms
have extra perks such as bathrobes.
As the hotel is near the Philharmonie
concert hall, the restaurant is popular
with concert-goers as well as business
people (see *Restaurants*). Gift shop,
florist, newsstand, • 7 meeting rooms
(capacity up to 200).

For general information about
German hotels, see the *Planning
and Reference* section.

OTHER HOTELS

Altea Baseler Hof [DM]||
Breslauer Pl 2, K1 ☎ *16540*
℡ *8886982* • *AE DC MC V.*
Convenient for the city centre and
within easy reach by ferry or
footbridge of the trade fair grounds.
Eden-Hotel [DM]|| *Am Hof 18, K1*
☎ *236123* ℡ *8882889* • *AE DC MC V.*
A small, privately owned hotel which
strives to give a personal

touch. Splendid views of the Dom.
Königshof [DM]| *Richartzstr 14–16,*
K1 ☎ *234583* ℡ *8881318* • *AE DC*
MC V. Comfortable but dull despite
exclusive touches; near cathedral and
shops.
Residence [DM]| *Alter Markt 55,*
K1 ☎ *235781* ℡ *8885344* • *Rema*
• *AE DC MC V.* Friendly, small hotel
with smart modern decor, pleasantly
situated in the Altstadt.

Restaurants

Many rate Cologne as the gastronomic capital of Germany. Its wide
choice of restaurants ranges from the very highly acclaimed Goldener
Pflug to the informal and lively brewery restaurants, where the food is
simpler and features local dishes. Many hotels offer fixed-price menus at
lunch time. Reservations are generally advisable.

Bado-La Poêle d'Or [DM]|||
Komödienstr 50–52 ☎ *134100* • *closed*
Sun, Mon L, 3 weeks in Jul–Aug and
hols (inc Christmas week) • *AE DC MC*
• *jacket and tie*
Its secluded courtyard setting and
restrained atmosphere make Bado-La
Poêle d'Or very suitable for detailed
discussions. Chef Jean Claude Bado's
nouvelle cuisine menus change with
the season, featuring dishes such as
duck in Burgundy sauce and salmon
mille feuilles. Four- and eight-
course gourmet menus are available at lunch
time and in the evening.

Bastei [DM]||
Konrad-Adenauer-Ufer 80 ☎ *122825*
• *closed Sat L* • *AE DC MC*
This large split-level restaurant
which juts out over the Rhein is the
city's most spectacular. Cooking is
mainly German with some Swiss and
Austrian dishes.

Bei Rino [DM]|||
Ebertpl 3 ☎ *721108* • *closed Sun and*
hols • *AE DC MC V*
Flemish tapestries hang on the walls
of this well-established Italian
restaurant, and pink and grey decor
and subdued lighting create a stylish
atmosphere. Owner-chef Geurino
Casati is known for his fish. The six-

course gourmet menu features perch
fillet and quail.

Chez Alex [DM]||||
Mühlengasse 1 ☎ *230560* • *closed Sat*
L, Sun and hols • *AE DC MC V* • *jacket*
and tie
This Altstadt restaurant is a
dependable place for business
entertaining. Divided into several
quiet rooms, it is in the grand style
with high ceilings, 18thC paintings
on panelled walls, plush dark
furnishings and deep-pink table linen
and candles. Considered by many to
be Cologne's best French restaurant,
the emphasis is on *nouvelle cuisine.* A
fixed-price four-course menu is
available at lunch time.

Goldener Pflug [DM]||||
Olpener Str 421, Merheim
☎ *895509/896124* • *closed Sun and*
hols • *no credit cards* • *jacket and tie*
Originally a traditional inn, the
Goldener Pflug is now one of
Germany's top restaurants, attracting
the highest praise from guides such
as *Michelin* for its rich, classic
German cuisine. Hard to beat if you
want to impress or celebrate with
important clients, but its location,
8km/5 miles out, makes it more
suitable for dinner than lunch.

Hanse-Stube   *[DM]||*
Excelsior Hotel Ernst, Trankgasse 1–5
☎ *2701 • closed Tue • AE DC MC*
• jacket and tie
Executives from the adjacent banking district are regularly to be found in the discreet alcoves of this wood-panelled restaurant. The menu has more seafood than meat, with salmon, sole and turbot invariably on offer. At lunch there is a buffet with German dishes. Wide selection of German wines.

St Georg   *[DM]||*
Kreishaus-Galerie, Magnusstr 3
☎ *218418 • closed Sun and hols exc during trade fairs • AE DC MC V*
Adjoining smart arcades of art and antique shops, this very striking circular modern restaurant is boldly decorated in white, black and maroon, with mirrored walls. Tables line the windows and there is a bar in the centre. The food is German with a strong French influence. A four-course business lunch and a seven-course gourmet dinner menu are available.

Good but casual
Cologne has many old-fashioned coffee-houses and restaurants which are agreeable rendezvous for informal meetings. *Em Krützche*, Am Frankenturm 1–3 ☎ 211432, is typical with blue and white tiles and a large collection of beer mugs over the bar. Of its several rooms, the Chippendale upstairs is the most suitable for talking business. Concert-goers favour the *Symphonie* in the Mondial hotel, Kurt-Hackenberg-Pl 1 ☎ 20630, opposite the new arts complex. It has a terrace overlooking the Rhein and at lunch time offers two special business menus. *Bado's Bistro*, Komödienstr 52 ☎ 134704, is the Bado-La Poêle d'Or's (see *Restaurants*) more informal and less expensive neighbour, while in the heart of the Altstadt an up market wine bar, *Im Walfisch*, Salzgasse 13 ☎ 219575, offers a small menu featuring fish. For watching the

world go by, there is no better place than the wide terrace of Cologne's most famous café, the *Café Reichard*, Unter Fettenhennen 11 ☎ 233892; inside, there are private alcoves.

Bars
As in most cities, the bars of the main hotels are the safest places to discuss business over a drink, but Kölner are gregarious people and colleagues might suggest a meeting in one of the city's hundreds of *Kölschlokale*, also called *Kneipen*. These are cheerful, friendly places where beer-drinking is taken seriously; the favourite brew is the locally made *Kölsch* which only 24 breweries are authorized to produce. You should also visit one of the drinking halls attached to breweries, old wood-panelled rooms with big scrubbed wooden tables, where beer and simple food are served by *Köbesse*, waiters in leather aprons. The most colourful of the brewery bars are the *Brauhaus Sion*, Unter Taschenmacher 5–7; *Früh am Dom*, Am Hof 12–14; and *Päffgen*, Friesenstr 64. They are open from mid-morning to around midnight.

Entertainment
The city has a reputation for theatre and music, recently boosted by the opening of an impressive arts complex beside the cathedral. Listings appear in *Kölner Leben* and *Kölner Woche*, both weekly, and the monthly *Köln-Monatsvorschau* and *Köln im...*, available from the tourist office and newsstands. For theatres and concerts, there is a 24hr information service ☎ 11517.
Theatre, dance, opera The repertoire of the *Opernhaus* (known as the *Oper*), Opernpl ☎ 212581, ranges from classical to contemporary works. Ballet and plays are also performed in the theatre in the same building ☎ 212651. The season runs Sep–Jun; seats are much in demand, especially for the opera. Ticket offices for all performances are in the Kaufhof department store in Hohe Strasse, at the Neumarkt *U-Bahn*

station and at the Opernhaus, Mon–
Fri, 11–2 and 4–6, Sat 11–2.

Non-German speakers might
prefer to take in a mime show at the
Pantomimentheater Kefka,
Albertusstr/Ecke Magnusstr
☎ 2401688. The humour and
colourful presentation of cabaret at
the *Senftöpfchen*, Brugelmannhaus,
Neugasse 2–4 ☎ 237980, also has
universal appeal.
Music The impressive new
Philharmonie concert hall,
Bischofsgartenstr 1 ☎ 204080, is the
main concert venue. Regular
performances are given by the
Gürzenich, West German Radio
Symphony and other leading
international orchestras.
Nightclubs The many discos
include *Filmdancing*, Im
Weidenbruch, where popular films,
particularly comedies, are shown in
three parts with dancing for all ages
in between; *Apropo*, Im Dau 17
☎ 311292; and *Subway Jazz*,
Aachener Str 82–84 ☎ 517969.
Respectable striptease clubs are the
Tingel-Tangel, Maastrichter Str 6–8
☎ 230161 and *Madame*, Klapperhof
49 ☎ 134306.

Carnival
Over several weeks before Lent,
Cologne gears itself up for the
annual *Karneval*. Every bar and
restaurant enters into the spirit of
the festival, while exuberant
formal balls are organized by over
100 special carnival clubs. During
the week before Lent begins,
there is much merrymaking
outdoors, culminating in the
Rosenmontag procession of
decorated floats. Stands are
erected for spectators along the
route, with the highest in the
cathedral square. Shop windows
are boarded up to protect them
from the hail of sweets and small
gifts thrown from the floats for
the crowd to catch. Carnival is not
the time to visit Cologne on
business.

Shopping
The city has a wide selection of
stores and shops, all within a
short walking distance of the
centre. The traffic-free Hohe
Strasse, which leads off the
cathedral square, has many
excellent small shops but they
tend to be overshadowed by pop
fashion boutiques. At its far end is
the broader Schildergasse where
all the large department stores are
situated, interspersed with
specialist shops. For toys,
especially model railways, try
Feldhaus. For crafts and gifts,
there are about 40 small shops
selling jewellery, leather and other
goods, gathered under one roof in
the *Kölner Ladenstadt* opposite the
Opernhaus. The Altstadt is a good
area for pottery and antiques, and
there are many art galleries and
small shops in the exclusive new
Kreishaus-Galerie off St-Apern-
Strasse. Nearby, the *Bazaar de
Cologne* is a modern shopping
mall with glass dome and chic
boutiques. It leads off
Mittelstrasse, which has a range
of smart fashion shops.

Sightseeing
The cathedral (*Dom*), whose twin
spires dominate the skyline, is
Cologne's main tourist attraction,
but within the old medieval walls
of the city are several excellent
museums and 12 Romanesque
churches. The paths along the
Rhein are ideal for leisurely
strolls, with plenty of activity to
watch on the river.
Dom It took over 600 years
(1248–1880) to complete the
city's most famous building, the
imposing and elaborate Gothic
cathedral beside the Rhein.
Astonishingly, it survived World
War II when the surrounding
area was almost completely
devastated. It is worth climbing
the 509 steps of the south spire for
the panoramic view. For guided
tours in English ☎ 2213340.

Domkloster. Closed during services; south spire open 9–5; Sun and hols from 1.

Ludwig and Wallraf-Richartz museums The new arts complex beside the cathedral includes two museums as well as the Philharmonie concert hall. The Museum Ludwig houses modern art including the collection of modern American paintings donated by Peter Ludwig, a millionaire chocolate manufacturer from Aachen. The Wallraf-Richartz-Museum has a major collection of 14th–19thC paintings, French Impressionists and 19thC sculptures. *Bischofsgartenstr 1. Open Tue–Thu, 10–8; Fri–Sun, 10–6.*

Rheinpark A large ornamental park on the right bank of the Rhein with colourful displays of bulbs in spring and fine views of the cathedral. It can be reached by the electric cablecar which runs from the zoo. *Open daily Easter–Oct; closed Fri.*

Römisch-Germanisches Museum This museum next to the cathedral houses the Dionysos Mosaic, the floor of a 3rdC Roman nobleman's villa which was uncovered there when an air-raid shelter was being dug in 1941. There are also displays of Roman domestic objects and glass. *Roncalliplatz 4. Open Tue–Sun, 10–5; Wed and Thu, 10–8.*

Schnütgenmuseum Religious art including madonnas and gold ornaments from the Middle Ages in the appropriate setting of the redundant St Cecilia church. *Cäcilienstr 29. Open Tue–Sun, 10–5.*

Zeughaus Former arsenal with an exhibition on city history, *Komödienstr 1–3. Open Tue–Sun, 10–5; Thu, 10–8.*

Guided tours
Two-hour city tours by bus depart from the tourist office ☎ 2213340 opposite the cathedral; tickets are available from the guide on board. There are also guided walking tours which take in churches and museums.

Out of town
Bergisches Land, the prettiest countryside across the Rhein, 32km/20 miles northeast of Cologne, is famous for its old black and white half-timbered houses and *Bergische Kaffee*, coffee served with black bread, cakes and waffles topped with sour cherries and cream. The village of *Altenberg* has a huge early Gothic cathedral. *Schloss Augustusburg* in Brühl, 19km/12 miles southwest in the Eifel foothills, is a splendid 18thC castle surrounded by a lake and spacious formal gardens.

Spectator sports
The tourist office ☎ 2213340 has a list of all sporting events.

Basketball The champion team, BSC Saturn, play in the *Sporthalle*, Deutz-Mulheimer Str ☎ 882031.

Horse-racing Races are held at Rennbahnverein, Rennbahnstr 152 ☎ 748074.

Ice hockey The local club, the "Hai" (Sharks), have frequently been national champions. They play in the *Eisstadion*, An der Lentstr ☎ 726026.

Soccer The FC Köln football team plays at the *Müngersdorfer Stadion* ☎ 4983222.

Keeping fit
Fitness centres Clubs have sprung up in most districts. One with a wide range of facilities is *Sport-, Fitness-und Freizeit-Park*, Aachener Str 76 ☎ 527513.

Jogging The *Stadtwald* in the suburb of Lindenthal is popular with local joggers, as are the banks of the Rhein around the Zoobrücke.

Squash and tennis *Center Kautz*, Rhondorfer Str 10 ☎ 411092.

Swimming The *Eis- und Schwimmstadion*, Lentstr 30 ☎ 726026 has a heated outdoor pool.

Local resources
Business services
Most top hotels have or can arrange a full range of business support services.

Photocopying and printing
Department stores have photocopying facilities. *Rank-Xerox*, Marzellen Str 3 ☎ 125120 offers a copying and printing service in the city centre, Mon–Sat.
Secretarial *Alpha-Zeitarbeit*, Zeppelin Str 2 ☎ 210996, Mon–Fri, 9–5.
Translation *Malcolm Mitchell Bureau*, Elisenstr 4–10 ☎ 217492, Mon–Fri, 8.30–5.30.

Communications
Local delivery For delivery by taxi ☎ 2882. Specialist firms include *Kölner Fahrradkurier* ☎ 131512, *Pervelo* ☎ 447244 and *Rapido* ☎ 5506196.
Long-distance delivery *Blitz-Kurier* ☎ 516081; *DHL* ☎ 36021.
Post office The main office is at An den Dominikanern 4 ☎ 1401.
Telex and fax At main post office.

Conference/exhibition centres
More than 30 international trade fairs take place in the city, attracting over 25,000 exhibitors in a typical year. Of the 1.5m visitors, a third are foreigners from 150 different countries. The largest fair is ANUGA, the food market (in Oct); others include furniture (Jan), home appliances, men's fashion (Feb), hardware (Mar), furnishings (May) and sports and camping (Sep). For general information ☎ 8212536. *KölnMesse*, Messe- und Ausstellungsgesellschaft, Köln, PO Box 210760, K21 ☎ 8212536 ⊠ 8873426 has the most important congress and exhibition facilities, with 27 meeting rooms (capacity up to 6,000). Of the several hotels with well-equipped rooms, the *Inter-Continental* offers the largest conference/banqueting room (capacity up to 1,000). Other useful centres include the *Gürzenich* buildings, Martinstr 29–37 ☎ 2213337 and the *Stadt-Halle Köln-Mulheim*, Jan-Wellem-Str 2 ☎ 622096.

Emergencies
Bureau de change At the main railway station, open daily, 7–9.
Hospitals 24hr emergency department at *Marien-Hospital*, Kunibertskloster 11–13 ☎ 16290. For information about doctors on emergency ☎ 720772.
Dental treatment Information ☎ 720772.
Pharmacies At the main railway station. For information on duty pharmacists and dentists ☎ 11500.
Police Am Waidmarkt ☎ 2291; emergencies ☎ 112.

Government offices
City administration: *Stadt Köln, Rat und Verwaltung*, Rathaus, Rathauspl ☎ 2211.

Information sources
Business information Advice is available from the chamber of commerce, *Industrie- und Handelskammer zu Köln*, Unter Sachsenhausen 10–26 ☎ 16400. Those who want to open a business should contact *Amt für Wirtschaftsförderung*, Richartzstr 2–4 ☎ 2213312. *Handwerkskammer Köln*, Heumarkt 12 ☎ 20221 gives advice on non-industrial crafts. The commercial library (*Wirtschaftsbibliothek*) is at Unter Sachsenhausen 29–31 ☎ 1640102; open Mon–Fri, 9.30–4.30.
Local media The main daily newspapers are the *Kölner Stadt-Anzeiger* (which has the best business coverage) and the *Kölnische Rundschau*. The *Express* and *Bild-Zeitung* are popular tabloids.
Tourist information The main tourist office is at Unter Fettenhennen 19 ☎ 2213340. (See also *Entertainment*.)

Thank-yous
Delicatessen *Hoss an der Oper*, Breite Str 25–27 ☎ 231292.
Florists *Blumen Klaus Pitschak* ☎ 134341, Hauptbahnhof.
Wine merchants *Feger und Unterberg*, Heumarkt 57 ☎ 213203.

DORTMUND

City codes zip 4600 ☎ 0231

Dortmund is West Germany's eighth largest city, with a population of 570,000, yet about half consists of parks, woods and fields. Historically, brewing is a major industry and 6,000 people are employed in its six breweries, of which the biggest is Union. For many years steel production has been the bulwark of the city's economy, providing around 10% of the national output. But the Ruhr has been hard hit by foreign competition in steel and the city's unemployment rate is 16%, the highest in West Germany. The recent restructuring of its biggest employer, Hoesch, which produces finished steel for the motor and electrical industries, has resulted in widespread redundancy, and the city's last colliery closed in 1987.

Over half of Dortmund's employees are now in service industries such as banking, commerce and insurance, in which it has become West Germany's third most important centre. A new casino contributes over DM10m to the city's economy and computer consultancy is a growing area. High hopes are placed on research and development in new technology, and applied engineering in particular has been encouraged at the technical high school and university.

Situated on two medieval trunk roads, Dortmund built its original prosperity on trade, becoming a leading member of the Hanseatic League. Today it is encircled by *Autobahnen* and has Europe's largest inland port, linked by the Dortmund-Ems canal to the Rhein and Rotterdam.

Arriving

Surrounded by the "Dortmund Ring" of *Autobahnen*, the city is at the heart of West Germany's road network. It has rail connections daily with nearly 40 cities, but no international airport. The nearest is Düsseldorf, from which there are hourly rail services (journey time 1hr 10min) to Dortmund Hauptbahnhof. Its port is the largest in Europe for freight.

Dortmund-Wickede airport

This new, small airport, a 10min drive to the northeast, is used by private aircraft, some regular commuters and services from cities such as Berlin, Frankfurt, Munich and Stuttgart. Information ☎ 218901.

Railway station

Dortmund Hauptbahnhof, modern and well-equipped, is in the city centre, a few minutes from the main shops and business areas. It has direct services to major West German towns (hourly to Frankfurt airport, 3hr 10min), as well as to Amsterdam, Brussels and Vienna. Local *S-Bahn* trains go to other Ruhr towns. InterRent car rental has a desk. Taxis are readily available and there are subway and streetcar links. Timetable inquiries ☎ 161011.

Getting around

The compact city centre can be crossed on foot within 15min. The suburbs are well served by public transport. *Autobahnen* circle the city and there are 12 access points.
Taxis There are ranks throughout the city, including at the Hauptbahnhof and the Westfalenhalle. For reservations ☎ 144444.
Limousines Avis ☎ 579357.
Driving The Ruhrschnellweg, the east-west expressway which crosses the city not far south of the centre,

leads directly onto the busy *Autobahn* ring. From the south the Ruhrwaldstrasse expressway leads straight into the centre, crossing the Ruhrschnellweg at the Westfalenpark, near the main exhibition halls. There are 15 parking sites within the city centre and extensive facilities at the exhibition halls and stadium. A car is an asset if you have appointments in the widely scattered industrial areas. Traffic is rarely heavy. Car rental firms include *Avis* ☎ 579357, *Hertz* ☎ 824044 and *interRent* ☎ 528086.

Walking Within the inner Wall ring road, distances are small and orientation easy.

Public transport The streetcar, bus and subway systems are straightforward. Single tickets can be bought from machines at main stops or from drivers. From the Hauptbahnhof to the new casino at

	HOTELS		RESTAURANTS
1	Drees	1	Edo
2	Lennhof	2	La Table
3	Parkhotel Landhaus	3	Mövenpick
	Syburg	4	Pfefferkorn
4	Parkhotel		Zum Widukind
	Westfalenhalle		(hotel 5)
5	Parkhotel	5	Hövels
	Wittekindshof	6	Krone
6	Römischer Kaiser	7	Rosenterrassen
7	Romberg-Park		

	BUILDINGS AND SIGHTS		
1	Chamber of	7	Post office
	commerce	8	Reinoldikirche
2	Hospital	9	Theatre
3	Marienkirche	10	Tourist information
4	Opera house	11	Westfalenhallen
5	Petrikirche		exhibition centre
6	Police		

Hohensyburg there are buses between noon and midnight. Local *S-Bahn* train services run about every 20min from the Hauptbahnhof to Bochum and Essen; 24hr tickets cover all services. For information ☎ 54343388 or go to the tourist office at Südwall 6.

Area by area
Post-World War II rebuilding is widespread and unremarkable. The heart of the city is the Alter Markt, bounded by the Wall ring road following the old city walls and punctuated by four gates: Westentor, Neutor, Ostentor and Burgtor.

In addition to traffic-free shopping streets, a cross-section of business and city administration is based within or just beyond the Wall. The Union brewery is immediately to the west of the Wall; the other breweries are dotted around the city.

The suburbs Heavy industry is mainly in the north and west around the suburb of Dorstfeld, with small pockets elsewhere, but the overall impression is not one of industry and grime.

There are desirable residential areas bordering attractive parkland throughout the suburbs, especially to the south, towards the hills in Syburg, 15min from the city centre on the Ruhrwaldstrasse.

Hotels
Many of Dortmund's best hotels are in the suburbs, often in rural settings, yet within easy reach of the city centre by car or public transport. Although major exhibitions and other events are held at the Westfalenhallen, there is never a severe shortage of accommodation. All hotels listed offer photocopying, currency exchange and parking.

Drees [DM]|
Hohe Str 107, D1 ☎ *103821/103824* ☎ *822490 • IHA • AE DC MC V • 153 rooms, 5 suites, 1 restaurant, 2 bars*
On a busy road halfway between the Westfalenhallen and the city centre, this modern hotel is unpretentious, practical and comfortable. Rooms overlooking the inner courtyard are quietest. It is linked to the Consul Hotel, with which it shares facilities. Gift shop, newsstand • pool, bowling, sauna, solarium, exercise equipment • 4 meeting rooms (capacity up to 100).

Lennhof [DM]|
Menglinghauser Str 20, D50 (Barop) ☎ *75726* ☎ *822602 • Romantik • AE DC MC V • 38 rooms, 3 suites, 1 restaurant, 1 bar*
The Lennhof is located in restful surroundings, yet industry is close, the centre is 10min away by car, and streetcars run nearby. The 300-year-old, half-timbered farmhouse retains its character despite modernization. The spacious guest rooms all have

safes and minibars. Six-course menus are offered in the restaurant, which provides a peaceful retreat for business meetings. Pool, sauna, solarium, tennis • 2 meeting rooms (capacity up to 30).

Parkhotel Landhaus Syburg [DM]|
Westhofener Str 1, D30 ☎ *774471 or 774476* ☎ *8227534 • HM Hotel-Management Gruppe • AE DC MC V • 60 rooms, 4 suites, 4 restaurants, 1 bar*
This 19thC converted farmhouse, with a large, modern extension, is in quiet countryside at Syburg, about 11km/7 miles from the city centre. In the original building, rooms are large and have an old-world atmosphere; those in the modern wing are plainer. But all are comfortable and have spacious, tiled bathrooms. The country-style restaurant with its tiled floor and open fire is good for relaxation. There is a nightclub and the casino bus stops outside. Pool, bowling, massage, sauna • 3 meeting rooms (capacity up to 80).

Parkhotel Westfalenhalle *DM/*
Strobelallee 41, D1 ☎ 1204230
℡ 822413 • AE DC MC V • 107 rooms,
1 suite, 1 restaurant, 1 bar
Part of the exhibition halls complex,
this modern hotel attracts business
people, top musicians and athletes.
The upper floors overlook an
extensive park, and the stylish rooms
are equipped with a desk unit in
addition to a table. Leisure centre
with pool, gym equipment, sauna
and solarium • fax, 12 meeting
rooms (capacity up to 800).

Parkhotel Wittekindshof *DM/*
Westfalendamm 270, D1 ☎ 596081
℡ 822216 • Top International Hotels
• AE DC MC V • 63 rooms, 2 suites,
2 restaurants, 1 bar
Built only ten years ago, the
Wittekindshof combines old country
character and modern facilities. The
lobby is baronial and bedrooms at the
back overlook pretty gardens, as does
the restaurant, Zum Widukind (see
Restaurants). The hotel is on the busy
Ruhrschnellweg but all rooms are

double-glazed and air-conditioned.
Newsstand, gift shop • sauna,
solarium • 5 meeting rooms
(capacity up to 200).

Römischer Kaiser *DM/*
Olpe 2, D1 ☎ 54321 ℡ 0822441 • AE
DC MC V • 160 rooms, 7 suites,
2 restaurants, 2 bars
Located near the city centre, the
Römischer Kaiser is typically North
German, with heavy dark furnishings
and a large, gloomy lobby. However,
it is well equipped for meetings and is
used as the base for a local business
club. Guest rooms are spacious but
unimaginatively decorated. Local
dishes feature in the restaurant which
is popular for business lunches.
Hairdresser • 9 meeting rooms
(capacity up to 300).

OTHER HOTELS
Romberg-Park *DM/* *Am
Rombergpark 67–69, D50
(Brünninghausen) ☎ 714073.* A
stylish modern hotel in a superb
lakeside setting.

Restaurants

Dortmunder tend to appreciate ample portions of plain home cooking,
but a few restaurants cater more adventurously for the special occasion.
Most hotel restaurants are suitable for business entertaining.

Edo *DM/*
*Westfalendamm 166 ☎ 597915 • D
only • AE DC MC*
Edo is a Japanese hotel offering both
Japanese and European food. The
result is ideal for visitors wanting a
smart, quiet restaurant with a
difference. A choice of three set
menus eases decision-making. A few
Japanese wines are available, with
more promised in the future, and a
range of German wines. Allow at
least two hours for a meal because the
Japanese chefs cook at a central grill
while customers watch.

La Table *DM/||*
*Spielbank Hohensyburg,
Hohensyburgstr 200 ☎ 774444 • D
only • AE DC MC • jacket and tie*

Business people wanting to hit the
high spots do so here, 244 metres up,
on a hill overlooking the Ruhr valley
in part of the new casino complex.
The clientele includes the area's
sophisticated jet set. Prices match the
plush surroundings but the French
food has a high reputation. Fresh fish
is particularly good and there is a
choice of 600 wines, with rarities
such as an 1894 St Emilion.

**Mövenpick Appenzeller-
Stube** *DM/*
*Kleppingstr 9–11 ☎ 579225 • closed
Dec 24 • AE DC MC V*
Not a sophisticated venue, but one
that attracts business customers by its
quality and value for money. It has a
rustic Swiss atmosphere, and seating

is around a central grill in high-sided alcoves which provide privacy. Regulars praise the fresh fish, lamb, and ice-cream sundaes. A range of wines is available by the glass, including several champagnes.

Pfefferkorn *DM*
Hoher Wall 38 ☎ *143644* • *AE DC MC*
This restaurant is in an unprepossessing building on the edge of the Wall but it has a tiled floor and old prints on the walls. Polished wooden tables and chairs set in alcoves provide quiet and privacy. Argentinian beef steaks and the seasonal dishes are recommended.

Zum Widukind *DM*||||
Parkhotel Wittekindshof ☎ *596081*
• *closed Sat* • *AE DC MC V*
Zum Widukind is one of the city's most stylish restaurants. The calm atmosphere, well-spaced tables, and the fact that it is convenient for the city centre, make it very suitable for business negotiations. The menu features lamb and fish.

Good but casual
A visit to one of the local brewery restaurants is a must. *Hövels*, Hoher Wall 5–7 ☎ 141044, is one of the best. The building is new but the atmosphere traditional, with dark wood alcoves, blue and white wall tiles and wooden tables. A big window looks onto a room containing copper vats and other beer-making equipment. Local dishes include plump, home-made sausages and a cutlet on toast with mushrooms. *Krone*, Alter Markt ☎ 527548, overlooks the old market square, and has sections for grills, snacks or cakes. *Rosenterrassen*, Strobelallee ☎ 1204245, serves the exhibition halls and Parkhotel Westfalenhalle.

Bars
Within the Wall, particularly around Olpe, there are many *Bierlokale*, which can be large brewery halls or small inns. Informal and often noisy, they stay open at least until midnight and serve snacks. The hotel bars are the best bet for meeting clients.

Entertainment
Listings appear in the weekly *Dortmunder Bekanntmachungen* and monthly *Blick in die Stadt* and *Blickpunkt*.
Theatre, dance, opera
Performances are staged mid-Sep–mid-Jul at the striking new *Opernhaus*, Hansastr, and adjacent *Schauspielhaus*, Hiltropwall ☎ 144431.
Music *Westfalenhalle* ☎ 12040 is the venue for large celebrity shows. There is an open-air festival in May at the *Alter Markt*.
Casino The new *Spielbank Hohensyburg*, Hohensyburgstr 200 ☎ 77400 offers roulette, blackjack and baccarat from 3pm. The decor is modern.

Shopping
Dortmund is the shopping centre for a wide area and reputed to have the keenest prices in West Germany. The main pedestrianized shopping streets, Westen- and Ostenhellweg, have a choice of six department stores.

Sightseeing
There are few historic buildings but some churches have been extensively restored. In Ostenhellweg are the Romanesque *Marienkirche*, formerly a monastery, with a 15thC carved altarpiece; and the fine 90-metre-high Gothic *Reinoldikirche*. In Westenhellweg, the *Petrikirche*, founded in 799, is the oldest church in Westphalia.
Hohensyburg A pretty, hilly, wooded area overlooking the Ruhr valley and Hengstey lake. Direct bus from the Hauptbahnhof every 30min, 12am–12pm.

Spectator sports
The *Westfalenhallen* complex, off the Ruhrschnellweg, includes ice and roller-skating rinks; the 54,000-seat Westfalenstadion, home of *Borussia*

Dortmund football club; the *Rote Erde* athletics track and facilities for basketball and show jumping. Information ☎ 12040; reservations ☎ 1204666. Horse-racing is at *Galoprennbahn Wambel* ☎ 597044.

Keeping fit

Fitness centres *Revierpark Wischlungen*, Höferstr 12, Dorstfeld ☎ 171994.
Golf *Dortmunder Golf-Club*, Reichsmarkstr ☎ 774133 (bring membership card of your own club).
Ice skating *Westfalenhalle* ☎ 12040.
Jogging The Romberg Park is conveniently near the city centre.
Squash and tennis *Tenniscenter Dortmund*, Bunsen-Kirchoff-Str/Ardeystr ☎ 104401.
Swimming Indoor pool at *Südbad*, Ruhrallee 3 ☎ 54223503. Open-air pool in the *Volkspark*, Schwimmweg 2 ☎ 54228743.

Local resources

Business services

Photocopying and printing Department stores have photocopying facilities. Express services are offered by *Sofortdruck Kordt*, Heiligenweg 17 ☎ 522610 and *Schnelldruck Service*, Rheinischestr 62 ☎ 146237.
Secretarial *Job-Vermittlung des Arbeitsamtes* ☎ 1203650.
Translation *Inlingua* ☎ 149966.

Communications

Local delivery Taxis will deliver.
Long-distance delivery *Kurierdienst*, Bahnhofstr 1 ☎ 1310 operates a national mail service. Train delivery ☎ 140064. International delivery: *DHL*, Beratgerstr 36 (Dortsfeld) ☎ 179711.
Post office Bahnhofstr 1 ☎ 1310.
Telex and fax At above post office.

Conference/exhibition centres

Besides hotel facilities, the main centre is the large municipal *Westfalenhalle*, Rheinlanddamm 200, to the south: five main halls (capacity up to 20,000), and several conference rooms (capacity up to 300) with full technical facilities. Parking for over 1,000 cars. Contact Westfalenhalle, Postfach 1130 ☎ 1204359 (large congresses and fairs) ☎ 1204521 (exhibitions) or ☎ 1204260 (conferences). The casino, *Spielbank Hohensyburg*, Hohensyburgstr 200 ☎ 77400 also has fully-equipped conference rooms for up to 480.

Emergencies

Bureau de change *Noris Bank*, Westenhellweg 108, is open normal shopping hours, including Sat, 9–1.
Hospitals *Städtische Kliniken*, Münsterstr 240 ☎ 84971. Dental and medical emergency services ☎ 435050.
Pharmacies At railway station, open Mon–Sat, 7am–9pm. Each pharmacy gives details of those on duty out of hours.
Police The main station is at Hohe Str 128 ☎ 10801.

Government offices

Local council: *Stadt Dortmund*, Südwall 2–4 ☎ 5421.

Information sources

Business information Chamber of commerce: *Industrie- und Handelskammer*, Märkische Str 120 ☎ 54170; handcrafts association: *Handwerkskammer*, Reinoldistr 7–9 ☎ 54930.
Local media There is good business coverage in the daily *Ruhr Nachrichten* and the *Westdeutsche Allgemeine Zeitung*.
Tourist information Tourist office with accommodation service at *Verkehrspavillon*, Königswall 18 ☎ 54222174, open Mon–Fri, 9–6; Sat, 9–1; also at *Dortmund Information und Presseamt*, Südwall 6 ☎ 54225666, open Mon–Fri, 8–4.

Thank-yous

Florists *Blumen Evels* ☎ 160181 at Hauptbahnhof, open daily.
Wine merchants *Hilgering*, Westenhellweg 114 ☎ 149027.

DÜSSELDORF
City codes zip 4000 ☎ 0211

In 1946 when the British forces occupying northwest Germany amalgamated two states to create North Rhine Westphalia, Düsseldorf became its capital, to the delight of its citizens.

Düsseldorfer like to be a step ahead, in business as in day-to-day living. Appearances matter and it is no coincidence that they are among the most fashion conscious in West Germany; the Königsallee is the country's smartest boulevard for buying and showing off fine clothes. Though lacking the reassurance of a long cultural history like Cologne's, they are proud that their city was the symbol of West Germany's postwar miracle and keen to exploit its convenient location. Though the population is only 650,000, the city is responsible for around 10% of West Germany's foreign trade, enabling its citizens to earn over 20% more than the national average.

The industrial revolution gave Düsseldorf its reputation as the *Schreibtisch* of the Ruhr, the administrative headquarters of Germany's traditionally most productive industrial area; two-thirds of its 350,000-strong workforce are white-collar workers. The city's prosperity has been closely linked with the Ruhr; in the buoyant years of steel and coal output it boomed. Today the unemployment rate is 11%, higher than the national average though lower than that of the Ruhr itself.

Chemicals, machinery, steel tubing and vehicle production are Düsseldorf's major industries, and Daimler-Benz, Henkel, Krupp, Salzgitter and Thyssen all have important centres there. Diversification has helped to cushion the recession in steel. Mannesmann, for instance, is now stronger in electronics than in heavy engineering. In banking and insurance, Düsseldorf trails behind Frankfurt and Cologne, though its commercial and service sectors – advertising and consultancy firms – are significant. Trade fairs, mostly in capital goods, are also big earners.

More than 3,000 foreign companies have an administrative base in the city, twice as many as in Frankfurt, its nearest rival. Most are American, the next most numerous being Dutch and Japanese companies. A DM180m Japan-Center has been built and sales by the 300 different Japanese enterprises, encompassing electronics, engineering and commerce, are valued at DM7bn. The city is now Japan's main European base, and about 6,000 Japanese live there. Significantly, Düsseldorf is actively pursuing links with the Chinese, hoping to become Europe's base for China as well.

Arriving

Düsseldorf is the gateway to north Germany, with its international airport 8km/5 miles south of the city centre. *Autobahnen* from Holland, Belgium and France join the busy German network near the city. Express trains run hourly to other major cities.

Düsseldorf-Lohausen airport
The airport, which handles nearly 10m passengers a year, half of whom are on charter flights, is Germany's third largest for freight. There are over 840 scheduled flights each week, connecting with 76 cities across four continents. The newly built terminal has two wings for scheduled flights

and one for charter. Distances between check-in and boarding are short. There is a bureau de change, open daily, 6.15–10, and a bank, open Mon–Fri, 6–10. Other facilities include post office, florist and hairdresser, conference and banquet rooms, and VIP lounge. Airport information ☎ 421223; freight inquiries ☎ 421551.

City link Train is the quickest transport into town but many business travellers prefer to take a taxi.

Taxi Cabs wait outside the terminal building. There are fixed fares to the city centre (DM16) and for the 5min ride to the NOWEA exhibition grounds (DM10).

Limousine Autohansa and Artus Buchholz have desks in the arrival hall.

Car rental Autohansa, Avis, Europcar, interRent, Hertz and Budget have desks. Only rent a car if you plan to go out of town.

S-Bahn Trains run every 20min to the Hauptbahnhof, journey time 13min, and then on to Solingen-Ohligs (36min).

Bus During fairs the 896 departs at 20min intervals for the NOWEA exhibition grounds 3km/2 miles away.

Railway station

Düsseldorf Hauptbahnhof is on the east side of the city centre, a 15min walk from the main shops and business areas. Intercity services run to some 60 major European cities; these include 13 daily to Amsterdam (2hr 40min), 16 to Brussels (3hr 20min), 14 to Milan (11hr 30min) and 9 to Paris (5hr 50min). Lufthansa operates express services for its passengers to Frankfurt airport (2hr 35min) four times daily. Local commuter *S-Bahn* trains run to 19 stations within the city and throughout the Ruhr area.

The smart, modern station has a large central concourse lined with an impressive array of shops and cafés, a post office, bureau de change, pharmacy, florist and photocopying

service; *interRent* car rental has a desk in the centre of the concourse. Buses and trams leave from the front of the main entrance. Timetable inquiries 6–8.30 ☎ 58228.

Getting around

Walking within the main business and shopping area centred on Königsallee is practical, but elsewhere take a taxi or use public transport which serves the main areas and hotels efficiently.

Taxis White Mercedes taxis can be picked up at the station, airport or NOWEA exhibition grounds and there are numerous ranks in the city centre. Reservations ☎ 33333.

Limousines The main car rental firms offer limousine service. Other companies are *Auto Posern* ☎ 423666 and *Artus Buchholz* ☎ 325040.

Driving Four *Autobahnen* run into the city across the Rhein from the east. There are also two from the north and one from the south. Heavy traffic frequently causes long delays on the bridges at rush hours, 7–8.30 and 4.30–6. Parking can be difficult in the centre, although the city has 48 parking areas, several beside the Rhein, in addition to meters and hotel garages. Car rental firms include *Autohansa* ☎ 325040, *Avis* ☎ 132055, *Budget* ☎ 360401, *Hertz* ☎ 357025, *interRent* ☎ 767261; and sports cars from *Erdmann* ☎ 375827.

Walking While it is easy and safe to find one's way round on foot, distances between different areas of the city can be considerable. The Altstadt is pedestrianized.

Public transport VRR (Verkehrsverbund Rhein-Ruhr) bus, streetcar and *S-Bahn* train services run efficiently between the city centre, suburbs, and the NOWEA exhibition grounds. They link up with Deutsche Bundesbahn train services throughout the Rhein-Ruhr region. Train tickets on the different services are interchangeable. Single bus or streetcar tickets can be bought from drivers, or from ticket offices.

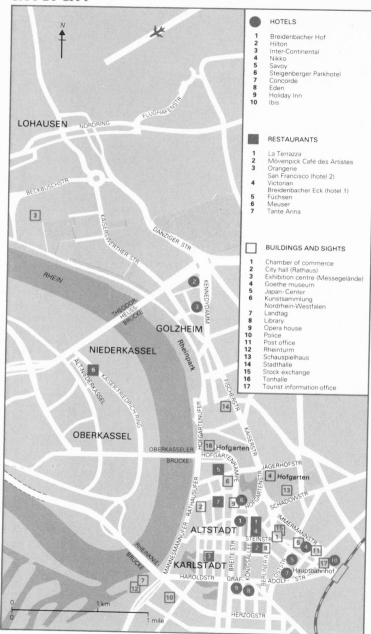

CITY BY CITY

HOTELS
1 Breidenbacher Hof
2 Hilton
3 Inter-Continental
4 Nikko
5 Savoy
6 Steigenberger Parkhotel
7 Concorde
8 Eden
9 Holiday Inn
10 Ibis

RESTAURANTS
1 La Terrazza
2 Mövenpick Café des Artistes
3 Orangerie
  San Francisco (hotel 2)
4 Victorian
  Breidenbacher Eck (hotel 1)
5 Füchsen
6 Meuser
7 Tante Anna

BUILDINGS AND SIGHTS
1 Chamber of commerce
2 City hall (Rathaus)
3 Exhibition centre (Messegelände)
4 Goethe museum
5 Japan-Center
6 Kunstsammlung Nordrhein-Westfalen
7 Landtag
8 Library
9 Opera house
10 Police
11 Post office
12 Rheinturm
13 Schauspielhaus
14 Stadthalle
15 Stock exchange
16 Tonhalle
17 Tourist information office

VRR 24hr passes are good value. Route maps are available from the tourist office opposite the Hauptbahnhof.

Area by area

The city centre is a 3km/2-mile area lying between the Rhein, on the west, and the main railway station. In the middle, Königsallee, the city's most famous boulevard, runs south from the extensive Hofgarten park to Graf-Adolf-Platz. The 200-year-old "Kö," as it is called, is lined with chestnut and plane trees, and smart shops and street cafés. The other main streets run parallel on either side. Postwar rebuilding followed the previous grid pattern of broad straight streets. Some old buildings were restored to their heavy Germanic style but many more were replaced by undistinguished modern buildings in the 1950s. The Thyssen headquarters, a slender mass of glass and concrete overlooking the Hofgarten park, was Germany's first skyscraper. Across the canalized river Düssel, on the western side, are the headquarters of many large companies. The city centre's business quarter is sandwiched behind them in Breite Strasse and Kasernenstrasse. Many banks cluster around Blumenstrasse, behind the Kö, to the east. Japanese businesses are concentrated on Immermannstrasse where the Japan-Center is situated.

The Altstadt, the oldest part of the city, between Heinrich-Heine-Allee and the Rhein, is a quaint pedestrianized area of narrow streets, baroque churches and old houses. It is particularly lively at night, as it is crammed with beer halls, restaurants and jazz cellars.

The suburbs

Almost a third of Düsseldorf's workforce commutes, some travelling as far as 65km/40 miles. Close to the trade fair grounds overlooking the Rhein, Lohausen and Kaiserswerth have remained sought-after residential areas despite the airport's proximity; and Angermund is an exclusive residential area just outside the city, 8km/5 miles north of the airport.

Japanese business people have moved in force into Oberkassel in a loop of the Rhein's west bank, while neighbouring Niederkassel has become a fashionable area for dining out.

In Golzheim, until recently farmland between the city and the airport, high-rise office blocks house insurance, computer and fashion companies.

Heavy industry is concentrated to the east of the main station in Flingern-Süd, Lierenfeld and Gerresheim. There are also large pockets of heavy industry in Derendorf and Rath, to the south and southeast of the airport, as well as on the city's southern borders at Holthausen and Benrath and on the west bank in Heerdt (ceramics).

Hotels

The city is keen to promote itself as a key business centre and has several very well-equipped hotels. Pride of place goes to the Breidenbacher Hof. The big modern hotels run by international chains are farther out, in the more recently developed business districts. The large number of foreign visitors, including many Japanese, helps to keep standards of service and prices high, especially during major trade fairs when it is essential to make reservations well in advance. The tourist office ☎ 350505 has a computer reservations service. Bedrooms usually have an IDD telephone, a minibar and multichannel TV. Most hotels offer secretarial and other office facilities. The main recommendations below have 24hr room service and parking space.

Breidenbacher Hof [DM]||||
Heinrich-Heine-Allee 36, D1 ☎ 8601
TX 8582630 • Regent International •
AE DC MC V • 140 rooms, 20 suites,
2 restaurants, 1 bar
Düsseldorf's oldest and most elegant
hotel, right in the city centre, in the
banking district, was family-run until
1985 but is now part of the Regent
International group. The large,
thickly carpeted lobby and bar-
lounge are furnished with antiques
and oil paintings, and uniformed
staff are on hand to attend to the
needs of guests, most of whom are
business people. Rooms are
individually decorated in lavish style,
with gold-leaf fittings as well as
practical details like good lighting
and spacious worktops. Airport
limousine service • 6 meeting rooms
(capacity up to 90).

Hilton [DM]||||
Georg-Glock-Str 20, D30 ☎ 43770
TX 8584376 • AE DC MC V • 376
rooms, 18 suites, 2 restaurants, 2 bars
This is the city's largest hotel, built
in 1970 and now surrounded by high-
rise office blocks. Its lobby buzzes
with business executives and show-
business personalities, and middle-
eastern royalty make frequent use of
the top-floor suites, one of which has
a grand piano. All bedrooms are air-
conditioned and have recently been
renovated. One floor is reserved for
nonsmokers. The San Francisco (see
Restaurants) is one of Düsseldorf's
leading restaurants. Shops • pool,
sauna, solarium, massage • in-house
secretaries and translators, extra
telephone lines available, 24hr
courier, Reuters service, fax, 14
meeting rooms including the 1,500-
seat Rheinlandsaal.

Inter-Continental [DM]||||
Karl-Arnold-Pl 5, D30 ☎ 45530
TX 8584601 • AE DC MC V • 290
rooms, 20 suites, 2 restaurants, 1 bar
Like the neighbouring Hilton, the
Inter-Continental is modern and
international in style, catering mainly
to business people visiting or working

in the immediate area. The new Les
Continents restaurant, with side
rooms available for small groups, is
eminently suitable for working meals,
with three- or four-course executive
menus at lunch time. The smart,
long lobby area, divided into sections,
is a useful meeting point and has
news and share-price monitors, as
does the adjoining pleasant Café de la
Paix. Hairdresser, gift shop,
newsstand, Lufthansa check-in
• pool, jacuzzi, gym, massage, sauna,
solarium • fax, 11 meeting rooms
(capacity up to 400).

Nikko [DM]||||
Immermannstr 41, D1 ☎ 8661
TX 8582080 • AE DC MC V • 285
rooms, 16 suites (3 Japanese-style),
2 restaurants, 1 bar
This modern luxury hotel is in the
district where many Japanese
companies have established their
offices. Standards of service are high
and there is a comprehensive range of
business facilities including news and
share-price monitors in the large
lobby area. There is an executive
floor and 10 rooms are reserved for
nonsmokers; the Japanese-style suites
have futon beds. The Benkay
restaurant has Japanese rooms where
diners sit on the floor, as well as
Western seating and set menus.
Hairdresser, gift shop, fashion
boutique, newsstand • pool, exercise
equipment, 2 saunas, solarium,
jacuzzi, Japanese massage • fax,
7 meeting rooms (capacity up to 700)
with simultaneous translation.

Savoy [DM]|||
Oststr 128, D1 ☎ 360336 TX 8584215
• AE DC MC V • Günnewig • 123
rooms, 1 suite, 1 restaurant, 1 bar
The centrally situated Savoy appeals
to those who demand high standards
of accommodation but prefer a
smaller, more individual hotel. Its
guest rooms have considerable charm
and the comfortable bar area is very
suitable for informal business
meetings. Another useful rendezvous
is the hotel's Konditorei-café, next

door. Newsstand • pool, gym, sauna, massage, solarium • fax, 4 meeting rooms (capacity up to 150).

Steigenberger Parkhotel [DM]||| *Corneliuspl 1, D1* ☎ *8651* ⒯⒳ *8582331* • *AE DC MC V* • *147 rooms, 13 suites, 1 restaurant, 1 bar*
The Parkhotel overlooks the wooded Hofgarten and is one of the city's finest old buildings. It offers an efficient, willing service that business visitors clearly appreciate. Bedrooms and extensive lounge areas were restored to their turn-of-the-century glory after World War II damage and are furnished in period. Rooms have cable TV; some also have safes and trouser presses. Suites have large drawing rooms, which are ideal for private conferences, and a second telephone in the bathrooms. Staff will arrange for the services of secretaries and interpreters or the despatch of

packages. Fax, 10 meeting rooms (capacity up to 150).

OTHER HOTELS
Concorde [DM]| *Graf-Adolf-Str 60, D1* ☎ *369825* ⒯⒳ *8588008* • *Rema* • *no credit cards.* Small hotel with well-equipped rooms.
Eden [DM]| *Adersstr 29–31, D1* ☎ *381060* ⒯⒳ *8582530* • *Best Western* • *AE DC MC V.* Situated close to the Kö, with newly renovated rooms and conference facilities.
Holiday Inn [DM]||| *Graf-Adolf-Pl 10, D1* ☎ *38730* ⒯⒳ *8586359* • *AE DC MC V.* At the end of the Kö, with the usual Holiday Inn facilities, including a pool, exercise equipment and good conference services.
Ibis [DM]| *Konrad-Adenauer-Pl 14, D1* ☎ *16720* ⒯⒳ *8588913* • *AE DC MC V.* No-frills accommodation in part of the main station building; rooms overlook a quiet courtyard.

Restaurants

It is fashionable to dine on *nouvelle cuisine* in up-to-the-minute surroundings, but many local business people prefer heartier indigenous dishes such as *Schweinshaxe,* knuckle of pork, *Sauerbraten,* a beef dish with a piquant sauce, or cabbage with *Mettwurst* – a local sausage – served in unpretentious beer hall restaurants. Few of the Altstadt's many restaurants are suitable for business entertaining. The main hotel restaurants are a safe choice and those on Königsallee usually reliable and more lively. Reservations are strongly advised, especially during trade fairs.

La Terrazza [DM]|| *Königsallee 30* ☎ *327540* • *closed Sun and hols* • *AE DC MC V* • *jacket and tie*
Well-spaced tables and an airy atmosphere with trailing plants, white wicker chairs on a black-and-white tiled floor and picture windows which overlook the Kö all help to make La Terrazza a favourite with business people. Italian food with an emphasis on regional and fish dishes.

Mövenpick Café des Artistes [DM]|| *Kö-Galerie, Steinstr 13* ☎ *320314* • *AE DC MC V*
The glittering modern Kö-Galerie, which contains several restaurants, is spread over two hexagonal floors decked with palms and linked by a striking perspex elevator. In a quiet corner on the lower floor is the Café des Artistes, which is popular with both local business people and shoppers. Good-value French menus with an Italian influence change every day depending on what is available at market, and the wine list is impressive.

> For general information about tipping in restaurants, see the *Planning and Reference* section.

Orangerie [DM]||||
*Bilker Str 30 ☎ 131828 • closed Sun
except during fairs • AE DC • jacket
and tie*
Serving classic *haute cuisine* in
commensurately rich surroundings,
the Orangerie is the place to be seen,
particularly during fashion fairs. It
attracts jet-setters and successful
business people out for a celebratory
evening. The recommended six-
course menu changes every day.
Special dishes include celery soup
with gorgonzola, lobster on vegetable
purée and poached veal with chervil
potatoes. Less expensive menus and *à
la carte* dishes are offered in the
Bistro section.

San Francisco [DM]||||
*Hilton hotel ☎ 43770 • AE DC MC V
• jacket and tie*
This restaurant is much used for
business entertaining by executives
from the nearby offices of
international corporations such as
IBM. The cuisine is American; prime
rib, imported direct from the USA
and carved on the trolley, is a popular
choice. Four-course lunches
including wine are particularly good
value.

Victorian [DM]||||
*Königstr 3a ☎ 320222 • closed Sun
and hols • AE DC MC V • formal
dress*
Günter Scherrer, one of Germany's
leading chefs, created the Victorian
in 1984 to meet the needs of business
people: quality cuisine at the right
price, an impressive wine list,
efficient service and quiet
surroundings. The upstairs Salon,
discreet in sober Victorian style,
offers a menu featuring German and
French dishes, with the emphasis on
nouvelle cuisine. A private room is
available and at lunch there is a
fixed-price three-course menu.
Downstairs there is a less formal
Lounge restaurant. If entertaining
important clients, be sure to specify
the Salon when making your
reservation.

Good but casual
The ambience and view from the café
restaurants along the Kö make them
very suitable for informal business
lunches. The *Breidenbacher Eck*,
Heinrich-Heine-Allee 36 ☎ 8601, is
as popular with executives working in
the neighbourhood as with opera-
goers in the evening. Its alcove
seating is informal but private.
Füchsen, Ratingerstr 28 ☎ 84062 is a
typical brewery beer hall with rows
of long, unvarnished wood tables and
tiled walls. *Meuser*, Alt-Niederkassel 75
☎ 51572, is an old country inn on
the fashionable west bank specializing
in *Speckpfannkuchen* (bacon
pancakes). *Tante Anna*, Andreasstr 2
☎ 131163, is the city's oldest wine-
cellar; straightforward Continental
food and beer as well as wine are
available until 3am.

Bars
The local beer is *Altbier*, a strong,
dark-brown brew with a malty
flavour, often served straight from
the barrel. It is drunk in large beer
halls, with stone floors and rows of
bare ashwood tables. They are
frequented by both managers and
workers, equally attracted by a love
of good beer. In the Altstadt,
nicknamed the "world's longest bar
counter," over 200 brewery bars,
restaurants, cafés and discos are
concentrated in a square kilometre
with not a strip club in sight. In
summer large numbers of tourists
join the regulars.
    The cocktail bars along the Kö are
much more sophisticated than those
in the Altstadt. Bankers mingle with
journalists at *NT*, short for
Nachtrichten Treff, beside newspaper
offices at Königsallee 77; electronic
news displays flash overhead and
newspapers are provided.

Entertainment
Düsseldorf's main cultural reputation
is for painting and sculpture but
its opera and music also attract
audiences from outside the city.
The Altstadt provides informal

Carnival
Hundreds of fancy-dress balls and other lively events take place in the weeks preceding Lent. During the last six days of the carnival season, colourful parades of decorated floats take over the streets. The main one, the Rosenmontag (Rose Monday) procession, is over 3km/2 miles long. Spectators watch from large stands erected along the route and also spend a lot of time on the streets, dancing and singing in fancy dress. Sweets and other small gifts are showered from the floats. Very little serious business is done during these few days. Most offices, shops and schools are closed on Rose Monday.

---

entertainment and the nightclubs around Königsallee a more sophisticated variety.

Listings appear in the monthly *Düsseldorfer Hefte*, available from newsstands, TOP *Tips* and *Düsseldorf-Führer*, available free at hotels, and in the daily newspapers. Information ☎ 11516. Opera and concert performances tend to get sold out well in advance, but the tourist office ☎ 350505 has a special allocation.

Theatre, dance, opera The *Deutsche Oper am Rhein*, Heinrich-Heine-Allee 16 ☎ 370981, has a combined Düsseldorf/Duisburg repertory company performing a wide-ranging programme (Sep–Jun), including ballet. The *Düsseldorfer Schauspielhaus*, Gustaf-Gründgens-Pl 1 ☎ 363011, has large and small theatres staging classic and modern plays. *Kom(m)ödchen*, in the Kunsthalle, Hunsrückenstr ☎ 325428, is famous for its political cabaret but a good knowledge of German is essential.

Music There are 20 concerts a month (Sep–mid-Jun), in the acoustically excellent *Tonhalle*, Ehrenhof 1 ☎ 8996123, beside the Rhein. The Düsseldorfer Symphoniker performs regularly, and leading

international orchestras on occasion. Classical concerts also take place in the *Robert-Schumann-Saal*, Ehrenhof 4a ☎ 8993829, and rock concerts in the *Philips-Halle*, Siegburger Str 15 ☎ 8993679, which seats up to 6,000.

Nightclubs The smartest nightclubs are in the Königsallee area and include *Chequers Club* at no. 28 ☎ 327521 with a cabaret, and *Sams West* at no. 27 ☎ 328171.

Shopping
Düsseldorf's claim to be the smartest, most fashionable city in West Germany is reflected in its shops. The east side of Königsallee is lined with exclusive fashion shops and jewellers, antique and bookshops. Several chic new shopping arcades lead off on either side, such as the Kö-Galerie and Trinkhaus Galerie.

Along Schadowstrasse are the largest department stores and as many as 20 shoe shops. There is also a compact new shopping precinct, Garsch-Hans, under the Heinrich-Heine-Allee.

Sightseeing
In addition to glamorous Königsallee (see above), the other main area which should be explored on foot is the Altstadt. The city has a long tradition as a major art centre. Many leading artists and sculptors have taught at its art academy. Special exhibitions are staged regularly in the *Städtische Kunsthalle*, Grabbepl 4 ☎ 8991 and also in the many smaller galleries, particularly around Bilker Strasse in the Altstadt.

Goethe Museum Devoted to Goethe and his time, featuring the writer's original manuscripts. *Jägerhof Str l. Open Tue–Sun, 10–5 (Sat, 1–5)*.

Hofgarten At the end of the Kö, a huge park with ornamental gardens and fountains. Most of the city's art galleries are around it.

Kunstsammlung Nordrhein-Westfalen State art collection, with a fine selection of modern paintings, notably works by Paul Klee but also

Pablo Picasso, Georges Braque and Marc Chagall. *Grabbepl. Open Tue–Sun, 10–5 (Wed, 10–8)*.
Rheinturm Just by the Rhein and the parliament buildings, this new telecommunications tower has a 234-metre high viewing platform, revolving restaurant and the world's largest decimal clock. *Stromstr 20. Open daily, 10–midnight*.
Schloss Benrath This 200-year-old castle has recently been magnificently restored. It is 12min by streetcar 701 from Jan-Wellem-Pl. *Benrather Schlossallee 104. Open Tue–Sun, 10–5.*

Guided tours
Bus tours depart daily at 2.30 mid-Apr–mid-Oct (otherwise Sat only) from Friedrich-Ebert-Str, opposite the Hauptbahnhof. The 2hr 30min tour includes a visit to the Rheinturm and a boat trip. Reservations at the tourist office ☏ 350505.

Out of town
The hilly countryside of *Bergisches Land* about 29km/18 miles to the southeast is dotted with half-timbered houses, country inns, picturesque churches and castles. Near Solingen, *Schloss Burg* ☏ (0212) 42098 is a medieval castle with fine views over the Wupper valley and a collection of antique furniture and weapons. *Neandertal*, the valley where prehistoric human remains were found, lies 18km/11 miles east of the city; museum ☏ (02104) 31149.

Spectator sports
Horse-racing The *Grafenberg* racecourse, 5km/3 miles out, has weekly meetings May–Oct ☏ 353666.
Ice hockey Federal League matches every week at the *Eisstadion Düsseldorf*, Brehmstr 27 ☏ 627101.
Soccer and football The home soccer team, Fortuna, plays at the *Rheinstadion*, Europapl 4 ☏ 8995216. There is a strong following here for the Panthers American football team.
Tennis Exhibition matches at the *Rochus Club*, Rolander Weg 15 ☏ 623676.

Keeping fit
Details of sports facilities are available from *Sportamt* ☏ 8995204. A useful leaflet is *Tips für Freizeit-Sportler* from the tourist office.
Fitness centres The newest and most luxurious centre is the *Kö-thermen*, inside the Kö-Galerie, Königsallee 80 ☏ 139950, which even has a jogging track. Others include the *Olymp-Fitness-Center*, Tempelforterstr 47 ☏ 354664, and the *Business-Communication-Club*, Graf-Adolf-Str 92 ☏ 353229, which has gym equipment, sauna and squash courts.
Golf West Germany's only public course (two 9-hole rounds) is *Golfplatz Lausward*, Auf der Lausward ☏ 396617; season Mar–Nov.
Ice skating *Eisstadion Düsseldorf*, Brehmstr 27 ☏ 627101.
Swimming *Wellenbad Stadtmitte* indoor pool is at Grünstr 15 ☏ 8216413. The Nikko and Savoy hotel pools are open to nonresidents.
Tennis Reservations for public courts at the *Freizeitpark*, Ulenbergstr ll ☏ 152520 and (summer only) the *Rheinstadion* ☏ 8995216.

Local resources
Business services
Photocopying Available at department stores and the Hauptbahnhof.
Printing *Druckerei Vialon*, Ronsdorfer Str 11 ☏ 7336139.
Secretarial *Arbeitsamt Düsseldorf*, Fritz-Roeber-Str 2 ☏ 8226513.
Translation *Messmer*, Hüttenstr 6 ☏ 379839. Also *Arbeitsamt Düsseldorf* ☏ 8226513.

Communications
Local delivery Taxis will deliver.
Long-distance delivery *City Cars Courier* ☏ 334471; *DHL* ☏ 49080 or 474081; *Postkurierdienst* at the main post office ☏ 19619 and *IC Kurierdienst* at the Hauptbahnhof ☏ 3680524. Also *Federal Express*, Wanheimer Str 61 ☏ 424632.

Post offices Main post office:
Immermannstr 51 ☎ 1630.
Telex and fax At main post office.

Conference/exhibition centres

Thirty major trade fairs attracting
nearly 22,000 exhibitors, over half
from abroad, take place each year in
Düsseldorf. They include four
international fashion fairs (IGEDO),
and those for footwear and catering.
The boat show and DRUPA (printing
and paper) are both the world's
largest.

The Düsseldorf trade fair
organization, *NOWEA*, Stockumer
Kirchstr ☎ 45601 or 4560555 (press
and information) has 15
interconnected halls with a total of
155,300 sq metres of exhibition space,
plus another 58,000 sq metres
outdoors. The connected exhibition
congress centre (*MKC*), between the
city and the airport, includes
conference rooms for up to 1,200. All
have simultaneous translation
facilities (6 languages) and video
transmission.

The numerous other conference
venues include the *Stadthalle*,
Fischerstr 20 ☎ 8993806, *Philips-
Halle*, Siegburger Str 15 ☎ 8993679
and the *Palais Wittgenstein*, Bilker Str
7–9 ☎ 89995781. The *Hilton* has the
biggest hotel conference complex.

Emergencies

Bureaux de change At the airport,
open daily 6.30–10, and at the
Hauptbahnhof, open daily 7.30–8.
Hospitals Emergencies ☎ 3888989.
24hr emergency *Städtische
Krankenanstatten*, Gräulinger Str 120
☎ 28001.
Pharmacies At the Hauptbahnhof,
open Mon–Fri, 8–9; Sat, 8–2. The
address of the nearest duty pharmacy
is posted up at other times.
Police Main station: Jürgenspl 5
☎ 8701.

Government offices

*Landesregierung des Landes Nordrhein-
Westfalen* (state government),
Haroldstr 2 ☎ 83701. The

Bezirksregierung (district government
offices) are at Cecilienallee 2
☎ 49771.

Information sources

Business information *Industrie-
und Handelskammer zu Düsseldorf*
(chamber of commerce), Ernst-
Schneider-Pl ☎ 35571. Stock
exchange: *Rheinisch-Westfälische
Börse*, Ernst-Schneider-Pl 1 ☎ 8621.
Central library: *Bücherei Stadtmitte*,
Bertha-von-Suttner-Pl ☎ 8994399.
Useful business listings appear in the
sales guide available free from the
Werbeamt, Mühlenstr 29 ☎ 8993864.
The editorial offices of *Handelsblatt*,
the leading business daily, are at
Kasernenstr 67.
Local media The serious-minded,
daily *Rheinische Post* carries extensive
national and local business coverage.
Tourist information
Verkehrsverein der Stadt Düsseldorf,
Konrad-Adenauer-Pl ☎ 350505,
opposite the Hauptbahnhof (open
Mon–Fri, 8–6, Sat, 8–1; closed Sun
and hols). Accommodation and
information office at Hauptbahnhof
(open Mon–Sat, 10–10; Sun, 4–10).

Thank-yous

Confectionery *Walter Cordes*, Im
Kö-Karree, Königsallee 58 ☎ 80246.
Florists Numerous shops in every
district. There is one at the
Hauptbahnhof, open 8–10; and
Blumen Muschkau is at the airport as
well as at Berliner Allee 48 ☎ 371702.
Gifts *Hella B*, Hohe Str 46
☎ 132626; and from several shops in
the Garsch-Hans basement,
Heinrich-Heine-Allee.

ESSEN

City codes zip 4300 ☎ 0201

West Germany's fifth largest city, with a population of 620,000, is having to come to terms with the decline in heavy industry and the need to diversify. Essen's coal and iron ore mines helped fuel Germany's industrial revolution and the Krupp company, founded in 1811, played a key role in the city's emergence as an industrial centre. Later, as a manufacturer of armaments, Krupp was central to Hitler's war plans. Today it no longer makes arms but is still one of the largest engineering companies in West Germany.

The city is West Germany's most important energy centre, distributing coal, water and nuclear-generated power throughout Europe, through RWE (Europe's largest electricity corporation), Ruhrgas and Ruhrkohle. But Essen's coal mines have closed, steel production has been severely hit and unemployment is 5% higher than the national average. The whole Ruhr area is similarly affected as its industries are interdependent in both materials and labour.

To offset mine closures, Essen council is actively promoting new technology, and a number of small enterprises, particularly in electronics, are joining established giants like Krupp, Thyssen, Hochtief, AEG, Ruhr Glass and Siemens. Research and development are backed by the expertise of the university, an institute for mining research and a power industry training centre. Twenty-five years ago, 60% of the workforce were in blue-collar production jobs and 40% in offices. Today the figures are reversed. Eleven of West Germany's 100 biggest companies have their headquarters in the city. They include Karstadt department stores and publishers Axel Springer.

The area has always accepted large numbers of "outsiders" from the rest of Germany and Eastern Europe during boom years, and trade fairs, particularly engineering and motor shows, now attract 1.7m visitors annually from 70 countries.

Arriving

Essen is served by three *Autobahnen*, one of which sweeps right across the city centre. Düsseldorf Rhein-Ruhr airport is a 30min drive away and there is a half-hourly bus service from the airport to Essen Hauptbahnhof. (By local *S-Bahn* train it takes about 45min, changing at either Düsseldorf Hauptbahnhof or at Unterrath.) Rail connections are excellent.

Railway station

Essen Hauptbahnhof, a modern station in the city centre, has direct express links with many European cities. *S-Bahn* commuter trains serve the Ruhr area including Düsseldorf, Mülheim and Dortmund every 20min. The station has a bureau de change (open Mon–Fri, 7.30–7; Sat, 7.30–5; Sun, 10–1), shopping arcades and a Hertz car rental desk. There are always taxis at ranks outside, and subway (*U-Bahn*) and bus connections are good. Timetable inquiries ☎ 7997421–3.

Getting around

The city centre is easily manageable on foot but the suburbs are spread out. They are well served by public transport but it is much quicker to get to them by car.

Taxis White Mercedes taxis are

HOTELS

1 Bredeney
2 Essener Hof
3 Handleshof
4 Sheraton
5 Arcade
6 Schloss Hugenpoet

RESTAURANTS

1 Au Premier (hotel 3)
  Saalbau
  Schloss Hugenpoet (hotel 6)
2 Walliser Stuben
  Bauern Stube (hotel 2)
  Bisou de Mer (hotel 1)
  Pfanne (hotel 1)
3 Maredo

BUILDINGS AND SIGHTS

1 Chamber of commerce
2 City hall
3 Folkwang Museum
4 Grugahalle exhibition centre
5 Hospital
6 Library
7 Münster
8 Opera house
9 Police
10 Post office
11 Saalbau conference centre & theatre
12 Tourist information

available at the Hauptbahnhof and in ranks in the city centre, including one at the opera. Reservations ☎ 667066.

Limousines Hertz ☎ 233066.

Driving The *Autobahn* network can be joined on the east-west Ruhrschnellweg (A430), the Haeseler Strasse (A52) 3km/2 miles to the south or the Emscherschnellweg (A42) 6.5km/4 miles to the north. There are plenty of parking spaces in the inner city. A car is an advantage for business visits beyond the centre but the *Autobahnen* and city-centre

roads are busy during rush hours, 7–8.30 and 4.30–6. The Gruga trade fair grounds, 4km/2.5 miles from the city centre, are an easy 20min *Autobahn* drive from Düsseldorf airport. Car rental from *Avis* ☎ 233911, *Europcar* ☎ 707064 or 707067, *Hertz* ☎ 233066, *interRent* ☎ 20851 or *top-cars Essen* ☎ 233333.

Walking Much of the city centre, encircled by a main ring road, is pedestrianized.

Public transport Buses, streetcars and a subway (*U-Bahn*) converge at the main station. Tickets are interchangeable and can be bought either from machines or on board. The Gruga trade fair grounds are 10min from the main station by *U-Bahn*. Local *S-Bahn* trains run every 20min to other Ruhr towns. Maps are available from the tourist office.

Area by area

Essen rises nearly 90 metres above the flat industrial North German plain. To the south are wooded hills through which the broad valley of the river Ruhr runs westwards. Despite the city's industry, there are extensive woodlands and parks and in the industrial zones to the north "green belt" areas are being created. The suburbs, which were once individual small towns and villages, have retained their separate characters, so there are marked

contrasts between old and new, industrial areas and countryside.

The rebuilt city centre has wide pedestrianized streets lined mainly by blocks of shops and offices. The heaviest industry lies to the north among redundant mines, but is broken up by the "green" working-class areas of Borbeck, Steele and Katernberg which were redeveloped after extensive war damage.

The banking and insurance areas have grown up in the modern Südviertel area immediately south of the city centre. The Gruga trade fair grounds are nearby, adjoining the lovely Gruga Park. Margarethenhöhe to the west is a particularly pleasant residential area. Another much sought-after district to the southeast is the Stadtwald, convenient for both the city centre and Lake Baldeney.

Hotels

Essen's main hotels are grouped around the Hauptbahnhof and during trade fairs are very busy. But there are many smaller hotels in the suburbs, often in rural surroundings and easily accessible by car. Telex and currency exchange are standard facilities and rooms have IDD telephone, TV and minibar. Normally, parking is no problem.

The tourist office at the Hauptbahnhof runs an accommodation reservations service.

Bredeney   *DM*//
Theodor-Althoff-Str 5, E1 ☎ *7690*
TX *857597* • *Scandic* • *AE DC MC V*
• *290 rooms, 10 suites, 3 restaurants, 2 bars*
This quiet modern hotel stands in its own large grounds, within a few hundred metres of the A52 *Autobahn* to Düsseldorf, and the Gruga fair grounds are a 10min bus ride away. The offices of IBM and Karstadt adjoin it. The spacious mirrored lobby with armchairs and low tables is smart and practical for informal meetings. Rooms are similarly stylish; eight, furnished in white with pink carpets, are set aside for women executives and 24 rooms are reserved for nonsmokers. The buffet breakfast includes a health food selection. 24hr room service, newsstand • pool,

massage, solarium, sauna, exercise equipment, bowling alley • fax, 11 meeting rooms (capacity up to 750).

Essener Hof   *DM*/
Teichstr 2, E1 ☎ *20901* TX *8579582*
• *VCH* • *AE DC MC V* • *130 rooms, 2 suites, 1 restaurant, 1 bar*
The Essener Hof, opposite the Hauptbahnhof, was Essen's first hotel, dating from 1883. The emphasis reflects the "caring hospitality" motto of VCH hotels, a Christian association which is Germany's oldest hotel chain. Rooms are comfortable, with good lighting and adequate desk-top space. Those overlooking the central courtyard are quietest. Room service is available until 11pm only. 5 meeting rooms (capacity up to 100).

Handelshof [DM]|
Am Hauptbahnhof 2, E1 ☎ *17080*
ⓉⓍ *857562 • Mövenpick • AE DC MC V*
• 190 rooms, 5 suites, 2 restaurants,
1 bar
The Handelshof Mövenpick is at the
hub of the city centre, opposite the
Hauptbahnhof. It was constructed in
1912, rebuilt after war damage and is
designated a historic building. All the
rooms have been refurbished since
1982, and have cable TV; those at the
back are larger and quieter. There are
21 nonsmoking rooms. No room
service • fax, 4 meeting rooms
(capacity up to 150).

Sheraton [DM]|||
Huyssenallee 55, E1 ☎ *20951*
ⓉⓍ *8571266 • AE DC MC V • 193*
rooms, 12 suites, 1 restaurant, 1 bar
The Sheraton is an imposing six-
floor, modern, mirrored building
overlooking the city park, beside the
Saalbau conference centre, only a
5min walk from the city centre and

the same by *U-Bahn* to the Gruga
fair grounds. Rooms are similar in
layout and decor, with king-size
beds, large windows and plenty of
well-lit working space. Top-floor
rooms at the back have the best
views; all have video. The Park-Suite
is suitable for small seminars. 24hr
room service, hairdresser, gift shop,
newsstand • pool, sauna, solarium,
massage, exercise equipment • fax,
3 meeting rooms (capacity up to
100).

OTHER HOTELS
Arcade [DM]| *Hollestr 50, E1*
☎ *24280* ⓉⓍ *8571133 • Pullman • MC*
V. Near the main station and offering
cheerful, no-frills good value.
Schloss Hugenpoet [DM]||
August-Thyssen-Str 51, E18
☎ *(02054) 6054 • gast im schloss • AE*
DC MC. A 300-year-old moated castle
in the Ruhr valley near Kettwig. One
of Germany's leading small hotels, it
has just 33 beds.

Restaurants

The safest choice for business entertaining is a hotel restaurant near the
city centre or Gruga fair grounds. Many serve simple Ruhr dishes, often
based on the local variety of sausages, as well as international menus.
Within a 15min drive of the city centre, there are numerous small
restaurants in rural surroundings, such as the Ange d'Or in Kettwig and
the Schwarze Lene overlooking Lake Baldeney. During trade fairs it is
advisable to make reservations.

Au Premier [DM]
Handelshof hotel, Am Hauptbahnhof 2
☎ *1708111 • AE DC MC V*
Au Premier's light, airy atmosphere
makes it very suitable for business
entertaining and a side room is
available for small groups. The beef is
outstanding and the menu also
features Swiss dishes such as veal
fillet with scampi, and a large
selection of Swiss wines.

Saalbau [DM]
Huyssenallee 53 ☎ *221866 • AE*
DC MC
The Saalbau, as part of the
conference centre, is convenient for

business lunches. Window tables in
separate alcoves overlook the city
park. The catering features Ruhr
dishes of plump sausages such as
Dicke Bohnen mit Mettwurst and
Blutwurst mit Apfel. There are also
seasonal choices such as Matjes
herrings.

Schloss Hugenpoet [DM]||||
August-Thyssen-Str 51 ☎ *(02054)*
6054 • AE DC MC V • jacket and tie; no
pipes
If you want to pull out all the stops,
there is no better place than this
elegant restaurant in superb
surroundings (see *Hotels*). It

serves classic French cuisine, accompanied by an impressive wine list. Discreet, attentive service.

Walliser Stuben   *DM*/
Arosa hotel, Rüttenscheider Str 149
☎ *72280* • *AE DC MC V*
Dark wood, rustic decor and a central serving area in Swiss style create a relaxed atmosphere. Tables in alcoves are ideal for private discussions. Two separate rooms are available for groups of up to 30. Grills and Swiss dishes are recommended.

Good but casual
Bauern Stube, Essener Hof hotel, Teichstr 2 ☎ 20901, is a traditional restaurant serving local dishes and beer from the barrel: it is open evenings only. The Bredeney hotel, Theodor-Althoff-Str 5 ☎ 714081, has two smart but unpretentious restaurants, the *Bisou de Mer* for fish and the *Rôtisserie Pfanne* for duck. *Maredo*, Kapuzinergasse 2 ☎ 227822, is a city-centre steak restaurant serving top-quality meat with salad.

Bars
Hotel bars are the best place for meeting a business client. For relaxing over a beer, bars throughout the city centre and suburbs are lively, often until the early hours. Rüttenscheider Strasse is popular for discos, as well as having a good selection of *Kneipen* (bars).

Entertainment
Essen has a professional symphony orchestra and opera company, as well as over 100 amateur choirs.
Theatre, dance, opera Opera, ballet and musicals are performed at the *Opernhaus/Grillobau* Am Theaterpl, and plays at the new *Stadt Theater*, designed by Alvar Aalto and opened in 1988. The *Rathaus-Theater* in the city hall, the *Casa Nova* centre and *Humboldt* hall are also used for performances. Tickets for all these venues ☎ 882828, 884216 or 884271.

Music The Essener Philharmonie orchestra, which performs at the *Saalbau* conference centre and the *Opernhaus*, has an international reputation. Programme information ☎ 882233. The Folkwang Kammer Orchester gives concerts at the *Villa Hügel* ☎ 49030. Rock concerts and musical spectaculars are staged in the *Grugahall* in Gruga Park ☎ 7244291.

Shopping
Essen is a major shopping centre, the main streets being Kettwiger Strasse, Viehofer Strasse and Limbecker Strasse. They are broad, straight and traffic-free and have open-air cafés.

Sightseeing
Much of the city, rebuilt since World War II, is unremarkable, but the old quarters in suburbs such as Werden and Kettwig have half-timbered houses and pretty market squares. In Werden, the *Luciuskirche* is the oldest parish church in Northern Europe (begun 995). *Lake Baldeney* is a particularly pleasant area for excursions. A tourist pass, DM7, available May–Sep, gives reduced admission to places of interest.
Münsterschatz The minster is famous for its Romanesque gold treasures including the Golden Madonna. *Burgpl. Open Tue–Sun, 10–4*.
Museum Folkwang Modern art gallery with an excellent collection, including works by Auguste Renoir and Paul Gauguin. *Bismarckstr 64–66. Open Tue–Sun, 10–6 (Wed, 10–8)*.
Villa Hügel Former home of the Krupp family, built in 1862 in extensive wooded grounds near Lake Baldeney, and now a cultural centre. Art exhibitions and concerts are held there. *Haraldstr, Bredeney. Open Tue–Sun, 10–6*.

Spectator sports
Ice hockey Matches at the *Eissporthalle*, Curtiusstr ☎ 744085.
Sailing International watersports events take place at *Lake Baldeney*. Information from the city public

relations office (*Werbe- und Verkehrsamt*) ☎ 882300.
Soccer Schwarz Weiss Essen plays at *Uhlenkrug stadium*, Am Uhlenkrug in Rüttenscheid ☎ 41161. Rot Weiss Essen plays at *Georg-Melches-Stadion*, Hafenstr in Borbeck ☎ 669660.

Keeping fit

Information on all sports and fitness facilities: *Sportbüro* ☎ 882958. The Gruga Park, Rüttenscheid ☎ 887807, is popular with joggers and has public tennis courts.
Fitness centres Nonresidents can use the *Sheraton* and *Bredeney* hotels' pools and fitness clubs. Also *Thumulla Fitness Center*, Planckstr 58 ☎ 777070.
Swimming *Hauptbad*, Steeler Str 38, and a pool in the *Gildehof Center* by the Hauptbahnhof ☎ 883823.
Tennis and squash *Tennis u. Squash Park*, Schürmannstr 15 ☎ 255871.
Watersports Sailing and boardsailing at Lake Baldeney.

Local resources

Business services

Photocopying and printing *City Copy*, Wegenerstr 1 ☎ 795165
Secretarial *Bürotel* ☎ 771011.
Translation *Zeitarbeit-Vermittlung des Arbeitsamts*, Limbecker Str 8 ☎ 87256.

Communications

Local delivery Taxis will deliver.
Long-distance delivery *West Air*, Geilinghausweg 26 ☎ 406564 or *DHL* in Düsseldorf ☎ (02102) 49080.
Post office Hachestr 1 ☎ 8191.
Telex and fax At main post office.

Conference/exhibition centres

Trade fairs attract 1.7m visitors a year to the fair grounds adjoining the Gruga Park. There are 13 exhibition halls and several conference rooms. The largest, the *Grugahalle*, seats up to 8,000. Information from Messe Essen, Messehaus, Norbertstr ☎ 72440. The other main conference centres are in the *Stadtgarten-*

Saalbau, Am Stadtgarten ☎ 510200 (capacity up to 600) and the *Haus der Technik*, Hollestr 1 ☎ 18031 (capacity up to 700).

Emergencies

Bureaux de change At the Hauptbahnhof, open Mon–Fri, 7.30–7; Sat, 7.30–5; Sun, 10–1.
Hospitals 24hr emergency department: *Klinikum der Gesamthochschule*, Hufelandstr 55 ☎ 79911.
Pharmacies At the Hauptbahnhof, open 7.30–9.30, with duty pharmacy at other times posted up.
Police *Polizeipräsidium*, Büscherstr 2 ☎ 72911.

Government offices

City administration: *Stadtverwaltung*, Rathaus, Porschepl ☎ 881.

Information sources

Business information Advice on business opportunities, exhibitions and city promotion/public relations at *Amt für Ratsangelegenheiten, Werbe- und Verkehrsamt*, Rathaus, Zimmer 230, Porschepl ☎ 883564. Open Mon–Fri, 8–1 and 2–4. Chamber of commerce: *Industrie- und Handelskammer*, Am Waldthausenpark 2 ☎ 18920. Central library (*Stadtbibliothek*), Hindenburgstr 25–27 ☎ 882665, has good scientific and technical sections and a large selection of periodicals.
Local media The *Westdeutsche Allgemeine* and *Neue Ruhrzeitung* newspapers have extensive local business coverage.
Tourist information Accommodation service and information at the south exit of the Hauptbahnhof; open Mon–Fri, 9–8; Sat, 10–8; Sun, 10–noon ☎ 235427 and 8106082. For daily events ☎ 11516.

Thank-yous

Florists At the main railway station, open daily; or *Blumen Maassen*, Frohnhauser Str 244 ☎ 701980. Both accept credit cards and will deliver.

FRANKFURT

City codes zip 6000 ☎ 069

Frankfurt am Main is not the largest city in Germany, but it is the centre of German business and, in particular, the undisputed centre of banking. Albert Speer once called Frankfurt a small provincial city town but, with a population of just over 600,000, its achievement in becoming the showcase of the West German economic miracle is impressive. The establishment here of the Deutsche Bundesbank (central bank) after World War II attracted the financial community. Today, 370 banks (many of them foreign), employing a total of 42,000 people, have headquarters or offices in Frankfurt, thus earning it the obvious nickname of "Bankfurt." The city's booming stock exchange (*Börse*) is the most important in West Germany, though its turnover is far short of that of New York, Tokyo or London.

Frankfurt benefited from the partition of Germany, becoming the geographical centre of the Federal Republic. Its already considerable role as a crossroads of European trade was thereby enhanced, which helps to explain its other economic successes: its Messe, one of Europe's leading trade fair centres; and its airport, which handles more freight than any other in Europe and employs over 40,000 people. It is also the home of a number of well-known companies, of which by far the largest is the big chemicals group Hoechst. Other international companies headquartered here include Metallgesellschaft, AEG (now a part of Daimler-Benz), Degussa and Philipp Holzmann. The reputation of Frankfurters for being hardworking, dour and hard-nosed is not entirely unjustified; local business people, for instance, do not like their day to be interrupted by too protracted a lunch.

For years, Frankfurt has suffered from a poor image. According to one opinion poll, 57% of its inhabitants would prefer to live somewhere else. It has been voted "Europe's most boring city" by readers of a business magazine. Yet the city council has lavished money on theatre and music and built a string of new museums along the Main river. More than 10% of the city's budget, which is partly funded by a local corporation tax, goes on culture. But Frankfurt's image is rapidly changing. A recent (1986) European Community study concluded that it is one of the most successful cities in the whole Community. The city is on the verge of a new building boom. Companies and financial organizations want to be in the centre, so the trend is to build upwards. The tallest building in Europe, the Messeturm, designed by the German/American Helmut Jahn, has already been started. When it is finished, at 250 metres tall, it will dwarf the buildings of today. By the mid-1990s there will be ten skyscrapers of a size equal to that of "Jahn Turm." Frankfurt will then really live up to its nickname "Mainhatten."

Arriving

Frankfurt is almost exactly in the middle of West Germany. It has first-class road and rail links with the rest of Germany and with neighbouring countries. Most visitors from abroad come in via Flughafen Frankfurt Main, the second largest airport in Europe after London's Heathrow.

Frankfurt Main airport

There are regular direct flights to Frankfurt Main airport from over 200 cities worldwide. Twenty million people use the airport annually and the rapid increase in numbers which has recently caused delays has led to an accleration of the plans for a new runway and terminal. It is difficult to find porters and trolleys and there is a long walk to the baggage claim area. But the facilities of this huge three-level terminal include 36 cafés and restaurants, over 100 shops, 5 banks, 2 post offices, 2 pharmacies, a clinic (☎ 6906767 ext. 3000), a dentist's surgery (☎ ext. 3228), a nursery, 3 cinemas, one of which shows English-language films, a police station, a non-denominational chapel and a discotheque (see *Entertainment.*) The airport's Europe City Club (ECC) provides a special lounge for first-class passengers of airlines which do not have their own VIP lounge ☎ 6903718. Also available are conference rooms with catering, telephones, telex and fax ☎ 69070066/7. In 1988 the 47,000-sq metre Frankfurt Airport Centre, a business, exhibition and communications complex, will be opened. The special "meeting point" between Halls A and B is a useful place for a rendezvous or from which to be collected. Airport information ☎ 6903051. Freight inquiries ☎ 6906969.

Nearby hotels **Sheraton,** Hugo-Eckener-Ring 15 Am Flughafen ☎ 69770 TX 4189294 • AE DC MC V. Connected by a covered passageway with the terminal, this Sheraton will become Europe's biggest hotel in 1988, following enlargements. *Steigenberger Airporthotel,* Unterschweinstiege 16, F75 ☎ 69851 TX 413112 • AE DC MC V. Large hotel 5min drive from the airport near the greenery of the Frankfurter

Stadtwald. Sauna and indoor pool. *Novotel Frankfurt Rhein-Main,* Am Weiher 20, Kelsterbach 6092 ☎ (06107) 75050 TX 4170101 • AE DC MC V. Quiet, 10min drive from the airport, with sauna, indoor pool, solarium and good conference facilities. A free minibus shuttle runs to the Steigenberger Airporthotel and the Novotel from the back end of the taxi rank to the left of the arrival level exits.

City link The airport is only 9km/5.5 miles southwest of Frankfurt. *S-Bahn* trains from the station underneath the terminal to the Hauptbahnhof main station are frequent and speedy (journey time 11min), if you have little baggage, although they are crowded in rush hours. If you are heavily laden, a taxi will be more convenient although it will take longer (journey time 20–35min). Renting a car can be useful if you have out-of-town places to visit. But the excellent network of fast *S-Bahn* trains should suffice for most destinations around Frankfurt.

Taxi There are usually plenty of taxis at the various exits of the arrival level; the downtown ride costs DM30–40. Reservations ☎ 230001. *Limousine* Avis ☎ 6902777.

Car rental All major car rental firms have desks on the arrival level of Section A.

S-Bahn The journey by the two *S-Bahn* lines into central Frankfurt costs about a tenth of the taxi fare. The S15 runs about every 15min to the Hauptbahnhof, while the slightly less frequent S14 serves both the Hauptbahnhof and Hauptwache, the centre of the city.

Railway station

Frankfurt's Hauptbahnhof, which is very large and very busy, has hourly mainline train connections over 18 hours of the day with all major German cities. It forms the hub of 14 *U-Bahn* (subway) and *S-Bahn* lines, reaching the whole city, the suburbs and most of the neighbouring towns. The Hauptbahnhof is quite central,

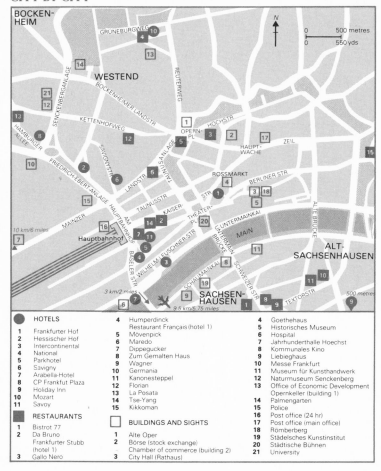

	HOTELS	4	Humperdinck Restaurant Français (hotel 1)		4	Goethehaus
1	Frankfurter Hof	5	Mövenpick		5	Historisches Museum
2	Hessischer Hof	6	Maredo		6	Hospital
3	Intercontinental	7	Dippegucker		7	Jahrhunderthalle Hoechst
4	National	8	Zum Gemalten Haus		8	Kommunales Kino
5	Parkhotel	9	Wagner		9	Liebieghaus
6	Savigny	10	Germania		10	Messe Frankfurt
7	Arabella-Hotel	11	Kanonesteppel		11	Museum für Kunsthandwerk
8	CP Frankfurt Plaza	12	Florian		12	Naturmuseum Senckenberg
9	Holiday Inn	13	La Posata		13	Office of Economic Development
10	Mozart	14	Tse-Yang			Opernkeller (building 1)
11	Savoy	15	Kikkoman		14	Palmengarten
					15	Police
	RESTAURANTS		BUILDINGS AND SIGHTS		16	Post office (24 hr)
					17	Post office (main office)
1	Bistrot 77	1	Alte Oper		18	Römerberg
2	Da Bruno	2	Börse (stock exchange)		19	Städelsches Kunstinstitut
	Frankfurter Stubb (hotel 1)		Chamber of commerce (building 2)		20	Städtische Bühnen
3	Gallo Nero	3	City Hall (Rathaus)		21	University

but is a good 20min walk, or more, from many of the leading hotels, the Messegelände (exhibition centre) and the banking quarter. A streetcar (*Strassenbahn*), which can be picked up outside the station, passes the Messe. On the three levels of the Hauptbahnhof are a wide range of shops, many cafés and brasseries, several banks, a post office and the tourist office, which will help you find a hotel room. The rank in the forecourt usually has plenty of taxis.

There are, however, no porters and the exit is a long walk from arrival platforms. There are no car rental offices in the station building. Timetable inquiries ☎ 230521.

Getting around

Distances between business districts in Frankfurt are too far to be covered on foot although, if you have appointments in the banking quarter and are staying at one of the central hotels, walking may be the best way of getting around. When visiting the suburbs, take either a taxi or an *S-Bahn* train to the station nearest your destination, then a taxi from there.

Taxis Taxis are available only from outside the Hauptbahnhof, outside the major hotels or by phoning for one, which may take 10min to arrive. They become very scarce at key hours during major trade fairs and a wait of anything up to half an hour outside the Messegelände in the evening is not unusual. Radio taxi ☎ 230001, 250001, 230033 or 545011.

Limousines *Limousine-Travel-Service* ☎ 230492/5.

Driving There are no particular problems here except for many one-way streets and the traffic-free streets in the centre. The map in the tourist office's useful *Information and Tips for the Visitor* indicates parking facilities. All the major car rental firms have offices in central Frankfurt. *Avis* ☎ 230101, *Budget* ☎ 290066, *Europcar* ☎ 234002, *interRent* ☎ 291028 and *Hertz* ☎ 233151.

Walking is generally safe, although single women should avoid the red-light district at night around the Kaiserstrasse.

Public transport Frankfurt has an integrated and interchangeable, although confusing, public transport system of *U-* and *S-Bahn* subway trains, trams and buses. When finding taxis is a problem (see above), public transport can be a lifesaver.

Buy a ticket from a vending machine at the stop before boarding. Fares vary depending on the time of day, so the simplest solution may be to buy a 24hr rover ticket valid for all forms of transport. Some maps provided by the tourist office are out of date because of extensions to the *U-Bahn* network and the phasing out of some bus and tram routes.

Area by area

The heart of Frankfurt is a compact area centred on the pedestrian square, Hauptwache. Only about

1.6km/1 mile across, it is bordered on three sides by a string of gardens where the city walls once stood and on its south by the river Main. It was almost totally rebuilt after World War II. Some corporations are based there, but the chief business and banking quarter, along Kaiserstrasse, is a little farther to the west, towards the Hauptbahnhof. Northwest of the main station is the vast Messegelände (exhibition centre).

Westend, which is north of the city centre, is a much sought-after residential area as well as the home of many publishers, advertising agencies and computer systems companies. Up-and-coming residential areas include Bockenheim, northwest of the centre which is conveniently connected with the banking quarter by the new *U-Bahn* lines 6 and 7, and the quiet district of Bornheim northeast of the centre.

Sachsenhausen, on the south side of the river, is partly residential and partly the entertainment quarter for Frankfurters and tourists alike.

The suburbs About half of the 400,000 people who work in Frankfurt commute daily from its extensive and often pleasant suburbs. Niederrad, on the immediate outskirts of the city south of the river, combines a new business district with an unspoilt old quarter. Similarly, Höchst, a little farther out to the west, is both the seat of the eponymous chemical giant (spelt Hoechst) and an old town with several historic buildings. To the northwest, the little town of Königstein and the fashionable spa of Bad Homburg in the Taunus hills are where many senior executives live.

Getting around Germany
Information on long-distance travel in Germany by air, train and car is given in the *Planning and Reference* section.

Hotels

The major hotels are scattered in or near the centre, the banking quarter and the Messegelände. Between major fairs half of the city's rooms are unoccupied (and special terms can often be arranged). But during the Motor Show or Book Fair it can be impossible to find accommodation in Frankfurt itself, and prices rise steeply. Rooms then have to be sought as far afield as Bad Homburg (17km/11 miles), Darmstadt (35km/22 miles), Mainz or Wiesbaden (40km/25 miles), but road and rail connections from these towns to Frankfurt are very good.

All the main hotels listed here have IDD telephones; currency exchange is standard and parking is generally available, but a charge may be made.

Frankfurter Hof [DM]||||
Bethmannstr 33, F1 ☎ *20251*
ⓉⓍ *411806 • Steigenberger • AE DC MC V • 360 rooms, 38 suites, 4 restaurants, 2 bars*
This is the doyen of Frankfurt's hotels (opened 1876) and undoubtedly offers the best and most comprehensive services of them all. Located not too far from the banking quarter, it provides a full range of in-house business facilities. The rooms, which are spacious and well soundproofed, are tastefully decorated in pink or green. The Aperitif Bar and especially the duck-blue Lipizzaner Bar (from 5pm), which sometimes has live music, are favourite spots for informal business discussions. Of the four restaurants, two, the Restaurant Français and the Frankfurter Stubb (see *Restaurants*), attract customers from outside the hotel, while the Roofgarten is a popular venue for business lunches. 24hr room service, hairdresser, newsstand • fax, 16 meeting rooms (capacity up to 500).

Hessischer Hof [DM]|||||
Friedrich-Ebert-Anlage 40, F1
☎ *75400* ⓉⓍ *411776 • AE DC MC V • 153 rooms, 7 suites, 1 restaurant, 2 bars*
A rather stern late-40s exterior, opposite the Messegelände, conceals a hotel that ranks near the Frankfurter Hof. Customers appreciate the staff's friendly and personal service, and the fact that their room preferences are noted down for next time. The decor of its spacious rooms is old-fashioned in the best sense. Public areas are almost museum-like in their decor, with several fine old masters, attractive prints and a collection of Sèvres porcelain as well as other antiques. The lobby bar is a favourite meeting place (from 3pm), while the other bar, Jimmy's, is one of the city's most elegant nightspots. The restaurant's well-spaced tables make for discreet business entertaining although it is too dark in the evenings for detailed negotiations. Newsstand • fax, 11 meeting rooms (capacity up to 300).

Intercontinental [DM]||||
Wilhelm-Leuschner-Str 43, F1
☎ *230561* ⓉⓍ *413639 • AE DC MC V • 750 rooms, 62 suites, 3 restaurants, 1 bar*
Close to the banking quarter, this recently renovated hotel has two wings. Business travellers are usually accommodated in the older building overlooking the river. In return for its high prices, the hotel offers comfortable rooms and the most modern conference rooms in Frankfurt. The other side of the coin is its rather dull, anonymous atmosphere. The Prolog/Epilog bar behind the lobby is a good place to meet. 24hr room service, hairdresser, florist, gift shop, newsstand • pool, sauna, solarium, gym, massage • fax, 11 meeting rooms (capacity up to 700).

National *DM*|*||*
Baseler Str 50, F1 ☎ *234841*
Ⓣ⌧ *412570* • *Best Western* •
AE DC MC V • *71 rooms, 1 restaurant,*
1 bar
Like the Hessischer Hof, the
National is housed in a rather
unprepossessing postwar building.
But its rooms and public areas have
antique furniture and carpets. Its
leisurely, discreet atmosphere,
friendly staff and very reasonable
prices obviously appeal to its regular
customers. The hotel is opposite the
main railway station and not very far
from the headquarters of the big
banks. The best rooms face the
back, but those overlooking the
busy station forecourt have
soundproofing. 24hr room service,
newsstand • 4 meeting rooms
(capacity up to 60).

Parkhotel *DM*|*|||*
Wiesenhüttenpl 28–38, F1 ☎ *26970*
Ⓣ⌧ *412808* • *Mövenpick* • *AE DC MC V*
• *263 rooms, 17 suites, 3 restaurants,*
1 bar
The Parkhotel, which is as usefully
located as its neighbour, the
National, is the choice for many
guests visiting the Messe. It has two
sections: the main body of the hotel
(built 1970), for which a major year-
long renovation from March 1988 is
planned, and the more exclusive and
expensive Tower (built 1905 and
refurbished), which is more suitable
for business travellers. The hotel is
notable more for its service, attention
to regular customers and comfort
than for its grandeur. There are 25
rooms for nonsmokers, and a
particularly helpful concierge. The
hotel's main restaurant, La Truffe
(closed Sat and Sun), which is highly
suitable for business entertaining, is
rather sombre but serves fine French
cuisine and remarkable wines. The
Casablanca piano bar, although
crowded, is a popular rendezvous.
Newsstand, gift shop • sauna,
solarium, exercise equipment • fax,
13 meeting rooms (capacity up to
230).

Savigny *DM*|*|||*
Savignystr 14–16 F1 ☎ *75330*
Ⓣ⌧ *412061* • *Pullman* • *AE DC MC V* •
120 rooms, 2 suites, 1 restaurant,
1 bar
This modern hotel is tucked away in
a quiet street halfway between the
Messe and the banking quarter. Since
being taken over by Pullman in 1986,
it has been refurbished in good taste
throughout. There is a large public
area with a relaxed light grey decor,
and many of the rooms have
balconies. The restaurant is good for
business meals of a very private
nature, as sections of it can be
partitioned off. Newsstand, gift shop
• fax, 4 meeting rooms (capacity up
to 80).

OTHER HOTELS
Arabella-Hotel *DM*|*||* *Lyoner*
Str 44–48, 71-Niederrad ☎ *66330*
Ⓣ⌧ *416760* • *AE DC MC V.* This
modern hotel is in the new business
district of Niederrad. Its facilities
include a large swimming pool and a
jogging track.
CP Frankfurt Plaza *DM*|*||||*
Hamburger Allee 2–4, F1 ☎ *79550*
Ⓣ⌧ *412573* • *Canadian Pacific* • *AE*
DC MC V. At the top of a skyscraper
(except for reception) and opposite
the Messe, it offers the usual facilities
of a luxury hotel but has little
character.
Holiday Inn City Tower *DM*|*|||*
Mailänder Str 1, F70 ☎ *68020*
Ⓣ⌧ *411805* • *AE DC MC V.* A 26-floor
tower with fine views, on the edge of
Sachsenhausen. Conference facilities
available.
Mozart *DM*|*|* *Parkstr 17, F1*
☎ *550831* • *closed Christmas–New*
Year • *AE DC MC V.* A modest,
modern and friendly hotel, in a leafy
street on the edge of the Westend
area. For those who prefer discretion
and quiet rather than business
facilities.
Savoy *DM*|*||* *Wiesenhüttenstr 42,*
F1 ☎ *230511* Ⓣ⌧ *416394* • *AE DC*
MC V. An attractive modern hotel,
near the station, with good business
facilities and a pool.

Out of town
There are two luxury hotels near
Frankfurt that appeal to those in
search of relaxation in a stylish
setting rather than a convenient
location. *Gravenbruch Kempinski*,
Frankfurt 6078/Neu-Isenburg 2
☎ (06102) 5050 is a large hotel, set
in spacious grounds, 11km/7 miles
south of the city and within easy
reach of the airport by *Autobahn* (free
shuttle service). It has a health farm,
indoor and outdoor pools, a tennis
court and excellent food at its
Gourmet-Restaurant. The *Schloss-
Hotel*, Kronberg im Taunus 6242
☎ (06173) 7011 is an imposing
19thC castle-hotel, surrounded by a
park with an 18-hole golf course. The
rooms are large and furnished with
antiques. Dining in its majestic
restaurant is a memorable event.
Kronberg is reached in about 20min
by *S-Bahn* 4 from Frankfurt. The

Sonnenhof, Falkensteiner Str 9
☎ (06174) 29080, although not quite
in the same class, is a pleasant hotel
in a very quiet location 23km/14
miles away in Königstein. It has a
pool and sports facilities.
In case you are unable to find
suitable accommodation in
Frankfurt, here are some suggestions
in nearby towns : the *Maritim-
Kurhaus-Hotel* in Bad Homburg
☎ (06172) 28051, a comfortable
hotel with sauna and pool a stone's
throw from the Kurpark, where
guests can take the waters, and visit
the casino; the *Mainzer Hof* in
Mainz; and the *Nassauer Hof* in
Wiesbaden, containing the best
restaurant in Wiesbaden, Die Ente
Vom Lehel (see *Mainz and
Wiesbaden*); and the *Maritim* in
Darmstadt ☎ (06151) 80041, a hotel
with sauna and pool, right next to the
station.

Restaurants

Hotel restaurants in Frankfurt offer remarkably high standards and
value for money. In addition to the Restaurant Français and Frankfurter
Stubb described below, the main restaurants of the Hessischer Hof, the
Parkhotel and the Savigny (see *Hotels*) are eminently suitable for
business entertaining. During major fairs service may be very slow,
restaurants crowded and reservations are essential.

Bistrot 77 [DM]/||
Ziegelhüttenweg 1 ☎ *614040 • closed
Sat L, Sun and 3 weeks Jun–Jul •*
AE DC MC
In Sachsenhausen, but well away
from the brash touristy quarter,
Bistrot 77 is one of the best French
restaurants in town. The cuisine of
its Alsatian chef, Dominique
Mosbach, is sensibly *nouvelle*. The
top advertising executives and
showbiz celebrities who dine at this
restaurant like its cool, white-tiled
modern decor and pleasant terrace.

Da Bruno [DM]/||
Elbestr 15 ☎ *233416 • closed Sun
(open Sun D during major fairs) and
Jul 15–Aug 15 • AE DC MC*
This restaurant has long been a

favourite with bankers (many of
whom work round the corner), no
doubt because of its almost club-like
atmosphere. Some of the tables are
set in private booths. The food is
straightforward, top-quality Italian,
the ambience perhaps more suitable
for a business lunch than an evening
out.

Frankfurter Stubb [DM]/
Frankfurter Hof hotel ☎ *215679 •
closed Sun (open Sun D during major
fairs), 3 weeks Jul and Dec 24–Jan 3 •*
AE DC MC V
This rustic cellar restaurant, with its
alcoves and waitresses in traditional
German costume, is very different in
style from the hotel in which it is
housed. It is the haunt of local

business people who like genuine German cuisine of the highest quality. In addition to Frankfurt's own herb sauce, the delicious *Grüne Sosse*, you can also sample dishes made from forgotten recipes dug up from old cookbooks.

Gallo Nero [DM]/
Kaiserhofstr 7 ☎ *284840 • closed Sun (exc during major fairs) • AE DC MC V*
Young executives like the terrace (weather permitting) of this Italian restaurant near the Alte Oper, and the small alcove tables inside are ideal for private meetings and negotiation. Both the very good and imaginative food and the service are typically Italian.

Humperdinck [DM]////
Grüneburgweg 95 ☎ *722122 • closed Sat L, Sun and 3 weeks Jun–Jul • AE DC MC V*
Some find Humperdinck's a bit pretentious, but there is no denying its very high standards and its suitability for the most important occasions. Good taste prevails throughout, from the mainly French cuisine to the restful decor and occasional live classical music. There are several interesting set menus, including a special business lunch. The restaurant, which is on the edge of the Westend business quarter, is in the house where the composer Engelbert Humperdinck, who wrote *Hansel and Gretel*, once lived.

Restaurant Français [DM]////
Frankfurter Hof hotel ☎ *20251 • closed Sun (except during major fairs) and Jul • AE DC MC V • jacket and tie*
A sumptuous yellow and green decor, oil paintings, very well-spaced tables, silver tableware and legions of well-trained waiters help to make the Restaurant Français *the* place for a really important business celebration. To top everything, the French cuisine is among the best in Frankfurt, and the wine list is staggering.

Good but casual
Many Frankfurt business people prefer not to linger over lunch, so they frequent quite simple restaurants. Two favourites, partly because of their convenient locations, are the *Mövenpick*, Opernpl 2 ☎ 20680, which is a cluster of different types of restaurant (including a nonsmoking one), and the *Maredo*, Taunusanlage 12 ☎ 7240795, a steakhouse on the first floor of the handsome two-towered Deutsche Bank building (from which it draws many of its customers: reservations advisable at lunchtime). A useful standby opposite the station is *Dippegucker*, Am Hauptbahnhof 4 ☎ 234947, which is more congenial than it seems from the outside and offers good, honest German fare. All these restaurants serve food continuously from noon to midnight.

For more relaxed eating out, locals often choose one of the taverns in Sachsenhausen to enjoy *Rippchen* (salted pork chops) and *Handkäs mit Musik* (cheese with onions), washed down with *Apfelwein* (*Ebbelwoi* or *Ebbelwei* in local dialect), a dry, almost still cider with a deceptively strong punch. They avoid Alt-Sachsenhausen (the northeast end), which is full of tourists and off-duty US soldiers, preferring instead the establishments on and off Schweitzer Strasse. These include: *Zum Gemalten Haus* ☎ 614559 and its neighbour *Wagner* (the most fashionable of all) ☎ 612565, at 67 and 71 Schweitzer Strasse respectively, and, round the corner, *Germania* ☎ 613336 and *Kanonesteppel* ☎ 611891, at 16 and 20 Textorstrasse.

For foreign food, there are two Italian restaurants worth a visit. In Westend, and frequented by the banking and advertising sets at both lunch and dinner, is *Florian*, Kettenhofweg 59 ☎ 722891. And *La Posata*, Schlossstr 126 ☎ 777274, is an atmospheric Italian restaurant only a few minutes' walk from the Messe. The best of those offering

Chinese food is *Tse-Yang*, Kaiserstr 67 ☎ 232541 and one of the newest Japanese restaurants *Kikkoman*, Friedberger Anlage 1 ☎ 4990021, which serves Washoku and Teppan, is also the most reliable.

Out of town
It is well worth going out of Frankfurt to the restaurant of the *Sonnenhof* in Königstein or to sample the superb food in three other hotels, the *Gravenbruch* at Neu-Isenburg, the *Nassauer Hof* in Wiesbaden, and the *Schloss-Hotel* in Kronberg (see *Hotels*). But for the special occasion, locals will suggest you go 13km/8 miles south of Frankfurt to *Gutsschänke Neuhof* in Dreieich-Götzenhain ☎ (06102) 3214, a 500-year-old half-timbered manor house, with log fires, lawns and weeping willows.

Bars
The bars of the major hotels are convenient and congenial places to meet, particularly the *Lipizzaner* in the Frankfurter Hof, the *Prolog/Epilog* in the Intercontinental and the *lobby bar* of the Hessischer Hof.

Besides the cider taverns (see *Restaurants*), two pleasant meeting places in the traffic-free centre which have terraces in summer are *Volkswirt*, Kleine Hochstr 9 (from 4pm), which provides 32 excellent wines (mainly German) by the glass and is usually jammed with yuppies, and *Das Cafehaus*, Grosse Eschenheimer Str 13, which, unusually for Frankfurt, is open 6am–3am.

Entertainment
Frankfurt has a lively and varied cultural life. Most listings except film programmes will be found in the tourist office's fortnightly *Frankfurter Woche*. Otherwise consult the local editions of *Frankfurter Allgemeine Zeitung* or the *Frankfurter Rundschau*.
Theatre, dance, opera Theatre, particularly of an experimental and avant-garde nature, has long

flourished in Frankfurt, and there is plenty for the playgoer who understands German. Of the three municipal companies (reservations ☎ 236061/3) based in the *Städtische Bühnen*, Theaterpl 1, the opera enjoys the highest international reputation.
Cinema Frankfurt has plenty of good cinemas, and, unusually for West Germany, shows some foreign films in their original versions. The *Kommunales Kino* is a cinema in the *Filmmuseum*, Schaumainkai 41 ☎ 628927.
Music The *Alte Oper*, Opernpl, for many years a bomb-scarred ruin, was converted in 1981 into a multipurpose, modular hall with superb acoustics for all kinds of concerts (classical, jazz, rock), as well as conferences. Concert reservations ☎ 1340400. Many other musical events are held in the *Jahrhunderthalle Hoechst*, Pfaffenwiese, Höchst ☎ 3601213.

Frankfurt is one of Europe's main jazz centres. A number of clubs regularly feature top performers. There are frequent jazz concerts in the *Opernkeller* (the bistro beneath the Alte Oper ☎ 13400), the courtyard of the *Historisches Museum*, Saalgasse 19 ☎ 2125599, and the *Palmengarten*, Palmengartenstr ☎ 2123382.
Nightclubs and casinos It is best to avoid the second-rate and sometimes risky nightlife in the notorious red-light area in and around Kaiserstrasse, which is due to be cleaned up (or moved to the other side of town) in the near future. Frankfurt's classiest nightspot is *Jimmy's* in the Hessischer Hof (see *Hotels*). But for a little more life – and noise, in its disco section – try the jet-setters' favourite, the *Dorian Gray* ☎ 6902212 in Terminal C of Frankfurt airport.

There are two famous casinos not too far away, in Wiesbaden ☎ (06121) 526954, and in Bad Homburg ☎ (06172) 20041, and frequent bus shuttle services to each casino leave from the Hauptbahnhof (south side), stopping on the way opposite the Messe.

Shopping

There are many large department stores as well as clothing and shoe shops in the pedestrianized Zeil, the shopping street with the highest turnover in West Germany. Fashion boutiques are in Schillerstrasse and especially Goethestrasse, though the really smart place to go is Bad Homburg. Frankfurt is renowned for its furs, and the best shops cluster around Düsseldorfer Strasse opposite the main railway station.

Sightseeing

Frankfurt's modern and largely traffic-free centre is pleasant enough, although the Römerberg, with its faithfully reconstructed 15thC houses, looks a little like a film set. Sachsenhausen has retained much of its prewar atmosphere, though its older part, Alt-Sachsenhausen, has become rather brash as a result of the tourist trade. But the lack of sights is amply made up for by the seven museums along the Schaumainkai, on the south bank of the river.

Goethehaus Goethe's birthplace (rebuilt after World War II), furnished in period, with memorabilia in the small adjoining museum, the Goethemuseum. *Grosser Hirschgraben 23. Open Apr–Sep, Mon–Sat, 9–5.50, Sun, 10–1; Oct–Mar, Mon–Sat, 9–4, Sun, 10–1.*

Liebieghaus A remarkable sculpture museum with exhibits from antiquity to the present day. *Schaumainkai 71. Open Tue–Sun, 10–5 (Wed, 10–8).*

Museum für Kunsthandwerk Arts and crafts exhibited in a beautifully designed new museum. *Schaumainkai 17. Open Tue–Sun, 10–5 (Wed, 10–8).*

Naturmuseum Senckenberg A natural history museum with an extraordinary paleontological collection. *Senckenberganlage 25. Open*

Mon, Tue, Thu, Fri, 9–5; Wed, 9–8; Sat, Sun, 9–6.

Städelsches Kunstinstitut One of the world's major collections of paintings from the Middle Ages to the 20thC. *Schaumainkai 63. Open Tue–Sun, 10–5 (Wed, 10–8).*

Zoologischer Garten Founded in 1858, Frankfurt Zoo has some 700 species of animal and is widely regarded as one of the finest in the world. The Exotarium re-creates suitable conditions for many species. *Alfred-Brehm-Pl. Open summer 8–7, spring and autumn, 8–6, winter 8–5. Exotarium open 8am–10pm.*

Guided tours

The Ebbelwei-Express (with cider and pretzels), a converted old tram which can be boarded anywhere on its circular route, is a good way of seeing the main sights. Inquiries: *Stadtwerke Frankfurt/Main* ☎ 13682425. The *tourist office* ☎ 2128849/51 or 2128708/9 organizes 2–3hr tours, starting from the Hauptbahnhof.

Out of town

The spa of *Bad Homburg*, 17km/ 11 miles north, with its chic boutiques, casino and park, is definitely worth a visit. Less well-known is the smaller spa *Bad Nauheim*, 36km/23 miles north, whose 1910 buildings form a perfect example of *Jugendstil* (German Art Nouveau). The celebrated part of the *Rhein valley* from Wiesbaden to the Lorelei rock can be explored by car or on a day trip by river cruiser. Boats leave from the footbridge on Mainkai. Operator: *Köln-Düsseldorfer* ☎ 282420.

Spectator sports

Horse-racing From March to November at the *Niederrad racetrack*, Schwarzwaldstr 125 ☎ 677018.

Soccer Eintracht Frankfurt plays at *Waldstadion*, Mörfelder Landstr 362 ☎ 678040. The tourist office's two branches also sell advance tickets.

Keeping fit

For general information on sports facilities, contact *Sport- und Badeamt* ☎ 2123565. Most of the major hotels are equipped with sports facilities.

Fitness centres *United Sporting Club*, Mainzer Landstr 150a ☎ 735050; *Sportstudio P&W*, Schwalbacherstr 54 ☎ 7380045.

Golf Players of a reasonable standard with their club card can play at *Frankfurter Golf-Club*, Golfstr 41 ☎ 6662318 and *Hanau Wilhelmsbad*, Wilhelmsbader Allee 32, 6450 Hanau 1 ☎ (06181) 82071. There are several courses in Bad Homburg.

Squash *City Squash und Body* (3 courts), Kaiserstr 73 ☎ 232527; *Squash Zentrum Ost* (9 courts), Ostparkstr 35 ☎ 434756.

Swimming Many hotels have pools. The heated 50-metre-long *Garten Hallenbad Rebstock*, August-Euler-Str 7 ☎ 708078/9, also has saunas and a solarium.

Tennis *Waldstadion* (20 outdoor courts), Mörfelder Landstr 362 ☎ 678040, or *Tenniszentrum Klüh* (2 indoor and 16 outdoor courts), Im Uhrig 29 ☎ 525118.

Local resources

Business services

The major hotels can provide or organize most of the services you will need. *Messe-Servis* ☎ 752339, caters particularly for trade fair visitors.

Photocopying and printing Photocopying facilities in the main hotels. Printing: *ABC Druck* ☎ (06196) 60050.

Secretarial *Das Textstudio* ☎ 288833

Translation *KERN* ☎ 740821

Communications

Local delivery *Non-stop Kurier* ☎ 610671

Long-distance delivery *Skypak* ☎ (06107) 61066

Post office At the Hauptbahnhof and airport Departure Hall B: open 24hr.

Telex and fax Main post office: Zeil 108 ☎ 2110; open Mon–Fri, 8–6, Sat, 8–noon. Airport reception hall (telex only): open Mon–Sat, 8–9, Sun, 8–5.30.

Emergencies

Bureaux de change Late opening: *Deutsche Verkehrs-Kredit-Bank*, Hauptbahnhof, daily 6.30–10. Some airport banks are open daily 7–9.30.

Hospitals 24hr emergency department: *Uniklinik*, Theodor-Stern-Kai 7 ☎ 63011. Emergency doctor ☎ 79502200. Emergency dental treatment ☎ 6607271.

Pharmacies To find out pharmacies open late ☎ 11500.

Police Main station: Friedrich-Ebert-Anlage 9–11 ☎ 25551.

Government offices

Wirtschaftsförderung Frankfurt GmbH (City of Frankfurt am Main's Office of Economic Development), Grüneburgweg 102 ☎ 2121, puts out an informative booklet called *Frankfurt – Preferred by Decision-Makers*. It also provides information and gives advice to incoming firms.

Information sources

Business information The *Industrie- und Handelskammer Frankfurt am Main* (chamber of commerce), Börsenpl 6 ☎ 21971, publishes *Metropole Frankfurt am Main* which gives a broad picture of local business activity and *Frankfurt – Das Wirtschaftszentrum* provides details of hundreds of leading companies based in Frankfurt.

Local media The *Frankfurter Allgemeine Zeitung* (*FAZ*) is the bible of the West German business establishment. The other locally based paper is the *Frankfurter Rundschau*.

Tourist information *Verkehrsverein* (tourist office) is at the Hauptbahnhof ☎ 2128849/51, open Mon–Sat, 8–9 (8–10 Apr–Oct), Sun, 9.30–8 and at Hauptwache, Hauptwache-Passage ☎ 2128708/9, open Mon–Fri, 9–6, Sat, 9–2. Its *Information and Tips for the Visitor* is a useful booklet.

Thank-yous
Confectionery *Plöger*, Grosse Bockenheimer Str 30 ☎ 282319.
Florists *Blumen Beuchert*, Rathenaupl 2–8 ☎ 282663.
Wine merchants *Frankhof* (in the Frankfurter Hof, see *Hotels*) ☎ 20251.

Messe Frankfurt

Messe Frankfurt is one of West Germany's top three trade fair and exhibition centres. Its fairs attract about 1m visitors annually, rising to 2m in the years when big biennial events are held. In addition to the Book Fair, Fur Fair, Music Fair, various textiles fairs and the biennial IAA (International Motor Show), there are many smaller, more specialized events. Since 1980 there has been a policy of steady investment: the *Festhalle* (built 1907) has been refurbished for use as a conference and concert hall; the Messe's exhibition halls are now linked by the Via Mobile, a covered system of travelators and escalators almost 1km in length: and work on Europe's highest office skyscraper, a 250-metre tower, should be completed in time for the Messe's 750th anniversary in 1990.

Getting there At Ludwig-Erhard-Anlage 1, F1 ☎ 75750 ⓉⓍ 411558, the Messe is a 5–10min taxi ride from the centre of town, the main station, the Westend and banking quarters. It can also be reached by trams 16 and 19 from the main station.

Clear signposts from the *Autobahn* network direct cars to the Messe's Rebstock parking facilities for over 20,000 vehicles. From there a bus shuttles to and from the fairground. There are 3,000 parking spaces (mostly booked by exhibitors) in or in front of the Messe itself.

Exhibition space The Messe's ten exhibition halls are divided into three self-contained sections, so that several small fairs can be held simultaneously. In all, there are about 260,000 sq metres/2.8m sq ft of display space.

Facilities The hub of the Messe is the recently built Galleria, where the facilities include a post office, a travel agency, a baby-minding service, a medical centre, several banks, and 27 bars and restaurants. Temporary office accommodation is available in the central Torhaus.

Conferences are an expanding part of Messe Frankfurt's business. There is a wide range of conference facilities, with 42 rooms and halls, including the Festhalle, which holds 4,000.

There are two large hotels opposite the Messe, the Hessischer Hof and the CP Frankfurt Plaza (see *Hotels*). Accommodation during major fairs is a problem, so contact the *Messe Frankfurt Accommodation Bureau*, Ludwig-Erhard-Anlage 1, F1 ☎ 75756222 ⓉⓍ 411558 in good time. The bureau puts out a very useful booklet called *Hotelania Frankfurt–Hotelania Rhein-Main*, which lists over 500 hotels in Frankfurt and the surrounding Rhein-Main area.

Additional conference facilities

Two other important venues in and around Frankfurt are: the *Alte Oper Frankfurt*, Opernpl, F1 ☎ 13400 ⓉⓍ 412890, which has rooms for up to 700 and a main hall with a capacity of 2,400; and the *Jahrhunderthalle Hoechst*, Pfaffenwiese 6230, F80 ☎ 3601132, which has rooms for up to 200 and a main hall with a capacity of 2,000.

HAMBURG

City codes zip 2000 ☎ 040

Hamburg is both a city and one of the ten *Länder* which go to make up the Federal Republic. With 1.6m people, it is second only to West Berlin in size, and as a port its pre-eminence remains unchallenged. It is also one of the greatest concentrations of commerce in the country, and its industrial base is substantial.

Hamburg has been an important port for 800 years, although it is 104km/65 miles from the open sea on the river Elbe. A leading member of the Hanseatic League in the 14th century, in the 19th century it expanded to become Europe's gateway to the United States and Latin America. It remains important for transhipment and is one of the world's largest free ports. Blohm u. Voss and Howaldtswerke are still major shipbuilders and repairers, but the focus of engineering has shifted : Airbus Industrie's German participant, MBB, has its main plant here and Lufthansa's technical centre is at Fuhlsbüttel airport. Electronics is well established ; Philips makes instruments, while Valvo, its component subsidiary, turns out silicon chips. Several international oil companies have their German headquarters in Hamburg, including BP, Conoco, Esso, Mobil, Shell and Texaco. The biggest firm is BAT, not only manufacturing cigarettes but diversifying into food processing. Another large employer in Hamburg is Unilever and its subsidiaries, making toiletries and cosmetics.

Forty per cent of Germany's magazines and newspapers are published in Hamburg, including *Stern*, *Der Spiegel* and *Bild-Zeitung*, and two leading record labels, Deutsches Grammophon and Polygram, have manufacturing plants locally.

Industrial activity is supported by excellent research facilities. There are three universities – Hamburg, Hamburg-Harburg technical university and that of the federal armed forces – in addition to DESY, Germany's nuclear physics centre. Bio-technology and lasers, oceanography, timber and soil sciences and process technology are just some of the wide range of disciplines that are researched by Hamburg institutions.

Unemployment is above the national average at 12%. Industrial growth has not matched decline because of containerization at the docks and the loss of shipbuilding contracts. Yet trade and industry have an international outlook : 200 US and 100 Japanese companies have their German headquarters here. Indeed, Hamburg sees itself as Germany's window on the world.

Arriving

Hamburg is the communications centre of northern Germany and is well served by road, rail, air and sea. Euroroutes E3 and E4 (*Autobahnen* A1 and A7) from the south meet at Hamburg and continue into Scandinavia. Euroroute E15 (*Autobahn* A24) brings traffic from Berlin and eastern Europe. Just south of the city is Maschen, site of one of the largest railway marshalling yards in Europe.

Hamburg-Fuhlsbüttel airport
A DM350m upgrade of the present
airport is in progress and this may
cause some disturbance. The terminal
facilities are relatively limited for the
airport of a city of Hamburg's size.

The main terminal is reserved for
international services and an
adjoining one is for domestic flights.
There are only two air jetties so
passengers are usually bussed
between terminal and aircraft.
Clearing the airport takes 20–30min
on average. The Deutsche Bank
bureau de change is open daily, 6.30–
10.30. Shops and stalls include a post
office, hairdresser and florist. The
duty-free shop is small but well
stocked. Passenger inquiries
☎ 5082557 or 5082558, freight
☎ 5082639 or 5082699.
Nearby hotel *Airlines Hotel*,
Zeppelinstr 12, H63 ☎ 505043 • AE
MC V. About 800 metres from the
airport.
City link The airport is 8km/5 miles
north of the city centre and a taxi is
the quickest way to get into town.
Taxi There are ranks outside each
section of the terminal with cabs
usually waiting. However, the ranks
officially close at 11pm. The fare to
the centre is around DM25 and the
journey takes about 20–30min,
depending on traffic.
Limousines Avis Chauffeur-Drive
☎ 6700308.
Car rental Auto-Hansa, Avis,
Europcar, Budget, Hertz and
interRent all have desks near
international arrivals. Renting a car
makes sense if your appointments are
in the outer suburbs.
Bus There are bus stops outside each
section of the terminal. The Airport-
City-Bus leaves every 20min for the
Hauptbahnhof (journey 35min),
stopping at Holiday Inn (Crowne
Plaza), Jungiusstrasse, Hamburg
Messe, Hamburg Plaza (Congress
Centrum), Atlantic hotel,
Schauspielhaus in Kirchenallee,
Pavillon in Brockesstrasse, and
Zentral-Omnibus-Bahnhof. The fare
is DM8.

Train and subway The Airport
Express (no. 110 bus) runs every
10min to Ohlsdorf station, with *S-
Bahn* and *U-Bahn* connections to the
centre. A through ticket costs DM2.80
and the total journey time is 30–
35min. The last bus to connect leaves
the airport at 11.14pm.

Railway stations
Hamburg has two main stations.
Direct hourly services run to the main
Ruhr cities and to Cologne (4hr),
Frankfurt (4hr 30min), Mannheim
(5hr 20min) and Munich (7hr
20min). There are also important
connections with Berlin and East
Germany and with Scandinavia.
Inquiries ☎ 19419 for both stations.
Hauptbahnhof The station is on the
eastern side of the inner city zone.
Originally the main station, the
Hauptbahnhof is now primarily used
for suburban lines, although intercity
trains stop at platforms 11–14.
Facilities include two bureaux de
change, a hotel reservations desk, an
interRent counter and several shops
and stalls. There are taxi ranks on
both sides of the building and two *U-
Bahn* stations.
Altona This extensive, modern
station is the main terminus, well to
the west of the inner city. Facilities
include information office, bureau de
change, florist, tobacconist,
refreshment stall, cafeteria,
newsstands, shoe repairer and
department store. It is also a motor
rail loading point.
Dammtor The station for the
Congress Centrum, with both *S-Bahn*
and mainline connections. Many
intercity trains stop here.

The Landungsbrücken
The passenger landing-stages in the
St Pauli district are used for local
river services and for the car ferry to
and from England. Within the ticket
hall are an information office, bureau
de change, refreshment stalls and
restaurants. Landungsbrücken station
has both *S-Bahn* and *U-Bahn*
services. Inquiries ☎ 313977.

Getting around

Hamburg's well-organized public transport system provides an easy method of getting around.

Taxis The cabs are all beige, usually Mercedes, and must be picked up at a rank or ordered by telephone. At peak times, try the ranks at the Hauptbahnhof; otherwise call *Autoruf* ☎ 441011, *Hansa* ☎ 211211, *Radio Taxi* ☎ 6562011 or *Taxiruf* ☎ 611061.

Limousines *Richter* ☎ 666670, *Telecar* ☎ 8401440.

Driving Traffic is rarely very congested but finding the way is not always easy. Three concentric ring roads are signposted to avoid the city centre, but at most times of the day it will prove quicker to select a direct route. The main car rental companies have offices in the city including *Avis* ☎ 341651, *Europcar* 244455, *Hertz* ☎ 230045, *interRent* ☎ 362221 and *Budget* ☎ 241466.

Walking The inner city is best covered on foot. It is generally quite safe, with the exception, particularly at night, of the St Pauli and St Georg districts.

Public transport *U-Bahn* and *S-Bahn* both come under the

HOTELS

1 Atlantic-Hotel Kempinski
2 Elysee
3 Hamburg Plaza
4 Inter-Continental
5 Ramada Renaissance
6 Reichshof
7 Vier Jahreszeiten
8 Crest
9 Europäischer Hof
10 Novotel Hamburg Nord
11 Prem

Hamburger Verkehrsverbund (HVV). There are three fare zones; ticket machines display the fares to most points and give change. Tickets, which can also be bought from bus drivers, are valid for transfers between bus, train and subway.

Plans of the train and subway network are displayed at all stations. There are three *U-Bahn* and six *S-Bahn* lines, with trains every 10min to all parts of the city. In the late evening you may be troubled by drunks; certain station passageways are especially hazardous. Inquiries ☎ 322911.

Area by area

The residential and business centres of Hamburg are concentrated to the north of the river Elbe, and the port occupies the southern bank where the river divides into two. This district is called Harburg. The inner suburbs around the Alster lake are the most prestigious.

Innenstadt The city centre, and chief business and shopping centre, lies between the river Elbe and the old city wall. It is split in two by the river Alster, with the Altstadt on the east and Neustadt on the west. The Binnenalster and the "Fleete"

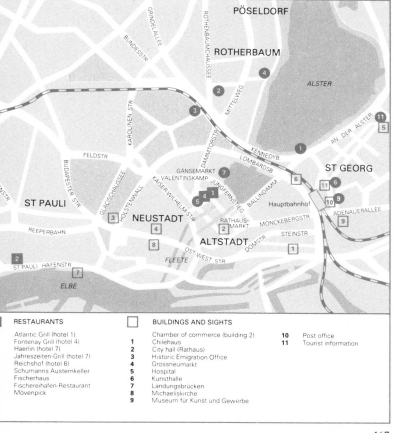

RESTAURANTS

Atlantic Grill (hotel 1)
Fontenay Grill (hotel 4)
Haerlin (hotel 7)
Jahreszeiten-Grill (hotel 7)
Reichshof (hotel 6)
Schumanns Austernkeller
Fischerhaus
Fischereihafen-Restaurant
Mövenpick

BUILDINGS AND SIGHTS

Chamber of commerce (building 2)
1   Chilehaus
2   City hall (Rathaus)
3   Historic Emigration Office
4   Grossneumarkt
5   Hospital
6   Kunsthalle
7   Landungsbrücken
8   Michaeliskirche
9   Museum für Kunst und Gewerbe
10 Post office
11 Tourist information

network of canals lend a Venetian flavour to the district. Little remains of the old city, save in areas such as Peterstrasse, with its brick and half-timbered houses.

The restored stock exchange on Adolphsplatz is the focus of the financial sector, and insurance and other commercial companies cluster around the Hauptbahnhof.

The most striking feature of the shopping district is the attractive network of *Passagen*, covered arcades where people can stroll, protected from traffic and the weather; the Alster arcades, lit by old-fashioned lanterns, date from the last century, while others, such as the Hanse-Viertel complex with its glass barrel roof and cupolas, are much more recent.

St Pauli and St Georg These two areas, respectively to the west and east of the city centre, exemplify the libertine atmosphere often unjustly attributed to the city as a whole. The main streets, the Reeperbahn and Steindamm, otherwise known as *Sündige Meile* (mile of sin), blaze with neon at night, offering all forms of entertainment from sex shows to the famous Hansa variety theatre.

Pöseldorf is a trendy part of the high-class residential area, Harvestehude, on the west of the Alster lake. Stylish boutiques, art galleries, discos and restaurants now occupy former sheds and stables centred on the Pöseldorf market.

Eppendorf, around the head of the lake, has attracted many quality shops and restaurants although it is not as affluent as Pöseldorf.

Uhlenhorst, on the eastern side of the lake, traditionally the "wrong" side, is nevertheless a select residential area and the base for many sailing and rowing clubs.

Altona The DESY nuclear research centre is here but it is mainly residential and, along the Elbchaussee, has some of the most expensive mansions in the city.

The outer suburbs

Blankenese The former fishing village of Blankenese is built on a steep and wooded hillside, 14km/9 miles west of the centre. It has been taken over by affluent commuters who have built splendid villas and gentrified the fishermen's cottages, but the old centre retains an attractive, rustic atmosphere.

City-Nord This area of high-rise office blocks around 5km/3 miles north of the city centre dates from the mid-1960s. More than 20 distinctive complexes house multinational companies such as BP, IBM, Hoechst, Esso, Shell and Texaco, altogether employing some 2,000 people.

Hotels

In a city where tourism is not highly developed, most hotel clients are business people. Recently there has been expansion at the top end of the scale and one hotel, the Vier Jahreszeiten, is ranked among the best in the world.

All of the main hotels listed have TVs and IDD telephones in the guest rooms and provide currency exchange and parking.

Atlantic-Hotel Kempinski [DM]||||
An der Alster 72, H1 ☏ *28880*
TX *2163297* • *AE DC MC V* • *265 rooms, 13 suites, 2 restaurants, 1 bar*
Built at the beginning of the century by the Alster lake, the Atlantic was originally intended to attract the North Atlantic luxury liner business and resembles "a glittering ocean liner at anchor." Its spacious lobby and public rooms are in a grand style, and its clients include political figures and leading business people. The corner bar, called Atlantic Brücke (bridge), and both restaurants overlook the Alster (see *Restaurants*). The suites are on the lakeside and all

of the elegantly furnished guest rooms have well-equipped bathrooms and video. 24hr room service, florist, gift shop, boutique, hairdresser, newsstand • pool, health club, massage, solarium; tennis and squash at a nearby club • fax, 15 meeting rooms (capacity up to 300).

Elysee *DM*////
Rothenbaumchaussee 10, H13
☎ *414120* ⓉⓍ *212455* • *AE DC MC V*
• *300 rooms, 6 suites, 2 restaurants, 1 bar*
This modern hotel, opened in August 1985, has light and streamlined decor. A brasserie and *Stube* provide informal meals. The clientele is half business and half leisure. 24hr room service • pool, sauna, jacuzzi, massage • 4 meeting rooms (capacity up to 750).

Hamburg Plaza *DM*////
Marseiller Str 2, H36 ☎ *35020*
ⓉⓍ *214400* • *Canadian Pacific* • *AE DC MC V* • *570 rooms, 20 suites, 2 restaurants, 2 bars*
The 32-floor Plaza is the biggest hotel in Hamburg. Well served by public transport, it is only a few metres from Dammtor station and the airport bus stops outside. It is in a complex which includes the Congress Centrum Hamburg and draws many of its clients from there. Two floors are reserved for nonsmokers, and all guest rooms are comfortable and furnished in a bright modern style. Extras include video. Hairdresser, gift shop, newsstand • pool with screened area for nude bathing, health club, jacuzzi, sauna, solarium, arrangements for golf, tennis and squash • fax, 9 meeting rooms (capacity up to 700).

Inter-Continental *DM*////
Fontenay 10, H36 ☎ *414150*
ⓉⓍ *211099* • *AE DC MC V* • *284 rooms, 6 suites, 3 restaurants, 1 bar*
The efficient 12-floor Inter-Continental stands in a quiet street at the edge of fashionable Pöseldorf. Its spacious entrance hall is flanked by a

small shopping arcade. There is a large ballroom and conference facilities are available on the tenth floor. The comfortable bedrooms, decorated in pastel shades, have cable TV. On the top floor are the Fontenay Grill (see *Restaurants*) and the Hamburg casino. 24hr room service, hairdresser, gift shop, shoe shop, men's outfitters, newsstand, hotel transport • pool, health club, massage, solarium • fax, 9 meeting rooms (capacity up to 450).

Ramada Renaissance *DM*////
Grosse Bleichen, H36 ☎ *349180*
ⓉⓍ *2162983* • *AE DC MC V* • *204 rooms, 7 suites, 1 restaurant, 1 bar*
The Renaissance is modern, but constructed in traditional Hamburg brick, blending into the adjacent Hanse-Viertel shopping arcade. The public rooms are furnished in sombre style; in contrast, the bedrooms are pleasantly light and spacious. One whole floor is given over to the Renaissance Club which has its own check-in service and lounge. 24hr room service, newsstand • sauna, massage, solarium • fax, 5 meeting rooms (capacity up to 200).

Reichshof *DM*//
Kirchenallee 34–36, H1 ☎ *248330*
ⓉⓍ *2163396* • *AE DC MC V* • *294 rooms, 6 suites, 1 restaurant, 1 bar*
The Reichshof, run by the third generation of the founding family, is right opposite the Hauptbahnhof. It has a fine Edwardian-style exterior and a spacious marble reception and lounge area. Rooms come in three grades: business, standard and economy. Business rooms are the best appointed, with larger TV, desk and additional seating; economy rooms have TV, radio, shower and minibar. The most spacious bedrooms are at the front. The restaurant (see *Restaurants*) has a gallery divided into a series of private rooms. Gift shop, newsstand • fax, 12 meeting rooms (capacity up to 40).

Vier Jahreszeiten [DM]/////
Neuer Jungfernstieg 9–14, H36
☎ *34941* TX *211629* • *AE DC MC V* •
175 rooms, 4 restaurants, 2 bars
This top-class hotel, with its white
façade, looks out over the inner
Alster lake. Founded in 1897 by Fritz
Haerlin, it is now run by the third
generation of the Haerlin family. The
six-floor building is on a triangular
site with an inner courtyard; outer
rooms are mainly doubles and inner
ones singles. The Vier Jahreszeiten is
furnished throughout in 19thC style,
with chandeliers, ormolu clocks, dark
paintings and tapestried chairs. The
impressive function rooms include
the appropriately named Gobelin-
Saal, which is lined with fine
tapestries. The Haerlin and
Jahreszeiten-Grill are both notable
(see *Restaurants*). 24hr room service,
newsstand, hairdresser • fax,
5 meeting rooms (capacity up to
120).

OTHER HOTELS
Crest [DM]/// *Mexikoring 1, H60*
☎ *6305051* TX *2174155* • *AE DC MC V.*
Well-equipped modern hotel,
adjacent to the City-Nord office
complex.
Europäischer Hof [DM]/
Kirchenallee 45, H1 ☎ *248171*
TX *2162493* • *Golden Tulip* •
DC MC V. The second biggest hotel
in Hamburg, opposite the
Hauptbahnhof. Comfortable, if a
little unimaginative.
Novotel Hamburg Nord [DM]/
Oldesloer Str 166, H61 ☎ *5502073*
TX *212923* • *MC V.* Modern, low-rise
hotel on the north side of the city,
next to *Autobahn* exit Schnelsen-
Nord.
Prem [DM]// *An der Alster 8–10,*
H1 ☎ *241726* TX *2163115* • *AE DC V.*
Very near the Atlantic and of the
same generation, but much smaller.
Popular with business people though
it lacks even basic business facilities.

Restaurants
Hamburg is famous for its seafood, although no fish now come from the
river Elbe because of pollution. Some fish restaurants are well-known
beyond the city limits but, generally, the best restaurants are in the main
hotels. Reservations are advisable.

Atlantic Grill [DM]////
Atlantic hotel ☎ *28880* • *AE DC MC V*
• *jacket and tie*
The Atlantic hotel's main restaurant,
with views across the Alster lake, has
a relaxed atmosphere which appeals
to both business and private patrons.
The menus are seasonal, with an
emphasis on fish dishes. A buffet
lunch is available in the grillroom.

Fontenay Grill [DM]////
Inter-Continental hotel ☎ *443430 or*
414150 • *closed Sat L* • *AE DC MC V*
• *jacket and tie*
This relatively small restaurant on
the top floor of the Inter-Continental
hotel is an appropriate choice for
business entertaining at the highest
level. The food is classic French and
the wine list includes some superb
Bordeaux wines.

Haerlin [DM]/////
Vier Jahreszeiten hotel ☎ *34941*
• *closed Sun* • *AE DC MC V* • *jacket*
and tie
The elegant Haerlin restaurant offers
a wide choice of international *haute
cuisine* and the equally diverse wine
list carries 300 labels. Well-spaced
tables, gilt mirrors and bronze-
coloured carpets, set off by white
walls, give it an air of opulence. It is
eminently suitable for top-level
business entertaining and a fixed-
price lunch menu is available.

Jahreszeiten-Grill [DM]/
Vier Jahreszeiten hotel ☎ *34941* • *AE*
DC MC V
The linen napkins and fine china
clearly indicate that this is not the
average *Stube*, though the rustic
furniture and oak fittings are in style.

The menu is similar to that of the Haerlin, but the atmosphere is more relaxed and less ostentatious. Prices are also lower.

Reichshof [DM]||
Reichshof hotel ☎ 248330 • *AE DC MC V*
The Reichshof is not suitable for entertaining top-rank executives, but it is well used by business people generally. One of its virtues is that the full menu is available continuously between noon and midnight. The food is German.

Schümanns Austernkeller [DM]|||
Jungfernstieg 34 ☎ 346265 *or* 345328 • *closed Sun and hols* • *no credit cards* • *reservations essential*
More than a century old, this restaurant is known for its unusual layout. It consists entirely of booths and private rooms seating up to 30, with names such as "Dutch Room" or "Hunter's Room" and with antique furnishings to match. The menu is German and the wines are mainly white.

Good but casual
There are dozens of good eating places all over Hamburg. *Fischerhaus*, St Pauli-Fischermarkt 14 ☎ 314053, heads the list of fish restaurants. Farther along the river at Grosse Elbstrasse 143, the *Fischereihafen-Restaurant* ☎ 381816, not exclusively for fish but with a fine view of the port, is just as popular. In the centre of town, in the basement of the Hanse-Viertel, is the Mövenpick which features four different theme restaurants: *Mövenpick, Café des Artistes, Backstube* and *Weinkeller* ☎ 351635.

Credit card abbreviations	
AE	American Express
DC	Diners Club
MC	Access/MasterCard
V	Visa

Bars
Bars range from elegant cocktail establishments to down-to-earth *Kneipen*. The cocktail bars in the main hotels – notably *Hansa Kogge* (Inter-Continental), *Simbari* (Vier Jahreszeiten), *Noblesse* (Ramada), *Piano Bar* (Reichshof) and the *Atlantic-Bar* (Atlantic) – are all suitable for drinks in the early evening. For the beer connoisseur, the *Börsen Treff*, Alten Wall 36, opposite the stock exchange, serves ten beers from the wood, and is quiet enough for informal business discussions. There are half a dozen casual bars on and near the Grossneumarkt, and Eppendorf is worth exploring for good *Kneipen*.

Entertainment
Hamburg is notorious for its striptease and sex shows, but it also offers classical music and drama performed to the highest standards. Many events are detailed in the monthly *Hamburger Vorschau*, which can be obtained from the tourist information offices at Bieberhaus am Hauptbahnhof (Kirchenallee exit), at the airport (Ankunftshalle D) and at the St-Pauli-Landungsbrücken 3. Tickets can be reserved from theatres and the following ticket agencies: *Collien*, Eppendorfer Baum 25 ☎ 483390, *Gerdes*, Rothenbaumchaussee 77 ☎ 453326, *Schumacher*, Colonnaden 37 ☎ 343044.

Theatre, dance, opera Out of some 40, the three main theatres are *Deutsches Schauspielhaus u. Malersaal*, Kirchenallee ☎ 248713, opposite the Hauptbahnhof, and *Thalia-Theater*, Raboisen 67 ☎ 330444, both with a repertoire of serious drama; and the *Hamburger Kammerspiele*, Hartungstr 9 ☎ 445162, which puts on lighter plays. The *Hamburgische Staatsoper* ☎ 351555, one of the world's leading opera houses, is located at Grosse Theaterstrasse. It also stages performances by the Hamburg Ballet company. Variety shows with international acts are presented at the *Hansa-Theater*, Steindamm 17 ☎ 241414. The *Operettenhaus* ☎ 311176, in the Reeperbahn, stages popular musicals.

Cinema There are many *Sex Kinos* in St Pauli and St Georg. Two downtown cinemas offering feature films are *Broadway* in Gerhofstrasse ☎ 343175, and *Metropolis* in Dammtorstrasse ☎ 342353, both near the Gänsemarkt. The *Amerika-Haus*, Tesdorpfstr 1 ☎ 4106292, shows American films in the original version. *The British Council Film Club* has shows (2–5) at Rothenbaumchaussee 34 ☎ 446057.

Music Concerts are regularly given by the three Hamburg orchestras – the Symphoniker, the Philharmonisches and the Sinfonie – at the *Musikhalle*, Karl-Muck-Pl ☎ 346920. Jazz is played mostly in *Kneipen* and small clubs. There are regular jazz, rock and pop concerts at *Fabrik*, Barnerstrasse ☎ 3915636.

Nightclubs and casinos The main districts for nightlife are St Pauli and St Georg. It is important to take care here: leave valuables in the hotel safe, do not go alone, carry money in small denominations, order your own drinks and pay for them on receipt. Less risky are the other nightlife areas: Pöseldorf, Eppendorf and Grossneumarkt, which is only an 8min walk from the Rathausmarkt and has plenty of cheerful bars and bistros in which to absorb the local atmosphere.

The only licensed casino in Hamburg is in the Inter-Continental hotel (other places are only fruit machine halls). It is open 3pm–3am and a passport is required. Roulette, baccarat and blackjack are played. Stylish discos include the one in the Vier Jahreszeiten hotel and *Blue Satellite*, on the 26th floor of the Hamburg Plaza hotel.

Shopping

The main shopping area is in the city centre. The big department and clothing stores such as *C&A, Hennes u. Mauritz, Horten, Jäger & Mirow,*

Karstadt and *Peek u. Cloppenburg* are along the Mönckebergstrasse, the wide street that runs from the Hauptbahnhof to Rathausmarkt. Across the Alster from the Rathaus is Neustadt, where you will find smaller, individual shops as well as *Alsterhaus*, an upmarket department store. *Schüler* is a men's tailor trading from an old-fashioned shop in the Alsterarkaden. The network of *Passagen* makes this the most pleasant part of the city for window shopping.

Sightseeing

Leaflets and maps are available from tourist offices at the main railway stations, the airport and St-Pauli-Landungsbrücken 3. The official free booklet, *Where to go in Hamburg*, is published monthly.

Historic Emigration Office This part of the Museum für Hamburgische Geschichte (Hamburg history museum) contains the names of all who emigrated to the USA via the port of Hamburg between 1850 and 1914. For a fee, any ancestors can be traced and details supplied of their journeys. *Holstenwall 24. Open Tue–Sat, 10–1, 2–5.*

Kunsthalle One of the most important collections in Germany, covering European art comprehensively to the 20th century. Of major interest are the world-famous 14thC altar paintings and the works from the German Romantic movement. *Glockengiesserwall. Open Tue–Sun, 10–5.*

Michaeliskirche This landmark, near the port, is considered to be the finest late-baroque church in north Germany. *Krayenkamp 4c. Open daily, 9–5.30 (summer); Mon–Sat, 10–4, Sun, 11.30–4 (winter).*

Museum für Kunst und Gewerbe The art and industry museum has a large collection of medieval, oriental and Islamic art. Of special interest are the rooms furnished in *Jugendstil* (Art Nouveau). *Steintorpl. Open Tue–Sun, 10–5.*

Port The port (*Hafen*) covers 100 sq km/39 sq miles and has berths for 500 ocean-going ships along 39km/24 miles of quayside. Guided tours (see below) depart from near the Landungsbrücken.

Rathaus The late-19thC city hall is a splendid example of the Nordic Renaissance style. It contains the seat of the Hamburg Senate and the city administrative offices. It has 647 rooms, including a series of noteworthy ceremonial halls. *Rathausmarkt. Open Mon–Fri, 10–3; Sat–Sun, 10–1; tours every 30min.*

Other notable buildings The curiously-shaped ten-floor office block in Burchardplatz, known as the *Chilehaus*, was built in the 1920s. The *St Pauli Elbtunnel*, constructed in about 1910, was featured in the film *The Odessa File*; this twin tunnel runs from near the Landungsbrücken into the free port area. Descent and ascent at each end is in cages for both people and vehicles (open Mon–Sat, 5am–10pm).

Guided tours
Boat trips *Alster Touristik* ☎ 341141 or 341145 operates sightseeing boats from Jungfernstieg on the Alster lake and canals from April to October. *HADAG Line* ☎ 37680024 and other operators run tours (1hr) around the port. All depart from jetty 2, St-Pauli-Landungsbrücken.
Bus tours *Jasper* ☎ 2201201, and others, operate 2hr or 2hr 30min bus tours of the city.

Spectator sports
Horse-racing The German Derby and other racing and showjumping events are held at the *Klein Flottbeck* racecourse, Derby Pl, Baron-Voght-Str 59 ☎ 828182, and trotting races at the *Trabrennbahn Am Volkspark*, Luruper Chaussee 30 ☎ 894004.
Soccer Hamburg's most famous team, HSV, plays at the *Volksparkstadion*, Sylvesteralle ☎ 837001.
Tennis The *Club der Alster* courts in Rothenbaum ☎ 445078 are used for the German open championships.

Keeping fit
Detailed advice on sports facilities may be obtained from *Hamburger Sportbund* ☎ 41211.
Fitness centres About 60 clubs in Hamburg offer fitness training, bodybuilding, sauna, solarium and even martial arts, all open to visitors. The Atlantic, Plaza, Inter-Continental, Elysee and Ramada hotels, in that order of preference, have fitness centres open to nonresidents.
Golf The most attractive course is the *Hamburger Golf-Club Falkenstein*, In de Bargen 59 ☎ 812177. The *Golf-Club auf der Wendelohe*, Oldesloer Str 251 ☎ 5505014, is open to nonmembers. Call *Hamburg Golf-Verband* ☎ 4121245 for details on other courses.
Squash Recommended clubs in the suburbs are *Squash-Hof*, Cuxhavener Str 66 ☎ 7962079, *Squashland*, Barsbütteler Str 33 ☎ 6530017, and *Squash Rackets Center*, Hans Henny Jahnweg 63 ☎ 2205519.
Swimming The best equipped public pool is the *Alster Schwimmhalle*, Ifflandstr 21 ☎ 223012. Also recommended are the *Bismarckbad*, Ottenser Hauptstr 2 ☎ 397601, and *Holthusenbad*, Goernerstr 21 ☎ 474754.

Local resources
Business services
Most of the larger hotels provide or will arrange photocopying and other business services. *Rent-an-Office*, Schauenberger Str 15 ☎ 3281080, can provide furnished or unfurnished offices for rental periods from a few hours to several weeks, supported by secretarial, telex and fax services.
Photocopying and printing *Fix Fotokopien* at Mönckerbergstr 11 ☎ 324709 is the most central. *G.F. Scharlau* has a shop at Hühnerposten 14 ☎ 231313 and three other branches. *Copyshop*, Grindelallee 132 ☎ 443679, also has a fast printing service.
Secretarial *Hamburg City Büro Service* at Spalding 1 ☎ 231175;

Multi-Büro-Service at Billstr 30
☎ 784449; both open Mon–Fri.
Translation *Büro R.K. Lochner*, An
der Alster 26 ☎ 244654.

Communications
Local delivery *Courier Express*
☎ 6770011, *Der Kurier* ☎ 291919.
Long-distance delivery DHL
☎ 55410, *XP* ☎ 501212, *Federal
Express* ☎ 5082941, *TNT* ☎ 7320626
and *World Courier* ☎ 505055 have
offices at the airport.
Post office Main office at
Hühnerpostern 12 ☎ 2395224. The
office in Hauptbahnhof is open 24hr.
Telex and fax *City Büro Service*
☎ 231175, Mon–Fri.

Conference/exhibition centres
The *Congress Centrum Hamburg*
(CCH) at Dammtor ☎ 35690
comprises 17 air-conditioned halls of
different sizes. On the other side of
the Botanical Gardens is the
Messegelände, Jungiusstr 13 ☎ 35690,
exhibition grounds with 13 halls. The
biggest fair held there is the annual
German international boat show.

Emergencies
Bureaux de change *Deutsche
Verkehrs-Kredit-Bank* upstairs in the
Hauptbahnhof is open daily, 7.30–10;
it provides emergency cash on all
credit cards.
Hospitals Nearest to the centre is
Allgemeines Krankenhaus St Georg,
Lohmühlenstr 5 ☎ 248801.
Emergency doctor ☎ 228022.
Emergency dental service ☎ 11500.
Pharmacies Police stations or the
emergency doctor can advise on
pharmacies that open late. Foreign
drugs are stocked by *Internationale
Apotheke*, Ballindamm 39 ☎ 335333
and *Roth's Alte Englische Apotheke*,
Jungfernstieg 48 ☎ 343906. Both are
near Jungfernstieg station.
Police Headquarters at Beim
Strohause 6 ☎ 2838520.

Government offices
Hamburg Information at Burchardstr
14, H1 ☎ 3005000 is the first source

of general guidance on business
matters in Hamburg. *Behörde für
Wirtschaft*, Hans-Ulrich Witt, Alter
Steinweg 4, H11 ☎ 34912427 is the
local department of trade and
industry. The *Behörde für
Wissenschaft u. Forschung*, Hamburger
Str 37, H76 ☎ 291881 deals with
science and research. Neither of these
bodies handles promotions or liaison,
which are the responsibility of the
chamber of commerce.

Information sources
Business information The
Handelskammer Hamburg (chamber
of commerce) is in the stock
exchange (part of the Rathaus) at
Adolphspl 1, H11 ☎ 361380.
Local media *Hamburger Abendblatt*
has the best local business coverage.
The national daily, *Die Welt*, has a
local section on Hamburg. The
regional radio and TV organization,
NDR, broadcasts from Hamburg.
Tourist information The main
office of *Fremdenverkehrszentrale
Hamburg e.V.* is in Bieberhaus,
opposite the Hauptbahnhof
☎ 24870245. The counter in the
Hauptbahnhof itself operates a hotel
reservations service ☎ 24870230.
Other tourist offices are at the airport
☎ 24870240, at Hanse-Viertel
☎ 24870220 and St-Pauli-
Landungsbrücken 3 ☎ 313977.

Thank-yous
Chocolates *Paulsen*, Poststr, sells
fine chocolates.
Florists *Blume Eppendorf*,
Eppendorfer Baum 20 ☎ 474793, is a
high-class florist with three other
branches. *Blumen Gaworski*,
Lübecker Str 85 ☎ 252918, is well-
established.
Gifts *Möhring*, Neuer Wall 25–31
☎ 367951, has a wide selection of
gifts; credit cards are taken.
Wine merchants *Cordx Stehr*,
Mohlenhofstr 3 ☎ 337961, and *C.C.F.
Fischer*, Hahntrapp 2 ☎ 3606924.

HANOVER
City codes zip 3000 ☎ 0511

Hanover's claim to fame in the business community arises from its Messe, or annual trade fair, held in April. It was started by the British during the Cold War of the late 1940s as competition to the centuries-old Leipzig Messe. The Hannover Messe has become the most important general trade fair in the world, with 406,000 visitors in 1986 to add to its normal population of 500,000. Several smaller exhibitions are also regular features.

Following the devastation of the Thirty Years' War (1618–48), the archduke Georg von Calenberg selected Hanover as his residence. His successors built palaces and gardens which attracted scholars and artists from other parts of the continent. One Hanoverian duke, Ernst August, became Elector of the Holy Roman Empire in 1692, and his son, Georg Ludwig, became King George I of England.

Industrialization came slowly, starting with the first ironworks in 1835, but during the 19th and early 20th centuries a mixture of industries was set up. When Volkswagen built its factory at nearby Wolfsburg, 60km/37 miles to the east of Hanover, the balance of manufacturing swung to the motor industry. An overdependence upon that sector is the main cause of Hanover's present economic difficulties. Employment has been running at a rate 50% higher than the national average since 1984. No vehicles are now made in Hanover, but Volkswagen has an engine factory here. Other major industries include Continental tyres, Varta batteries, VDO instruments and Wabco-Westinghouse electrical equipment. The long-established Hanomag makes construction machinery, another sector which has declined, and several Hanover-based companies are in the oil exploration business, which has slumped with the price of oil. Businesses less affected by economic decline are Siemens, making domestic appliances, Pelikan, office drawing equipment, and Bahlsen, one of Germany's biggest bakers.

Over the last 15 years Hanover has made considerable investment in its infrastructure, with new roads, city centre rebuilding, a new subway and airport terminal, for example. Yet employment has dropped by one-fifth. Local economists pin their hopes on structural changes to industry as part of a package which will resuscitate the north of Germany. The sectors for emphasis are marine research, air and space travel, communications and services.

Arriving

Hanover is on the North German plain, midway between Berlin and the Ruhr. Euroroutes E4 and E8 (*Autobahnen* A7 and A2) pass through Hanover. Rail routes also cross here, and it has an important international airport.

Hannover-Langenhagen airport
The airport terminal was completed in 1973. The main building is divided into two triangular sections with a central link. Lufthansa, Air France, Swissair, Alitalia, NFD and ESS share one half, British Airways, SAS, KLM, THY-Turkish Airlines and charter

carriers the other. Facilities can be stretched during major trade fairs because of special charters. Shops in the central link include a hairdresser, amusement arcade and newsstand. There is multilevel car parking and a filling station within the complex. The international courier services of DHL, TNT, XP, UPS and World Courier are available.

Clearance through customs and baggage collection normally takes 10–15min. There are lounges for Lufthansa's Senator Club and British Airways Executive Club. A Mövenpick restaurant opens daily until 10.30pm. As there is no general departure lounge, passengers are not called for security and customs checks until shortly before departure. Duty-free goods are sold at each boarding gate about 45min before departure of international flights. Bureau de change open Mon–Fri, 6.30–9; Sat, 9–5.30; Sun 10–6.30. Airport information and freight inquiries ☎ 7305224.
Nearby hotel Holiday Inn Hanover airport, Petzelstr 60 ☎ 730171 ⓉⓍ 924030 • AE DC MC V. Minibus service from airport.
City link The airport is 12km/7 miles north of the city. There is no rail link, and roads can be congested during the rush hours (7–9 and 4–6).
Taxi There is a rank immediately in front of the terminal and cabs can normally be obtained without difficulty. It usually takes about 25min to the centre, but nearer 35min during rush hours. The fare is typically DM30.
Car rental Autohansa ☎ 7305463, Avis ☎ 7305454, Europcar ☎ 7305575, Hertz ☎ 730544310, interRent ☎ 7305451, and Sixt (Budget) ☎ 7305408 have desks at the airport.
Bus Route no. 60 buses start from the front of the terminal, next to the taxi rank. They run direct to the city air terminal behind the Hauptbahnhof ☎ 1682801, open Mon–Thu and Sat, 9–6.30; Fri, 9–9; closed Sun. Buses run every 30min up to 10.30. The

journey takes 25min and the fare is DM4.40. This route is recommended even with baggage as a taxi can be picked up easily at the town terminal. A special bus also runs direct to the Messegelände (exhibition grounds) during major events.
Helicopter During important exhibitions, Luftreederei Meravo ☎ 892725 operates an air taxi service to and from the Messegelände.

Railway station
Hauptbahnhof The baroque-style main station is the central focus of Hanover. The façade is restored but the interior was completely rebuilt a few years ago. Regional, national and international services call at Hanover and there are direct hourly services to all main cities.

Platforms have underground access, as is usual in Germany, here linked with the nearby shopping mall. Below are the platforms for the *Stadtbahn*, which connects directly with the Messegelände as well as many other parts of the city. Behind the station is the in-town air terminal with connecting buses to the airport. The main taxi rank is at the front of the station with a smaller one at the rear. Rail information ☎ 16111.

Getting around
During major exhibitions taxis and/or public transport are strongly recommended. At other times you can choose. Roads are wide and clearly laid out and there are adequate parking facilities.
Taxis There is a tremendous demand for taxis during exhibitions, but at other times there is no shortage. Service is from ranks only, or by telephone request to *Taxi-ruf* ☎ 3811 or 2143.
Limousines Uni Rent ☎ 805444.
Driving There is a *Hertz* counter ☎ 324036 at the railway station but it is easiest to arrange car rental at the airport.
Walking An extensive traffic-free area and shopping mall make walking the easiest option in the centre.

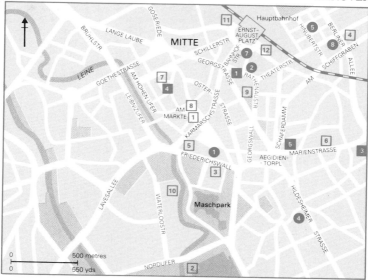

HOTELS

1 Inter-Continental
2 Kastens Hotel Luisenhof
3 Landhaus Ammann
4 Maritim
5 Schweizerhof
6 Congress-Hotel am Stadtpark
7 Grand Hotel Mussmann
8 Königshof
9 Parkhotel Kronsberg
10 Queen's Hotel am Tiergarten

RESTAURANTS

Ammann (hotel 3)
1 Baron de la Mouette
2 Georgenhof
Orchidee (hotel 2)
Schu's (hotel 5)
3 Sternchen Restaurant
Härkestuben
4 Altstadt
5 Ristorante da Lello

BUILDINGS AND SIGHTS

1 Altes Rathaus
2 Casino
3 City hall
4 Chamber of commerce
5 Government offices
6 Hospital
7 Kreuzkirche
8 Marktkirche
9 Opernhaus
10 Police headquarters
11 Post office
12 Tourist information
13 Congress-Centrum

Hanover is reasonably safe at night but be careful in underground shopping arcades.

Public transport The extensive *Strassenbahn* (streetcar) system is fast and efficient. In the central area, it largely runs underground and is also referred to as the *Stadtbahn*. In the suburbs the cars surface. Services on most routes run every 7–10min. The Hanover area is divided into three zones. A trip in zones 1 and 2, or 2 and 3, costs DM2.40, and a trip through all three zones costs DM4 (multiride tickets called *Sammelkarten* give six rides for DM10 and DM12 respectively). Tickets are bought from station machines and have to be cancelled in a machine before starting a trip. Route diagrams are displayed on stations and at stops. Information offices in the Hauptbahnhof and in Kröpcke station.

Area by area

Hanover is an industrial city. The larger business and residential areas are described below.

Mitte The central area is given over almost entirely to shopping, and commercial and cultural activities. It is delineated by a ring road on which the main public buildings are clustered and which changes its name every few blocks. The shopping streets are largely traffic-free. Most of the architecture is postwar but tiny pockets of the medieval town survive, and the old buildings have been lovingly restored.

Herrenhausen and Nordstadt Northwest of the centre are the parklands *Georgengarten* and the enclosed *Grosser Garten.* Georgengarten consists of a large area of grass with tree-lined avenues; Grosser Garten is a superb example of baroque horticultural art (see *Sightseeing*). In this area are the university, other academic institutions and many fine modern and period houses, some used as offices.

Eilenriede This district of natural woodland, to the east of the centre, has select residential areas, mainly in List to the north and around the zoo on the south.

Stöcken To the northwest of Herrenhausen is industrial Stöcken, along the bank of the Mittelland Kanal, which connects the Ruhr with Berlin. Volkswagen, Continental and Varta are all located here.

Hotels

For many years Hanover lacked the hotel accommodation required during major exhibitions, and families were encouraged to take in visitors. Although the number of hotel rooms has increased, it is perfectly acceptable to take private accommodation at the time of the Messe.

Most of the best hotels are in the central area and standards are high. During exhibitions rates may be increased by up to 20% and it is common practice to make reservations 12 months in advance. All hotels listed below offer currency exchange and room service at least until 11pm. Parking is generally not a problem.

Inter-Continental [DM]||||
Friedrichswall 11, H1 ☎ *16911*
[TX] *923656 • AE DC MC V • 285 rooms, 14 suites, 2 restaurants, 2 bars*
One of the first of the new hotels to be built in Hanover, the Inter-Continental has recently been refurbished. Although no longer the largest hotel, it is still considered to have the best position, facing the Rathaus across Friedrichswall. The ten-floor hotel is faceless on the

outside, but guest rooms are spacious and tastefully furnished. Thirty rooms are reserved for nonsmokers. Of the two restaurants, one has an international menu and the other serves German food, but neither is regarded as smart. 24hr room service, florist, newsstand • solarium, bicycles in summer, jogging suits loaned • fax, 8 meeting rooms (capacity up to 300).

Kastens Hotel Luisenhof [DM]//
Luisenstr 1–3, H1 ☎ *12440* ⊤ⓧ *922325* • *AE DC MC V* • *160 rooms, 4 suites, 2 restaurants, 1 bar*
The Luisenhof is a family-run hotel with high standards. It is within 150 metres of the railway station but on a quiet street. The public rooms are lofty but the mirrored surfaces and glittering lighting seem out of keeping with the traditional image fostered by the owners. All the bedrooms are individually furnished, some with antiques. The Orchidee (see *Restaurants*) features international cuisine, and there is a *Stube* offering country fare. 10 meeting rooms (capacity up to 300).

Landhaus Ammann [DM]//
Hildesheimer Str 185, H1 ☎ *830818* ⊤ⓧ *9230900* • *AE DC MC* • *14 rooms, 3 suites, 2 restaurants, 1 bar*
This pretty, modern hotel is situated in a pleasant area halfway between the city centre and the Messegelände. The exterior is painted white and the upper floor has attractive dormer windows. The atmosphere is restful and the furnishings include original oil paintings. Service is polite and discreet, and the Ammann restaurant is highly regarded (see *Restaurants*). Newsstand, gift shop • fax, 3 meeting rooms (capacity up to 100).

Maritim [DM]///
Hildesheimer Str 34–40, H1 ☎ *16531* ⊤ⓧ *9230268* • *AE DC MC V* • *294 rooms, 6 suites, 1 restaurant, 1 bar*
The Maritim, opened in 1983, is the largest hotel in town. It is on the edge

of the central area only 50 metres from Schlägerstrasse subway station. Many business clients come for the seminars held in the hotel. The entrance is opulent and dark, with black glass and chandeliers. The comfortably furnished rooms are decorated mostly in warm tones. Newsstand • pool, sauna, solarium • 8 meeting rooms (capacity up to 500).

Schweizerhof [DM]//
Hinüberstr 6, H1 ☎ *3495151* ⊤ⓧ *923359* • *AE DC MC V* • *104 rooms, 2 suites, 2 restaurants, 1 bar*
Hidden away in a quiet street behind the station, this independent hotel opened in 1983. The building was originally planned as an apartment block but was converted to a hotel before completion. This accounts for the bare brick walls in the corridors and the interesting layouts of the large rooms. The major appeal of the hotel is its restaurant, Schu's (see *Restaurants*). Sauna, squash court • 4 meeting rooms (capacity up to 130).

OTHER HOTELS
Congress-Hotel am Stadtpark
[DM]// *Clausewitzstr 6, H61* ☎ *28050* ⊤ⓧ *921263* • *AE DC MC V* Next to the Congress-Centrum, 3km/2 miles east of the centre.
Grand Hotel Mussmann [DM]////
Ernst-August-Pl 7, H1 ☎ *327971-5* ⊤ⓧ *922859* • *AE DC MC V*. An old hotel opposite the Hauptbahnhof.
Königshof [DM]/ *Königstr 12, H1* ☎ *312071* ⊤ⓧ *922306* • *AE DC MC V*. A modern hotel near the centre, with reproduction antique furnishings.
Parkhotel Kronsberg [DM]/
Laatzener Str 18, H72 ☎ *861086* ⊤ⓧ *923488* • *AE MC V*. Comfortable accommodation within walking distance of the Messegelände but far from anywhere else. Car essential.
Queens Hotel am Tiergarten
[DM]/ *Tiergartenstr 117, H71* ☎ *51030* ⊤ⓧ *922748* • *AE DC MC V*. Near *Autobahn* exit Hanover-Anderten 8km/5 miles east of the centre.

Restaurants

There is a wide choice of national restaurants in Hanover but most are unmemorable. The best hotel restaurants are suitable for business; those listed below are most likely to impress. Reservations are advisable.

Ammann   *DM*////
Landhaus Ammann hotel ☎ 830818 • closed Dec 24 • AE DC MC • jacket and tie
The small restaurant in the Landhaus Ammann displays a quiet elegance. The cuisine might be described as *nouvelle* in its artistry and fine ingredients but the portions are generous. The well-balanced wine list carries 500 labels.

Baron de la Mouette   *DM*///
Mövenpick Café Kröpcke, Georgstr 35 ☎ 326285 • AE DC MC V
The Kröpcke Café, on a main junction in the centre of Hanover, has been a feature of city life since 1878, although the present building was opened in 1976. It consists of a large, high-class café/*Konditorei* at street level and the smaller Baron restaurant upstairs. The restaurant's seasonal menus, together with beef from the trolley, make it always popular for business lunches, as for social occasions.

Georgenhof   *DM*/////
Herrenhäuser Kirchweg 20 ☎ 702244 • closed Dec 24 • no credit cards
This suburban restaurant was the first in the area to earn a Michelin star, in 1968. Under its new owner, Heinrich Stern, one of Hanover's most respected restaurateurs, it will not rest on its laurels. The menu, like that of his Sternchen Restaurant (see below), features regional dishes with a *nouvelle* emphasis. Comprehensive wine list.

Orchidee   *DM*/
Kastens Hotel Luisenhof ☎ 16151 • closed Sun in Jul and Aug • AE DC MC V
The Orchidee is a good choice of restaurant for business lunches. It is right in the centre of town, in an attractive hotel, and serves international dishes. Tables are sufficiently well-spaced to give a feeling of confidentiality.

Schu's   *DM*///
Schweizerhof hotel ☎ 34950 • closed Sat L • AE DC MC V • jacket and tie
Schu's (named after the chef) has a Michelin star and is well patronized by Hanover's business community. The unostentatious dining room is open to the hotel lobby. The cuisine, using fresh ingredients, is French with a German flavour; the wine list is firmly international.

Sternchen Restaurant Härkestuben   *DM*///
Marienstrasse 104 ☎ 817322 • closed Sat in Jun–Sep • AE DC MC V • jacket and tie
Despite its unpromising exterior, this family-run restaurant, conveniently placed for the Congress-Centrum, is one of the best in the city. Evenings are less crowded than lunch times. The menu is short, and the food modern German. Private dining room available.

Good but casual
If you hanker after the traditional generous German helpings, aim for places described as *bürgerlich*, such as *Altstadt*, Knochenhauerstr 42 ☎ 328732, in the old market. They provide hearty, if unimaginative, meals at reasonable prices. Italian and Greek restaurants are popular but standards are not always very high. Try *Ristorante da Lello* ☎ 320705 in Marienstrasse, near to Aegidientorplatz.

> For general information about German restaurants, see the *Planning and Reference* section.

Bars

It is best to keep to the main hotels if you want sophistication. The *Inter-Conti Bar* is spacious and pleasant. There are several respectable bars in the Altstadt that serve decent drinks, such as *Dortmunder Treff*, Ihmepl 2c. If you want to sample the local brew, ask for a *Lüttje Lage*.

Entertainment

Entertainment tends to be rather conventional although street and beer festivals occur sporadically. The tourist office issues a monthly guide *Hannover Vorschau* and the weekly magazine *Hannover Woche* is available from newsstands.

Ticket agencies *Verkehrsbüro*, Ernst-August-Pl 8 ☎ 1682800 and *Besucherring*, Georgstr 36 ☎ 326245.

Theatre, dance, opera The *Staatsoper*, Opernplatz ☎ 1686140, a fine neo-classical building, is the most prestigious theatre, putting on chamber music, opera, operetta and orchestral works. The *Staatsschauspiel*, Ballhofstrasse ☎ 1686142 has a repertory of established drama from Feydeau to Shakespeare. Performances change daily.

Music An open-air summer programme of classical music and drama is produced in the graceful surroundings of the *Grosser Garten*, Herrenhäuserstr ☎ 1687593. *Jazz Club*, Am Lindener Berge 38 ☎ 454455 has performances about three times a week.

Nightclubs and casinos The casino *Spielbank Hannover*, Arthur-Menge-Ufer ☎ 804018, has roulette, blackjack and baccarat. There are cabarets at *Alcazar*, Leonhardtstr 11 ☎ 344610 and *Amourette*, Asternstr 11 ☎ 717182.

Shopping

Around the Marktkirche and by the river there are interesting small shops including some selling antiques. At the other end of the scale is the flea market, held every Saturday on the Hohes Ufer.

Sightseeing

A continuous red line on the street indicates a tourist route.

Altes Rathaus 15thC brick building with stepped gable end, now used for city archives. *Köbelingerstr 59. Open daily, 8.30–3.30; Tue and Thu, until 6.*

Grosser Garten A formal, early baroque garden with flowers, statues, fountains and a maze. *Herrenhäuser Str. Open daily, 8–dusk; open late for special summer events.*

Kreuzkirche The oldest church in the city, begun in 1333; altarpiece by Lucas Cranach the Elder. *Goldener Winkel. Open during services.*

Marktkirche Its high tower has become the emblem of Hanover. 14thC stained-glass windows. *Am Markte. Open Mon–Sat, 10–5; Sun 11–4.*

Guided tours

The tourist office ☎ 1682319 has a 2hr 30min tour at 1.30 and 4 every afternoon in the summer, Wed and Sat in winter.

Out of town

Southwards along the Weser valley, 45km/28 miles southwest of Hanover, is *Hameln*, of Pied Piper fame, with many medieval and baroque buildings.

Spectator sports

Football Hannover Broncos play American football at the *Leinestadion* ☎ 1683424.

Soccer Hannover 96 plays at the *Niedersachsen-Stadion* ☎ 1684574.

Keeping fit

Most participating sport in Hanover needs club membership. The largest fitness centre is the *Sport und Sauna Studio*, Badenstedterstr 60 ☎ 2107312; day membership available.

Squash *Club Langenhagen*, Kopernikusstr 30 ☎ 776030.

Swimming The two main public indoor swimming pools are *Stadionbad*, Arthur-Menge-Ufer ☎ 1685411 and *Vahrenwalder Bad*, Vahrenwalder Str 100 ☎ 1684629.

Local resources

Business services
Photocopying and printing *City Copy*, opposite the Hauptbahnhof ☎ 332640.

Secretarial *Schreibbüro Foss*, Bahnreihe 7 ☎ 6040267, work in English and French as well as German.

Translation *Bruno Berger*, Max-Born-Weg 35, 3014 Laatzen (just south of Hanover) ☎ 824682 and *Buglass u. Long*, Gustav-Adolf-Str 11 ☎ 717051 (English) or ☎ 7000070 (French, Spanish, Italian).

Communications
Local delivery *Krüger* ☎ 6477744.
Long-distance delivery *DHL* ☎ 740060, *TNT* ☎ 743061 and *World Courier* ☎ 774577 at the airport. Services throughout northern Germany from *Schenkers* ☎ 736034.
Post office Main post office in Ernst-August-Platz next to the Hauptbahnhof. Open Mon–Fri, 8–6; Sat, 8–1. Late counter open Mon–Fri, 6–10; Sat, 1–10; Sun, 7–10.
Telex and fax Main post office ☎ 1271 and *Ingeborg Buczilowski*, Jägerweg 6 ☎ 737567.

Conference/exhibition centres
The *Messegelände*, D-3000 Hannover 82 ☎ 891 ⓉⓍ 922728 to the south of the city includes 25 separate halls and extensive grounds. Special trains run during exhibition times direct to Messegelände station. Many extra cars on the *Stadtbahn* provide fast and frequent services. The *Congress-Centrum Stadtpark*, Theodor-Heuss-Pl 1–3 ☎ 810031 ⓉⓍ 0923198, 3km/2 miles east of the city centre, has capacity for up to 4,000.

Emergencies
Bureaux de change *Deutsche Verkehrs-Kredit-Bank* in the Hauptbahnhof, open Mon–Fri, 7.30–9; Sat, 7.30–6; Sun, 10–5.
Hospitals Emergency doctor ☎ 314044. *Unfallklinik* (accident hospital) Marienstr 37 ☎ 12431. Emergency dentist ☎ 311031, Mon–Fri, 5–7; Sat–Sun, 3–6.
Pharmacies All give details of pharmacies on duty out of hours.
Police Headquarters Hardenbergstr 1 ☎ 1090.

Government offices
The Ministry of Commerce and Trade (*Ministerium für Wirtschaft und Verkehr*) at Friedrichswall 1 ☎ 1201 provides business information about Niedersachsen (Lower Saxony). For city government information contact the Press and Information Office (*Presse- und Informationsamt*) at the Neues Rathaus ☎ 1681.

Information sources
Business information The local chamber of commerce (*Industrie- und Handelskammer Hannover-Hildesheim*), Schiffgraben 49 ☎ 31070, also provides information on the Messe. City library (*Stadtbibliothek*), Hildesheimer Str 12 ☎ 1682169.
Local media The main local paper for business coverage is *Hannoversche Allgemeine*. The *Braunschweiger Zeitung* and the *Hildesheimer Allgemeine* may also be relevant for business activities in the neighbouring towns. *NDR* broadcasts TV and radio from the city.
Tourist information *Verkehrsbüro*, the main tourist office, is opposite the station at Ernst-August-Platz 8 ☎ 1682319.

Thank-yous
Chocolates *Henf*, opposite the Hauptbahnhof ☎ 320527.
Florists *Floristen Messe Service* Alte Döhrener Str 97 ☎ 800021 will deliver.
Wine merchants *Weinhandelshaus Bernhard Kasselbring*, Laportestr 20 ☎ 441725 arranges gift-packed wine.

KIEL

City codes zip 2300 ☎ 0431

Kiel promotes itself as the "breezy city" (*die Stadt im frischen Wind*); this is an accurate physical description rather than a metaphorical one. The city is at the head of a large fjord, 17km/10.5 miles from the open sea, and it has a population of almost 250,000. Shipping and marine engineering have dominated the local economy since the last century, when the Nord-Ostsee Kanal or Kiel Canal was cut to enable the Prussian navy to sail unhindered between the Baltic and North seas. It is now used by commercial vessels. But the military element is still strong as there are both German and British bases here. The ruins of the massive U-boat pens from World War II still dominate the view from the quayside and near the mouth of the fjord stands the German naval memorial.

The big firms in Kiel today are still involved with the defence industry. Howaldtswerke and MaK (Krupp) are the leading shipbuilding and heavy engineering companies. Hagenuk is a manufacturer of communications and navigation equipment, but major German firms such as AEG and Siemens also have plants in the city. The new industrial areas at Kiel-Mettenhof and Kiel-Wellsee have attracted companies such as Bosch and Philips. One of Germany's leading medical firms, Ortopedia, is based here; and there are several small boatyards.

Kiel is the seat of government and therefore of the administration of the *Land* (province) of Schleswig-Holstein. The port is the southern terminus of car ferry routes to Denmark, Norway and Sweden. The sailing events of the 1936 and 1972 Olympics were held at Kiel, which has become increasingly important as a centre for this sport. The annual *Kieler Woche* is the highlight of the sailing calendar in northern Europe. Government, shipping and sailing provide more than twice the employment opportunities of the manufacturing sector.

Arriving

Kiel has a small airport at Holtenau with limited services, including flights to Frankfurt and Copenhagen by Cimber Air and to Berlin by PanAm. Flight inquiries ☎ 323656. Air taxis *Ohlair* ☎ 323828. Hamburg is the nearest international airport; a special coach connects with Kiel (90min). The A215 *Autobahn*, a branch of Europe's E3 north–south artery, runs to Kiel, whose main station is the junction for trains from the south.

Railway station

Hauptbahnhof is in the south of the central business district, beside the bus station and quayside. It has rail

and city information stalls and a cab rank directly outside. There are regular Intercity services to Hamburg in the mornings, several going on to Bonn and Frankfurt and others to Mannheim and Nuremburg. There are other services to Flensburg and Lübeck with connections to Berlin. Inquiries ☎ (040) 11532 (Hamburg and south) or (040) 11533.

Getting around

The city centre is within a few minutes' walk of the station. Most of the big industrial complexes are some distance away and you will need a car or taxi. For some journeys, such as to the shipyards at Wellingdorf, a ferry

can be quicker than a car.
Walking is both safe and pleasant in all areas, by day or night.
Taxis There are several ranks in the centre and in the suburbs. For collection within the Kiel area ☎ 680101.
Driving is fairly straightforward despite many one-way streets and some pedestrianized zones. There are several multilevel garages, but these can be full. The main rental offices are *Autohansa* ☎ 672011, *Avis* ☎ 94028, *Europcar* ☎ 524052, *Hertz* ☎ 676554 and *interRent* ☎ 675030.
Ferries The main passenger route along the fjord runs every 50min, and this connects at Seegarten and Reventlou with another route that crosses the fjord to the Wellingdorf shipyards. Tickets, sold from machines on the jetties or by the ticket attendant on board, must be cancelled in the *Entwerter* machine by the gangway. Inquiries ☎ 701234.

Local buses Kieler Verkehrs-AG (KVAG) operates both the local orange buses and the ferries. The busiest bus routes run every 10min to and from the centre. A zonal fare system operates, with the basic fare DM2, rising in stages to DM4. These fares include free transfer to the ferry or another bus within a set period (60min for the basic fare, longer for the more expensive). A 24hr ticket (*Netzkarte*) can be bought for DM8. Buy single tickets from the driver or a more economical carnet from kiosks. Passengers must cancel tickets in the *Entwerter* inside the door. Route diagrams are displayed at most stops. Inquiries ☎ 701234.

Area by area
Much of the centre of Kiel lacks any feeling of intimacy following post-World War II rebuilding along straight wide streets. The main business in the central area is that of

HOTELS
1 Conti-Hansa
2 Maritim-Bellevue
3 Astor
4 Kieler Kaufmann
5 Kieler Yacht-Club
6 Wiking

BUILDINGS AND SIGHTS
1 Canal High Bridge
2 Chamber of commerce
3 Government Office for Economic Promotion
4 Hospital
5 Kieler Schloss
6 Nikolai-Kirche
7 Opera house
8 Ostseehalle
9 Police station
10 Post office
11 Schiffahrtsmuseum
12 Tourist Information

RESTAURANTS
Fayence (hotel 1)
Maritim (hotel 2)
Hansa-Pavillon (hotel 1)
1 Angus Steakhaus
Normandie (hotel 6)

government administration, both city and *Land*. A smallish pedestrian precinct has been created around the Alte Markt and an attractive park lies behind the old Nikolai-Kirche.

A few hundred metres from the centre is the Schwedenkai for the roll-on/roll-off ferries. On the other side of Sartorikai is Kiel's red-light district.

Bellevue The university and government buildings are north of the city centre. Beyond that, by the fjord, lies the Hindenburgufer, the most prestigious residential area.

The suburbs
Kiel has developed along both sides of the fjord and the coastal suburbs are the most sought-after. On the eastern shore, opposite the city centre, is Mönkeberg and farther north are Heikendorf and Laboe, popular summer resorts and high-class residential areas for commuters.

Holtenau, on the western shore, has some charming 19thC town houses by the canal. Farther out are the rather modern and characterless Friedrichsort, Strande and Schilksee, where the Olympic village is situated.

Hotels

Only the Maritim-Bellevue and the Conti-Hansa offer the standard of accommodation and facilities expected by most business travellers. Both provide IDD telephones and currency exchange. Rooms have minibars and sometimes hairdryers.

Conti-Hansa [DM]|
Schlossgarten 7, K1 ☎ *51150*
TX *292813* • *AE DC MC V* • *164 rooms, 1 suite, 2 restaurants, 1 bar*
The plain brick exterior of the Conti-Hansa belies its elegant, well-equipped interior. It was substantially enlarged in 1984. The guest rooms are comfortable and decorated in a conservative but pleasant style. Extras include trouser presses and cable TV. The hotel is in a green setting overlooking Oslokai. The Fayence restaurant, open in the evenings only (see *Restaurants*), and the Hansa-Pavillon are very suitable for business entertaining.
Hairdresser, gift shop, newsstand • sauna, solarium, jacuzzi • 6 meeting rooms (capacity up to 280).

Maritim-Bellevue [DM]||
Bismarckallee 2, K1 ☎ *35050*
TX *292444* • *AE DC MC V* • *85 rooms 4 suites, 1 restaurant, 1 bar*
The Maritim is the most important business hotel in Kiel. It is about 3km/2 miles from the city centre, in the prestigious Bellevue district. A modern, white building, it stands ten floors high on rising ground, giving

superb views across the fjord from the restaurant (see *Restaurants*) and from the balconied rooms on the east side of the hotel. The other side of the building looks out on woods. The guest rooms are spacious and comfortable. Hairdresser, wine shop, newsstand • pool, sauna, solarium, gym • 7 meeting rooms (capacity up to 800).

OTHER HOTELS
Astor [DM]| *Holstenpl 2, K1*
☎ *93017* TX *292720 AE MC V.*
Modestly priced in a central location close to the convention centre, but with rather small, plainly furnished rooms and lobby.
Kieler Kaufmann [DM]|
Niemannsweg 102, K1 ☎ *85011*
TX *292446* • *Ringhotel* • *AE DC MC V.*
Pleasantly situated in Bellevue parkland.
Kieler Yacht-Club [DM]|
Hindenburgufer 70, K1 ☎ *85055*
TX *292869 AE DC MC V.* Nautical atmosphere and fresh location on the fjord.
Wiking [DM] *Schützenwall 1, K1*
☎ *673051.* On the street leading to the *Autobahn*, yet close to the centre.

Restaurants

Eating establishments in Kiel are mainly geared to the tourist trade. Most business entertaining is done at the leading hotel restaurants.

Fayence *DM*||
Conti-Hansa hotel ☎ *51150* • *closed L and Sun* • *AE DC MC V* • *jacket preferred*
The Fayence is a good choice for smart business entertaining. It is stylish and comfortable, with dark panelling and tapestried chairs and banquettes. The cuisine is international but with a good leavening of local Schleswig dishes such as elderberry soup, Kiel sprats and pike with raisins. The wine list consists of mainly German vintages.

Maritim *DM*|
Maritim-Bellevue hotel ☎ *35050* • *AE DC MC V*
A plainly furnished modern restaurant with spectacular views of the fjord. The cuisine is generally international with a German flavour and the fish dishes are based on local Baltic recipes. The Maritim is an acceptable venue for normal business entertaining, but it may be a little too public for confidential discussions.

Good but casual
The *Hansa-Pavillon*, Conti-Hansa hotel ☎ 51150, open from early morning until 11, offers a wide menu, and is a regular choice by local business people. Also well patronized is the *Angus Steakhaus*, Kehdenstr 24 ☎ 93919. Steaks are good and the table arrangement permits fairly private discussions. An Italian restaurant, *Claudio's*, Königsweg 46 ☎ 676867 (closed Sun) is highly regarded. The *Normandie*, Wiking hotel ☎ 673424, (evenings only) offers a completely French cuisine.

Bars

The bars of the main hotels are the principal meeting places for business people. The *Conti-bar* in the Conti-Hansa hotel has a piano and dancing.

The centrally located *King George* bar at Lange Reihe 23 doubles as a disco later in the evening. Another popular bar is on top of the Astor hotel (see *Hotels*).

Entertainment

A free monthly pocket guide to local entertainment is available from the information centre at the Sophienblatt-Sophienhof. It lists events at the two theatres and the multipurpose *Ostseehalle*, Europapl ☎ 9012305 (information) or 92900 (tickets).
Music *Opernhaus*, Fleethörn ☎ 92100 stages popular classics and lesser-known works.
Nightclubs There is little nightlife. Leaving aside the unappealing establishments along the Sartorikai, the entertainment in the Maritim-Bellevue hotel is the most promising.

Shopping

Around the Markt and along Holstenstrasse, Dänische Strasse, Schloss Strasse and Flämische Strasse there are the usual department stores. Sailing equipment shops are out of town at Schilksee.

Sightseeing

The 90min ferry journey to the mouth of the fjord passes the naval base, the canal locks, the various yachting harbours, the U-boat memorial at Möltenort and the naval memorial at Laboe. A return by road (local bus nos 44, 64 and Express-Bus no. 40) goes over the canal high bridge with spectacular views along its length.
Kieler Schloss Kiel Castle contains the Schleswig-Holstein collection of 17th–20thC European old masters. *Dänische Str 44. Open Tue–Fri, 10–5, Sat, Sun 2–6.*
Schiffahrtsmuseum The shipping museum is near Oslokai, with three

historic ships alongside. *Wall 65. Open daily 10–6; Oct–Apr 10–5, closed Mon.*

Spectator sports
Sailing The main events take place during *Kieler Woche* in June. There are national, European or world event water sports throughout the summer ☎ 62230.

Keeping fit
Fitness centres *Fitness Center California*, Ringstr 37–39 ☎ 62625, is open to nonmembers on a daily basis. The best-equipped sports centre is at the university on Olshausenstrasse ☎ 8801.
Cycling Cycles can be rented from *Rahefs* ☎ 555159.
Gliding Gliding and parachuting clubs at Kiel aerodrome ☎ 322066.
Sailing Try *Baltic Yachtservice* ☎ 334969 or *Happy Sailing* ☎ 371163 for crewing or renting sailing boats.
Swimming *Brest-Halle*, Lautziusstr ☎ 9011151, a sports complex, has an indoor pool. There are superb bathing beaches around the fjord. The nearest beach is at Heikendorf with others at Laboe, Schilksee and Strande.
Water sports *Surf City Kiel* ☎ 63063 provides facilities for parasailing, waterskiing and surfing.

Local resources
Business services
The Maritim and Conti-Hansa hotels provide comprehensive business facilities with secretaries and translators by arrangement.
Photocopying *Franke u. Möhring*, Küterstr 13 ☎ 98060, plus most department stores.
Printing *Repro-Renard*, Ringstr 41 ☎ 675252.
Secretarial *Franke u. Möhring* ☎ 98060.
Translation *Dr W. Brorsen*, Schillerstr 25 ☎ 551816.

Communications
Local delivery *C.D. Weber* in Henri-Durant-Allee ☎ 549700.
Long-distance delivery *DHL* ☎ 51272.

Post office Main office in Stresemannplatz ☎ 5910. Open Mon–Fri, 8–6; Sat, 8–1.
Telex and fax At the main post office ☎ 5911; telex at hotels.

Emergencies
Bureau de change The main post office in Stresemannplatz has a special counter (*Spätschalter*) open until 9pm Mon–Fri; until 6 Sat, Sun, hols.
Hospitals *Universitäts-Klinik*, Hospitalstr 21 ☎ 5970; ambulance ☎ 19222. Emergency dental service (weekends) ☎ 30759; medical stand-by service 6pm–6.30am ☎ 19292.
Pharmacies All give details of pharmacies open out of hours.
Police Main station: Blumenstr 2 ☎ 5981; emergency calls ☎ 110. Lost property ☎ 9012184.

Government offices
The Office for Economic and Communications Advancement, foreign department (*Amt für Wirtschafts- und Vekehrsförderung, Abteilung Fremdenverkehr*), Sophienblatt-Sophienhof ☎ 9012300 provides helpful information.

Information sources
Business information The local chamber of industry and commerce (*Industrie- u. Handelskammer*) is at Lorentzendamm 24 ☎ 59041.
Local media Business people read *Die Welt* rather than local papers. The Kiel office of *NDR* (Nord Deutscher Runkfunk) radio is at Wall ☎ 9870.
Tourist information Public inquiries at the office (Verkehrsverein) opposite the railway station at Sophienblatt-Sophienhof ☎ 62230.

Thank-yous
Grossman, florists, Kleiststr 55 ☎ 802006, will deliver. Try *Hohwü Delikatessen*, Holstenstr 80 ☎ 91038 for food and wines; *Geschenkstudio-Barbara*, Brunswiker Str 46 ☎ 567551 for gifts; and for chocolates, go to *Most*, Holstenstr 43 ☎ 94925.

MAINZ/WIESBADEN *City codes* (Mainz) zip 6500 ☏ 06131; (Wiesbaden) zip 6200 ☏ 06121

Mainz and Wiesbaden, separated by the Rhein, are both overshadowed by Frankfurt, but they are state capitals, and each plays an individual part in German cultural and economic life. Mainz is the seat of Germany's Catholic hierarchy and centre of the wine trade, while wealthy Wiesbaden produces the champagne-like Sekt.

From the Middle Ages until the early 19th century, Mainz was a major political, ecclesiastical and commercial centre, but the industrial revolution saw its relative decline. However, its central location, near Frankfurt and rail, road and river routes to all parts of Germany, eastern France and Switzerland, has recently attracted industry, most of it around the two Rhein docks. Leading companies with plants here include Nestlé, Degussa, MAN, IBM and Schott, the glassmakers. Printing, the making of paper, cement, textiles, electrical goods and chemicals are also carried out here, and a new industrial zone, away from the river, is planned.

Gutenberg invented printing in Mainz, and the regional broadcasting station and ZDF, the second national TV channel, are based here. Since its recent renovation, the big Rheingoldhalle has become an important conference centre. Mainz has been capital of Rheinland-Pfalz since 1949; but, with 186,000 inhabitants to Wiesbaden's 268,000, it is the smaller of the two cities.

Downstream across the Rhein, Wiesbaden is a 19th-century creation, a spa with thermal baths, casino, elegant shops and hotels, and superior entertainment. The local tax system, favourable to investment income, drew many wealthy industrialists who settled and built imposing villas, which still stand along leafy avenues. The curative waters brought invalids and their doctors, and the city now has several clinics. Wiesbaden's chief activity is administration; it is the capital of Hessen, a large *Land* which includes Frankfurt, and as well as state ministries there are federal institutions like the Bundeskriminalamt (German FBI) and a regional command of the Bundeswehr.

Arriving

Frankfurt airport is about 40km/25 miles to the east. The best rail connections are with Mainz, but Wiesbaden is served by some Intercity trains. *Autobahnen* encircle Mainz, pass close to Wiesbaden and link both to the main routes up and down the Rhein and through Frankfurt to north Germany.
City link From Frankfurt airport the choice is train or taxi. To Mainz, trains leave hourly, on the hour, 8–10 (journey time 20min). The more frequent *S-Bahn* service takes 40min.

Wiesbaden has no Intercity train connection with the airport and the *S-Bahn* takes about 50min. The Deutsche Bundesbahn ticket office, directly below the terminal, covers both Intercity and *S-Bahn* trains. The taxi journey to either city takes 20–25min (fare about DM60).

Railway stations

Mainz Hauptbahnhof is an important junction. There are dozens of trains from Frankfurt Hauptbahnhof (30min) and Düsseldorf (2hr 15min) and at least hourly connections with Mannheim (40min), Stuttgart (2hr 5min) and Saarbrücken (2hr 20min). The station is at the west of the city centre, not far from the business area. There is a bureau de change and a taxi rank, and the tourist office is just outside, at Bahnhofstrasse 15. Inquiries ☎ 233741.

Wiesbaden Hauptbahnhof About 1.5km south of the city centre, this is a terminus, but the Intercity connections are poor. Apart from hourly direct trains to Frankfurt (40min), Bonn (1hr 40min) and Düsseldorf (2hr 35min), most destinations involve a change at Mainz or Frankfurt. There is a bureau de change, tourist office and a taxi rank. Inquiries ☎ 312847.

Getting around

Mainz can be covered from a hotel in Wiesbaden and vice versa, though this makes a car almost essential. They are about 10km/6 miles apart. In Mainz, the banks and government offices are 1km from the big hotels, but in Wiesbaden offices and businesses are widely dispersed.

Taxis Radio taxis ☎ 60011 (Mainz) and ☎ 39911 or 444444 (Wiesbaden). A taxi from one city centre to the other takes 10–15 min and costs DM25.

Limousines HTS Limousine-Service, Wiesbaden ☎ 410900.

Driving The narrow streets of Mainz Altstadt make driving and parking difficult. Car Raule Autovermietung has offices in Mainz ☎ 682030, and Wiesbaden ☎ 422055; Avis ☎ 609041 (Wiesbaden); Hertz ☎ 374073 (Wiesbaden).

Walking Safety is not a problem.

Streetcars, buses In Mainz most of the frequent services pass the Hauptbahnhof. Route maps at each stop give details. Buses run from Mainz station to Wiesbaden (journey time 25min) which has fewer buses and no streetcars. For information ☎ 124664 (Mainz) ☎ 3692205 (Wiesbaden).

S-Bahn Half-hourly trains run between the two and link both to Frankfurt, and to the riverside industry in Amöneburg (Hoechst), Kastel, Gustavsburg and Rüsselsheim (Opel).

Area by area

The centre of Mainz is a rough triangle. Most banks and business offices are around Kaiserstrasse, to the northwest. Government buildings cluster between Kaiserstrasse and, to the southeast, the Grosse Bleiche. The Höfchen and Markt, in front of the Dom (cathedral), are the focus of city life and to the north and south are pedestrianized shopping and entertainment streets. The modern Rathaus, Rheingoldhalle and Hilton hotel overlook the Rhein quays.

Wiesbaden is a rectangle of wide streets, wooded parkland and prosperous suburban avenues. From the station, the Friedrich-Ebert-Allee slopes gently up to the Rhein-Main-Halle, where it becomes Wilhelmstrasse, a promenade of smart shops facing parkland. It culminates in the Kurhaus casino, and opposite on Kaiser-Friedrichs-Platz is the prestigious Nassauer Hof hotel. The Landtag (parliament house) and the Altes and Neues Rathaus are in the old, traffic-free centre. The business, legal and other professional and Land government offices are on and near Rheinstrasse; the federal offices are more scattered.

Residential areas On the heights to the south of Mainz are some exclusive avenues by the Drususwall park and the citadel. The extensive wealthy suburbs of Wiesbaden, with their clinics and thermal baths, are to the east and north of the city.

Industrial areas The two docks north of Mainz, the Binnenhafen and Industriehafen, are the site of paper, glass and chemical plants. At Gonsenheim, near the Autobahn, a new industrial area is planned. IBM is in the south at Weisenau, and across the Rhein in Ginsheim-Gustavsburg MAN is a big employer.

189

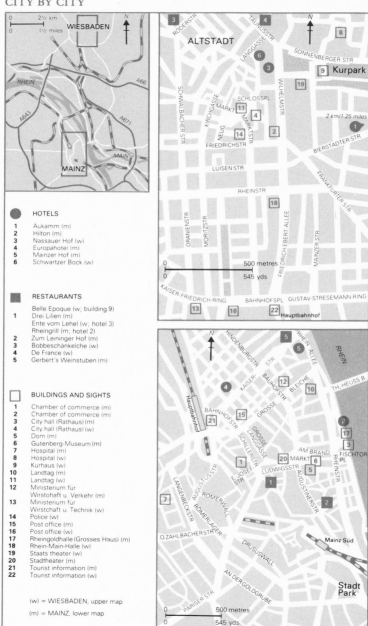

HOTELS

1 Aukamm (m)
2 Hilton (m)
3 Nassauer Hof (w)
4 Europahotel (m)
5 Mainzer Hof (m)
6 Schwartzer Bock (w)

RESTAURANTS

1 Belle Epoque (w; building 9)
Drei Lilien (m)
Ente vom Lehel (w; hotel 3)
Rheingrill (m; hotel 2)
2 Zum Leininger Hof (m)
3 Bobbeschänkelche (w)
4 De France (w)
5 Gerbert's Weinstuben (m)

BUILDINGS AND SIGHTS

1 Chamber of commerce (m)
2 Chamber of commerce (m)
3 City hall (Rathaus) (m)
4 City hall (Rathaus) (w)
5 Dom (m)
6 Gutenberg-Museum (m)
7 Hospital (m)
8 Hospital (w)
9 Kurhaus (w)
10 Landtag (m)
11 Landtag (w)
12 Ministerium für Wirstohaft u. Verkehr (m)
13 Ministerium für Wirstchaft u. Technik (w)
14 Police (w)
15 Post office (m)
16 Post office (w)
17 Rheingoldhalle (Grosses Haus) (m)
18 Rhein-Main-Halle (w)
19 Staats theater (w)
20 Stadtheater (m)
21 Tourist information (m)
22 Tourist information (w)

(w) = WIESBADEN, upper map

(m) = MAINZ, lower map

Hotels

For first-class hotels in Mainz look no further than the Hilton, but in Wiesbaden there is a choice of three. All hotels listed have radio, TV, bath or shower and IDD telephone. Currency exchange is standard and parking not a problem. Modern business hotels in a lower price bracket are few but adequate in both cities.

Aukamm   *DM*///
Aukamm-Allee 31, Wiesbaden ☎ *5670* ⊤ₓ *4186283 • AE DC MC V • 160 rooms, 14 suites, 2 restaurants, 2 bars*
The most modern of Wiesbaden's major hotels, the Aukamm was fully renovated in 1987. It is about 2km east of the casino and 3km from the Rhein-Main-Halle and office area. Business guests (from Siemens, Hoechst, Opel and others) account for about two-thirds of the total. The Japanese restaurant and Suaheli (Swahili) bar provide an exotic air. The rooms are spacious and welcoming, all with balcony, video and minibar; suites have hairdryers. Florist, pharmacy, gift shop, newsstand • pools, access to thermal baths, exercise facilities, cosmetic studio • fax, 8 meeting rooms (capacity up to 300).

Hilton   *DM*///
Rheinstr 68, Mainz ☎ *2450* ⊤ₓ *4187570 • AE DC MC V • 418 rooms, 15 suites, 3 restaurants, 2 bars*
On the Rhein, not far from the business district and the Theodor-Heuss bridge (convenient for Wiesbaden), this hotel, built in 1969, has no competitor in Mainz. Its clientele is very international but not predominantly business oriented. The original building (*Rheinflügel*) has direct access to the Rheingoldhalle concert and conference venue, and to the *Domflügel* wing across Rheinstrasse. Most of the rooms in this new ziggurat-shaped building have flower-bedecked balconies. It has a piano bar, disco and bistro but for the best meals cross to the Rheingrill (see *Restaurants*). The rooms vary widely in price (avoid those overlooking Rheinstrasse), but all are spacious, well equipped for working, decorated in warm pastel colours, and have soundproofing. 24hr room service, hairdresser, newsstand, gift shop • sauna, solarium, gym, massage • 12 meeting rooms (capacity up to 700), plus up to 3,000 in the Rheingoldhalle.

Nassauer Hof   *DM*////
Kaiser-Friedrich-Pl 3–4, Wiesbaden ☎ *1330* ⊤ₓ *4186847 • AE DC MC V • 188 rooms, 21 suites, 4 restaurants, 1 bar*
In existence since 1819, this is one of Germany's most famous hotels, and witness to many historic encounters, such as the Franco-German armistice commission in 1940. The unashamed luxury and superb food attract a wealthy, jet-set clientele, but 70% of guests are on business. Media folk and politicians are also much in evidence. The rooms are large, stylish and comfortable, and the suites provide an ideal setting for informal but important business meetings. The Ente vom Lehel restaurant is famous (see *Restaurants*). 24hr room service, hairdresser, gourmet shop, boutiques, newsstand, airport bus • thermal pool, sauna, massage, beauty farm • fax, 8 meeting rooms (capacity up to 200), 250-seat banqueting room.

OTHER HOTELS
Europahotel   *DM*/   *Kaiserstr 7, Mainz* ☎ *6350* ⊤ₓ *4187702 • AE DC MC V.* Fully renovated in 1987, this hotel aims to attract a business clientele. Rooms are adequate and have 24hr room service. 3 meeting rooms (capacity up to 100).
Mainzer Hof   *DM*/   *Kaiserstr 98, Mainz* ☎ *233771* ⊤ₓ *4187787 • AE DC MC V.* Fully renovated in 1987. Close to business and government

buildings. 1 meeting room (capacity up to 30).

Schwarzer Bock *DM*|| *Kranzpl 12, Wiesbaden* ☎ *3821* ☎ *4186640* • *AE DC MC V*. In the old part of town and near the casino, theatre and Wilhelmstrasse. Ornate 1870s decor and small rooms but clients include major companies. 6 meeting rooms (capacity up to 250).

Restaurants

In Mainz, only the Hilton's Rheingrill is entirely suitable for formal business occasions. In Wiesbaden you have grander surroundings and a couple of the best restaurants in the area; always make reservations.

Belle Epoque *DM*||
Kurhauspl 1, Wiesbaden ☎ *525942* • *D only; closed Mon* • *AE DC MC V* • *jacket and tie*
This attractive restaurant is inside the casino. The space, *fin-de-siècle* elégance and first-class French cuisine make dinner here a memorable and not overpriced experience.

Drei Lilien *DM*||||
Ballpl 2, Mainz ☎ *225068* • *closed 3 weeks in summer* • *AE DC MC V*
In a charming cobbled square the husband-and-wife owners have a reputation for serving the best food in Mainz. Local ingredients, salads and seafoods are all handled imaginatively in short but frequently changed, fixed-price menus. It is usually full of business people.

Die Ente vom Lehel *DM*||||
Nassauer Hof hotel, Wiesbaden ☎ *133666* • *closed Sun, Mon and hols* • *AE DC MC V* • *jacket and tie*
This highly praised restaurant is very fashionable and frequented by the jet-set. The cuisine is *nouvelle* with Bavarian overtones. For lunch, the satellite Bistro Ente is almost as luxurious, with selections from the same menu and wine list, at much lower prices.

Rheingrill *DM*||
Hilton hotel, Mainz ☎ *2450* • *AE DC MC V* • *jacket and tie*
Fellow guests at this large and elegant restaurant will include TV executives from ZDF and politicians. The skills of the chef, Pierre Pfister, of France's Académie Culinaire, ensure that the international cuisine has a *nouvelle* French emphasis.

Zum Leininger Hof *DM*||
Weintorstr 6, Mainz ☎ *228484* • *closed Sun* • *AE MC*
This intimate, candle-lit cellar restaurant is in one of the oldest houses in Mainz. It is frequented by business and media people, though only for more informal occasions. The *nouvelle* French menu is highly rated. The nine tables are widely spaced and a private room is available.

Good but casual
Bobbeschänkelche, Röderstr 39, Wiesbaden ☎ 527959 is a small, old and crowded *Weinlokal*, where local beer, wine and simple food are served in the evenings. One of the top dozen restaurants (in terms of food) in Germany, *De France*, in a small hotel, Taunusstr 49, Wiesbaden ☎ 51251, is sadly marred by an unimposing entrance, flashy decor and intrusive muzak. *Gebert's Weinstuben*, Frauenlobstr 94, Mainz ☎ 611619, owned and run by Wolfgang Gebert, formerly a chef at the Hilton, is a popular lunch-time haunt of bankers and politicians.

Bars

The big hotels provide almost the only sophisticated bars. Wine bars are more plentiful, including the *Weinstube am Brand*, Mailandgasse 2, Mainz; and the *Wiesbadener Weingewölbe*, Sonnenberger Str 80a, Wiesbaden.

Entertainment

The range of events is small because of Frankfurt's proximity. *Terminus*, a listing guide, is published monthly.

Theatre, dance, opera Theater der Landeshauptstadt Mainz, based in the *Grosses Haus*, Gutenbergpl, Mainz ☎ 123366, performs opera, operetta, drama and cabaret.

In Wiesbaden, the *Grosses Haus* in the *Hessisches Staatstheater* stages opera and ballet. The International May Festival of music and drama, with top-class international artists, is held in the theatre and *Kurhaus*. Information and reservations ☎ 1321 (Staatstheater) and *Kurbetrieb*, Rheinstr 15 (corner of Wilhelmstr) ☎ 374353 (Kurhaus).

Music Concerts are given in Mainz at the *Grosses Haus*, the *Eltzer Hof*, Bauhofstr, the *Kurfürstliches Schloss* and the *Rheingoldhalle*. All tickets from the Verkehrsverein, Bahnhofstr 15 ☎ 233741 or Kartenhaus, Schillerstr 11 ☎ 228729.

Nightclubs and casinos In Mainz, the *Terminus Disco*, Rhein-Allee-Zentrum ☎ 688847, is recommended. Wiesbaden's casino, in the *Kurhaus*, is open daily, 3pm–2am ☎ 526954.

Shopping

The main shops in Mainz are in the Grosse Bleiche, the Am Brand complex, Ludwigstrasse and the attractive Augustinerstrasse.

Wiesbaden is famous for luxury goods like jewellery, antiques and gourmet foods. The main shopping streets are Wilhelmstrasse and the pedestrian Langgasse, with its extension, Kirchgasse.

Sightseeing

Mainz has an attractively restored 18thC quarter of narrow streets and squares around Augustinerstrasse, just south of the chief sight, the Dom.

Dom (Cathedral of St Martin), Mainz. The many-spired, red sandstone, Romanesque cathedral (dating from 975) dominates the city skyline.

Gutenberg-Museum, Mainz. In a restored 1660 house, this museum has exhibits from the history of printing. *Liebfrauenpl 5. Open Mon–Fri, 10–6; Sun and hols, 10–1.*

Kurhaus, Wiesbaden. The casino (1904–07) has a vast marble lobby, with columns and friezes and an attractive setting of ornamental pools and fountains flanked by colonnades and the Staatstheater.

Out of town

From the Mainz quays and from Biebrich, steamers leave on Rhein trips downstream to Koblenz, taking in the gorge, the Lorelei, cliff-top castles, terraced vineyards and pretty waterside villages. Köln-Düsseldorfer line ☎ 224511 (Mainz), ☎ 600995 (Wiesbaden).

Keeping fit

Fitness centre *Bienefeld Fitness-Center*, Grosse Langgasse, Mainz ☎ 231661.

Golf *Golf Club Main-Taunus*, Wiesbaden-Delkenheim ☎ (06122) 52399.

Jogging In Mainz there are paths in the Stadtpark, Volkspark, the Römerwall and Drususwall. Wiesbaden's Stadtwald is north of the city.

Squash, tennis *Tennisquash Center*, Dotzheimer Str 174, Wiesbaden ☎ 421026.

Swimming *Thermalschwimmbad*, Aukammallee, Wiesbaden; *Am Taubertsberg*, Wallstr, Mainz ☎ 122174.

Local resources

Business services

Büro Full Service, Eibenweg 16, Mainz ☎ 3010612, and *Büroservice-Center*, Weidenbornstr 8a, Wiesbaden ☎ 79010.

Photocopying and printing *J.B. Heim*, Flachsmarktstr 28–30, Mainz ☎ 233718; *Lang Kopierzentrum*, Karlstr 5–7, Wiesbaden ☎ 305361 (photocopying); *wds Sofortdruck*, Schwalbacher Str 46, Wiesbaden ☎ 409667 (fast offset printing).

Translators and interpreters
Inlingua, Friedrichstr 31–33,
Wiesbaden ☎ 3735.

Communications
Local delivery *Kurierdienst*
Wiesbaden ☎ 51591.
Long-distance delivery DHL
☎ (06107) 7541.
Post offices Bahnhofstr 2 ☎ 149458
(Mainz), Fischerstr 2–4 ☎ 1301
(Wiesbaden). Both open Mon–Fri,
8–6 (late desk till 9pm); Sat, 8–1pm
(late desk till 8pm); Sun, 8–8.
Telex and fax At both post offices.

Conference/exhibition centres
The *Rheingoldhalle* in Mainz is run
by the Hilton. Recently refurbished
and re-equipped, it is ideal for
staging elaborate presentations
(capacity up to 3,000). Its lobby has
4,000 sq metres/43,100 sq ft of
exhibition space. Information from
Kongressdirektion Mainz, Rheinstr
66 ☎ 232881.

In Wiesbaden, apart from the
hotels and the *Kurhaus*, the modern
Rhein-Main-Halle has a floor area of
18,500 sq metres/199,100 sq ft.
Information from Presse- und
Informationsamt, Rathaus,
Wiesbaden ☎ 31326.

Emergencies
Bureaux de change *Deutsche
Verkehrs-Kredit-Bank*, Mainz
Hauptbahnhof, open Mon–Sat, 7.30–
12, 12.30–7.45; Sun and hols, 10–
1.45. Wiesbaden Hauptbahnhof, open
daily, 8–12, 12.30–7.45.
Hospitals Emergency doctor
(*Notarztwagen*), ambulance and
address of nearest hospital ☎ 232323
(Mainz) ☎ 48081 (Wiesbaden).
Doctors on call after hours
(*Ärztlicher Bereitschaftsdienst*)
☎ 679097 (Mainz) ☎ 461010
(Wiesbaden); Mon–Fri, 7pm–7am;
Wed, from 2pm; Sat, Sun and hols,
24hr. Dental emergencies: ☎ 173041
(Mainz); ☎ 461010 (Wiesbaden).
Pharmacies *Mercator*, Ludwigstr
12, Mainz ☎ 234368; *Apotheke Am
Kochbrunnen*, Taunusstr 11,

Wiesbaden ☎ 529565.
Police Main stations: Valenciapl 2,
Mainz ☎ 651; Friedrichstr 25,
Wiesbaden ☎ 3451.

Government offices
City administration: *Stadtverwaltung*,
Rathaus, Mainz ☎ 121; Rathaus,
Wiesbaden ☎ 311. State offices:
*Ministerium für Wirtschaft und
Verkehr* (Economics, Trade and
Tourism), Rheinland-Pfalz,
Bauhofstr 4, Mainz ☎ 161;
*Ministerium für Wirtschaft und
Technik* (Economics and
Technology), Hesse, Kaiser-
Friedrich-Ring 75, Wiesbaden
☎ 8151.

Information sources
Business information The
chambers of commerce are *Industrie-
und Handelskammer für Rheinhessen*,
Schillerpl 7, Mainz ☎ 2620; and
*Industrie- und Handelskammer
Wiesbaden*, Wilhelmstr 24,
Wiesbaden ☎ 150026.
Local media Each city has two local
newspapers: the *Allgemeine Zeitung
Mainz* and *Mainzer-Rhein-Zeitung*;
and the *Wiesbadener Tagblatt* and
Wiesbadener Kurier. ZDF (*Zweites
Deutsches Fernsehen*), the second
national TV channel, is based in
Mainz-Lerchenberg. *Südwestfunk*,
the regional radio and TV station, has
studios in Mainz.
Tourist information *Mainzer
Verkehrsverein*, Bahnhofstr 15
☎ 233741; *Wiesbadener
Verkehrsverein*, Rheinstr 15
☎ 374353.

Thank-yous
Florists *Blumen-Wolf*, Grosse
Langgasse 16, Mainz ☎ 222427;
Blumenhaus Voigt, Bahnhofstr 16,
Wiesbaden ☎ 372526.
Wine merchants *Burgeff & Co*,
Walpoldenstr 5, Mainz ☎ 235962.

MANNHEIM/LUDWIGSHAFEN   *City codes* (Mannheim)
zip 6800 ☎ 0621; (Ludwigshafen) zip 6700 ☎ 0621

Although belonging to different *Länder*, the two cities effectively form a single unit, densely industrialized and diversified, with a population of 470,000. Mannheim, on the east bank of the Rhein, is the second city of Baden-Württemberg, and has a variety of industries; while Ludwigshafen, on the west bank in Rheinland-Pfalz, is dominated by BASF. Mannheim has a history and culture; Ludwigshafen has not.

Mannheim was created as the Elector Palatine's new capital, in 1720, on the spit of land where the Neckar joins the Rhein. Its importance as a river trading town was enhanced during the 19th century when it became a free port. The inland harbour with 60km/37 miles of waterfront is now the second largest in Europe. Mannheim prospered under the Kaiser's empire. The population trebled between 1871 and 1900, and most of its important buildings date from around 1900.

The cities are at a nodal point in the national and European rail networks, and *Autobahnen* converge from Germany, eastern France and Switzerland. Industrial activity includes electrical engineering (Brown, Boveri and Siemens), automotive products (Daimler-Benz and John Deere), advanced medical equipment (Boehringer), and petro-chemicals, paper and glass. Boehringer is one of several large German companies with headquarters here. In Ludwigshafen, BASF, the Badische Anilin- und Soda-Fabrik, is Germany's largest chemical producer, and one of Europe's leading companies. Ludwigshafen has its own civic buildings and shopping centre, but looks to Mannheim for entertainments, services and culture.

Arriving

Frankfurt is the nearest international airport (75km/47 miles to the north). Take the *S-Bahn* from the airport to Frankfurt Hauptbahnhof, where you can take an Intercity to Mannheim, at roughly half-hourly intervals between 6am and 11pm (a few stop at Ludwigshafen). The fastest journey time is about 40min. Consider renting a car at Frankfurt; the cities are at a junction of major routes. The small but busy airfield at Neuostheim (3km/2 miles southeast of Mannheim) is used by executive aircraft, and Pegasus operates a service from Munich ☎ 474844.

Railway stations
Mannheim Hauptbahnhof This is a large through station on the south side of the city, a few minutes' taxi ride from the main hotels and business area. Intercity connections include hourly direct trains to Heidelberg (12min), Frankfurt (40min), Stuttgart (1hr 27min) and Düsseldorf (3hr). Several trains a day leave for Basel, Switzerland (2hr 15min), and eastern France and Paris (5hr 30min). Outside is a large taxi-rank and stops for many streetcar and bus routes. The station has a bureau de change, florist, bookshop and other shops. The *Verkehrsverein* (tourist office) is at Bahnhofspl 1 ☎ 101011 (Mon–Fri, 8–6; Sat, 8–12). Train inquiries ☎ 19419.
Ludwigshafen Bahnhof This is a much smaller station at the western edge of the town, near the Ramada (see *Hotels*). Streetcars connect with Mannheim every 5–10 min. There is a bureau de change and a taxi rank. Train inquiries 511880.

Getting around

The long straight streets of the Quadrate, or central Mannheim, are wearying to foot and eye. Only two streetcar routes cross it. The hotels, conference hall, best restaurants and many banks and businesses are clustered around Friedrichsplatz. A car or taxi is advisable for visits outside the Quadrate.

Taxi Hard to find, apart from ranks at the two stations. Radio-controlled taxi centre, Mannheim ☎ 444044; Ludwigshafen ☎ 522061.

Driving The Quadrate streets are narrow and parking is difficult here. The main axes are pedestrianized and the rest are alternately one-way. There are many parking garages. The *Stadtführer* (city guide) from the tourist office (Bahnhofpl 1) lists their addresses and opening hours. The wide perimeter avenue gives access to two Rhein bridges and three over the Neckar, and outside the Quadrate driving and parking are easy. Offices are maintained by *Avis* ☎ 442091 and *Europcar* ☎ 851047 in Mannheim, and by *Avis* ☎ 553061 and *Raule* ☎ 522002 in Ludwigshafen.

Walking Within the Quadrate, a map is needed to master the street numbering system (available from the station bookshop or tourist office). Briefly, each block is given vertical and horizontal coordinates, such as Q4; the addresses are numbered round all sides of each block, so that Q4, 27 could be on any of four streets.

Public transport In addition to buses and city streetcars, two long-haul streetcar lines run through central Mannheim every 15min on the same tracks. The OEG (Upper Rhein railway) goes to Heidelberg, and the RHB (Rhein-Haardt railway) runs through Ludwigshafen west to Bad Dürkheim.

Area by area

Mannheim's Quadrate The dome-shaped area of geometric streets,

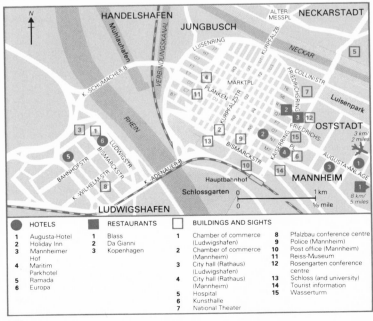

	HOTELS		RESTAURANTS		BUILDINGS AND SIGHTS		
1	Augusta-Hotel	1	Blass	1	Chamber of commerce (Ludwigshafen)	8	Pfalzbau conference centre
2	Holiday Inn	2	Da Gianni			9	Police (Mannheim)
3	Mannheimer Hof	3	Kopenhagen	2	Chamber of commerce (Mannheim)	10	Post office (Mannheim)
4	Maritim Parkhotel			3	City hall (Rathaus) (Ludwigshafen)	11	Reiss-Museum
5	Ramada			4	City hall (Rathaus) (Mannheim)	12	Rosengarten conference centre
6	Europa			5	Hospital	13	Schloss (and university)
				6	Kunsthalle	14	Tourist information
				7	National Theater	15	Wasserturm

rebuilt after World War II, is bounded by the Rhein to the southwest, the Neckar to the north and the docks to the northwest. Near the Rhein is the huge, baroque Schloss, now the university. In front of it, on and around Bismarckstrasse, are the chamber of commerce, the law courts and Finanzamt (revenue office). The western half of the Quadrate is cultural and residential. To the east is the shopping and commercial area. The main axes, Kurpfalzstrasse and the "Planken," are largely pedestrianized. The latter leads into the eastern perimeter street, Friedrichsring, and beyond it to Friedrichsplatz.

Oststadt East of Friedrichsring the street plan is less rigid, there are more trees and many 19thC buildings have survived. The buildings around Friedrichsplatz, with its ornamental gardens and Wasserturm (water tower), are a good example of *Jugendstil*, Germany's Art Nouveau. Among them are the Rosengarten conference centre and the Kunsthalle. One of the best hotels, the Maritim, is here. Banks, professional offices and the Mannheimer Hof and Augusta hotels are on or just off the main thoroughfare, Augusta-Anlage. A few blocks north is an exclusive residential area near the Luisenpark

botanical gardens.

Ludwigshafen is reached either by the impressive Kurt Schumacher suspension bridge, spanning the docks and the Rhein, or by the Konrad Adenauer bridge, near the Schloss. Between the two are offices, shops and civic buildings, including the Pfalzbau conference centre.

Residential areas Heavy industry is never far away but there are a few pleasant suburbs, such as Almenhof to the south. The many *Autobahn* exits enable executives to live farther out, towards Heidelberg, in the Odenwald hills, or in the wine-growing district of Haardt, west of the Rhein.

Industrial areas The heart of the industrial area is at the river junction, near the extensive docks. Pharmaceuticals, cellulose and textiles are manufactured; MWM (Motoren-Werke Mannheim) is in Neckarstadt, and north in Luzenberg is Daimler-Benz; Boehringer is nearby in Waldhof and Brown, Boveri in Käfertal to the northeast. South of the city, one of Germany's largest railway marshalling yards stands beside John Deere and other industrial plant. More factories are sited north and south of Ludwigshafen, and the vast BASF plant stretches for about 4km/2.5 miles downstream to the north.

Hotels

For such an important business and industrial conurbation, hotels are limited. Most business people stay in Mannheim, but Heidelberg and Frankfurt, which is less than an hour away, are more attractive possibilities. The Europäischer Hof in Heidelberg is one of Germany's best hotels. Standard facilities in the hotels listed are bath/shower, TV/radio, IDD telephone, minibar and currency exchange. Room service is 24hr only where stated.

Augusta-Hotel [DM]/
Augusta-Anlage 43–45, Mannheim
☏ *408001* ⊤ˣ *462395 • Best Western • AE DC MC V • 105 rooms, 1 suite, 2 restaurants, 1 bar*
On a quiet corner, within walking distance of banks, conference centre

and shops, this small hotel is well patronized by local business people. The rooms are comfortable. The modern American Bar leads off the lobby. In the basement, the Mannemer Stubb has a typically German atmosphere. Newsstand •

health club with sauna, steambath, jacuzzi, solarium, exercise equipment • 5 meeting rooms (capacity up to 150).

Holiday Inn *[DM]||*
Kurfürstenarkade N6, Mannheim
☎ 10710 ℡ 462264 • AE DC MC V •
146 rooms, 1 suite, 1 restaurant, 1 bar
This modern hotel occupies a block within the Quadrate, with the entrance on a main shopping street. All the leading Mannheim companies use it; nearly half the guests are from abroad, and most are on business. The interior evokes *Jugendstil*. There are 15 rooms reserved for nonsmokers. Rooms have trouser presses, hairdryers, bathrobes and toiletries, and adequate working space. The hotel has no parking. Shopping arcade, newsstand • pool, sauna, exercise equipment • 7 meeting rooms (capacity up to 180).

Mannheimer Hof *[DM]||*
Augusta-Anlage 4–8, Mannheim
☎ 45021 ℡ 462245 • Steigenberger •
AE DC MC V • 197 rooms, 3 suites,
2 restaurants, 1 bar
Belonging to one of Germany's top chains, this is a spacious, comfortable and very professionally run hotel. It is also conveniently sited for business purposes and 80% of the clientele are guests of local companies. Built in the 1920s, the interior shows the uncluttered Bauhaus influence. There is a wide variation in the quality and price of rooms, but all have working space; the quietest are those facing south across the courtyard. The rather grand restaurant, with an international cuisine, lacks atmosphere, but the Holzkist is an attractive cellar restaurant. 24hr room service, hairdresser, travel agent • 6 meeting rooms (capacity up to 300).

Maritim Parkhotel *[DM]||||*
Friedrichspl 2, Mannheim ☎ 45071
℡ 463418 • AE DC MC V • 184 rooms,
3 suites, 2 restaurants, 1 bar
With its imposing neo-classical façade, on Mannheim's main square,

this is an elegant hotel that enjoys a long-established reputation for personal attention and individuality. It has an international business clientele and many major German companies use it, as do bankers, media and insurance people and the medical profession. It has spacious function rooms. There is a restaurant downstairs, and the Weinstube is reached by a back staircase. The large bedrooms have modern decor and adequate work space. Those overlooking the street are soundproofed and they also have air conditioning. The separate floor of suites has a conference room. There are 5 rooms for nonsmokers. 24hr room service, boutique, jeweller, gift shop, newsstand • pool, sauna, exercise equipment, steambath • 6 meeting rooms (capacity up to 120).

Ramada *[DM]||*
Pasadena Allee, Ludwigshafen 4
☎ 519301 ℡ 464545 • AE DC MC V •
195 rooms, 2 suites, 3 restaurants, 1 bar
This modern tower is in a bleak and windy triangle between urban throughways and the station (with which it is linked by a short footpath). By contrast, following complete renovation in 1987, the interior is decorated in soft pinks and browns with velvet furnishings. Guests are usually here on business, and well over half are from abroad. Major clients include Boehringer, BASF and John Deere. All rooms have video and self-adjusting air conditioning; 40 rooms are reserved for nonsmokers. Giftshop, newsstand, • pool, sauna, solarium • 6 meeting rooms (capacity up to 200).

OTHER HOTEL
Europa *[DM]| Ludwigspl 5–6,*
Ludwigshafen ☎ 519011 ℡ 464701 •
AE DC V. A functional 1960s block, renovated in 1986, in central Ludwigshafen, with a mainly German business clientele. The rooms are small, brightly decorated and well equipped. Limited garaging.

Restaurants

There are few excellent restaurants in Mannheim and those in the centre are very busy at lunch time, but the hotel restaurants provide a quiet, pleasant atmosphere.

Blass [DM]//
Langlachweg 30, Friedrichsfeld
☎ *472004 • closed Sat L, Mon •*
no credit cards
Kurt Blass, the chef-owner, is famous throughout Mannheim. His restaurant is 9km/6 miles by *Autobahn* southeast of the city. The short menu is full of originality and the wine list offers good-value wines.

Da Gianni [DM]//
R7, 34, Mannheim ☎ *20326 • closed Mon, 3 weeks in Jul • AE MC*
Near Friedrichsplatz, this Italian restaurant is one of the two most popular for business entertaining. The restful pastel decor sets off the crisp white table linen and the tables are widely spaced in two rooms, of which the inner is the quieter. The wine list is mainly Italian.

Kopenhagen [DM]///
Friedrichsring 2a ☎ *14870 • closed Sun • AE DC MC V*
Next to the Rosengarten conference hall, this crowded restaurant is the most fashionable and expensive place in Mannheim, best suited to informal occasions. The menu, which is strong on fish, includes German, Danish and international dishes, and there is a good, if pricey, wine list.

Bars

The bars of the best hotels, notably in the Holiday Inn, Maritim Parkhotel and Augusta-Hotel, are the only appropriate places for discussions. But good wine bars serving the local vintages from the Baden and Pfalz districts are plentiful. Popular bars are *Weinkelter*, Augusta-Anlage, Mannheim; *Weinprobe*, Humboldstr 1, Neckarstadt; and the *Weinkistl*, Maxstr 47, Ludwigshafen.

Entertainment

Information on theatre and cinema is available ☎ 11512 (Mannheim) and ☎ 11511 (Ludwigshafen), and on all events from the *Verkehrsverein* (tourist office) ☎ 101011, Mannheim.

Theatre, dance, opera
Mannheim's *Nationaltheater*, over 200 years old, is the oldest municipal theatre company in Germany, and is the unofficial home of Schiller productions. At the postwar theatre in Goetheplatz it stages classical drama, opera and operetta. Advance reservations, Collinistr 26 ☎ 248447 (open Sat–Mon, 11–1; Tue–Fri, 11–1, 2–6), and at the theatre.
Cinema Every October Mannheim hosts an international Film Week, attended by young progressive film-makers; avant-garde films are always on show at the *Cinema Quadrat*, L7, 12, Mannheim ☎ 2932745. Mainstream movies can be seen at the 6-screen *Planken Kino-Center*, P4, 13, Mannheim ☎ 25151.
Music Visiting orchestras and performers often appear in the *Mozartsaal* of the Rosengarten conference centre, and the regional Kurpfalz Chamber Orchestra performs regularly in the *Rittersaal* of the Schloss. The best jazz is at the *Miljöö*, U1, 23, Mannheim ☎ 15809.
Nightclubs and casinos There is some tawdry glitter around Dalbergstrasse, near the docks. There is a floor show (Mon–Sat, 9pm–5am) at the *Haus Imperial* restaurant, J1, 6, Mannheim ☎ 23762. In Bad Dürkheim, 22km/13 miles west of Mannheim, the *Kurhaus Casino*, Schlosspl 1 ☎ (06322) 7970 is open daily, 2pm to 2am.

Shopping

Mannheim's shops are concentrated on three streets of the Quadrate between blocks N and P, the north/south pedestrianized Breite Strasse and the adjoining Marktplatz. Big department stores are represented here as well as shops selling jewellery, glass and china, leather goods and furs. The *Stadtgarten*, N5, is a striking arcade with two floors of boutiques and stalls. Gifts can be bought at *Cri-Cri*, 06, 2 and *Präsent*, 07, 11.

Sightseeing

Mannheim's city bus tour (May 1–Sep 30 daily at 10 from the Wasserturm, Friedrichspl) visits all the more important sights. The impressive inland harbour can be seen by boat (Jun–Aug), starting from the Kurpfalz bridge. An unusual view of the unique street pattern can be seen from a balloon or on 15min flights from Neuostheim airfield (Sun, 10–1). Details from the *Verkehrsverein* (tourist office), Bahnhofpl 1 ☎ 101011.

Kunsthalle An important collection of 19thC and 20thC European art. *Moltkestr 9, Mannheim. Open Tue–Sun, 10–5 (Thu, 10–8).*

Reiss-Museum Mannheim's history, and a collection of archeology, anthropology, porcelain and faïence, are on view in the Zeughaus (arsenal) and in a striking new building. *Open Tue–Sat, 10–1, 2–5 (Wed, 2–8); Sun, 10–5.*

Schloss This 18thC palace, with its 1.3km-long façade, is one of the largest baroque buildings in Europe. *Bismarckstr, Mannheim. Open Apr–Oct, Tue–Sun, 10–12, 3–5; Nov–Mar, Sat–Sun, 10–12, 3–5.*

Out of town

Within easy driving distance are some beautiful historic towns, set in attractive countryside. The most important is *Heidelberg*, best visited in spring or late autumn when it is less crowded. From the romantic Schloss and its hillside gardens there are beautiful views over the Altstadt; the Kurpfälzisches Museum contains paintings from the Romantic period; and the Haus zum Ritter has a fine Renaissance façade.

Other towns worth a visit include *Ladenburg* (13km/8 miles east), on the Neckar, a well-preserved medieval town with 12thC walls and a Roman museum; *Schwetzingen* (16km/9 miles south), with its 18thC Schloss and theatre (venue for a drama festival every May and June); the ancient cathedral town of *Speyer*, 22km/13 miles upstream on the Rhein; and downstream, *Worms*, with its 12thC cathedral.

Spectator sports

Football SV *Waldhof-Mannheim*, in the *Bundesliga* 1st Division, plays at the Südweststadion, Erich-Reimann-Str, Ludwigshafen-Süd ☎ 563101.

Horse-racing There is regular flat-racing at the *Badischer Rennverein*, in Seckenheim. Tickets and information from the *Verkehrsverein*, Bahnhofspl·1 ☎ 101011.

Ice hockey The local team, MERC, plays at the Eisstadion, Bismarckstr, Mannheim ☎ 2932291.

Motor-racing The German Formula 1 Grand Prix is held (Jul or Aug) at the *Hockenheim* circuit, 24km/15 miles south of Mannheim ☎ (06205) 7021.

Keeping fit

Fitness centres *Fitness-World*, Pfingstweidstr 186, Mannheim ☎ 856080.

Golf The *Mannheim-Viernheim* club, Alte Mannheimer Str, Viernheim ☎ (06204) 71313 has a nine-hole course, 11km/7 miles to the southeast. Contact the secretary, at the Deutsche Bank ☎ 199332.

Jogging The *Luisenpark* in Mannheim, with 10km/6 miles of paths, charges a modest entrance fee. Gates on Otto-Beck-Str.

Squash *Squash-Center*, Bad Kreuznacher Str 34, Mannheim-Käfertal ☎ 736700. TVG *Squash und Tennis-Center*, Saarburger Str 28, Ludwigshafen ☎ 523030.

Swimming *Herschelbad*, Mannheim U3 ☎ 2932439 has three indoor pools.

Tennis Indoor courts at *Tennis-Center Marquet*, Paul-Martin-Ufer 4a, Mannheim-Neuostheim ☎ 403818. TVG *Squash und Tennis-Center* (see above).

Local resources

Business services
TEXTA Büroservice, Mannheim
☎ 28822 provides secretarial and
office services.
Photocopying and printing *Copy
Shop*, Bismarckpl 15, Mannheim
☎ 408767; *Sofort-Druck-Service
M. Heid*, Ziethenstr 39, Mannheim
☎ 797540. *BB Copy-Shop*, Bahnhofstr
42, Ludwigshafen ☎ 518658.
Secretarial Contact the chamber of
commerce (see below) for advice.
Translators and interpreters
Bruno Hochreiter, Ludwigshafen
☎ 563933 (Mon–Fri, 9–12, 2–5).

Communications
Local delivery *RNX Express Kurier*,
Mannheim ☎ 14237.
Long-distance delivery *TNT
Skypak*, Mannheim ☎ 738075.
Post offices Main offices:
Bahnhofspl 13, Mannheim ☎ 2940;
Rathauspl 21, Ludwigshafen ☎ 5071.
Telex and fax At main post offices.

Conference/exhibition centres
Mannheim has hosted the annual
congresses of both the major political
parties, and is used by medical,
scientific and industrial groups. The
enlarged *Rosengarten* conference
centre, Rosengartenpl 2 ☎ 414061,
opened in 1974. The Mozartsaal seats
2,300, smaller halls seat 150–1,400
and there are many small meeting
rooms, all served by two restaurants
and parking space for 500 cars. In the
Luisenpark, the *Festhalle Baumhain*
☎ 411087 seats 390. Information
about other conference facilities from
the *Verkehrsverein*, Bahnhofspl 1
☎ 101011. Ludwigshafen has
conference facilities in the *Pfalzbau*,
Berliner Str 30 ☎ 518307.

Emergencies
Bureaux de change *Deutsche
Verkehrs-Kredit-Bank*, Mannheim
and Ludwigshafen, open Mon–Sat,
7.30–12, 12.30–7.45; Sun and hols,
10–1.45.
Hospital *Klinikum der Stadt
Mannheim*, Theodor-Kutzer-Ufer

☎ 3831. **Emergency doctors**
☎ 11500. Doctors on weekend and
night-call (Sat, 8am– Mon, 7am;
Wed, 1pm–11pm; hols): Joseph-
Meyer-Str 17 ☎ 19292
(Mannheim); August-Heller-Str 12
☎ 571051 (Ludwigshafen). Dental
emergencies ☎ 22525 (Mannheim).
Pharmacies *Wasserturm-Apotheke*
P7, 16, Mannheim ☎ 25510; *Post-
Apotheke* Ludwigspl 13,
Ludwigshafen ☎ 513434.
Police Headquarters, L6,
Mannheim ☎ 1740; Wittelsbachstr 3,
Ludwigshafen ☎ 56130.

Government offices
Contact the *Bürgermeisteramt* in each
city: Rathaus, Mannheim E5
☎ 2931; Rathaus-Center, Jägerstr
Ludwigshafen ☎ 5041. At *Land* level
refer to the Staatsministerium in
Stuttgart (for Mannheim) and in
Mainz (for Ludwigshafen).

Information sources
Business information The
chamber of commerce in Mannheim
is *Industrie- und Handelskammer
Rhein-Neckar*, L1, 2 ☎ 17091 and in
Ludwigshafen *Industrie- und
Handelskammer für die Pfalz*,
Ludwigspl 2–3 ☎ 59040.
Local media The three local daily
papers are the *Mannheimer Morgen*,
the *Rhein-Neckar-Zeitung*, published
in Heidelberg, and the *Rhein-Pfalz* in
Ludwigshafen. In 1986 *Handelsblatt*
opened an editorial office in
Ludwigshafen.
Tourist information
Verkehrsverein Mannheim, Bahnhofpl
1 ☎ 101011; *Verkehrsverein
Ludwigshafen*, Am Hauptbahnhof
☎ 512035.

Thank-yous
Florists *Blumen-Ecke*,
Friedrichsring 46, Mannheim
☎ 25292; *Weidemann*, Wormser Str
68, Ludwigshafen ☎ 672667.
Wine merchants *Le Tonneau*, E2,
9, Mannheim ☎ 22354; *Wein- und
Töpferladen*, Maxstr 46,
Ludwigshafen ☎ 510684.

MUNICH

City codes zip 8000 ☎ 089

If you ask Germans where, if they had to move, they would most like to live and work, München comes top of the list. The city is a cultural and economic magnet. The beautifully restored architecture, the choice of theatre, music, art galleries, restaurants and shops, and the nearby Alps all give Munich a head start. Add to that the dynamic Franz Josef Strauss, Bavaria's minister-president for the past 15 years, who has lobbied tirelessly to bring in leading-edge industries, and you have a city that is go-ahead as well as attractive.

Munich's success dates back over a century to when the Wittelsbach kings promoted education and science; the technical university was founded in 1868 and later a great scientific library and museum, and the German patent office. Mechanical and electrical engineering, alongside brewing and insurance, became Munich's chief industries. Siemens, BMW and MAN had plants here before World War II, and Siemens moved its headquarters from Berlin to Munich in 1945, bringing suppliers in its wake. Later BMW concentrated its operations on Munich. Today, major companies in the city include aerospace specialists Deutsche Airbus and MBB, and Motorola and Texas Instruments in the field of electronics, as well as much of Germany's software industry. At the research complex at Garching 4,000 scientists and technicians work with some of the world's most powerful experimental hardware. In manufacturing output, Munich is now the top city in Germany, and the insurance giants, Allianz and Münchener Rückversicherung (or Munich Re), with their vast investment funds have helped make the city a major financial centre. Additionally, Munich leads in Germany's softer industries, notably fashion, advertising, printing and publishing, and the country's biggest film studios, Bavaria-Film, are also located here.

Tourism is a big revenue earner, particularly since the 1972 Olympics, and Munich is an important venue for congresses and trade fairs. The city has invested heavily in infrastructure to serve its population of 3m. The problem now is an acute shortage of office and industrial space. A new business park is being developed in north Munich, and fully equipped small-business "nurseries" are being created in a run-down pocket of the city, but the long-term solution lies with the closure in 1991 of the existing airport to which the exhibition centre and several of the breweries will move, releasing valuable inner-city sites. This is typical of Munich's ambitious and far-sighted approach. Yet underneath the glitter, the old Munich is still very much alive, with its Fasching (carnival), Oktoberfest and seasonal markets.

Arriving

Munich is Germany's second busiest airport in scheduled passenger volume, after Frankfurt. There are direct international flights from 70 cities world-wide, and domestic links with 15 cities are excellent, with about 20 flights a day from Frankfurt. The main Intercity railways from Hamburg, the Rhein-Ruhr area and Frankfurt terminate here, and five *Autobahnen* converge.

Munich airport (Riem)

The 1939-built airport, which is 8km/5 miles east of the city, is too small. It will be closed in 1991 and replaced by a new, larger one at Erding, 30km/20 miles northeast of Munich. Departing and arriving passengers use separate buildings. On arrival, immigration and customs clearance takes 10–40min. In the arrivals hall there are information desks for Lufthansa and general flight information, and a city tourist office (*Fremdenverkehrsamt*) which provides a hotel reservations service. The bureau de change is open daily, 7.30–10. A snack bar is open daily, 7–12. The departure building has more extensive and better facilities including a large restaurant and two smaller adjoining ones. In addition, there are four snack bars open daily, 4.30am–9pm. Several airlines have lounges and there is a choice of shops, with a modest duty-free section. Airport information ☎ 92110. Freight inquiries ☎ 92118528.

City link For the short ride into the centre a taxi is best.

Taxi The journey takes 15–25min and the fare is DM20–25. There are always cabs outside the terminal.

Car rental It is not worth renting a car unless you have appointments in the industrial suburbs. Hertz, Avis, Europcar and several German firms have desks at the airport.

Bus and train. A shuttle bus service between the airport and the Hauptbahnhof, which takes about 25min, leaves every 15min or so, 6–9.30 (airport), 5–9 (Hauptbahnhof). The fare is DM5.

Railway stations

München Hauptbahnhof This is a terminus for many Intercity routes from northern and central Germany, and trains to and from Italy and Austria stop here. There are almost hourly services to many central and southern German cities. The station has a restaurant, shops, a DB (Deutsche Bundesbahn) travel centre, city tourist office, Bavarian state travel agency and bureau de change with a Eurocard cash dispenser. Taxis are plentiful and there are ranks and bus and streetcar stops in front of the main exit. An underground concourse of shops leads to the *U-Bahn* and *S-Bahn* station. Timetable inquiries ☎ 592991.

Bahnhof München-Pasing A busy junction in the western suburbs where Intercity trains from Stuttgart and the Rhein stop. It is also served by four *S-Bahn* lines.

Getting around

The city is large and distances between centres of activity are considerable. In the Altstadt (part of which is pedestrianized) and within the government and banking districts it is practical to walk between appointments. If venturing farther afield take a taxi (expensive) or get to know the excellent public transport system; a map and timetable can be obtained from the city tourist office at the Hauptbahnhof or most bookshops. All public transport has an interchangeable automated ticket system. A 24hr unlimited ticket covers a 10km/6-mile radius; cost DM6.50.

Taxis can be picked up at one of 150 ranks (identified on easily available street maps) or called ☎ 21611 (24hr). Note that some drivers are *Gastarbeiter* (foreign workers) or students, with a hazy knowledge of the city.

Driving Traffic flows freely at most times, except on Friday afternoons. The fast outer city ring road links all five *Autobahnen*. Driving in the Altstadt is not recommended. There are parking facilities, many multilevel, particularly west of the Altstadt, off Sonnenstrasse. Car rental: *Avis* ☎ 12600020, *Budget* ☎ 223333, *interRent* ☎ 557145.

Walking The city centre, formerly a haunt of prostitutes, is now safe at all hours, but along Goethestrasse and on the western edge of the city, sex clubs and hookers are much in evidence. Another hazard is cyclists.

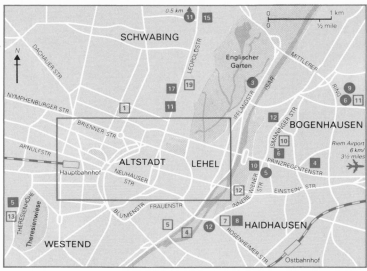

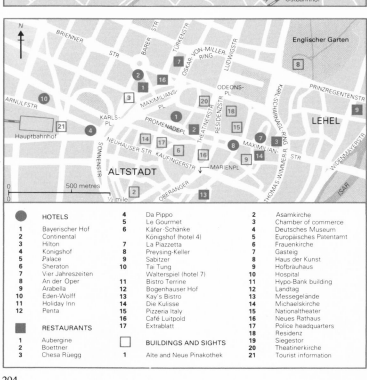

HOTELS			4	Da Pippo	2	Asamkirche
			5	Le Gourmet	3	Chamber of commerce
1	Bayerischer Hof		6	Käfer-Schänke	4	Deutsches Museum
2	Continental			Königshof (hotel 4)	5	Europäisches Patentamt
3	Hilton		7	La Piazzetta	6	Frauenkirche
4	Königshof		8	Preysing-Keller	7	Gasteig
5	Palace		9	Sabitzer	8	Haus der Kunst
6	Sheraton		10	Tai Tung	9	Hofbräuhaus
7	Vier Jahreszeiten			Walterspiel (hotel 7)	10	Hospital
8	An der Oper		11	Bistro Terrine	11	Hypo-Bank building
9	Arabella		12	Bogenhauser Hof	12	Landtag
10	Eden-Wolff		13	Kay's Bistro	13	Messegelände
11	Holiday Inn		14	Die Kulisse	14	Michaelskirche
12	Penta		15	Pizzeria Italy	15	Nationaltheater
			16	Café Luitpold	16	Neues Rathaus
	RESTAURANTS		17	Extrablatt	17	Police headquarters
					18	Residenz
1	Aubergine				19	Siegestor
2	Boettner			BUILDINGS AND SIGHTS	20	Theatinerkirche
3	Chesa Rüegg		1	Alte and Neue Pinakothek	21	Tourist information

Subway and rapid transit The *U-Bahn* (white "U" on blue sign) and the *S-Bahn* (green "S" on white) use the same stations in the centre, with *S-Bahn* routes running east-west between the Hauptbahnhof and Ostbahnhof (by a large industrial zone to the east). The *U-Bahn* routes run mainly north-south, with interchanges onto the *S-Bahn* at the Hauptbahnhof Karlsplatz, Marienplatz and Ostbahnhof. An important new route, for completion in 1988, will link the centre with residential Bogenhausen and the office and hotel complex at Arabellapark, to the northeast.

The *S-Bahn* lines run out to commuter towns and industrial areas, roughly within a 35km/22-mile radius. *U-Bahn* inquiries ☎ 238030; *S-Bahn* inquiries ☎ 557575.

Streetcars and buses
Strassenbahnen (streetcars) are slow and generally to be avoided, but bus 55 is the only public transport route (until the *U-Bahn* is finished) from the Hauptbahnhof to Bogenhausen and Arabellapark.

Area by area
The city owes its present shape to the post-1945 policy of re-creating its historic form. There are no skyscrapers and office and hotel development has had to find space where it can, often in outer districts. Most of the city lies west of the small river Isar but, with improved public transport, business, hotels and entertainments are spreading to east-bank Bogenhausen and Haidhausen.
City centre The Altstadt (old town), with its narrow winding streets and buildings dating from the Middle Ages to the Renaissance, is still defined by three ancient gates and a ring road following the old walls. In the centre is a pedestrianized area around Marienplatz, where beautiful old churches and public buildings blend with shops, restaurants and *Bierkeller*. The main shopping street, Kaufingerstrasse, and its

continuation, Neuhauser Strasse, run west to the Karlstor and Karlsplatz (or Stachus), the hub of city traffic. Running north from Marienplatz, another traffic-free shopping street, Theatinerstrasse, leads into the main north-south axis, Ludwigstrasse, flanked by formal public buildings as far as the Siegestor which looks like a triumphal arch.

To the east of Marienplatz a maze of narrow streets, now being restored to create studios and boutiques, surrounds the famous Hofbräuhaus beer hall. Just north of this is Maximilianstrasse, Munich's most exclusive shopping street, which runs east from the Residenz palace and opera house, past the very grand Vier Jahreszeiten hotel, to the Bavarian parliament building across the Isar.
Business districts Business is scattered throughout the city, although traditionally the banking, insurance and professional district is the area west of Ludwigstrasse. The headquarters of Siemens is also here, in Wittelsbacher Platz, and the striking dark-blue steel and glass complex of the Landesbausparkasse (LBS) is on Oskar-von-Miller-Ring. Other prestigious addresses are Barer Strasse, Brienner Strasse and Jägerstrasse. Some of the best restaurants and nightclubs, as well as the Continental hotel, are on or near Maximiliansplatz; to its south, Promenadeplatz, with the elegant Bayerischer Hof hotel, has some of the oldest private banks.

Another business and administrative area is the Lehel, the former Jewish quarter between the Altstadt and the river, where the fairly narrow streets are lined with ornate late-19thC houses. Several state government offices are here, including the Staatsministerium für Wirtschaft und Verkehr (Ministry of Economics).

Across the river, on the far side of Bogenhausen, an important new development is under construction at Arabellapark. Already completed are the Sheraton and Arabella hotels, a conference centre, the startlingly modern high-tech headquarters of the Hypo-Bank (now the tallest building in Munich) and many other office blocks.

Schwabing This is Munich's Latin quarter. North of the Siegestor, Ludwigstrasse becomes tree-lined Leopoldstrasse with pavement cafés; the university, Academy of Arts, boutiques and small theatres are all here, as well as an increasing number of businesses and many restaurants. In the quiet side streets are sought-after 19thC apartment houses, once occupied by artists and writers such as Thomas Mann.

Theresienwiese and Westend On the west side of the city is the Theresienwiese, site of the annual Oktoberfest. Next to it is the Messegelände (exhibition centre), and the surrounding district is home for many foreign workers. The city council is rejuvenating the area with small enterprise zones and townscaping.

The suburbs
The most exclusive inner suburb is Bogenhausen, across the Isar.

Haidhausen, just south of it, is being gentrified and is the site of an impressive new cultural complex, the Gasteig. Nymphenburg, near the royal palace, is another desirable residential area a couple of miles to the west.

Many executives live farther out, particularly in Grünwald to the south, or along the *S-Bahn* line to Starnberg or in the eastern suburbs beyond the airport.

Industrial areas Industry is spread right around the perimeter and along the main railway lines. Siemens' main plant is at Obersendling in the south, but it also has works at Neuperlach in the southeast and at Freimann in the north, and it is building a big new plant at Poing in the northeast. Also at Freimann is the Euro-Industriepark. At Karlsfeld in the northwest are MAN and MTU; Junkers and Krauss-Maffei are at Allach in the west, and BMW is near the Olympiapark in the north of the city. New industries are being established in the northern corridor of the two *Autobahnen* to Landshut and Ingolstadt, both important industrial centres.

Hotels

The 1972 Olympics gave a great boost to Munich's hotel building; there then followed a lull, but new hotels are opening again, particularly in the northeast around Bogenhausen. In the city centre a handful of long-established German-owned hotels with both charm and cachet dominate the scene.

All rooms in the hotels listed have bath or shower, an IDD telephone and TV. Most hotels offer exchange facilities for major currencies. Parking is not a problem.

Bayerischer Hof/Palais Montgelas [DM]//
Promenadepl 2–6, M2 ☎ *21200*
🆃🆇 *523409* • *AE DC MC V* • *440 rooms, 45 suites, 3 restaurants, 4 bars*
This busy hotel is one of the hubs of Munich's social and commercial life. At the edge of the Altstadt, the main hotel has a postwar façade, but the adjoining neo-classical Palais

Montgelas was acquired in 1969 and has been lavishly restored to provide palatial reception rooms. The public areas are furnished with antiques and tapestries, and the guest rooms, though not spacious, are comfortable; those facing south over the square are best. The Grill restaurant is very popular as a business lunch venue, and the Palais-

Keller serves Bavarian food. There is also a nightclub and a theatre (the Kleine Komödie). Hairdresser, beauty salon, gift shop, jeweller, newsstand, fashion boutiques, fur shop, travel agents • rooftop pool, solarium, sauna, jacuzzi, massage • fax, 17 meeting rooms (capacity up to 1,280), 11 other banqueting rooms.

Continental   [DM]////
Max-Joseph-Str 5, M2 ☎ *551570* ⊤ *522603* • *Royal Classic* • *AE DC MC V* • *143 rooms, 14 suites, 2 restaurants, 1 bar*
The "Conti," convenient for the business district, was acquired in 1986 by a Scandinavian group and substantially renovated. The accent now is on understated luxury and attentive service, and regular guests include big names in fashion, finance and industry. The rather utilitarian architecture is well disguised with antiques, paintings, tapestries and oriental rugs and the larger guest rooms are elegant, often with wood panelling or fabric-covered walls. All have video with a choice of English or German films, and 80% look onto a grassy courtyard. The Conti-Grill restaurant has a big open fire. Hairdresser, florist, newsstand • fax, 4 meeting rooms (capacity up to 160).

Hilton   [DM]////
Am Tucherpark 7, M22 ☎ *38450* ⊤ *5215740* • *AE DC MC V* • *480 rooms, 21 suites, 2 restaurants, 1 bar*
Built in 1972 and refurbished in 1987, this is probably now the best Hilton in Europe. Just a 10min drive from the centre, it has superb views, proximity to the lovely Englischer Garten and access to all of the suburbs using the ring road. The lobby with its tapestries, mirrors and gilding is undeniably flamboyant, but the pastel decor of the guest rooms is more restful, and the suites range in style from Laura Ashley to Royal Bavarian. All of the rooms have scenic views either to the Alps or over river and parkland. 24hr room service, hair and beauty salons, boutiques, newsstand,

gift shop, medical centre, shuttle-bus to the city • pool, sauna, solarium, massage, gym, free loan of golf clubs, other sports available locally • fax, courier, 9 meeting rooms (capacity up to 1,000).

Königshof   [DM]////
Karlspl 25, M2 ☎ *551360* ⊤ *523616* • *AE DC MC V* • *97 rooms, 9 suites, 1 restaurant, 1 bar*
The Köngishof, on Munich's busiest square, close to the Altstadt and Hauptbahnhof, more than compensates for its undistinguished exterior with *trompe-l'oeil* panelling, leather seating and much gilt. This decor extends to the guest rooms (which vary widely in price according to size and comfort) but not to the bar or to the restaurant, which is one of the best in Munich. Rooms have air conditioning and soundproofing. Fax, 4 meeting rooms (capacity up to 100).

Palace   [DM]////
Trogerstr 21 (corner Prinzregentenstr), M80 ☎ *4705091* ⊤ *528256* • *AE DC MC V* • *67 rooms, 6 suites, 1 restaurant, 1 bar*
Opened in September 1986, this is one of Munich's newest luxury hotels, in Bogenhausen, a 7min drive from the airport and 8min from the city centre. It has grandeur on an intimate scale, with marble floors, classical statuary and spotless white decor, and is already establishing a reputation. International musicians are among the regular guests. Most of the rooms overlook a central courtyard and are decorated in pastel colours. Some suites have a private sauna. 24hr room service • terrace with solarium and jacuzzi, exercise equipment, massage • 6 meeting rooms (capacity up to 100).

Credit card abbreviations	
AE	American Express
DC	Diners Club
MC	Access/MasterCard
V	Visa

Sheraton $\boxed{DM}$ ||||
Arabellastr 6, M81 ☎ *924011*
TX *522391* • *AE DC MC V* • *650 rooms,*
3 restaurants, 2 bars
This 22-floor tower is in the rather
bleak Arabellapark complex, about a
10min drive from the airport and the
city. The rooms are pleasant and
functional, and it has extensive
conference facilities. Nightclub,
hairdresser, shops, Avis desk • pool,
sauna, exercise room • 10 meeting
rooms (capacity up to 1,200).

Vier Jahreszeiten $\boxed{DM}$ ||||
Maximilianstr 17, M22 ☎ *230390,*
TX *523859* • *Kempinski* • *AE DC MC V*
• *316 rooms, 25 suites, 2 restaurants,*
1 bar
The Vier Jahreszeiten is the grandest
hotel in Munich. It was acquired by
the Kempinski group in 1973 and,
since then, there has been some
necessary refurbishment of its
time-honoured decor. On the
city's most exclusive shopping street,
conveniently close to the opera house
and national theatre, its original mid-
19thC frontage has been carefully
preserved and its softly lit, panelled
lounge is a society haunt. The
bedrooms, however, are rather airless
and heavily furnished; the best
overlook the Residenz. Even the suites
lack glamour and some of the
corridors are distinctly shabby, but
the service is civilized and welcoming.
The famous Walterspiel restaurant is
not for everyday eating (see
Restaurants), whereas the cheaper

Jahreszeiten-Eck is popular
for business lunches. The ornate
private rooms are better for
receptions than conferences. 24hr
room service, hairdresser, gift shop,
newsstand, Lufthansa check-in desk
• pool, sauna, massage, exercise
equipment • fax, 10 meeting rooms
(capacity up to 450).

OTHER HOTELS
An der Oper $\boxed{DM}$ | *Falkenturmstr*
10, M2 ☎ *228711* TX *522588* • *AE DC*
MC. A small hotel with comfortable,
modern rooms and a good restaurant.
Arabella $\boxed{DM}$ |||| *Arabellastr 5,*
M81 ☎ *92321* TX *529987* • *AE DC*
MC V. A 300-room tower near to the
Sheraton, adjoining the congress
centre. Pool and exercise centre.
Eden-Wolff $\boxed{DM}$ |||| *Arnulfstr*
4–8, M2 ☎ *551150* TX *523564* • *AE*
DC MC V. Big, comfortable hotel
beside the Hauptbahnhof. Rooms
vary widely in price; the best are
away from the street and station.
Well-equipped meeting rooms.
Holiday Inn $\boxed{DM}$ |||| *Leopoldstr 194,*
M40 ☎ *340971* TX *5215439* • *AE DC*
MC V. North of Schwabing, near the
ring road and Nuremberg *Autobahn.*
Pool and usual Holiday Inn facilities.
There is a cheaper Holiday Inn in
Sendling, near the Siemens plant.
Penta $\boxed{DM}$ |||| *Hochstr 3, M80*
☎ *4485555* TX *529046* • *AE DC MC V.*
Big, modern tower in Haidhausen,
handy for the airport and close to the
centre. Pool, sauna and well-
equipped meeting rooms.

Restaurants

There is a wide choice of foreign cuisine – French, Italian, Balkan and
Chinese – in the city centre, Schwabing and Bogenhausen and all levels
of formality are catered for. Bavarians are fond of meat and fish; local
dishes include *Leberkäse*, a liver pâté often served in hot slices, and fish
grilled on a skewer, *Steckerlfisch*. Reservations up to two days in advance
for the main restaurants described are strongly advised.

Aubergine $\boxed{DM}$ ||||
Maximilianspl 5 (entrance in Max-
Joseph-Str) ☎ *598171* • *closed Sun,*
Mon, 3 weeks in Aug, hols • *MC*
• *jacket and tie*

Master chef Eckart Witzigmann, ex-
Paul Bocuse and Washington's
Jockey Club, owns and sometimes
cooks in this restaurant, which is
famous throughout Germany. This is

the place to celebrate a major coup or give a big thank-you, but you must reserve 2–3 weeks ahead. The costly decor of deep purple carpet, chandeliers, mirrors, white and metallic walls is a blend of classic and high-tech modern. The dozen tables are well spaced, and there is a small upstairs bar (with a selection of 80 whiskies). The *nouvelle cuisine* fixed-price menu is slightly cheaper for lunch than dinner. The wine list is superb and the service impeccable.

Boettner   [DM]///
Theatinerstr 8 ☏ *221210* • *closed Sat D, Sun, hols* • *AE DC MC V* • *jacket and tie*
This central restaurant, club-like and intimate, and furnished with antiques, has been a lunch-time watering-hole for top business people and politicians since 1906. It still retains the atmosphere of those days, and the founder's grandson, Roland Hartung-Boettner, is in genial attendance. Although busiest at lunch, the ten tables are often full during the evening interval of the nearby opera house. The rich menu offers old-fashioned German and French *haute cuisine*. The bar doubles as a wine shop and delicatessen, where you can buy oysters and caviar to eat there or take away.

Chesa Rüegg   [DM]/
Wurzerstr 18 ☏ *297114* • *closed Sat, Sun, hols* • *AE DC MC V* • *jacket and tie*
The Chesa Rüegg has become a popular lunch and dinner haunt of the business and media fraternity, with its rustic Alpine decor, reasonable prices and convenient location just off Maximilianstrasse. But its 30 tables are closely spaced and it can be noisy. Mainly Swiss menu, strong on veal and steaks.

For general information about German hotels, see the *Planning and Reference* section.

Da Pippo   [DM]/
Mühlbaurstr 36 ☏ *4704848* • *closed Sat L, Sun, Aug 1–21, Dec 23–Jan 2* • *DC MC*
This spacious, informally elegant restaurant in a leafy Bogenhausen street is for social rather than business entertaining. In the evening, mirrors and candlelight give it a romantic atmosphere. Sophisticated Italian cooking and good Sicilian wines.

Le Gourmet   [DM]////
Ligsalzstr 46 ☏ *503597* • *D only; closed Sun and 2 weeks in Jan* • *AE DC MC V*
The only good restaurant close to the Messegelände (exhibition centre), Le Gourmet's ten tables are in two small ornately furnished rooms. The top-class cooking is both *nouvelle* and Bavarian. The cellar has over 300 French classified *crus*.

Käfer-Schänke   [DM]///
Prinzregentenstr 73 ☏ *41681* • *closed Sun, hols* • *AE DC MC*
A large, old-established, family-owned restaurant, the Käfer-Schänke is a Munich institution and is usually crowded and noisy. It is better for a lively evening than a working lunch, though it has private rooms. Famous faces are seen here. The food is good value though prices are fairly high.

Königshof   [DM]///
Königshof hotel, Karlspl 25 ☏ *551360* • *AE DC MC V* • *jacket and tie*
Probably the best hotel restaurant in town, the restfully decorated and spacious dining room of the Königshof has a soundproofed picture window overlooking the Stachus. The cuisine is *nouvelle*, with dishes like coquille St Jacques and calf's liver with shallots in red wine sauce. A wide selection of excellent wines.

La Piazzetta   [DM]/
Oskar-von-Miller-Ring 3 ☏ *282990* • *closed Sat L* • *AE DC MC V*
A relatively new restaurant in the business district (in the LBS

building). Comprising three adjoining rooms and a separate brasserie, many of its tables are in alcoves, ideal for a discreet business rendezvous. The Florentine menu allows a wide choice of antipasti and fish dishes. The extensive Italian wine list includes reasonably priced bottles.

Preysing-Keller [DM]//
Innere Wiener Str 6 (Haidhausen)
☎ *481015 • D only; closed Sun and Dec 22–Jan 6 • no credit cards*
This spacious restaurant, deep in a 300-year-old vault, with bar and comfortable lounge, is a splendid refuge on a winter's night. Near the parliament house and Gasteig arts centre, it is only a short ride from the city. The food is international and ambitious and the wines excellent.

Sabitzer [DM]////
Reitmorstr 21 ☎ *298584 • closed Sat L, Sun • AE DC MC*
This is one of Munich's most respected establishments. Recently refurbished, on the outside it sports gleaming stucco and awnings, while inside there are sparkling chandeliers and flowers on every table. The cuisine is *nouvelle* Bavarian with dishes such as soufflé of pike with basil sauce and haunch of rabbit with tarragon. The wine list is appropriately grand. A good choice for a business meal.

Tai Tung [DM]/
Prinzregentenstr 60 ☎ *471100 • closed Sun • AE DC MC*
The oldest and best Chinese restaurant in southern Germany, Tai Tung is in an inviting scarlet and black lacquer basement beneath the Stuck Villa, a *Jugendstil* (Art Nouveau) museum and gallery.

Walterspiel [DM]////
Vier Jahreszeiten hotel ☎ *23039599 • closed Mon L and Sat L, Aug • AE DC MC V • jacket and tie*
This elegant rococo restaurant has long been patronized by members of the government and aristocracy, but lately there have been mutterings that it is guilty of culinary backsliding. As a business venue, it still has considerable cachet.

Good but casual
Bistro Terrine, Amalienstr 89 (entrance Amalien-Passage) ☎ 281780 is newish but much praised. In Bogenhausen, the *Bogenhauser Hof*, Ismaningerstr 85 ☎ 985586, is an old hunting lodge where Bavarian food is served in traditional surroundings. *Kay's Bistro*, Utzschneiderstr 1 ☎ 2603584, has a showbiz clientele, live music and good food. *Die Kulisse*, Maximilianstr 26 ☎ 294728, is a busy after-theatre restaurant in the style of a Viennese coffee-house. The popular *Pizzeria Italy*, Leopoldstr 108 ☎ 346403, offers Italian cooking at reasonable prices.

Cafés
The Münchner has a habit of sitting down to eat, drink and talk at any time of the day, and there are numerous rendezvous. In the business district, the *Café Luitpold*, Brienner Str 11 ☎ 292865, is somewhere to drink coffee and read the papers among potted palms from 9am, with the restaurant opening at 11.45. The trendier *Extrablatt*, in Schwabing, Leopoldstr 7 ☎ 333333, is furnished with original pieces from long gone *belle époque* hotels. For a drink at any time of day the *Augustiner-Gaststätte*, Neuhauser Str 16, has spacious rooms and a leafy beer-garden behind a small 16thC façade.

Bars
Early evening drinking is not a common habit in Munich. The bars of the top hotels are a good rendezvous. *Harry's New York Bar* in Falkenturmstrasse is old-established and more Munich than

Manhattan. Probably the most "in" place is *Schumann's*, Maximilianstr 36, which is open to the small hours.

Entertainment

Munich has the richest variety of opera, theatre and music of any city in Germany, particularly during the festival months of June and July. The best source of information is the official monthly programme, *München: offizielles Monatsprogramm*. Tickets for theatre, concerts and sports events (but not for the Staatsoper, Staatstheater and Kammerspiele) can be bought from agencies including *ABR-Theaterkasse*, Neuhauser Str 9 ☏ 1204421, and *Max Hieber*, Liebfrauenstr 1 (by the cathedral) ☏ 226571.

Opera, musicals, dance Richard Wagner and Richard Strauss still feature strongly in the repertoire of the Staatsoper at the *Nationaltheater*, Max-Joseph-Pl (box office Maximilianstr 11 ☏ 221316), and occasional productions are staged in the beautiful *Cuvilliéstheater*, Residenzstr 1 ☏ 221316. The *Staatstheater am Gärtnerplatz*, Gärtnerpl 3 ☏ 2016767, offers a wider range of opera, ballet and musicals, and the *Deutsches Theater*, Schwanthalerstr 13 ☏ 592911, has a programme of operetta, musicals and international solo stars.

Theatre Traditional productions of the classics are staged by the Staatsschauspiel company at the *Residenztheater*, Residenzstr 1, and *Marstalltheater*, Max-Joseph-Pl ☏ 225754 (for both), and more adventurous stagings of classic and contemporary plays are performed by the Kammerspiele at the *Schauspielhaus*, Maximilianstr 26 ☏ 237210. For satirical comedy, there is the famous *Münchner Lach- und Schiessgesellschaft*, Ursulastr 9 ☏ 391997. More in vogue is the *Münchner Rationaltheater*, Hesselohestr 18 ☏ 334050.

Cinema Most of the popular cinemas are to the west of the city or in Schwabing. Foreign-language films are shown at *Europa-Fremdsprachenkino*, Arnulfstr 8–9 ☏ 593406.

Music The recently opened *Gasteig* centre, Rosenheimer Str 5 ☏ 41810, stages international concerts and recitals. The Bavarian Radio Symphony Orchestra under Rafael Kubelik gives concerts (Thu, Fri) in the *Herkulessaal* of the Residenz, and chamber music is performed in the *Max-Joseph-Saal*, Residenzstr 1 ☏ 224641. There are summer concerts in the *Schloss Nymphenburg* ☏ 179081.

Nightclubs Munich's nightspots are numerous but mainly aimed at the young. Perennially "in" despite or because of its spartan interior is *P1* (pronounced *peh eins*), Prinzregentenstr 1 ☏ 294252 (open 9.30–4, closed Mon), once the tea rooms of the Haus der Kunst. In summer, drink on the terrace overlooking the Englischer Garten. *Eve*, Maximilianspl 5 ☏ 554070 (open 10–4, closed Sun), is a superior striptease club, where politicians and celebrities are seen.

Shopping

Munich is Germany's headquarters for the fashion industry, art and antiques. The most exclusive shops are in Maximilianstrasse and adjoining streets.

Department stores For less expensive shops, try Kaufinger and Neuhauser Strasser; *Karstadt*, *Kaufhof* and *Woolworth* are here. *Hertie* is in Schützenstrasse.

Gifts *Dallmayr*, Dienerstrasse, is a fresh food shop and delicatessen that once supplied royalty.

Fashion In Maximilianstrasse *Gucci*, *St Laurent* and *Jil Sander* are represented; *Guy Laroche* is in Falckenbergstrasse, along with top names in shoes, jewellery and men's clothes. Traditional dirndls are stocked at *Beck am Rathauseck*, Marienplatz.

Sports equipment The superb *Sport-Scheck*, Sendlinger Str 85, also leases equipment.

Antiques The antiques trade clusters around the Viktualienmarkt; art dealers are in Ottostrasse (Kunstblock), north of Maximiliansplatz. The top art auctioneers, *Neumeister*, is in Barerstrasse.

Schwabing is known for antiquarian books and prints (Amalienstrasse), and it has dozens of boutiques and galleries.

Sightseeing

The galleries, museums, churches and palaces are among the finest in Europe. For recorded information in English ☎ 239162 (galleries and museums) ☎ 239172 (other sights).

Altstadt landmarks Within a short walk of Marienplatz are the earliest royal residence, the *Alter Hof*, a quiet medieval courtyard open at all times; the *Altes Rathaus*, the old town hall, from Gothic to baroque in style; the red-brick Gothic cathedral and centrepiece of the city, *Frauenkirche*; the 16thC *Hofbräuhaus*, Platzl 9, with its oom-pah band; and the *Michaelskirche* in Neuhauser Strasse, the greatest Renaissance church north of the Alps. On the Marienplatz is the ornate neo-Gothic *Neues Rathaus*, whose famous Glockenspiel draws a big crowd every day at 11am (also 12am and 5pm in summer).

Alte Pinakothek Built in 1827 to house the royal collection, this is now one of the world's foremost art galleries, with virtually all major 14th–18thC painters represented. *Barer Str 27. Open Tue–Sun, 9–4.30; also Tue and Thu, 7pm–9pm.*

Asamkirche The narrow 18thC façade of this church conceals a riot of pink, white and gold stucco. *Sendlingerstr. Open daily.*

Deutsches Museum Built in 1903 on an island in the river, and dedicated to science and technology, it ranks with the Smithsonian. *Isarinsel. Open 9–5.*

Englischer Garten This informal park, so named because an Englishman advised on its layout in

1785, is a haven for cyclists, joggers, sunbathers (often nude) and lovers; drinkers gather at the *Chinesischer Turm* pagoda. *Entrance in Prinzregentenstr. Open 24hr.*

Haus der Kunst In one of the few surviving public buildings of the Nazi era, where the notorious "Decadent Art" show was held, there is now an excellent 20thC collection from Pablo Picasso and Marc Chagall to Pop and Minimal art. *Prinzregentenstr 1. Open Tue–Sun, 9–4.30; also Thu, 7pm–9pm.*

Neue Pinakothek A striking modern building, completed in 1980, housing late-18th and 19thC works, including some by the German Romantics, English landscape painters and French Impressionists. *Theresienstr. Open Tue–Sun, 9–4.30.*

Nymphenburg palace The Bavarian Versailles. Built as a royal summer residence between 1664 and 1715, its ornate public rooms look onto an ornamental park. *In M19, 6km/4 miles west of centre. Open May–Sep, Tue–Sun, 9–12.30, 1.30–5; Oct–Apr, 10–12.30, 1.30–4.*

Olympiazentrum Impressive sports complex open to the public (see *Spectator sports*), built for the 1972 Olympics. The huge tent-like roof, made up of 8,000 acrylic plates, is 75,000 sq metres in area. *On U-Bahn 3.5km/2 miles north of centre. Guided tours on request.*

Residenz Max-Joseph-Pl 3. A collection of imposing 16th–19thC buildings where the Wittelsbach kings lived. The *Cuvilliéstheater* (Residenzstr 1, entrance in Brunnenhof) is a sumptuous red and gold rococo auditorium with four tiers of balconies (*open Mon–Sat, 2–5; Sun, 10–5*). North of the Residenz, the *Hofgarten*, Hofgartenstr, is a formal 17thC garden enclosed by colonnades on two sides (*open 24hr*). The magnificent courtyards and state apartments of the palace now form the *Residenzmuseum*, housing the crown jewels and other treasures (*Max-Joseph-Pl, open Tue–Sat, 10–4.30; Sun, 10–1; guided tours*).

Schwabing Just north of the pagoda in the Englischer Garten, Thiemestrasse takes you into the side streets of Schwabing. If you have a spare hour, walk up to Wedekindplatz, then through to Münchener Freiheit and back down Leopoldstrasse.

Siemens-Museum Has several thousand exhibits connected with the development of electronics. *Prannerstr 10. Open Mon–Fri, 9–4; Sat–Sun, 10–2.*

Theatinerkirche An elegant ochre-washed baroque basilica with twin spires. *Theatinerstr. Open May–Sep, 10–1, 3–5.*

Guided tours

Panorama Tours City & Country ☏ 5904248 runs daily 2hr 30min bus tours of main city sights from Bahnhofplatz. *Rema-Reisen* ☏ 595831 runs tours by car with a guide lasting 2hr 30min (or 4hr with lunch).

Out of town

Dachau, 17km/10.5 miles northwest of city, is the site of the notorious concentration camp. The one remaining building is a museum ☏ (08131) 1741.

Starnbergersee 30km/19 miles southwest of Munich. The most easily reached of Munich's lakes, set in wooded hills with a view of the Alps. A steamer leaves on regular trips ☏ Starnberg Staatliche Schiffahrt (08151) 12023.

Munich's festivals

Oktoberfest is an annual beer-drinking festival at the end of September, which has developed from celebrations held in 1810 to mark a royal wedding and now attracts some 6m visitors.
Fasching, Munich's carnival season, runs from January 6 until Shrove Tuesday, four to six weeks later, and includes some 2,000 costume balls. Outdoor events take place around the Viktualienmarkt.

Spectator sports

Athletics, cycling, soccer Soccer is predominant and Bayern-München is one of the strongest teams in Europe. Their home ground is the *Olympiastadion,* also used for major athletic and cycling events. Tickets ☏ 30613577.

Horse-racing Meetings are held on Wed and Sat at *Daglfing* (trotting) and *Riem* (flat racing) ☏ 9300010.

Skiing International competitions in downhill, slalom amd jumping are held at *Oberstdorf,* 160km/100 miles southwest of Munich. Klinker organizes excursions ☏ 263093.

Keeping fit

Fitness centres *Club Vitaprop,* Berg-am-Laimstr 91 ☏ 433061. *Fitnessstudio Arabellapark,* Arabellastr 15 ☏ 911891. *Body Up,* Dachauer Str 50 ☏ 596293.

Golf A most attractive course is at *Feldafing* on the Starnbergersee ☏ (08157) 1305.

Jogging The Englischer Garten offers ample scope.

Skiing *Sport-Scheck* ☏ 21660 organizes day and weekend excursions.

Squash *Bavaria Squash Center,* Bavariastr 16 ☏ 774181, has 14 courts.

Swimming The open-air pool at *Prinzregentenbad,* Prinzregentenstr 80 ☏ 474808, is fashionable and has a restaurant. Visitors can use the pool at the *Olympiazentrum* ☏ 30613390.

Tennis *Sport-Scheck* ☏ 21660 runs courts, now as popular as the private clubs, especially the ones at *Herzogpark* in Bogenhausen.

Local resources

Business services

Companies offering fully furnished, equipped and staffed offices for short-term use include *Günther Bureau Service System,* Leopoldstr 28 ☏ 333200.

Photocopying and printing
Hansa-Print, Thalkirchner Str 72 ☏ 530195; *Top Kopie,* Gabelsberger Str 73 ☏ 5234598; *Copyland,*

Amalienstr 46 ☎ 288275.
Secretarial *Petra Fischer*,
Einsteinstr 111 ☎ 4707071 (Mon–
Fri, 8.30–5.30); *Lydia Morawietz
Büro-Service*, Zeppelinstr 73
☎ 4488496 (Mon–Fri, 8.30–5.30).
Allround ☎ 8595055 for English and
foreign languages (Mon–Fri, 10–8).
Translation The *Industrie- und
Handelskammer* ☎ 51160 can
recommend interpreters and
translators.

Communications
Local delivery *City Car* ☎ 555444;
CentroCar ☎ 770077.
Long-distance delivery *DHL*
☎ 909050; *TNT* ☎ 2012290.
Post office Main post office:
Residenzstr 2 ☎ 2177302; 24hr
service at Bahnhofpl 1 ☎ 5598406.
Telex and fax *Günther Bureau
Service* ☎ 333200 handles telex, fax
and data processing; also *International
Business Services* ☎ 4313005
TX 5213379.

Conference/exhibition centres
The *Messegelände* beside the
Theresienwiese, on the west side of
the city, comprises 19 halls with a
total of 105,000 sq metres, and a
further 200,000 sq metres of open-air
space. It hosts some 20 fairs and 60
conferences each year. Contact
*Münchner Messe- und Ausstellungs
GmbH*, Theresienhöhe 13, M72
☎ 51070. The *Arabella Konferenz-
Zentrum*, in Arabellapark, M81, has
11 rooms on two floors, seating up to
560. For audiences of up to 2,400, the
Kongresssaal of the *Deutsches Museum*
☎ 2179241 is often used. For all
conference information contact
Fremdenverkehrsamt, Rindermarkt 5
☎ 2391216.

Emergencies
Bureau de change Hauptbahnhof
(railway station), open daily, 6–11.30.
Hospitals Emergency admissions at
Krankenhaus Rechts der Isar,
Ismanninger Str ☎ 41401. Heart
emergencies ☎ 41402239. Ambulance
☎ 222660. Doctors on emergency

☎ 558661, and dentists ☎ 7233093.
Pharmacies For pharmacies open
after hours and on Sun ☎ 594475.
Police Ettstr 2 ☎ 2147211.

Government offices
The economic department of the
City Council, *Wirtschaftsamt der
Landeshauptstadt München*,
Blumenstr 17, M2 ☎ 2334872, deals
with companies wanting to set up
here. At state level, contact the
*Staatsministerium für Wirtschaft und
Verkehr*, Prinzregentenstr 28, M22
☎ 216201.

Information sources
Business information The
Industrie- und Handelskammer, Max-
Joseph-Str 2, M2 ☎ 51160, runs a
computer database of products and
suppliers in Oberbayern and
Munich, and advises on all
regulations. *Europäisches Patentamt*,
Erhardstr 27, M5 ☎ 23990, is the
central patent office for the EC, and
the *Deutsches Patentamt*,
Zweibrückenstr 12, M2 ☎ 21951 for
the Federal Republic. *Bayerische
Staatsbibliothek*, Ludwigstr 16, is the
central reference library.
Local media The *Süddeutsche
Zeitung* is one of Germany's leading
papers. Its politics are liberal, left of
centre and its business coverage is
excellent. The *Münchner Merkur* has
a more regional appeal and is loyal to
the CSU government. *Bayerischer
Rundfunk* is the local station for both
radio and TV.
Tourist information *Amtliches
Bayerisches Reisebüro* for tours
outside Munich, at the
Hauptbahnhof ☎ 12040.
Fremdenverkehrsamt München for the
city, at the Hauptbahnhof, south exit
☎ 2391256.

Thank-yous
Confectionery *Café Kreutzkramm*,
Maffeistr 4.
Florists *Blumen-Schmidt*, in the
precinct under Karlspl ☎ 597739.
Wine merchants *La Maison du
Vin*, Hohenzollernstr 34 ☎ 341400.

NUREMBERG
City codes zip 8500 ☏ 0911

Today, Nürnberg gives place to Bavaria's capital, Munich, and locally to Ansbach, the administrative centre of Mittelfranken. But its proud early history – Dark Ages fortress of the Franks and imperial capital in the 11th and 12th centuries – has given it legendary status.

At an important crossroads of trade, Nuremberg's natural sphere of influence reached east to Bohemia and north to Saxony. Commerce and culture prospered in the hands of merchants and metalworkers, men such as Albrecht Dürer, Hans Sachs and the Meistersingers, craftsmen and artists. Its artisans developed brassfounding and invented the gunlock, pocket watch and clarinet. For 600 years, Nuremberg was a self-governing Free City; this ended with the annexation by Bavaria in 1806, and its ingenuity was applied to emerging technology. In 1835, the first railway in Germany was built from Nuremberg to nearby Fürth.

Later history has not been so inspiring. Under the Third Reich the city was again prominent and in 1945 played its final part as venue of the war trials. The Allies flattened all but its great walls, the Iron Curtain separated long-standing trading partners like Dresden, Leipzig and Prague, and advanced industry has gone elsewhere. Even so – and despite the slow rise in its population to 480,000 – today Nuremberg is an industrial and business centre. It is the home of Adidas, Grundig and Triumph-Adler, and the site of plants built by the electrical giants AEG, Bosch and Siemens and by MAN, the big truck and bus company. Companies headquartered here or in Fürth include Diehl, Flachglas and Philips Kommunication. It has superb exhibition and congress facilities, and by the end of the century the new Europa Canal, which now connects into the Main and Rhein, will link it to the Danube. By that time, relations with the Eastern Bloc may have improved sufficiently to restore Nuremberg to its former importance.

Arriving
There are flights from the most important German cities and from some European capitals and business centres. From Frankfurt, there are five 45min flights daily and an hourly train service from the airport station, usually with a change at Würzburg (journey time 2hr 40min). Other rail links are good, and the city is at the Munich–Berlin, Frankfurt–Vienna and Mannheim–Prague *Autobahn* intersections.

Nürnberg airport
This small airport, 7km/4 miles north of the city, is busy only during big trade fairs. It has a restaurant, bureau de change and car rental desks for

Avis, Hertz, interRent, Budget and Europcar. Flight information ☏ 3506200; freight information ☏ 3506344.
City link A taxi takes 10min (fare DM20) into town (more in rush hours). There is a bus service to and from the Hauptbahnhof, linked to departure and arrival times. During the big trade fairs, *Aero-Dienst* ☏ 52080 runs a helicopter shuttle to the exhibition centre.

Railway station
Hauptbahnhof This imposing 19thC main station is at the southeast of the city centre, close to the big hotels and business area. There are hourly services to Munich (1hr

215

40min) and Mannheim (3hr), as well as Frankfurt, and routes radiate to all parts of north Bavaria. It has a bureau de change, tourist information, a bookstand, food shop and pharmacy. It is on the *U-Bahn* and cabs are always available. Train information ☎ 19419.

Getting around

The Altstadt (old city) and Marienplatz business district are walkable (about 1.5km end to end). Elsewhere you need transport, preferably taxis.

Taxis There are ranks at the station and, in the Altstadt, at Lorenzer Platz, Hauptmarkt and Innere Laufer Platz. Otherwise ☎ 20555.

Limousines Avis ☎ 49696 (city) and 528966 (airport).

Driving Most cross-town journeys involve a detour on the inner ring road of Frauentorgraben, Neutorgraben and Marientorgraben, in order to avoid pedestrian and one-way streets, and the massive walls. There are parking facilities in the Altstadt and in Marienplatz. A fast outer ring links the city, *Autobahnen* exits and a throughway, the Frankenschnellweg, to adjacent

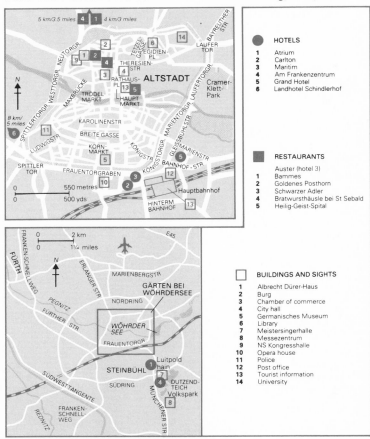

HOTELS
1 Atrium
2 Carlton
3 Maritim
4 Am Frankenzentrum
5 Grand Hotel
6 Landhotel Schindlerhof

RESTAURANTS
Auster (hotel 3)
1 Bammes
2 Goldenes Posthorn
3 Schwarzer Adler
4 Bratwursthäusle bei St Sebald
5 Heilig-Geist-Spital

BUILDINGS AND SIGHTS
1 Albrecht Dürer-Haus
2 Burg
3 Chamber of commerce
4 City hall
5 Germanisches Museum
6 Library
7 Meistersingerhalle
8 Messezentrum
9 NS Kongresshalle
10 Opera house
11 Police
12 Post office
13 Tourist information
14 University

towns such as Fürth and Erlangen. Inner city car rental: *Avis* ☏ 49696.
Walking At any hour, walking is perfectly safe.
Subway The *U-Bahn* is useful for getting to the Messezentrum (southeast) and Fürth (northwest).
Buses and streetcars Streetcar no. 9 links the Hauptbahnhof and Meistersingerhalle.

Area by area
The recreated Altstadt, within its red sandstone ramparts, is primarily devoted to shopping and entertainment. Bisected by the pretty river Pegnitz, its northern half is dominated by the forbidding castle, beneath which huddle streets of antique shops and *Weinstuben*. South of the river, around Lorenzer Platz with its tall Gothic church, are the main traffic-free shopping streets and, beyond the Königstor gate, Bahnhofsplatz, the main traffic fulcrum. Banking, insurance and other businesses are concentrated around Marienplatz and along the inner ring road. The Meistersingerhalle and adjoining Atrium Hotel, the Dutzendteich lakes, and the exhibition centre (Messezentrum) are to the southeast.

Most industry is at a radius of 3km/2 miles or more from the city, but there are plants closer in at Steinbühl. The canal docks and Frankenschnellweg are sites of new development.

The most desirable residential area is on the east side, by the Wöhrder See, in Gärten, St Jobst and Mögeldorf.

Hotels
The choice of top-class hotels is limited, with two main clusters around the Hauptbahnhof and near the Messezentrum; none is in the Altstadt. All those listed have a TV and IDD telephone in every bedroom, and most have currency exchange and parking facilities.

Atrium [DM]||
Münchener Str 25, N50 ☏ *47480*
TX *626167* • *AE DC MC V* • *200 rooms, 3 suites, 2 restaurants, 1 bar*
A pleasant, modern low-rise building in parkland, adjoining the Meistersingerhalle concert and congress venue, it is a 5min drive from the station, the Messezentrum, and from the *Autobahn*. Though restful and spacious, with function rooms, it lacks atmosphere. It is almost exclusively used by German business and conference visitors. The adjacent Park Restaurant has more exciting food than the hotel. Bus at airport by arrangement • pool, sauna • 5 meeting rooms (capacity up to 250).

Carlton [DM]||
Eilgutstr 13–15, N70 ☏ *20030*
TX *622329* • *Best Western* • *AE DC MC V* • *124 rooms, 6 suites, 2 restaurants, 1 bar*

Built in 1948, in a quiet square near the station, this hotel was expensively refurbished in 1986 to compensate for its unprepossessing appearance. From the very modern silver-grey lobby you enter a tartan and black-leather bar, which at night is a popular rendezvous. Clients are international, mainly business, and include many big companies. The rooms vary in comfort and price, the most pleasant being at the top; all have hairdryers. The Swiss-style Chesa restaurant is warmly inviting and the Zirbelstube has pine panelling, cane furniture and a terrace. Gift shop, newsstand • sauna • 5 meeting rooms (capacity up to 120).

Maritim [DM]|||
Frauentorgraben 11, N70 ☏ *23630*
TX *622709* • *AE DC MC V* • *307 rooms, 9 suites, 2 restaurants, 1 bar*
This first-class hotel by the city walls opened in 1986. The decor is warm, colourful and elegant. Extras

in the bedrooms include hairdryers and toiletries. Over 40 rooms are reserved for nonsmokers, and there is a VIP floor. It has a fashionable bar with resident pianist, open until 3am, the top-class Auster restaurant (see *Restaurants*) and the 40-table Nürnberger Stuben, which does a good-value business lunch. Courtesy bus, car rental • pool, exercise equipment, massage, sauna, solarium, steambath • typewriter rental, 9 meeting rooms (capacity up to 800).

OTHER HOTELS
Am Frankenzentrum [DM]/
Görlitzer Str 51, N51 ☎ *89220*
ⓣ *9118494* • *AE DC V*. Near the

Messezentrum and *Autobahn*, this is a 1986-built, well-equipped business conference hotel.
Grand Hotel [DM]// *Bahnhofstr 1, N1* ☎ *203621* ⓣ *622010* • *Penta* • *AE DC MC*. Recently refurbished hotel close to the business district, with two useful restaurants.

Out of town
The *Landhotel Schindlerhof*, Steinacher Str 8, Nürnberg-Boxdorf N70 ☎ 302077, north of the city, 10min from the airport and centre, consists of an attractive group of 400-year old buildings. It is popular with young executives, so reserve well ahead for the restaurant.

Restaurants

The produce of the fields, forests and streams is the basis of Franconian cuisine, with freshwater fish, such as carp, featuring particularly. It is well worth trying. Most of the top restaurants, like business and industry, are in the village-like suburbs. In the centre, first-class entertaining is limited to the Maritim (see *Hotels*). Reservations are recommended for the main entries.

Auster [DM]//
Maritim hotel ☎ *23630* • *AE DC MC V* • *jacket and tie*
This opulent new restaurant, with widely spaced tables, is well placed to attract international business clients. The dark green and white decor, with mirrors and candelabras, is a suitable backdrop for the imaginative *nouvelle cuisine* of chef Wolfram Bartz, formerly at the famous Ente vom Lehel in Wiesbaden.

Bammes [DM]//
Bucher Hauptstr 63 ☎ *381303* • *closed Sun* • *AE DC MC*
In the village of Buch, 5km/3 miles north of the city, this pleasant, old, timbered house is well patronized by people from industry, banking and the professions. The chef-owner's excellent Franconian cooking is based on local ingredients, such as poached *Waller* (river fish) in wine sauce. It serves fine local, French and Italian wines. Private dining rooms cater for

up to 40, and a conference room will open in 1988.

Goldenes Posthorn [DM]//
Glöckleinsgasse 2–4 ☎ *225153* • *closed Sun* • *AE DC MC*
One of the few good restaurants in the Altstadt, it is more for tourists than business people, being reputedly the oldest eating-house in Germany (1498), where Albrecht Dürer and Hans Sachs were regulars. The ambitious menu includes quail and char in Riesling sauce.

Schwarzer Adler [DM]//
Kraftshofer Hauptstr 166, Nürnberg-Kraftshof ☎ *305858* • *closed Dec 22– Jan 3* • *DC MC*
Suitable for all special occasions, this is the grandest and most adventurous of the *Gasthäuser*. The 1752 building has been restored to its former glory, with decor and furnishings in a sophisticated country style. The wine list is mainly Franconian.

Good but casual

The traditional Nuremberg hostelries are called the *Bratwurst-Lokale*. At *Bratwursthäusle bei St Sebald*, Rathauspl 1 ☎ 227695, in the heart of the Altstadt, tasty home-made sausages are grilled over an open fire in a low-ceilinged *Stube*. The monastic *Heilig-Geist-Spital*, Spitalgasse 12 ☎ 221761, built over the river, serves traditional dishes, with wine and beer from the barrel, until late.

Bars

To talk in quiet and comfort, choose the bars of the *Grand, Carlton* and *Maritim*, but in the Altstadt two attractive *Weinstuben*, among many, are the *Trödelstuben*, Trödelmarkt 30, and *Weinkrüger*, Wespennest, on the south bank of the river.

Entertainment

Bayreuth is 83km/52 miles north by *Autobahn* or train. *Monatsspiegel*, from newsstands, lists events. Opera tickets at *Fränkischer Besucherring*, Lessingstr 1 ☎ 22990 (two weeks ahead). Other tickets from *ABR* in the Hauptbahnhof.

Theatre, opera The *Opernhaus*, Richard-Wagner-Pl ☎ 163808, has a resident company and visiting international productions.

Cinema American films, old and new, can be seen on Mondays at the *Deutsch-Amerikanisches Institut*, Gleissbühlstr 13 ☎ 203327.

Music Concerts and recitals at the modern *Meistersingerhalle*, Münchener Str ☎ 492011.

Shopping

This is one of the least expensive cities in Germany for shopping. The main shops are in Kaiserstrasse, Karolinenstrasse and Königstrasse, the trendier ones in Breitegasse. In the little streets between the castle and the Hauptmarkt, with its food and flower stalls, are specialist shops, such as jewellers *Robert Ertel*, Bergstr 16, and the antique dealers *Ebersbach u. Franzisi*, Albrecht-Dürer-Str 12.

Sightseeing

The interest of Nuremberg is its Gothic purity, although the Altstadt is really only an echo of the Middle Ages, except for the old riverside houses and covered bridges, and the narrow streets below the Burg. The massive 14th–15thC walls are 5km/3 miles long and have 80 watch towers. A curiosity is the brooding *NS Kongresshalle*, which was built at Hitler's behest as a meeting-place for the National Socialist Party.

Albrecht-Dürer-Haus The artist's tall 15thC house has some period furniture, but little of his art. *Am Tiergärtnertor. Open Mar–Oct, Tue–Sun, 10–5 (Wed, 10–9); Nov–Feb, Tue–Fri, 1–5 (Wed, 1–9); Sat–Sun, 10–5.*

Burg Fortified complex of three castles; the Kaiserburg (12thC) has the apartments and chapel of the Hohenstaufen emperors. *Vestnertor. Open Apr–Sep daily, 9–12, 12.45–5; Oct–Mar, 9.30–12, 12.45–4.*

Germanisches Museum Major collection of early paintings by Albrecht Dürer, Lucas Cranach and Albrecht Altdorfer. *Kornmarkt. Open Tue–Sun, 10–5; Thu, 8–9.30.*

Out of town

Within 100km/62 miles is the *Romantische Strasse*, with its perfectly preserved medieval towns of *Dinkelsbühl, Creglingen* and *Rothenburg ob der Tauber*. In *Würzburg* you can see the baroque *Residenz* of the prince-bishops, and from here you can take a steamer to the summer palace and rococo gardens at *Veitshöchheim. Bamberg* has a 1,000-year-old cathedral.

Sports and keeping fit

Both *Tennis-Zentrum Altdorf*, Jakob-Ellenberg-Str, Altdorf ☎ 09187 and *Squash Freizeit Park*, Andernacher Str 15 ☎ 527753 are multisports centres.

Fitness centre Star Fitness Studio, Oedenberger Str 149 ☎ 563007.

Jogging The Luitpoldhain park and Volkspark offer plenty of scope.

Soccer FC Nürnberg play at the *Städtisches Stadion am Dutzendteich*. Tickets from FCN, Valznerweiherstr 200 ☎ 404045.
Swimming *Naturgartenbad*, Schlegelstr 20 ☎ 592545 (outdoor pool).

Local resources

Business services
Hofmann Büro und Service, Königstr 26 ☎ 232372 (office and conference room rental and services).
Photocopying and printing *Copyland* ☎ 557770; *Druck + Kopier-Service* ☎ 549773.
Translation *Anüfa Übersetzungsdienst* ☎ 558559.

Communications
Local delivery OKT *Kurierdienste* ☎ 435925.
Long-distance delivery DHL ☎ 36644.
Post office Main office: Bahnhofspl 1 ☎ 2171. Telecommunications office: *Fernmeldeamt*, Karolinenstr 32 ☎ 1301.
Telex and fax At main post office.

Conference/exhibition centres
The *Messezentrum*, Münchener Str, N50 ☎ 86060, on the *U-Bahn*, is 5km/3 miles southeast of the centre, with space for 10,000 cars. The 11 interconnecting exhibition halls, and large multipurpose hall, give a total floor space of 86,000 sq metres. The conference rooms give a seating range from 30 to 3,000.

The elegant *Meistersingerhalle*, Münchener Str 21 ☎ 492011, is for conferences and music. The large hall seats up to 2,100 and the small one up to 400. There are four conference rooms for 30–120, a spacious exhibitions lobby, and a restaurant. Contact Verkehrsverein Nürnberg e.V., Frauentorgraben 3 ☎ 23360 ⓉⓍ 623558.

Emergencies
Bureau de change *Hauptbahnhof*, open Mon–Sat, 7.45–7.45; Sun, 9.15–12.30.

Hospitals *Klinikum der Stadt Nürnberg*, Flurstr 17 ☎ 3980. Ambulance and emergency medical help ☎ 533211. Doctors on emergency call at Kesslerpl 5 ☎ 533771: Fri 8pm–Mon 7am; Wed, 3pm–midnight; other times ☎ 3980.
Pharmacies *Apotheke*, Frauentorgraben 67 ☎ 222419. All display notices of the nearest late-opening pharmacy.
Police Headquarters at Jakobspl 5 ☎ 2111.

Government offices
Decisions are made in Bonn or Munich but the city administration is at *Bürgermeisteramt*, Rathauspl 2 ☎ 161 (town hall exchange). If planning to set up a factory or office, contact its development and economic division (*Referat Stadtentwicklung und Wirtschaft*), Hauptmarkt 18 ☎ 161.

Information sources
Business information *Industrie- und Handelskammer Nürnberg*, Hauptmarkt 25 ☎ 13350 is the chamber of commerce. For press information covering economics, the Nuremberg office of the *Vereinigte Wirtschaftsdienste* is at Frauentorgraben 43 ☎ 203061.
Local media The Munich-based *Süddeutsche Zeitung* gives some local coverage and is widely read by the business community. The daily *Nürnberger Nachrichten* covers regional economic and business news.
Tourist information *Verkehrsverein* (tourist office): Hauptbahnhof ☎ 233631, open Mon–Sat, 9–8 (Fri, 9–9); Hauptmarkt 18 (city hall) ☎ 233634, open Mon–Sat, 9–1 and 2–6; Sun, 10–1 and 2–4.

Thank-yous
Florist *Blumenhaus Blank* at the Hauptbahnhof ☎ 227297.
Gifts *Geschenkhaus Leykauf*, Hauptmarkt 16 ☎ 224729.
Wine merchant *Deschermeyer*, Breitscheidstr 55 ☎ 452549.

SAARBRÜCKEN
City codes zip 6600 ☎ 0681

Saarbrücken is the capital of Saarland (population 1m), a *Land* of the Federal Republic since 1957 but disputed between France and Germany for many centuries, latterly because of its important coal mining and iron and steel manufacture. In the 20th century, two periods of quasi-autonomy, but virtual annexation to France, have ended with Saarländer voting to be reunited with Germany. Although German in culture and language, about 50% of its trade is with France. Some 10,000 French workers cross the border daily, and there are several bilateral institutions.

Saarbrücken's economy, based on the Saar valley's nationalized coal and steel industries, suffered during the 1970s with the dramatic decline in steel production. By 1987 only two steel works and eight rolling mills were still operational. Unemployment is about double the national average. But active encouragement of investment has brought new industries, notably electrical and mechanical engineering, car manufacturing (Peugeot, Mercedes-Benz, ZF Gears and Brown, Boveri), clothing and food-processing. Ford has been in nearby Saarlouis for over 20 years. In the city, 70% of the workforce is employed in commerce, services and administration and the city's well-promoted conference and exhibition venues are bringing new trade and visitors.

Saarbrücken has good road and rail communications with central Germany and eastern France and, with its population of nearly 200,000, aims to be the commercial and cultural centre for a region extending into Lorraine (France) and Luxembourg. The city exudes an air of prosperity, generated partly by investment in public works under the Social Democrats, such as building restoration, a new road bridge and a city park. The Saarbrücker takes a relaxed, optimistic view of life which makes business contacts easy to establish.

Arriving

Saarbrücken is near the geographical centre of the European Community and has good road and rail connections with south and central Germany (via Mannheim), the Rheinland and north Germany (via Koblenz), and with eastern France and Switzerland. New sections of *Autobahn* will improve links with Luxembourg and Belgium. The city's small airport is only served by domestic flights and the nearest international airport is at Luxembourg, 100km/63 miles to the northwest, with direct flights to European capitals and the United States.

Saarbrücken airport
Scheduled flights arrive from eight German cities and from Lyon. The small terminal building has a restaurant and a bank, only open 2–4. The airport office changes dollars and sterling; ask at the information desk. Flight inquiries ☎ (06893) 831.
City link The airport is at Ensheim, 12km/7 miles southeast of the city. Taxis are plentiful. The fare for the 15–25min journey is DM20–25. Car rental is recommended as driving in Saarbrücken is easy, public transport is inadequate and the region's industries are well outside the city. Car rental firms with desks at the airport are Avis, Hertz and Europcar.

Railway station

The recently rebuilt Hauptbahnhof is north of the city centre, close to the two best hotels, and shopping and business streets. Most journeys, for example to Düsseldorf (4hr 20min), involve a change of trains. But an hourly service runs to Mannheim (1hr 25min) and continues to Frankfurt (via Mannheim – 2hr 30min). There are several direct daily trains to Paris (3hr 48min). Metz (France) is 55min and Luxembourg around 2hr 30min. Trains leave hourly for nearby industrial towns like Saarlouis, Völklingen, Dillingen and Neunkirchen. The station has a restaurant, a florist, other shops, a bureau de change and a large taxi rank. Deutsche Verkehrs-Kredit-Bank is on the right as you leave the station (open Mon–Sat, 7–7.45; Sun, 11–3). Train inquiries ☏ 19419.

Getting around

Businesses and shops are concentrated in a few streets north of the river Saar, and distances here are short enough for walking. An urban highway with two-level intersections runs along the south bank, where government buildings and more offices are located, and for journeys to this area taxis or cars are advisable.

Taxis These are difficult to find but there is a large rank outside the Hauptbahnhof, and another is situated to the east of the Wilhelm-Heinrich bridge. Radio taxis are also available ☏ 33033.

Driving Traffic flows freely in Saarbrücken and there are quick exits via the urban highway. Parking is easily available in multilevel garages and in a large open space near the Kongresshalle. Car rental firms include *Avis* ☏ 65571, *Hertz* ☏ 32238 and *interRent* ☏ 61056.

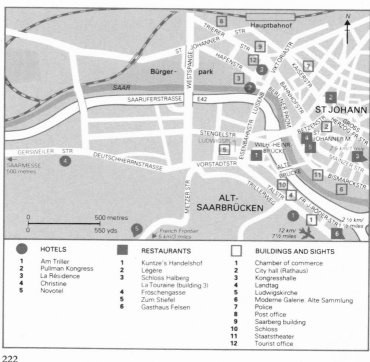

	HOTELS		RESTAURANTS		BUILDINGS AND SIGHTS
1	Am Triller	1	Kuntze's Handelshof	1	Chamber of commerce
2	Pullman Kongress	2	Légère	2	City hall (Rathaus)
3	La Résidence	3	Schloss Halberg	3	Kongresshalle
4	Christine		La Touraine (building 3)	4	Landtag
5	Novotel	4	Fröschengasse	5	Ludwigskirche
		5	Zum Stiefel	6	Moderne Galerie. Alte Sammlung
		6	Gasthaus Felsen	7	Police
				8	Post office
				9	Saarberg building
				10	Schloss
				11	Staatstheater
				12	Tourist office

Area by area

Commercial activity shifted, with the arrival of the railway, from the original town, now Alt-Saarbrücken, to St Johann, north of the river.

St Johann The prosperous and busy main shopping street, Bahnhofstrasse, near the station, runs southeast roughly parallel with the river. Northeast and parallel to it is Kaiserstrasse, where most of the banks are situated. Faktoreistrasse runs from Bahnhofstrasse to the river. Here are the two biggest hotels, Pullman-Kongress and La Résidence, the Kongresshalle, the Commerzbank and the mock Florentine headquarters of Saarberg, the state-owned coal-mining concern. Extending westward along the river is Hafenstrasse, lined with offices, and nearby a large city park is emerging on the site of the former docks. East of the city centre, the restored *Altstadt* of St Johann is an attractive precinct of cobbled squares and lanes lined with 18thC houses, now boutiques, restaurants, jazz clubs and *Kneipen*.

Alt-Saarbrücken The neo-classical Landtag (state parliament), the law courts and other government buildings face the river, along Franz-Joseph-Röder-Strasse. The nearby chamber of commerce occupies a modern block. Ludwigsplatz, a little way from the river, is a fine, large square of elegant 18thC houses, with the Ludwigskirche in the centre.

Residential areas

On the heights around this wooded city are some of the most exclusive districts, especially Triller, with its steep streets and stairways. East of Alt-Saarbrücken is St Arnual, which keeps its village-like charm. Facing it across the river is Am Staden.

Industrial areas

The Saar valley industrial area, downstream from the city, takes in the steel towns of Völklingen and Dillingen, where a new inland harbour is taking shape, and Saarlouis with its Ford plant. To the north are other industries at Quierschied, Sulzbach, Merchweiler and Neunkirchen. ZF Gears and Mercedes-Benz have established plants in the new industrial zone to the south, near the French border.

Hotels

Saarbrücken's only hotel of international standard is the Pullman Kongress, but several others offer pleasant surroundings and adequate business facilities. Unless otherwise stated, all rooms have bath or shower, TV/radio, minibar and IDD telephone. All the hotels listed provide room service but none 24hr.

Am Triller [DM]|

Trillerweg 57 ☎ 580000 ℡ 4421123 •
IHA • AE DC MC V • 120 rooms, 10
suites, 2 restaurants, 1 bar
In a quiet, steep street within walking distance of offices in Alt-Saarbrücken, the Am Triller is patronized by German businessmen with companies such as Ford, ZF and Brown, Boveri. The postwar building extends up the hillside so that some rooms are below the main entrance, but the suites at the top have grand views over the whole city. The mixed-style decor shows signs of wear, but the spacious rooms are well equipped; all have electric trouser presses and some have hairdryers. The restaurant Chez Marianne has a pleasant outlook but the Pilsstube is cramped. Newsstand • pool, sauna • 6 meeting rooms (capacity up to 130).

Pullman Kongress [DM]||

Hafenstr 8 ☎ 30691 ℡ 4428942 •
AE DC MC V • 145 rooms, 5 suites,
1 restaurant, 1 bar
This hotel was re-designated to the top Pullman class in spring 1987 and all the rooms have been renovated. It

is the most suitable hotel for senior executives. The outside elegance of this modern 10-floor building is not matched by the fussy lounge-reception area, but it is near the river and the Kongresshalle and has a large, comfortable bar, the Faktorei. There is an executive "Privilège" floor. Hairdresser, newsstand, gift shop, • pool, sauna, massage, exercise equipment • fax, 3 meeting rooms (capacity up to 120)

La Résidence _[DM]/_
Faktoreistr 2 ☎ 33030 ℡ 4421409 •
AE DC MC V • 70 rooms, 3 suites,
2 restaurants, 1 bar
This 1960s 10-floor block, situated opposite the Kongresshalle and conveniently near to the station, is much used by business people, some from abroad, and by Saarländischer Rundfunk personnel, politicians and bankers. The large rooms were fully renovated in 1984. The in-house Casablanca restaurant is run by an outside firm. The Touraine, which is owned by the hotel, is in the Kongresshalle opposite and has a reputation for being one of the best business restaurants in town (see _Restaurants_). Limited parking, newsstand, gift shop, hairdresser • sauna, solarium, exercise equipment • simultaneous translation equipment, 4 meeting rooms (capacity up to 150).

OTHER HOTELS
Christine _[DM]/_ _Gersweilerstr 39_
☎ _55081_ ℡ _4428736 • AE DC MC V._
West of town, a short walk from the western Saarmesse, this hotel has an unattractive location but the interior is welcoming. Mainly used by German executives. Some rooms are without bathroom or TV. Business facilities include 2 meeting rooms (capacity up to 70).
Novotel _[DM]/_ _Zinzingerstr 9_
☎ _58630_ ℡ _4428836 • AE DC ME V._
Near the Saarmesse but 6km/4 miles from the city. 8 meeting rooms (capacity up to 280).

Restaurants

French influence means that eating out in Saarbrücken is a more rewarding experience than in most German cities of comparable size. Reservations a few days ahead are generally essential. The best restaurant in the whole area, Hostellerie Bacher, is only 23km/14 miles north in Neunkirchen.

Kuntze's Handelshof _[DM]//_
Wilhelm-Heinrich-Str 17 ☎ 56920 •
closed Sun D and Mon • AE DC MC
Jutta and Peter Kuntze offer classic French cuisine with complementary wines in a discreet and elegant restaurant with antique furniture and prints. Set among period houses near Ludwigsplatz, this restaurant is high on the list for a business meal in civilized surroundings.

Légère _[DM]//_
Cecilienstr 7 ☎ 35900 • closed Sat L,
Sun, 3 weeks in Aug • AE DC MC V •
jacket and tie
Close to Bahnhofstrasse and Kaiserstrasse, this attractive French restaurant is much used by business people. A private dining room seats up to 35. The short menu, changed daily, is based on fresh, seasonal ingredients. There is also a good list of French wines.

Schloss Halberg _[DM]//_
Auf dem Halberg ☎ 63181 • closed
Sun • AE V
This baronial mansion, a 10min drive east of the city, shares its grounds with the studios of Saarländischer Rundfunk. The spacious restaurant is popular with bankers, industrialists and broadcasters, and offers a predominantly French menu, attentive service and a wine list that will be appreciated by connoisseurs.

La Touraine *DM*||
*Kongresshalle, Hafenstr 2 ☎ 49333 •
closed Aug 16–30 • AE DC MC V*
A large modern restaurant in the
Kongresshalle, the Touraine is used
by the city and *Land* for official
occasions, and is convenient for
business meals. It has a classic, well-
prepared French menu. There is a
good wine list, strong on French
vintages.

Good but casual
St Johann's Altstadt is full of wine
and beer *Kneipen*, many of which also
serve food. The lively *Fröschengasse*,
Fröschengasse 24 ☎ 371715, which is
particularly popular with the more
informal professionals, offers
enterprising French cooking. *Zum
Stiefel*, St Johanner Markt ☎ 31246,
is the best-loved traditional *Gasthaus*
in town where, at plain wooden
tables, you drink beer or the earthy
white wine of the Saar and eat rich
and filling local dishes featuring ham,
cream, dumplings and potatoes.
People who really know the area
make a pilgrimage to sample the fish
at *Gasthaus Felsen*, Feldstr 17
☎ 851931 in St Arnual, where the
chef is Hubert Müller, one of the
pioneers of French cuisine in
Germany.

Bars
The Pullman Kongress hotel's
Faktorei bar is the obvious choice
when meeting clients, but *Henry's*, in
nearby Kohlwaagstrasse, offers a
pleasant alternative. Like *Zum Stiefel*,
Hauk's Weinstube, which is also in St
Johanner Markt, is regularly
patronized by local officials and
business people.

Entertainment
Mainstream cultural events are
limited, although there are fringe
theatres, concerts, cabarets and jazz.
Classical theatre, dance and opera are
performed at the *Staatstheater*,
Tbilisser Pl 1 ☎ 30920. The monthly
listing *Salü Saarbrücken* is found in
hotels and tickets are available at the

tourist office ☎ 36515 and at the
Pressecenter, Diskonto-Passage
☎ 399606. Saarbrücken is a
surprisingly late-night city. The
Altstadt is known as the *Lange Theke*
(long bar) because of its many bars
and the number that stay open until
the small hours. There are quite a
few strip-clubs, the most respectable
being *Chez Albert*, Wilhelm-
Heinrich-Str 2 ☎ 51494. The most
sophisticated nightclub, with piano
and disco, is *Schicki-Micki*,
Kohlwaagstr 1 ☎ 31789.

Shopping
Saarbrücken's shops lack
sophistication, but *Kaufhof*, *Karstadt*
and *Peek & Cloppenburg*, all big
department stores, are on
Bahnhofstrasse and there are
numerous fashion boutiques and
galleries in the *Altstadt*, particularly
in Fröschengasse and the passages off
it, and on the raised walkway of the
Berliner Promenade.

Sightseeing
In Alt-Saarbrücken, the rococo
buildings by the 18thC architect F.J.
Stengel are a delight. They include
the *Schloss* in its own park and those
in *Ludwigsplatz*, especially the
church.
  The hills and valleys of the
Saarland have great charm and there
are many old towns to visit. Take the
route north along the Saar valley to
Trier on the Mosel, 93km/58 miles
away, to see the greatest gateway in
the Roman Empire, Porta Nigra.

Spectator sports
Soccer The local team plays at
Ludwigspark Stadium, north of the
city centre.
Horse-racing At Pferderennbahn
Güdingen, 3km/2 miles from
Saarbrücken ☎ (06894) 8289.

Keeping fit
Fitness centre Sport Fitness
Centrum, Beethovenpl ☎ 3713171.
Jogging Paths are laid out in woods
to the north and south of the city.

Swimming *Stadtbad St Johann*,
Richard Wagner-Str ☎ 34022.
Tennis and squash *Ball & Hall*,
Mainzer Str 187 ☎ 67272.

Local resources
Business services
Photocopying and printing *COD
Kopierzentrum und Druckzentrale*,
Bleichstr 22 ☎ 39351 (Mon–Thu,
8–6; Sat, 9–1).
Secretarial *Metenko*, Am Schillerpl
14 ☎ 35058 (Mon–Fri, 8–5).
Translation *Bender und Partner*,
Mainzer Str 159 ☎ 66001 (Mon–Fri,
8.15–4.45).

Communications
Long-distance delivery *Argus*,
Bahnhofstr 101 ☎ 39471, 24hr
international service.
Post office Main office: Trierer
Str 33 ☎ 4011, open Mon–Fri, 8–6;
Sat, 8–11.30.
Telex and fax Available at the main
post office.

Conference/exhibition centres
The city is actively promoting its
facilities. The *Kongresshalle*, Hafenstr
☎ 48074, has a large and a small
auditorium (capacity up to 1,200)
and three conference rooms, 2,000 sq
metres of exhibition space, a 120-seat
restaurant and catering for up to
1,000. North of the city,
Saarlandhalle, Ludwigspark
☎ 48051, can seat up to 6,000, has
smaller rooms for up to 400 and can
cater for 4,000. *Saarmesse* centre, Am
Schanzenberg ☎ 53056, to the west
of the city, has covered space of over
24,000 sq metres and the same area in
the open. For information on all
these facilities contact Amt für
Öffentlichkeitsarbeit, Kongress und
Touristik, Rathaus ☎ 3001304.

Emergencies
Bureau de change *Deutsche
Verkehrs-Kredit-Bank* ☎ 39601 at the
Hauptbahnhof (Mon–Sat, 7–7.45;
Sun, 11–3).
Hospital *Städtische Klinik
Winterberg* ☎ 6031. Red cross

ambulance ☎ 55555. Dental
emergencies ☎ 1150.
Pharmacies Those open late and at
weekends are listed at each pharmacy
and published in the *Saarbrücker
Zeitung*.
Police Main station: Karcher Str 5
☎ 6051.

Government offices
The body most directly concerned in
attracting industry and developing
trade is the quasi-governmental
*Gesellschaft für Wirtschaftsförderung
Saar Gmbh*, Bismarkstr 39–41
☎ 687990. The specific city authority
is *Amt für Wirtschaftsförderung und
Industrieansiedlungen*, Rathauspl 8
☎ 3001875; and at *Land* level, the
*Ministerium für Wirtschaft des
Saarlandes*, Hardenbergstr 8
☎ 5014177.

Information sources
Business information *Industrie-
und Handelskammer* (chamber of
commerce), Franz-Josef-Röder-Str 9
☎ *508265*.
Local media The quality daily is
*Saarbrücker Zeitung. Saarländischer
Rundfunk* broadcasts both TV and
radio and *SR1 Europawelle* and *SR3
Saarlandwelle* are commercial stations
run by Werbefunk Saar, with an
audience of 1.24m.
Tourist information *Städtisches
Verkehrsamt*, Faktoreistr, is open
Mon–Fri, 7.30–8; Sat, 7.30–4
☎ 3098222, 36515, 35197.

Thank-yous
Florists *Koehler*, at the
Hauptbahnhof ☎ 33884; *Storb*,
Bahnhofstr 38 ☎ 36588 (both
Fleurop).
Wine merchant *La Vinothèque*,
Türkenstr 2 ☎ 398907.

STUTTGART

City codes zip 7000 ☎ 0711

Stuttgart is a comparative latecomer to the league of big German cities, having neither a long mercantile tradition, nor, until just a century ago, any industrial importance. It began to emerge around 1750 when it became the permanent seat of the dukes and, in 1806, the kings of Württemberg. Several palaces were built, a bureaucracy was established, and an excellent educational system was set up. The poet Schiller and Hegel the philosopher were both pupils here. In the early 19th century Stuttgart was still chiefly a market for local farmers and wine-growers; publishing was the only organized industry of national importance. The advent of the railway ended the city's relative isolation, and its advanced schools produced two of Germany's great industrial pioneers, Gottfried Daimler and Robert Bosch. Their companies, founded in the 1880s, still dominate Stuttgart's industry. Today, about 80% of the city's output is in engineering – automobile, electrical and mechanical – represented by Daimler-Benz, Porsche, Bosch, SEL and Bauknecht. Other industries include optics, instrumentation, furniture, textiles, chemicals and food processing. The German headquarters of IBM is here, and Nixdorf has a plant. Yet Stuttgart is still an important centre for agriculture and for publishing, with more than 170 firms including the Holtzbrinck-Gruppe, Klett and the Deutsche Verlagsanstalt.

The old kingdom of Württemberg has become the federal *Land* of Baden-Württemberg (population 9.3m) and Stuttgart remains the region's political and administrative capital. Although the city itself has only 550,000 inhabitants, its immediate hinterland, the economically buoyant mid-Neckar region, has a population of 2.3m. It is being said that West Germany's future economic growth will be based on a Stuttgart–Munich corridor, well away from the Rhein-Ruhr area. Stuttgart is already a cultural rival to Munich, with two universities, theatre, opera and a world-class ballet company. Under the enlightened Oberbürgermeister Manfred Rommel, son of the World War II general, an elegant, efficient city has risen from the ruins of 1945. Yet it is still undeniably provincial, and its people, the Swabians, who have a strong sense of identity, are akin to the Swiss in their Protestant tradition, capacity for hard work and technical aptitude. Despite a wariness of outsiders, they have made Stuttgart a significant international business centre; of all German cities it is second only to Munich in the value of its exports, and hosts many major trade fairs and exhibitions.

Arriving

There are scheduled air services from about 25 cities outside Germany, mainly via Frankfurt or other major German airports. Direct connections exist with Brussels, Copenhagen, London, Madrid, Milan, Nice, Paris, Turin, Vienna and Zürich.

Domestic air links with major cities are comprehensive, with 6 flights a day from Hamburg (1hr 10min), 7 from Düsseldorf (1hr), 5 from Frankfurt (45min), though only 2 from Munich (55min). Rail links are also good: 24 services a day from Munich (2hr 12min), 22 from Mainz (2hr 8min), and 23 from Mannheim (1hr 27min). Stuttgart is well placed in the *Autobahn* network at the junction of E11 Karlsruhe–Munich and E70 Würzburg–Switzerland but traffic congestion is a problem, especially in summer.

Stuttgart airport

The airport is small and inadequate. Plans for a new terminal and longer runway are in hand, and a rapid-transit rail link to the city is being constructed, for completion in the early 1990s. Checking-in can be slow at peak times (7–9 and 3.30–6), but flight arrival procedures rarely take more than 30min. Facilities include a modest restaurant, the Top Air, a buffet, coffee shops and a bureau de change, open Mon–Sat, 7.30–10; Sun, 8.30–10. Flight information ☎ 7901388.

Nearby hotel *Mövenpick*, Flughafen, S23 ☎ 79070 ⓉⓍ 7245677 • AE DC MC V. Less than 200 metres from the terminal, with a free bus connection, the Mövenpick was renovated in 1986 and the rooms are all well equipped.

City link The airport is at Echterdingen, 13km/8 miles south of the city. Until the *S-Bahn* link is ready in 1990, the alternatives are airport bus or, probably more convenient, taxi (about 25min, 35min in rush hours).

Taxi Cabs line up outside the terminal; there is rarely a shortage.
Car rental Avis, Hertz and interRent offices are in huts facing the terminal exit, but driving is not recommended unless you have an appointment outside the city centre.
Bus Services, operated by Stuttgarter Strassenbahnen (SSB), run every 20–30min, 4.55am–12.15am; fare DM6. The pick-up point is outside the exit. Drop-off points are the city air terminal in Lautenschlagerstrasse and the main railway station.

Railway station

The *Hauptbahnhof* is the hub of the city, close to the two best hotels and

main shopping and business areas. More than 1,000 trains a day serve the 16 platforms, including the recently completed rapid-transit (*S-Bahn*) links to the industrial suburbs. The entrance to this system is down an escalator, where you also find the *U-Bahn*. At ground level in front of the station there are stops for many city buses including those to the airport and exhibition centre. There are always taxis in three ranks in front and beside the country bus terminus. In the concourse is a bureau de change, open Mon–Sat, 8–8.30, Sun, 9–8; and an information desk with English-speaking staff, open daily 6–10 ☎ 19419.

A large underground shopping precinct is immediately outside the station in the Arnulf-Klett-Platz, where there is a helpful city tourist office (*Verkehrsamt*) ☎ 2228240.

Getting around

The centre of Stuttgart is fairly compact, and short-term visitors should rely on walking or taxis. The city and inner suburbs are served by the rapid and cheap streetcar (*Strassenbahn*) system, part of which runs underground. Driving in the city is difficult, and for journeys to industrial suburbs such as Zuffenhausen, Feuerbach, Untertürkheim and Vaihingen, the *S-Bahn* is quicker (but note that it does not go to Sindelfingen).

Taxis It is best to pick up a cab at one of the many ranks at places in the centre, including the railway station, the Planie and the Rotebühlplatz. Otherwise call *Taxi-Auto-Zentrale* ☎ 566061.

Limousines *Rolf Brunold* ☎ 771992.

Driving As much of the centre is traffic-free and other streets are congested, driving in Stuttgart is not easy. The main traffic arteries are Konrad-Adenauer-Strasse and Theodor-Heuss-Strasse, linked by Schlossstrasse which crosses the centre in an underpass with complex multilevel junctions at either end. Street parking is very limited, but

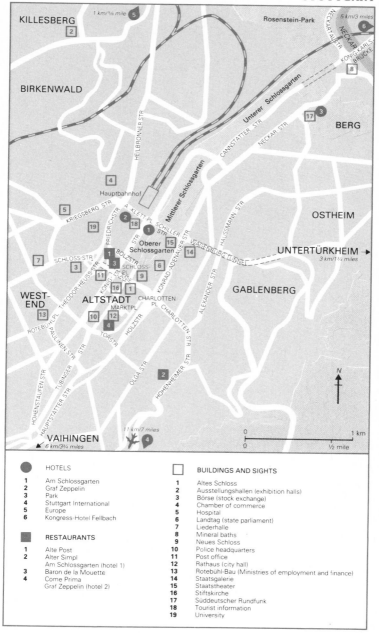

HOTELS

1 Am Schlossgarten
2 Graf Zeppelin
3 Park
4 Stuttgart International
5 Europe
6 Kongress-Hotel Fellbach

RESTAURANTS

1 Alte Post
2 Alter Simpl
   Am Schlossgarten (hotel 1)
3 Baron de la Mouette
4 Come Prima
   Graf Zeppelin (hotel 2)

BUILDINGS AND SIGHTS

1   Altes Schloss
2   Ausstellungshallen (exhibition halls)
3   Börse (stock exchange)
4   Chamber of commerce
5   Hospital
6   Landtag (state parliament)
7   Liederhalle
8   Mineral baths
9   Neues Schloss
10 Police headquarters
11 Post office
12 Rathaus (city hall)
13 Rotebuhl-Bau (Ministries of employment and finance)
14 Staatsgalerie
15 Staatstheater
16 Stiftskirche
17 Süddeutscher Rundfunk
18 Tourist information
19 University

there are over 30 multilevel or underground garages whose addresses are on a list obtainable from the tourist office. The main car rental firms all have city centre offices, including *Hertz* ☎ 643044.

Walking A large part of the city centre is accessible only on foot. The main axis, Königstrasse, is traffic-free as are Schlossplatz and many adjoining streets and squares. Walking at night presents no problems, but you might want to avoid the sex-bars around Leonhardsplatz.

Streetcars Streetcars and stops (marked either by "U" or "H" signs) are being modernized. A map is available from the vvs (Stuttgart transport) office in the Arnulf-Klett-Passage. Tickets for all public transport are sold only from orange vending machines at streetcar and *S-Bahn* stations and bus stops.

Buses There is a frequent service from the railway station to the exhibition centre at Killesberg.

Trains The *S-Bahn*, identified by green "S" signs, can be picked up for the industrial suburbs at the railway station or Rotebühlplatz; and taxis are available at main suburban stations.

Area by area

Stuttgart lies in a narrow valley. Its compact centre divides neatly into four zones. East of Königstrasse, Schlossplatz and Oberer Schlossgarten provide a setting for the Staatstheater, Landtag (state parliament), Neues Schloss and other impressive public buildings. South of this are the most exclusive shopping streets such as Calwer Strasse, Marktplatz and Hirschstrasse, on both sides of the Königstrasse. To the east, beyond the main traffic route of Holzstrasse, is the "low-life" area, with remnants of the old Stuttgart still visible. To the west of the pedestrianized shopping district is the main business area, between Schlossstrasse and Theodor-Heuss-Strasse, where 1970s glass and steel

mingle with 19thC neo-classical buildings. The stock exchange and state ministries of finance, economics, and employment are here, together with banks, insurance companies and professional offices.

The suburbs
The steep valley sides have winding streets of expensive and sober suburban houses only a few minutes from the city. Gablenberg, Degerloch on the east side, and Birkenwald and Killesberg on the west, are desirable places to live. In Killesberg, the Weissenhof-Siedlung is a famous estate of houses designed in 1927 by Le Corbusier, Walter Gropius, Mies van der Rohe and other leading architects. On the surrounding plateau, woods or agricultural land provide an attractive backdrop for commuter villages like Botnang and Sillenbuch.

Just north of the city, not far from the working class suburbs and gasworks and stockyards of Ostheim and Gaisburg, is the Berg district, an elegant enclave around the Villa Berg palace and gardens. Across the river is ancient Bad Cannstatt, whose warren of narrow old streets is popular with the young.

The industrial areas
The older industrial areas are along the Neckar. At Untertürkheim, upriver, is the main Daimler-Benz plant, and at Obertürkheim an inland harbour built in 1958 gives Stuttgart access to the Rhein and North Sea. Down the valley are Feuerbach (Bosch) and Zuffenhausen (Porsche). On the high ground to the south, Vaihingen has an important new industrial zone and the IBM headquarters. Linked to the city by the *S-Bahn* are the industrial outer boroughs – or mid-Neckar region – including Fellbach, Esslingen and Waiblingen to the east, Böblingen to the southwest, Leonberg to the west and Kornwestheim and Ludwigsburg to the north.

Hotels

No great hotels in Stuttgart survived the war, and well-known international chains are not yet represented, though an Inter-Continental is due to open in late 1988 and a Holiday Inn in late 1989. The current choice comprises German-owned hotels, most of which were built in the 1950s and 1960s.

All the hotels listed are well maintained and comfortable. They have room service to 11pm or later, with TV/radio in every room and a choice of *en suite* bath or shower.

Am Schlossgarten [DM]///
Schillerstr 23, S1 ☎ *299911* ⊤ₓ *722936*
• *LEGA* • *AE DC MC V* • *118 rooms,
7 suites, 2 restaurants, 1 bar*
Close to the railway station and Königstrasse, with views over the park and the Staatstheater, this discreet, courteously run hotel is the first choice for visiting politicians, celebrities and senior executives. The wood-panelled public rooms and lobby are in an elegant, modern and sober style. The lounge and bar are useful for informal discussions, while the main restaurant (see *Restaurants*) has an excellent reputation in the local business community. Bedrooms are light and attractively decorated, though not very spacious; the most pleasant overlook the park. 4 meeting rooms (capacity up to 120).

Graf Zeppelin [DM]////
Arnulf-Klett-Pl 7, S1 ☎ *299881*
⊤ₓ *722418* • *Steigenberger* • *AE DC MC
V* • *260 rooms, 20 suites, 4 restaurants,
2 bars*
Almost next door to the Am Schlossgarten, the Graf Zeppelin is less prestigious but larger and caters more directly for business people. Behind its bleak modern exterior an effort has been made to re-create the grand style, with mirrored surfaces, high-quality reproduction furniture and a wealth of textures and colours. Bedrooms are comfortable and well equipped, with cable TV, soundproofing and individual air conditioning. Two of the four restaurants in the hotel specialize in local cuisine, and there is a nightclub with live entertainment. Currency

exchange • pool, sauna, massage • fax, 11 meeting rooms (capacity up to 500).

Park [DM]//
Villastr 21, S1 ☎ *280161* ⊤ₓ *723405*
• *AE DC MC V* • *80 rooms, 3 suites,
2 restaurants, 1 bar*
This hotel in Berg, 2.5km/1.5 miles from the centre and midway to Daimler-Benz, attracts a clientele which includes business and media people; Süddeutscher Rundfunk (South German Radio and TV) is next door. It is also used regularly by the local CDU party. It is owned and run by a husband-and-wife team, with an accent on personal service. The public areas are predominantly white, with oriental rugs and simple, modern furnishings, while the bedrooms are light and welcoming; ask for one overlooking the park. One of the two restaurants is Swabian-style, and the snug bar in the basement is agreeable for informal conversation. Newsstand • 4 meeting rooms (capacity up to 80).

Stuttgart International [DM]//
Plieninger Str 100, Möhringen, S80
☎ *72021* ⊤ₓ *7255763* • *AE DC MC V*
• *LEGA* • *167 rooms, 33 suites,
3 restaurants, 1 bar*
This 1960s high-rise hotel has the most comprehensive facilities of any in the Stuttgart area, but is 8km/5 miles south of the city. The airport and the *Autobahn* are only 5min by road, and it is handy for the Vaihingen industrial area and IBM. The hotel's excellent conference facilities are much used. There is a

nightclub with cabaret and, in summer, an open-air beer garden. Hairdresser, newsstand, currency exchange • pool, sauna, solarium, exercise equipment, massage, bowling • fax, 13 meeting rooms (capacity up to 1,000).

OTHER HOTELS

Europe *DM*/ *Siemensstr 26, Feuerbach, S30* ☎ *815091* TX *723650* • *Europe Hotels International* • *AE DC MC V*. The nearest hotel to the

Killesberg exhibition complex and to Bosch but not within easy walking distance of either. A modern tower with a rather ugly mix of decors. Much used for conferences.
Kongress-Hotel Fellbach *DM*/ *Tainerstr 7–9, 7012 Fellbach* ☎ *58590* TX *7254900* • *AE DC MC V*. About a 10min drive east of Stuttgart, this spacious, low-rise hotel built in 1984 caters specifically for visitors to the new Schwabenlandhalle exhibition and conference centre.

Restaurants
There are few restaurants in Stuttgart that will suit a major occasion and for more routine business meals some Italian ones are reliable. The native Swabian cuisine is among the best in Germany, being lighter and more varied than elsewhere, with less *Wurst* and pickled products and, as in Switzerland, more emphasis on eggs and cheese. People working in the suburbs tend to eat at country inns.

Alte Post *DM*/
Friedrichstr 43 ☎ *293079* • *closed Sun, Mon L, Sat L, hols* • *AE MC V* • *jacket and tie* • *reservations essential*
This panelled restaurant in the heart of the city is the most exclusive in town, with a mainly dark-suited and earnest clientele. Although it is generally full, it is never noisy and is an eminently suitable venue for important business meals. The menu is international *haute cuisine*, with dishes like mousseline of turbot with caviar butter, and medaillons of venison in cranberry sauce.

Alter Simpl *DM*///
Hohenheimer Str 64 ☎ *240821* • *D only, closed Sun* • *no credit cards*
The intimate Alter Simpl, with its beams and paraffin lamps, is just a 5min taxi ride from the city centre. Its thick 19thC walls muffle the noise of the traffic on the busy road outside. The cooking is *nouvelle* German, based on skilful use of fresh seasonal ingredients. Suitable for either business occasions or relaxation, the restaurant stays open till 1am.

Am Schlossgarten *DM*///
Schillerstr 23 ☎ *299911* • *AE DC MC V* • *jacket and tie*
This restaurant is an absolutely dependable choice for an important lunch or dinner, and you can use the hotel's elegant bar and lounge for discussions before and after your meal. The large, panelled restaurant overlooks the gardens. The tables are widely spaced and the service polished. The menu includes international and local dishes, and the wine list is well chosen.

Baron de la Mouette *DM*//
Kleiner Schlosspl 11 ☎ *220034* • *AE DC MC V*
In the pedestrianized centre of Stuttgart the Swiss Mövenpick group runs a complex of five restaurants, of which the Baron de la Mouette is the most stylish. Many local business people eat here, attracted by the good-value, light international cuisine, with its emphasis on fresh ingredients. The restaurant is a useful choice for a working meal, especially if time is limited.

Come Prima [DM]||
Steinstr 3 ☎ *243422* • *closed Mon*
• *AE DC MC V*
Media and theatre people in
particular frequent Maurizio
Olivieri's light, uncluttered Italian
restaurant in a quiet location not far
from the Rathaus. The short, well-
chosen menu includes home-made
pasta and interesting fish dishes;
in summer there are tables
outside.

Graf Zeppelin [DM]|
Arnulf-Klett-Pl 7 ☎ *299881* • *closed
Sat, Sun, mid-Jul–early Aug, and
hols* • *AE DC MC V* • *jacket and
tie*
The Graf Zeppelin hotel's spacious,
elegant and international restaurant
is used almost exclusively by business
people. Its seasonally changed menu
ranges from classic to *nouvelle*,
with dishes such as quails with
marinated chanterelles, medaillons
of lobster with basil and noodles
and, for the more diet-conscious,
poached veal fillet in vegetable
stock. The excellent wine list
includes some agreeable local bottles,
and the service is discreet and
attentive.

Out of town
Country restaurants and inns are
very popular, especially when time is
not pressing. Visitors, however, may
feel uneasy entertaining a client on
his or her home ground, but two
places can be recommended for a
gastronomic treat.
  The *Ulrichshöhe*, in Nürtingen-
Hardt ☎ (07022) 52336, is about a
30min drive southeast of Stuttgart. It
has a terrace with a splendid view
and a menu which has earned a
Michelin rosette, including *loup de
mer* in olive sauce and rack of lamb
with rosemary. The *Traube* (closed
at weekends) is an 18thC inn in the
semi-rural suburb of Plieningen
☎ 454833. It serves such dishes as
quail consommé with truffles, ragout
of crayfish with chanterelles and
passion fruit sorbet.

Weinstuben
Weinstuben are a special feature of
the Stuttgart scene. Open only in
the evenings, they are cheerful,
noisy places, often in attractive
old buildings with rough wooden
furniture, where local wines are
served from the barrel. The food
is exclusively Swabian and
includes such dishes as
Maultaschen (like large ravioli) or
Spätzle (buttered noodles).
  Zur Kiste, Kanalstr 2
☎ 244002, is the best known, but
it is small and usually crowded.
In the same area, near
Charlottenplatz, is the
Schellenturm, Weberstr 72
☎ 234888, a 16thC tower with
rough stone walls and beamed
ceilings. Just 3.5km/2 miles out of
town, at Bad Cannstatt, is
another cluster of *Weinstuben*
including the *Klösterle*, Marktstr
71 ☎ 568962, a former monastery
which claims to be the oldest
occupied building in the
Stuttgart area.

Bars
For a quiet discussion, there are
really only the bars in the *Am
Schlossgarten* and *Graf Zeppelin*
hotels. Fashionable wine bars include
Emilie, Mozartstr 49 ☎ 6491900,
which is popular with artists,
journalists and students; and *Fresko*,
Konrad-Adenauer-Str 28 ☎ 233613,
in the avant-garde new wing of the
Staatsgalerie, which is candlelit at
night and has a grand piano for
customers to play.

Entertainment
For German-speakers and music-
lovers, Stuttgart offers top-class
theatre, opera, dance and concerts.
Tickets (except for the
Staatstheater) and a free listings
booklet, *Monatsspiegel*, with English
text, from the tourist office in
Arnulf-Klett-Passage ☎ 2228243.

Like all big German cities, Stuttgart also has a large number of sex-bars with live or filmed entertainment.

Theatre, dance, opera The *Staatstheater*, Oberer Schlossgarten 6 ☎ 2032444, is used for opera, with orchestras and singers of international standing, and for productions by the Stuttgart Ballet, founded by Britain's John Cranko, and now, under Marcia Haydée, one of the world's best. The *Kleines Haus* and the *Kammertheater* (in the new Staatsgalerie) offer outstanding German and international drama of all periods. The home of satire and cabaret is the *Renitenz-Theater*, Königstr 17 ☎ 297075.

Classical music Stuttgart has its world-famous chamber orchestra, its Melos Ensemble, and is the base for Helmut Rilling's Bach choral festival. *Liederhalle*, Berliner Pl 1 ☎ 2589710.

Cinema Most of the big cinemas are on or close to Königstrasse.

Nightclubs Stuttgart's nightlife lacks variety and sophistication. Apart from the *Scotch Club* in the Graf Zeppelin hotel, the only chic nightspot is the exclusive *Perkins Park*, Stresemannstr 39, Killesberg ☎ 252062. Two notable exceptions to the rather sleazy establishments around Leonhardsplatz are *The Four Roses*, Leonhardspl 24 ☎ 242837 and the *Moulin Rouge*, Kronprinzstr 15 ☎ 294705.

Shopping

All the best shops are concentrated around Königstrasse, near the south end of which is the attractive Calwer Passage, a restored period arcade of small boutiques. Porcelain, glass, furs, leather goods and jewellery are very good quality, though expensive. *Hertie*, on the corner of Schulstrasse and Königstrasse, and *Breuninger* in Marktplatz, are the most notable department stores. *Kamal und Silbermann*, Hindenburgbau, sells simple modern jewellery, while *Maas*, Schillerplatz, has antique jewellery and silver. *Schatzinsel*, Untere Königstrasse, is a leading oriental antique dealer; and among dozens of private art galleries, *Valentien* in Königsbau is one of the best-known. *Spielwaren-Kurtz*, Marktplatz, offers a wide selection of toys. For designer clothes, try *Modus* in Klett-Passage and *Uli's*, Stiftstrasse.

Sightseeing

The 217-metre-high Fernsehturm (television tower) in the hilltop suburb of Degerloch provides an impressive view of the whole city. Its important historical buildings, such as the Altes Schloss and the Neues Schloss, a late-18thC royal palace, have been restored since World War II and are within walking distance of each other.

Motor Museums There are two in the area: the *Daimler-Benz Museum*, Mercedesstr 136, Untertürkheim (open Tue–Sun, 9–5); and the *Porsche Museum*, Porsche-Str 42, Zuffenhausen (open Mon–Fri, 9–12, 1.30–4).

Staatsgalerie Important collections of medieval German, Dutch and Italian painting and, in the new wing designed by James Stirling, of 20thC art, with German artists well represented. *Konrad-Adenauer-Str 30–32. Open 10–5; Tue and Thu, 10–8; closed Mon.*

Stiftskirche Late-Gothic premier Protestant church of Württemberg. In a side chapel is the tomb of Count Ulrich (d.1265) and his wife, founders of the Württemberg dynasty. *Schillerpl. Open daily, 8–5.30 (Thu, 12–5.30). Church music performed Fri 7pm.*

Württembergisches Landesmuseum in the Altes Schloss, a handsome Renaissance castle with a central galleried courtyard. Mainly archeological and regional exhibits. *Schlosspl/Karlspl. Open Tue–Sun, 10–5 (Wed, 10–7). Guides available.*

Out of town

Burg Hohenzollern ☎ (07471) 2428, 60km/37 miles south near Hechingen, is a vast castle (completed 1867) with a panoramic view, and custodian of imperial treasures such as the Prussian crown of 1889. *Esslingen*, 14km/9 miles southeast, has a picturesque marketplace, a 15th–16thC former town hall and two interesting Gothic churches. At *Ludwigsburg*, 16km/10 miles to the north, there is a magnificent baroque palace and gardens ☎ (07141) 1411. Northeast of the city, *Maulbronn Zisterzienser-kloster* ☎ (07043) 7454, founded in 1147, is the best-preserved monastery in Germany. And the old university town of *Tübingen*, 40km/25 miles south of Stuttgart, has medieval buildings, many half-timbered.

Spectator sports
Details of fixtures from the *Sportamt*, Eberhardstrasse 33 ☎ 2162141.
Athletics International events are held at two venues. *Neckarstadion*, Mercedesstr ☎ 2164661, seats 70,000; tickets from the tourist centre ☎ 2228243 or *Kartenhäusle*, Kleiner Schlosspl. A new covered stadium next door, the *Hanns-Martin-Schleyer-Halle*, box office ☎ 561565, is also used for tennis, gymnastics, show-jumping and indoor soccer.
Soccer VFB Stuttgart plays at *Neckarstadion*.

Keeping fit
The clubs listed below do not require membership.
Fitness centres Sportstudio City Fitness Pfarrstr 1 (off Leonhardsplatz) ☎ 243327.
Golf The *Stuttgarter Golf Club* is 40km/25 miles away at Mönsheim ☎ (07044) 5852.
Jogging Stuttgart's forest jogging tracks (*Waldsportpfade*) are marked with posts. Nearest to the city, one starts and ends at Geroksruhe, in Gablenberg, at the terminus of the no. 15 streetcar.
Mineral baths Stuttgart has a greater volume of natural spring water than anywhere else in western Europe. *Mineralbad Leuze*, An der

König-Karls-Brücke ☎ 283224, is open daily, 6–8; the warm, invigorating, carbonated water feeds 6 swimming and plunge pools; saunas, solarium and restaurant.
Swimming In addition to the pool at the *Stuttgart International* hotel, which is open to non-residents (see *Hotels*), there are indoor public pools in the suburbs, but none in the city. In Killesberg, the *Höhenfreibad* is an outdoor pool, near the exhibition centre.
Tennis, squash The *Rems-Murr-Center* ☎ 582868 has 6 tennis and 6 squash courts. Nearer the city are the public courts of *Tennisanlage Cannstatter Wasen* ☎ 2164181.

Local resources
Business services
Of the various conference centres, only the Messe- und Kongresszentrum at Killesberg (see below) offers the fullest range of business services including word processing, modems, audiovisual equipment, tele-conferencing, secretaries, translators and interpreters.
Photocopying and printing Copy-Shop ☎ 225391, near the railway station.
Secretarial Mon–Fri, *Büro-Service Burth* ☎ 769067; *ib personal* ☎ 220059.
Translators and interpreters Kern GmbH Language Services ☎ 235066, Mon–Fri.

Communications
Local delivery Tele-car ☎ 561104.
Long-distance delivery Express Parcels Systems ☎ 8567666.
Post office Hauptpostamt, Kleiner Schlosspl/Fürstenstr ☎ 20671, open Mon–Fri, 8–6, Sat, 8.30–12.30; also at the railway station, open Mon–Sat. 7–11, Sun, 8–10..
Telex and fax At the station post office above.

Conference/exhibition centres
Stuttgart now hosts important trade events. A booklet from the Kongress-

und Tagungsbüro Stuttgart, Villa Scheuffelen, Stafflenbergstr 37 ☎ 233988, gives full details of 9 major venues and lists over 40 other conference sites, including hotels.

The main venue is the *Messe Stuttgart*, Am Kochenhof 16 ☎ 25891 ⊠ 722584, which is 4km/2.5 miles north of the centre, in Killesberg. It has 36,500 sq metres of exhibition space. Annual fairs include GARN (yarn and fibre), CAT (computer-aided technology), and INTERGASTRA (hotels and catering). The conference centre has 7 rooms seating 50–990 and a hall for 8,000. *Hanns-Martin-Schleyer Halle*, Mercedesstr 69 ☎ 552067/69 is a covered arena 3km/2 miles from the city centre, which can seat 3,000–10,000 in different configurations, with 4 smaller rooms for 50–200. Right in Stuttgart, the *Liederhalle* at Berliner Pl 1 ☎ 2589710 has 2,000 sq metres of exhibition space, 3 rooms for 150–2,000, audiovisual equipment and a restaurant. *Medienzentrum Alte Stuttgarter Reithalle*, Forststr 2 ☎ 22144043, also centrally located, offers 4 rooms for 30–800, full audiovisual equipment, 2 sound studios and film and video editing facilities. *Schwabenlandhalle* in Fellbach, Tainer Str 7 ☎ 580055 is 10km/6 miles east of the city. Its superbly designed, asymmetrical halls can seat up to 1,400 in different configurations.

Emergencies

Bureaux de change *Deutsche Verkehrs-Kredit-Bank* at the airport and railway station, open late and at weekends.

Hospitals In the city centre: *Katharinenhospital* ☎ 20341. Serious emergencies ☎ 280211. Dental treatment ☎ 7800266.

Pharmacies Every pharmacy (*Apotheke*) displays a notice with the address of the nearest all-night pharmacy.

Police Headquarters: Schmale Str 11 ☎ 89902101.

Government offices

Staatsministerium Baden-Württemberg, Richard-Wagner-Str 15 ☎ 21531 deals with very big projects only. The *Ministerium für Wirtschaft und Technologie, Baden-Württemberg*, Kienestr 18 ☎ 1230 handles import, export, cooperation between foreign and local companies, and foreign companies setting up subsidiaries locally. Those setting up in the city should consult the *Bürgermeisteramt der Stadt Stuttgart* (*Wirtschaftsreferat*), Marktpl 1 ☎ 2163570.

Information sources

Business information The regional chamber of commerce is the *Industrie- und Handelskammer Mittlerer Neckar*, Jägerstr 30 ☎ 20051. A documentation centre and patent library, showing the best of local products, is provided by the *Landesgewerbeamt Baden-Württemberg*, Kienestr 18 ☎ 1230. Public libraries include the *Württembergisches Landesbibliothek*, Konrad-Adenauer-Str 8 ☎ 2125424 and the *Universitätsbibliothek*, Holzgartenstr 16 ☎ 1212222.

Local media The *Stuttgarter Nachrichten* has excellent economic, political and arts coverage. *Süddeutscher Rundfunk* (South German radio and TV) is based in Stuttgart.

Tourist information The Verkehrsamt *i-Punkt* (information point) ☎ 2228240 is in the Arnulf-Klett-Platz, the precinct in front of the railway station. At the east exit of the precinct is the city transport information office, VVS ☎ 66061.

Thank-yous

Florists *Blumen-Gugeler* in the railway station and also in the Arnulf-Klett-Passage ☎ 295690; *Blumen-Fischer* in the Königsbau arcade, Schlosspl ☎ 295833. Both will deliver.

Wine merchants *Benz-Wein*, Urbanstr 1 ☎ 240947.

Planning and Reference

Entry details

The details which follow apply to visitors regardless of port of entry.

Documentation

Identity cards An alternative to passports for nationals of the following European countries: Austria, Belgium, Denmark, France, East Germany, Greece, Ireland, Italy, Liechtenstein, Luxembourg, Malta, Monaco, Netherlands, San Marino, Spain and Switzerland.

Passports A valid passport is required by all other visitors.

Visas For nationals of most countries, no visa is required for a visit of up to three months. Nationals of EC countries, Australia, Canada, Japan or the USA, for instance, will not require a visa. Holders of British passports with the endorsement "British Citizen," and those issued before 1 January 1983 with the endorsement "Holder has the right of abode in the United Kingdom" do not require a visa either. However holders of other British passports may do so and are advised to consult the German embassy or high commission in their country. Visitors from Australia, Canada, USA and Japan will also need a return ticket. Visas are normally valid for up to three months, transit visas for 48 hours.

Travel to Berlin (West) No transit visas are required if you travel by air. But they are required if you are travelling by road or rail. You must have a valid passport for them to be issued. If you are travelling by rail, the visa will be issued free of charge on the train. For those travelling by road, transit visas are issued at the checkpoints and cost DM5 for a single journey. It is best to take out a return visa; this does not oblige you to return through the same checkpoint. All transit visas are only valid for nonstop journeys through the German Democratic Republic to Berlin.

Work permit Members of EC countries may look for work or take up a job without a work permit, but for stays of more than three months they must obtain a residence permit. These can be obtained from the Aliens Office (*Ausländerbehörde*) at the regional police office or the consulate of the area where they intend to reside. Nationals of non-EC countries must obtain valid residence and work permits before entering the country, ideally through the future employer. However, the issue of such work permits is now restricted.

Driving licence You can drive in Germany for up to one year if you possess a current national or international driving licence.

Customs regulations

You may bring into Germany without any formality any item and equipment intended for your personal use.

You may bring in a limited amount of alcohol, perfume and tobacco products without paying tax or duty. If you buy goods in a duty-free shop, or in a non-EC European country, the allowances are given under Group A below. If goods are bought in an EC country where tax and duty has already been paid, see under Group B below.

Alcoholic drinks Group A: 2 litres of sparkling or liqueur wine to 22% or 1 litre if over 22% and 2 litres of table wine. Group B: 3 litres of sparkling wine to 22% or 1.5 if over 22% and 5 litres of table wine.

Tobacco products Group A: 200 cigarettes or 50 cigars or 100 cigarillos or 250 grammes of tobacco. Group B: 300 cigarettes or 75 cigars or 150 cigarillos or 400 grammes of tobacco.

Perfume Group A: 50 grammes of perfume and 0.25 litres of toilet water. Group B: 75 grammes of perfume and 0.375 litres of toilet water.

Other goods Group A: 100 grammes of tea or 40 grammes of extract; 250 grammes of coffee or 100 grammes of extract and goods to the value of DM115. Group B: 200 grammes of tea or 60 grammes of extract; 1,000 grammes of coffee or 300 grammes of extract and goods to the value of DM780.

If you are taking goods from West Germany back to another EC country, you can reclaim the VAT on arrival there at the customs point by producing a signed receipt. For other countries, apply at the German customs on departure.

Climate

The climate is fairly temperate and mild. Winters are generally dull and wet with average temperatures in January dropping to 1.5°C/35°F in lowland areas, with sharp daytime frosts, and much lower in the mountain regions (around -6°C/18°F in the Bavarian Alps), causing a considerable snowfall. The northern areas are milder than the south but have more rain. Summers are hot in the south and east, but cooler and more changeable in the north with less sunshine. July is the warmest with average temperatures ranging from 17°C/62°F in the North German lowlands to over 20°C/70°F in protected valleys of the south. Spring and autumn can be particularly pleasant. Generally it is a good idea to take a raincoat, and in winter very warm clothing is essential.

Holidays

The main holiday period is in July and August; some companies close for a complete month, particularly manufacturing companies. During the Christmas and New Year period many business people take a whole week off. At Easter and Whitsun also, it may be difficult to arrange appointments. It is always advisable to make appointments well in advance and to notify any change of schedule immediately. Punctuality is also important. Even being ten minutes late is considered not merely impolite but indicative of a positive lack of interest.

The main national public holidays are listed below. On these days all shops, stores and banks are closed, except at main railway stations.

Jan 1 New Year's Day
Late Mar/early Apr Good Friday and Easter Monday
May 1 Labour Day
May Ascension Day
Late May/early Jun Whit Monday
Third Wed in Nov Buss und Bettag, Day of Prayer and Repentance
Dec 25–26 First and second Christmas Days

In parts of Germany which are predominately Roman Catholic some religious festivals are also marked by a public holiday. These are:
Jan 6 Epiphany (Baden-Württemberg and Bavaria)
May/Jun (depending on the date of Easter) Corpus Christi Day (Baden-Württemberg, Hessen, Saarland, North Rhine-Westphalia, Rhineland-Palatinate, Catholic areas of Bavaria)
Aug 15 Assumption (Saarland and Catholic areas of Bavaria)
Oct 31 All Saints Day (Protestant areas: Schleswig-Holstein, southern Germany)
Nov 1 All Saints Day (Catholic areas: Baden-Württemberg, Saarland, . North Rhine-Westphalia, Rhineland-Palatinate and Bavaria)

Carnival Monday (*Rosenmontag*) Feb/Mar, before Lent, is not an official holiday, but most offices in carnival areas around the Rhein are closed on this day.

Money
Local currency

The currency is the *Deutschmark* (DM). The mark is divided into 100 *Pfennige* (Pfg). You will find notes for DM5, 10, 20, 50, 100, 500 and 1,000, although DM500 and 1,000 notes can be difficult to change in shops. Coins are available for 1, 2, 5, 10 and 50 Pfg and DM1, 2, and 5.

Most public telephones take 10 Pfg and DM1 and 5 coins. Parking meters usually take 10 Pfg and DM1 coins. DM2 or 5 are useful for tipping.

There are no restrictions about how much German or foreign currency you may bring into or take out of Germany.

Cheques Traveller's cheques normally provide the best rates of exchange. Eurocheques are also accepted and you can cash up to £100 per cheque at the banks that participate in the scheme. Many shops, hotels and restaurants will accept Eurocheques with a cheque card. Post offices with an "ec" sign cash Eurocheques, also Post Cheques (issued by a non-German Giro service and payable with a guarantee card) and traveller's cheques. Many post offices have Eurocheque cash dispensers.

Credit and charge cards
Acceptance of cards is not as widespread as in some other Western European countries. Large bills are often paid in cash although major cards are accepted by most hotels, large stores and car rental firms, but not by smaller shops.

Changing money
Banks are the best places to change money. Several banks have branches at the international airports and larger railway stations; they offer the official rate of exchange set by the Bundesbank and are often open outside normal banking hours. At bureaux de change (*Wechselstube*), the rate will not be as favourable. All big hotels, many post offices (*Postamt*) and a few travel agents also change money.

Banks
There are many private, commercial and state banks (*Landesbank*) throughout Germany. The big three are Deutsche Bank, Dresdner Bank and Commerzbank. Most of the foreign banks are based in Frankfurt.

There are regional variations, but banks generally open Mon–Fri,

8.30–1 and 2.30–4. Most open on Thu, until 5.30 or 6. All banks are closed on Saturdays.

Tipping
Hotels Hotels include service charges (*Bedienung*) of 10% in their bills, although it is usual to tip porters DM1–2 per bag or service. If the head porter (*Chef-Portier*) has gone out of his way to help you, he should also be tipped.

Restaurants and bars A 10% service charge is included in bills, but you may want to leave an additional cash tip in appreciation of especially good service, food or wine. About 5% is normal or rounding the bill up with loose change. If served by the owner, no tip should be left.

Taxis It is usual to round up the fare to the nearest mark.

Other Tip hairdressers and barbers about 10% of the bill and cloakroom attendants about 50 Pfg

Getting there
Germany is well served by over 80 airlines and has excellent road, rail and, in the north, sea connections with neighbouring countries.

Gateway airports
Although all the major airlines fly to Germany, its own international airline, Lufthansa, provides the most frequent and comprehensive service, linking Germany with over 160 cities worldwide. It is one of the few airlines to offer a first-class service on European and internal routes.

There are 12 airports (*Lufthafen*) that receive both international and domestic flights. Internal flights, except those to Berlin, are operated by German commuter airlines (DLT) which are associated with Lufthansa. If you need to transfer to a domestic flight, Frankfurt is very often the airport to use. All German airports can be reached in about 1hr flying time from Frankfurt and there are at least four flights daily from Frankfurt to each.

Köln/Bonn airport is now linked

with Düsseldorf and Frankfurt by the Lufthansa Airport Express, which travels in both directions four times daily. Passengers holding valid air tickets may use this train at no extra cost. The service is first class and includes meals and drinks.

Ferry ports

It is possible to reach North Germany by ferry (*Schiff*) from the UK and Scandinavia. DFDS Seaways operates a direct link between Harwich and Hamburg; the journey takes 21 hours and the service runs every other day. The ferries are comfortable, offering accommodation and food. If you are travelling by car from the UK, the alternative is to cross to one of the Belgian or Dutch ports, which have the best motorway links into Germany. The short cross-Channel routes take between four and five hours. Although the journey time from England to the French Channel ports is shorter, highway links into Germany are poorer. Cross-channel ferry services operate daily but it is advisable to make reservations well ahead during the summer months.

Getting around

In Germany, business executives tend to use cars for any journey of less than 200km/124 miles city to city. For journeys up to 450km/279 miles they may use trains, particularly between main towns. For longer distances air travel is usually favoured and may also be used on shorter journeys if there are convenient flights.

Air

Frankfurt is both the national and international hub of Lufthansa services, and the importance of other airports can be measured by the frequency of the number of flights to and from Frankfurt. There are 20 flights each weekday (each way) between Frankfurt and Munich, 18 between Frankfurt and Hamburg, 9 between Frankfurt and Düsseldorf and 6 between Frankfurt and

Hanover. Berlin is served direct from 16 German airports, but only airlines of the allied powers – France, the UK and the USA – are permitted to operate these domestic routes.

Reservations It is important to make reservations about two days ahead for early morning flights; for other flights it is advisable. Lufthansa has local offices in all cities: Frankfurt ☎ 25701, Hamburg ☎ 35955, Munich ☎ 51138.

Fares Few concessionary fares are available with Lufthansa. There are 40% discounts on internal journeys when combined with an international ticket, but inquire about the many additional restrictions that limit their usefulness to business travellers. First-class fares are 50% higher than economy, but Lufthansa and Swissair are the only European airlines offering this service.

Standards Lufthansa has an enviable record for punctuality, although the rapid increase in domestic air travel does lead to delays during peak travel times. In terms of service the reputation is one of brisk efficiency. On many flights there is no in-flight catering, but you can pick up a Lufthansa Snack at the departure gate.

Train

German Federal Railways (Deutsche Bundesbahn or simply DB) trains are graded acccording to speed and/or importance of the route. At the pinnacle are the EC (EuroCity) trains, travelling the length of the country. Business travellers normally use IC (Intercity) trains. These run between the main cities at regular hourly intervals. They have telephones on which calls can be made and received (at twice call-box rates). Outside the Intercity network are FD or long-distance expresses. Other fast trains are labelled *D-Zug* and ordinary trains *E-Zug*. Within the five main conurbations of Hamburg, the Ruhr, Frankfurt, Stuttgart and Munich the local rail networks, known as *S-Bahn*, provide frequent services which are integrated with local public transport.

The average speeds on IC trains range from 100kmph to 130kmph/60mph to 80mph. Frankfurt–Bonn takes 2hr, Hanover–Düsseldorf 2hr 20min, Mannheim-Stuttgart 1hr 27min and Munich-Nuremberg 1hr 40min.

DB has Park & Rail and Rail & Road schemes which operate at 41 Intercity stations. Reservations are advisable. Parking is free with a rail ticket covering more than 100km/62 miles. The Rail & Road scheme is organized through the interRent car rental firm. Counters are open at certain stations from 7.30 to 6.

Reservations Tickets can be bought on the spot or in advance at stations or the many DER travel agencies. Seat reservations are recommended when travelling at peak times. They may be made for part of a train's journey and a ticket is fixed to the seat giving the details. On platforms at main stations a *Wagenstandanzeiger* provides a pictogram of each train and indicates where each coach will stop at the platform in relation to suspended signs lettered A to E. Match reservation ticket with coach number to find your seat easily.

Fares Fares are based strictly on distance, going up in 10km steps (which average about 20 Pfg per kilometre) for the first 100km, after which they go up in 5km steps. Tourist cards (*Tourist Karte*) are good value for extensive rail travel. They cover 4, 9 or 16 days and are available in first or second class. A supplement or *Zuschlag* is payable on IC and some FD trains, except when travelling on a tourist card. This costs DM5 at the ticket office or DM6 if you pay the ticket inspector on the train. The timetable and the platform indicator show which trains require a *Zuschlag*.

Standards IC trains are very comfortable. Both first and second class sections have restaurant cars and some have a buffet car as well. Other trains are more basic but all have toilets. Some FD trains and *D-Züge* also have restaurant or buffet cars.

Car

The extensive (8,200km/5,080 miles) network of *Autobahnen* reaches to all important towns in Germany and links up with highways in neighbouring countries. Each is identified with a blue sign and numbered in an A series. Some *Autobahnen* constitute part of the trans-European routes. These are identified with a green E number. The *Autobahnen* tend to be very busy; trucks are banned at weekends and they are never permitted in the fast lane. There are local, signed and enforced speed limits but no general mandatory limit on *Autobahnen*. The recommended speed limit of 130km/81mph is largely disregarded and speeds in excess of 180km/110mph are not at all uncommon. The fast lane of an *Autobahn* is a hazardous place. Statistics show that driving in Germany is twice as dangerous as in the UK or the USA.

Information on road congestion is broadcast on local radio. Prominent road signs advise the relevant frequencies. There are filling stations every 30–40km/20–25 miles, usually with a refreshment kiosk, sometimes with a restaurant. Simple rest areas are every 5km/3 miles or so.

Ordinary roads are of good standard but not very fast. On-street parking can be very limited in city centres. Garage parking is usually expensive.

Car rental *Avis* has offices in the main cities and all airports ☎ (069) 730505. *Budget* is associated with *Sixt*, under which name it is often known in Germany, with offices in all large towns and at main airports ☎ (089) 791071. *Europcar* has about 80 outlets in Germany ☎ 0130 3151. *Hertz* offers its wide range of cars from in-town and airport locations ☎ (069) 730404. And *interRent* has a special arrangement with DB that enables it to have counters at over 40 stations. It is also represented at main airports ☎ 0130 2211.

Legal requirements Drivers must possess a current driving licence or international driving permit; those issued by most Western countries are accepted. Third-party insurance is compulsory. Seat belts must be worn by front and rear-seat passengers and the limit on alcohol consumption before driving is equivalent to about a half litre/1.1 pint of beer.

There are no general speed limits on *Autobahnen*, but the police pay considerable attention to vehicles travelling too close to the one in front. Most traffic police use green patrol cars but some travel in unmarked vehicles. Normal roads have a maximum speed limit of 100kmph/62mph. In built-up areas the limit is 50kmph/31mph.

Emergencies The emergency number in towns is ☎ 110. You are legally required to assist anyone who is injured. German highway law is completely unambiguous: an accident cannot occur without someone being at fault, so the police make a detailed report. They must be called in the event of personal injury or serious damage. Emergency telephones are situated every 2km along both sides of *Autobahnen*. Allgemeiner Deutscher Automobil-Club (ADAC) ☎ (089) 76760, together with Automobil Club von Deutschland and Deutscher Touring Automobil Club, operate patrols (*Strassendienst* or *Strassenwacht*) on all main roads, and provide an information and breakdown service. There is a charge for nonmembers. In the event of breakdown or accident the law requires the placing of a warning triangle, which all vehicles must carry, 150–200 metres before the incident.

Local transport

In the major cities well-organized systems integrate the railways with the subway (if any), buses and trams or streetcars. You should buy tickets at kiosks or from ticket vending machines before getting on. It is worthwhile buying a multiride ticket called a *Mehrfahrtenkarte* or *Streifenkarte* at around DM15. This is a strip of 10 or 12 tickets that must be cancelled either before boarding or on the vehicle. The cancellers, called *Entwerter*, are fixed near the entrances. One-day tourist tickets costing from DM6 to DM10 give complete freedom of public transport during the 24-hour period.

S-Bahn and *U-Bahn* (subway) systems are well publicized. In a large city or conurbation it is quite normal in business circles to travel by rail and pick up a taxi for the last stage of the journey. During major exhibitions everyone travels by tram. Bus routes are always more complicated to use but during fairs buses often provide transport between airport or station and fair grounds.

Bus

It is unlikely that business travellers will use bus services outside the main towns; it is normally quicker and far more convenient to rent a car. Each town is the centre for routes which radiate out to places within 50km/30 miles. Usually the bus station is next to the railway station and is described as a *Busbahnhof*.

Taxis

Taxis are remarkably uniform in appearance in all parts of Germany. Diesel-engined Mercedes are the most favoured vehicle although some drivers have Ford Taunus or Opel saloons. The colour is always beige or white. Cabs are generally picked up at recognized ranks or by telephone reservation. Only rarely can they be hailed on the street. Fares are always metered and quite expensive, typically DM3–4 per kilometre. It is common to give a few pfennigs as a tip, rounding up the fare to the nearest mark. Drivers are quite used to giving receipts for taxi fares; ask for a *Quittung*.

Hotels

A high standard of accommodation of all grades can be relied on in West Germany. Even the smallest guest house is invariably comfortable and clean.

This results largely from the country's widespread network of trade fairs and the importance which its companies place on sales and management conferences. Both factors generate a significant business clientele for hotels of all sizes. In addition, a remarkably high percentage of hotels are still privately owned and run by families who maintain high standards.

Also, international chains such as Hilton, Holiday Inn, Inter-Continental, Pullman and Ramada are adding more capacity at the top end of the market. Their hotels tend to be modern sky-scraper blocks in which the facilities and decor conform to their own particular style.

By contrast, private hotels often reflect local style, such as bedrooms with traditional furnishings (including plump *Federbett* covers instead of sheets and blankets) and restaurants with alcove seating.

Categories There are no official categories of hotels in Germany, but the following names give a general indication of facilities. *Hotel* (at least 20 rooms, most with bathroom); *Hotel garni* (providing breakfast and snacks but without a restaurant); *Hotelpension* (limited services with meals only for guests); *Fremdenheim* (a simpler pension); *Gasthof* and *Gasthaus* (bedrooms often without private bathroom, mainly catering to the tourist market); *Kurhotel* (found in spa resorts and providing medical services and special diets); and *Aparthotel* (self-catering suites with hotel facilities).

Grading German hotels are not obliged to advertise any particular grade to indicate standards. The most influential guide is published by Varta, whose staff regularly inspects every hotel it features.

In their own brochures, hotels often grade themselves with unofficial star-ratings: 1 and 2 stars cover guest-house accommodation used mainly by tourists; 3 and 4 stars are small hotels in the medium price and facilities bracket; 5-star ones have "first-class" facilities for business people; and "luxury" hotels are those with the highest grade of facilities and comfort.

Facilities Most of the better hotels are geared to business travellers' needs. In all business class hotels telex and photocopying facilities are available and an increasing number also have fax. Word processing, translating, printing and other secretarial services can usually be organized.

All or most rooms have private bathrooms, most with bath as well as shower, colour TVs, minibars and international direct-dial telephones (IDD).

Hairdryers and irons are not widely provided, though guests can usually borrow these from reception. The voltage is 220 AC so you may need a transformer as well as an adaptor for the shaver socket. Rooms do not have facilities for making tea or coffee, which are usually available in the coffee shop or lobby. Spirits tend to be expensive in hotels compared with inns or bars, but wines are sold at average prices.

Breakfast is increasingly buffet-style. Except at large international chains, it does not include anything hot other than hard-boiled eggs. Instead there is a choice of cold meats, cheese and bread and tea/coffee/chocolate, also fruit juices and yoghurts. Fresh fruit is featured at the most upmarket hotels. A few have a "bio" section of healthy raw ingredients.

Large hotels all have lobby areas, frequently suitable for business discussions. Many also have rooms available for conferences. These are invariably equipped with screens, overhead projectors, flip charts and microphones. For an additional charge, most hotels will organize more sophisticated services, including closed-circuit television and simultaneous translation.

Making reservations

Many privately owned hotels belong to international networks or to a service that will arrange reservations. Local tourist offices will find vacancies either on the spot, by telephone in advance or through a travel agent.

Reservations should be made well ahead during trade fairs. Many exhibitors at particularly busy ones book for the following year while there. At those times, rooms command top prices.

It is worth asking whether corporate rates are available and if reductions are made for visits of three days or more. Discounts vary but, for ten or more people, some hotels will offer 30%. Prices drop at weekends and during July and August, except in tourist areas such as Bavaria and the Rheinland. They also tend to be significantly lower in small towns.

Hotel groups

This list includes Germany's main hotel chains mentioned in the guide. Telephone callers to numbers with the prefix 0130 are charged at local rate only.

Best Western ☎ (06196) 47240 ᵀˣ 4072795. Central reservations ☎ 0130 4455 ᵀˣ 4072795. Seventy of the consortium's private hotels are in Germany, ranging from 3-star to luxury-class. Each has an individual style and most have pools and leisure facilities. Those in cities are particularly geared to the business traveller.

Canadian Pacific ☎ 0130 6116 ᵀˣ 416745. Intended for senior rather than top executives, the three hotels put emphasis on meeting facilities and on their restaurants.

Gast im Schloss ☎ (05675) 331 ᵀˣ 994812. Fifty-three hotels in the exclusive Castle chain are in Germany. All are historic buildings, comfortably transformed into hotel accommodation. Renowned for a high standard of cuisine and selection of wine, their settings are invariably spectacular and rural.

Hilton ☎ 0130 2345 ᵀˣ 413890 or ☎ 0130 2424 ᵀˣ 4189575 (group reservations). Its three modern tower-block hotels are efficient and comfortable, and provide a good range of facilities.

Holiday Inns International ☎ 0130 5678 ᵀˣ 412617. The 17 hotels in city centres or near airports have standard decor and facilities including leisure centres with pools. Several more are opening shortly.

Inter-Continental ☎ 0130 3955 or (01) 941 9751 (UK). Its 10 large hotels in major cities, including Berlin, all have extensive business and leisure facilities. Continuous refurbishment programmes ensure that standards of decor remain high. Two belong to its less expensive Forum Hotels division.

Kempinski ☎ (06102) 50020 ᵀˣ 411222. This is a leading chain of four luxury hotels each with a few spacious Presidential Suites and leisure facilities, and individual character. It is are also part of the Leading Hotels of the World chain ☎ 0130 2110 ᵀˣ 411592.

Maritim ☎ 0130 6969 ᵀˣ 8587964 or (06151) 81067 ᵀˣ 419313 (group reservations). Its 17 modern, medium-priced hotels have been built in smaller towns with the business traveller in mind. They have similar, functional standards, and a few have impressive sports facilities.

Mövenpick ☎ 0130 2217 ᵀˣ 773998. This Swiss-owned chain has 10 hotels in Germany, each in its own style but with similar facilities. All put strong emphasis on their restaurants. Affiliated to Radisson and linked with the Utell reservations network ☎ (0211) 369903.

Novotel ☎ (069) 742598 ᵀˣ 411053. The French company has 28 of its 155 European hotels in Germany. Conforming to similar, no-nonsense standards, most have been built near major approach roads rather than in city centres. World-wide reservation system, Resinter.

Pullman International ☏ (069) 230858 ⊤ⓧ 413727. Formed in 1986 as part of the Wagons-lits group, it has 13 of its hotels in Germany. Most are in city centres near to the railway station. There are three types: Pullman, geared to business people, located in either a completely new or an older, refurbished building and including a floor of "privilege rooms" with superior facilities; Altea, often a refurbished older establishment with a business and tourist clientele; and Arcade, newly built with plain, no-frills rooms.

Ramada ☏ 0130 2340 ⊤ⓧ 27607 (UK). The 11 hotels vary in style and age but all put an emphasis on service. Four are in the Renaissance category, having pools and Executive Club floors with hostess service.

Rema ☏ (0211) 379007 ⊤ⓧ 8582145. Expanding new chain of nine medium-sized, first-class hotels in North Germany. Some are in refurbished old buildings; others are completely new. Decor is modern and the facilities efficient.

Romantik ☏ (06188) 5020 ⊤ⓧ 4184214. About one-fifth of the 61 first-class Romantik hotels in Germany are in cities and exclusively serve business people. Another 20 have a half business, half tourist clientele. They are medium sized and privately owned. The settings all have a "romantic" aspect. Food tends to be above average.

Sheraton ☏ 0130 3535 ⊤ⓧ 261534 (UK). Has three of its modern luxury hotels in Germany, each built with the business traveller in mind.

Steigenberger ☏ (069) 295247 ⊤ⓧ 414697. Germany's most prestigious chain of 30 luxury hotels. The nine city ones are mostly in older buildings, extensively refurbished, and have good conference facilities. The spa hotels have treatment facilities and are also suitable as conference venues. Those at resorts specialize in the tourist trade.

Our recommended hotels

The hotels given full entries in this guide are the most comfortable and stylish in their area and do a thoroughly professional job of accommodating business visitors.

Listed under "Other hotels" are establishments which do not achieve such high standards but offer perfectly adequate accommodation. In contrast, the establishments listed under "Out of town" often have considerable character and charm.

The price symbols have the following meanings:

DM	up to DM 75
DM /	DM 75–150
DM //	DM 150–200
DM ///	DM 200–275
DM ////	over DM 275

These reflect the price at the time of going to press for one person occupying a standard room, including service and tax at 15%.

Restaurants

Germans have a reputation for liking to eat *gutbürgerlich* food, meaning plenty of plain, solid, well-cooked fare, normally including substantial portions of meat and potatoes. When entertaining on business, they like to eat somewhere reliable and safe, so shun adventurous food and surroundings unless they are already familiar with the menu and service.

When their local hotel or the nearest *Gasthof* satisfies these requirements, this is where business clients are likely to be taken. French and Italian cuisine are also regarded as safe, but Oriental varieties decidedly less so.

To impress a customer from abroad – and to show what Germany has to offer – they may search out a restaurant featuring *nouvelle cuisine.*

Social conventions

Meal times are 12–3 for lunch and 6 onwards for dinner with the most popular period being up to 9 to leave time for informal drinking later.

There is no need to wait to be

seated. Find an empty table and signal to the waiter (*Herr Ober*) or waitress (*Fräulein*). Meals begin with the greeting *Guten Appetit*, and the host must lift his glass to his guests before anyone drinks.

Local dishes

Gutbürgerlich food features all the regional dishes. Pork is served everywhere: boiled with *Sauerkraut* in Frankfurt, roasted with dumplings in Munich and as a ham in Westphalia. Lamb is much more of a delicacy but plenty is available in the north thanks to the excellent grazing pastures of the Lüneburger Heide. Fish is particularly good in North Sea areas like Hamburg and also Bavaria where trout is caught locally. Every region has its own type of sausage (*Wurst*): long coiled ones in Nuremberg which are roasted for lunch or dinner and white ones in Munich, eaten for breakfast or as a mid-morning snack.

In a country of eaters who enjoy their meat, vegetarianism is tolerated, but sometimes with a smile. Vegetarians can usually eat best at a Chinese restaurant or by choosing non-meat dishes from a standard menu. However, "bio" food is increasingly found on hotel menus with healthy items like raw vegetables, fruit and cheese. *Kurhotels* serve special diets.

Prices

Restaurants are required to display a printed menu and show that tax and service (*Mehrwertsteuer und Bedienung*) are included. Most feature *à la carte* dishes which change frequently, as well as fixed-price meals with a small choice for each course. They may also have a seasonal menu of fresh ingredients such as asparagus, fish or venison. City hotels often offer inclusive business lunches (*Geschäftsmenu*).

Bills should itemize each dish ordered and also include service. Additional tips need only be left as a gesture of appreciation after

particularly good service or specifically for the wine waiter. (See also *Money* for more on tipping.)

Reservations

It is always advisable to reserve ahead, at the latest in the morning for dinner, though longer notice may be required for groups of more than four. During trade fairs, city restaurants are particularly busy.

Our recommended restaurants

The restaurants given full entries in this guide have been selected for business entertaining, reflecting their quality of service, atmosphere, decor and reputation. Quality of food, while important, has not been given priority, though many of the restaurants in this category also feature in leading restaurant guides.

The establishments listed under "Good but casual" are useful for more informal occasions, when impressive service and surroundings are not important. Prices are usually lower.

In most cities, "good but casual" restaurants greatly outnumber the smarter choices. Occasionally, the classiest restaurants are not in the city itself, but out of town.

The price symbols used in the guide have the following meanings:

DM	up to DM 45
DM I	DM 45–70
DM II	DM 70–90
DM III	DM 90–120
DM IIII	over DM 120

These reflect the price at the time of going to press of a typical meal, including half a bottle of house wine, coffee and service.

Bars

There are various types of drinking establishments.

Bar Hotel bars are respectable places for a drink before or after a meal and also provide a suitable meeting point on business occasions. However "bars" elsewhere range from the small and sleazy to nightclubs with an entrance fee, expensive drinks and striptease for entertainment. Piano and cocktail bars provide smart surroundings for drinking but may not open before 4pm.

Other names *Kneipe* is often used to denote a bar in Northern Germany. These have a jolly, informal atmosphere and simple furnishings. A *Bierlokal* is similar.

Bavaria has many open-air *Biergarten* where customers can bring their own food. *Gaststätte* have the cheapest prices but tend to be the roughest places to drink.

Local breweries frequently have beer halls beside them in which beer is served straight from the barrel. In Bavaria they are called *Bierkeller*, but elsewhere *Brauereikeller* or simply *Brauerei*. Wine-growing areas have *Weinstuben* specializing in wine from local vineyards. Cider is drunk at an *Apfelweinwirtschaft*. Snackbars, called *Imbiss*, are found everywhere.

Types of drink

The popularity of beer, wine and cider (*Apfelwein*) depends on the area; local brews vary a good deal.

Cologne's *Kölsch* is a dry pale beer, while *Rauchbier* from the Franconia area has a smokey flavour. Munich's special *Weissbier* is made from wheat.

The heaviest wine-drinking areas are beside the Rhein and Mosel. Around Frankfurt, cider is very common. Spirits, fruit juices or coffee are invariably available. Drinking toasts are *"Zum Wohl,"* *"Prost"* or, very formal, *"Prosit."*

Vintage chart

A chart which dictates good and bad years for wine is inevitably inexact because it denies the possibility of exceptions: a talented producer can sometimes make better wine in a so-called "bad" year than his less able neighbour in a "good" one. However, a vintage chart does provide some guidelines.

Very good years are indicated by ★
Years to avoid are given in *italics*
Too young (n) indicates those wines which are not yet ready for drinking; (w) indicates those wines which are ready for drinking but which will improve.

German white (Riesling)
Rhein   86 85★ 83★ 82 81 76★ 75★ 73 71★
Mosel   86 85★ 83★ 82 81 79 76★ 75★ 71★
Baden   87 86 85 83 82 81 80
Franconia   86 85 83 82 81 79

French red
Bordeaux (classed growths)   87(n) 86★(n) 85★(n) 83(n) 82★(n) 81 80 79 78★ 76 75 71 70★; *77 74 72*
Burgundy (Côte d'Or)   87(n) 86(n) 85★(n) 83(w) 82 80 79 78★ 76 72 71★ 70; *84 81 77 75 74*
Rhône (Côte Rôtie/Hermitage)   87(n) 86(n) 85★(n) 83★(n) 82(w) 80 79 78★ 76 72 71★ 70★; *84 77*

French white
Bordeaux (top dry Graves)   87(n) 86★(n) 85★(n) 83★(n) 82★ 81 80 78★ 76★ 75★ 71★ 70★
Bordeaux (Sauternes)   86(n) 85(n) 83★(n) 81 80★ 78 76★ 75 71 70; *84 77 74 72*
Burgundy (Côte d'Or)   87(n) 86(n) 85★(w) 83 82 79 78★ 75 73★ 71★ 70; *77 74 72*
Rhône (north)   87(n) 86(w) 85★ 83★ 82 81 80 78★ 71★ 70★
Loire (dry)   87 86 85 83; *84*
Loire (sweet)   85★ 83★ 82 79 78 76★; *84 80*
Alsace   87 86 85★ 83★ 81 79 76★ 71★
Champagne   83(n) 82★(w) 81(w) 79★ 78 76 75★ 73 71 70★

Bar food

Menus particularly feature local dishes and snacks. In Berlin, *Frikadelle* or *Bouletten* (small tasty meatballs) are frequently served with beer, while Frankfurt's cider comes with *Handkäs mit Musik* – cheese, onions and bread. By law, establishments must have a printed menu. If it is not on show, it should be asked for before ordering to avoid any confusion over price.

Licensing laws

Most establishments open around 11.30am but have to close by 1am, unless a special licence to stay open later has been granted. The exception is Berlin where *Kneipen* only have to close for one hour in 24 for cleaning. Some only close half their premises at a time, so that customers can continue to drink in the other.

Shopping

Generally, shopping hours are from 9 to 6.30, Mon–Fri, although there can be regional variations. In smaller towns shops may be closed for lunch (Mon–Fri, 1–3). Throughout Germany, however, shops are closed on Saturday afternoons at 1 or 2 and Sundays, with the exception of the first Saturday in the month, when stores will stay open until 4 or 5.
Tax Value added tax (*Mehrwertsteuer*) is charged on most goods and services, currently at the rate of 14%. Some items, such as food products, attract the lower rate of 7%. If you wish to reclaim tax at customs on your return, keep the receipts.

Information sources

In your own country

The overseas section of your own Department of Trade should be able to provide helpful information. The German embassy in your country may have a commercial section and you may also have a branch of the German chamber of commerce. In Britain the *German Chamber of Industry and Commerce* is at 12 Suffolk St, St James's, London SW1Y 4HG ☎ 930 7251. The *German American Chamber of Commerce* has offices at 666 5th Ave, New York, NY 10103 ☎ 974 8830 and 3250 Wilshire Blvd Suite 2212, Los Angeles, Ca 90010 ☎ 381 2236. For general information, contact the German National Tourist Office, which has offices in over 20 countries.

In Germany

It is worth while contacting your own embassy or consulate-general in Germany, and the following organizations are also useful sources of information.
Ausstellungs- und Messe-Ausschuss der Deutschen Wirtschaft e.V. (AUMA) (Confederation of German Trade Fair and Exhibition Industries), Lindenstr 8, D-5000 Köln 1 ☎ (0221) 209070 publishes a twice yearly handbook (*Messehandbuch*) listing in five languages all the trade fairs in Germany. It also has an *Information Guide* in English with hints on taking part in trade fairs, statistical information, slides and videos. Details of fairs' programmes are available three years ahead.
Bundesverband der Deutschen Industrie (BDI) (Federation of German Industry), Gustav-Heinemann-Ufer 84-88, Postfach 510548, D-5000 Köln 51 ☎ (0221) 370800 publishes *Made in Germany*, a booklet on the country's economy and society and the International Economic Indicators (*Internationale Wirtschaftenszahlen*).
Deutscher Industrie- und Handelstag (DIHT) (Federation of German Chambers of Commerce), Adenauerallee 148, D-5300 Bonn 1 ☎ (0228) 104186, publishes a booklet listing all its overseas offices.
Zentralverband Elektrotechnik- und Elektronikindustrie e.V. (ZVEI) (German Electrical and Electronics Manufacturers Association), Stresemannallee 19, D-6000 Frankfurt am Main 70 ☎ (069) 63021, provides information and a

directory of manufacturers in new technology (*Taschenbuch der Elektropresse*); also the annual ZVEI Buying Guide (*Elektro Elektronik Einkaufs Führer*).

Local information
Business information Most local government bodies have a department responsible for encouraging the economic growth of the area. The administrative centre of each *Land* has a ministry of industry and technology (*Ministerium für Wirtschaft und Technologie*) to advise on questions concerning import and export. Each chamber of commerce (*Industrie- und Handelskammer*) can provide information about the services and products of its members, and the main reference library (*Bibliothek*) in every city generally has a commercial section.
Tourist information You will find local tourist information offices (*Verkehrsamt*) throughout Germany, generally at airports, railway stations, town halls or important tourist attractions.

Crime
It is only in certain areas of major inner cities that crime is a problem, but you should always still take sensible precautions. Keep wallets in inside jacket pockets and carry bags close to the body. Avoid carrying lots of cash. Deposit valuables in the hotel safe.

Always lock your car (you can be fined if you do not). Do not leave baggage visible inside and do not keep the car documents in it.

At night, avoid unlit areas and empty train compartments.

If you are robbed, report the loss to the police immediately. Dial 110 (calls are free); otherwise, go to the nearest police station. If you lose credit cards or traveller's cheques, notify the issuing bank immediately. Your embassy will help you get a new passport and airlines or travel agencies can assist with lost or stolen tickets.

If you are arrested
Although you will normally wish to cooperate with the police if you are arrested, you are not legally obliged to answer any questions (except in some cases to give your name and address). You will be allowed an interpreter if you need one but you are not obliged to give a statement. The exception is if you have information about terrorism, which you must give to the police. You must be told the reason for your arrest and cautioned that anything you say may be used as evidence, and you have the right to make a telephone call, to a friend or lawyer, once you get to the police station. There will be a duty lawyer on call to advise you. The police cannot hold you for more than 24 hours without charging you, except for terrorist offences.

Embassies
Most embassies (*Gesandtschaft*) are in Bonn, although some countries have consulates in other cities too.
Australia Godesberger Allee 107, D-5300 Bonn 2 ☎ (0228) 81030
Austria Johanniterstr 2, D-5300 Bonn 1 ☎ (0228) 230051
Belgium Kaiser-Friedrich-Str 7, D-5300 Bonn 1 ☎ (0228) 212001
Canada Friedrich-Wilhelm-Str 18, D-5300 Bonn 1 ☎ (0228) 231061
Denmark Pfälzer Str 14, D-5300 Bonn 1 ☎ (0228) 729910
Finland Friesdorfer Str 1, D-5300 Bonn 2 ☎ (0228) 311033
France Kapellenweg 1a, D-5300 Bonn 2 ☎ (0228) 362031
German Democratic Republic Godesberger Allee 18, D-5300 Bonn 2 ☎ (0228) 379051
Greece Koblenzer Str 103, D-5300 Bonn 2 ☎ (0228) 355036
Ireland Godesberger Allee 119, D-5300 Bonn 2 ☎ (0228) 376937
Italy Karl-Finkelnburg-Str 49, D-5300 Bonn 2 ☎ (0228) 820060
Japan Am Bundeskanzlerpl, D-5300 Bonn 1 ☎ (0228) 5001
Netherlands Strässchensweg 10, D-5300 Bonn 1 ☎ (0228) 238091

New Zealand Am Bundeskanzlerpl,
D-5300 Bonn 1 ☎ (0228) 214021
Norway Mittelstr 43, D-5300
Bonn 2 ☎ (0228) 374055
Portugal Ubierstr 78, D-5300
Bonn 2 ☎ (0228) 363011
Spain Schlossstr 4, D-5300
Bonn 1 ☎ (0228) 217094
Sweden Allianzpl, Haus 1, An der
Heuss Allee 2-10, D-5300
Bonn 1 ☎ (0228) 260020
Switzerland Gotenstr 156, D-5300
Bonn 2 ☎ (0228) 810080
UK Friedrich-Ebert-Allee 77, D-
5300 Bonn 1 ☎ (0228) 234061
USA Deichmannsaue 29, D-5300
Bonn 2 ☎ (0228) 3392286
Yugoslavia Schlossallee 5, D-5300
Bonn 2 ☎ (0228) 344051

Health care

In Germany health care is privatized.
The standard of health care is
generally high. Medically it is one of
the best-equipped countries in the
world.

Germany also has over 250
officially recognized spas and health
resorts. Further information can be
obtained from the Deutscher
Bäderverband (DBV), 111
Schumannstrasse, D-5000 Bonn, or
from the German National Tourist
Board.

If you fall ill

It is a good idea to bring with you
any medicine you take regularly. If
you have a particular health problem,
also bring a letter from your doctor
outlining your medical history and
treatment. Do try to have it
translated. If you need to bring
equipment such as syringes with you,
an explanatory letter from your
doctor, translated into German, may
save time at customs.
Pharmacies (*Apotheke*) You can
buy some medicines without a
prescription and there is always at
least one pharmacy in each city
district open 24hr. This information
is available from hotels, the police
and also from the local paper. Every
pharmacy will display details of

which *Apotheke* are open 24hr.
Seeing a doctor (*Arzt*) Doctors'
surgeries have a receptionist and
nurse permanently on duty. Doctors
will also visit you at your hotel if
necessary, although this will
obviously be more expensive.

Doctors' hours are usually 8–12
and 2–6. There is always a doctor on
call 24 hours a day. Information
about which doctor is on duty can be
found from the same sources given
above (see *Pharmacies*).
Emergency treatment If you
need treatment urgently, go to
the emergency department
(*Unfallstation*) of the nearest hospital
(*Krankenhaus*). Taxi drivers will
know where it is. In case of utmost
emergency, contact the police by
dialling 110. Calls are free and in
some phone booths you simply pull
the lever beside the phone to be in
direct contact with the police.
Rabies Rabies is present in
Germany. As yet there is no known
vaccine to provide complete
immunity. Any bite or scratch which
you get through contact with a wild
or stray animal should be cleaned and
medical advice sought urgently.
Dental treatment All dental
treatment in Germany is provided
privately and it can be very
expensive. But there is an emergency
dentist (*Zahnarzt*) available 24 hours
a day. Details can be found in your
hotel, in the local newspaper and
from the police.

Paying for treatment

Many countries have reciprocal
health care agreements with
Germany which will entitle you to
treatment free of charge or at a
reduced rate. However, the
procedures involved are often
tiresome, so it is always best to take
out adequate insurance; include
cover for emergency repatriation.

Communications
Telephones
The German Post Office operates the
national telephone service.

Numbers, which range from three to eight digits in Germany, can be dialled direct. They all have a trunk call dialling code, which can be found next to the place name in the telephone directory. A full list of national and international codes is given in the booklet of codes (*Vorwahlnummern*), known as AVON. You can dial direct numbers in most European countries and some intercontinental numbers.

Cheap rates operate between 6pm and 8am, Mon–Fri, and throughout the weekends. Calls inside Germany are divided into three chargebands, up to 50km/30 miles, up to 100km/62 miles and over 100km, which includes Berlin, East Germany and international calls. Charge units are for 12 seconds, or 16 at cheap rate. Local calls are not timed. Public telephone booths are yellow and labelled *Telefon* or *Fernsprecher*. The minimum charge is 20 Pfg. There are also some card phones. Charges can be reversed by asking the operator for an "*R*" *Gespräch*. Telephone numbers with the prefix 0130 indicate that callers will be charged at the local rate only, the rest of the cost being borne by the number's subscriber. Companies offering this cheap-call service include several major hotel and car rental groups.

International calls can be made from booths with a green sign, marked *Inlands und Auslandsgespräche*. Some telephone booths, named *anrufbares Telephon*, can now receive calls as they have a number. Often located at railway stations, they have a red bell sign.

Emergency services Dial 110 for the police (*Polizei*) and in case of medical emergency, and dial 112 for the fire department (*Feuerwehr*). In some cities for the emergency doctor (*Arzt*) ☎ 19292. Emergency calls are free.

Operator services Local calls ☎ 010, for international calls ☎ 0010.

Directory inquiries For directory information within Germany ☎ 1188

(in smaller towns ☎ 01188) and 00118 for international inquiries.

Telex and fax

Telex facilities are usually available at the main railway station, hotels, conference centres, trade fairs and at post offices. The use of fax is rapidly increasing and 1,000 post offices provide a service called *Telebrief* for documents up to A4 size.

Mail

Main post offices are open Mon–Fri, 8–6 (though smaller ones may close 12–2) and Sat, 8–12. Mail boxes are yellow. There is no mail delivery on Sundays but there is a collection in the morning.

The post office offers registered mail, proof of delivery for registered letters and goods of value. Express letters and packets, called *Eilbrief* or *Eilpaket*, go by normal mail but are delivered on arrival by a special service between 6am and 10pm and, for an additional charge, between 10pm and 6am. There is also an international express delivery service, *Datapost*. For information on postal services ☎ 011605 or 11605.

Addressing letters A four-digit postal code system is in operation in the Federal Republic and each town has a number which must appear as a prefix (eg 5000 Köln). In this guide, these prefixes are shown at the top of each city section. Larger cities are also subdivided into postal areas and this number appears after the name of the city (eg 1000 Berlin 62). Street numbers are always put after the name of the street.

Couriers and express services As well as the Post Office express services, German Federal Railways operates an express parcel and package service, *Kurierdienst*, at 50% of stations for same-day delivery, Mon–Fri. *Expressdienst* delivers the same day or the following morning, depending on the destination. Parcels up to 100 kilos/220lb can also be sent before 5.30pm by *Termindienst* with arrival guaranteed by 8am. Parcels can either be handed in and collected at stations, or collection and delivery can be arranged. Courier services are listed in Yellow Pages (*Gelbe Seiten*).

International dialling codes
Before dialling the country's code dial 00. The figures in brackets indicate how many hours the country is ahead or behind Central European Time (one hour ahead of Greenwich Mean Time). In Mar–Sep, clocks are put forward one hour.

Australia	61	(+7–9hr)
Austria	43	
Belgium	32	
Canada	1	(-4hr 30min–9hr)
Denmark	45	
France	33	
Germany East	37	
Greece	30	(+1hr)
Hong Kong	852	(+7hr)
India	91	(+4hr 30min)
Ireland	353	(-1hr)
Israel	972	(+1hr)
Italy	39	
Japan	81	(+8hr)
Netherlands	31	
New Zealand	64	(+11hr)
Norway	47	
Pakistan	92	(+4hr)
Portugal	351	(-1hr)
Singapore	65	(+7hr)
Spain	34	
Sweden	46	
Switzerland	41	
UK	44	(-1hr)
USA	1	(-6–11hr)

Conversion charts
Germany uses the metric system of measurement. In this guide, metric measurements are always used except in the case of distances, which are given in both miles and kilometers.

Length

centimeters (cm)	cm or in	inches (in)
2.54	= in 1 cm =	0.394
5.08	2	0.787
7.62	3	1.181
10.16	4	1.575
12.70	5	1.969
15.24	6	2.362
17.70	7	2.756
20.32	8	3.150
22.86	9	3.543
25.40	10	3.937
50.80	20	7.874
76.20	30	11.811
101.60	40	15.748
127.00	50	19.685

Mass (weight)

kilograms (kg)	kg or lb	pounds (lb)
0.454	= lb 1 kg =	2.205
0.907	2	4.409
1.361	3	6.614
1.814	4	8.819
2.268	5	11.023
2.722	6	13.228
3.175	7	15.432
3.629	8	17.637
4.082	9	19.842
4.536	10	22.046
9.072	20	44.092
13.608	30	66.139
18.144	40	88.185
22.680	50	110.231

Distance

kilometers (km)	km or miles	miles
1.609	= mi 1 km =	0.621
3.219	2	1.243
4.828	3	1.864
6.437	4	2.485
8.047	5	3.107
9.656	6	3.728
11.265	7	4.350
12.875	8	4.971
14.484	9	5.592
16.093	10	6.214
32.187	20	12.427
48.280	30	18.641
64.374	40	24.855
80.467	50	31.069

Volume

liters (l)	liters or US galls	US galls
3.79	= l 1 gall =	0.26
7.58	2	0.52
11.37	3	0.78
15.16	4	1.04
18.95	5	1.30
22.74	6	1.56
26.53	7	1.82
30.32	8	2.08
34.11	9	2.34
37.90	10	2.60
75.80	20	5.20
113.70	30	7.80
151.60	40	10.40
189.50	50	13.00

Temperature

°F 32 40 50 60 70 75 85 95 105 140 175 212
°C 0 5 10 15 20 25 30 35 40 60 80 100

Index